SO-AHR-233

KF
4541   Crosskey   21.343
.C8   Politics and the
1978   Constitution in
V.2   the history of
P.   the United States

DATE DUE

Politics and the Constitution in the his
KF4541.C8 V2P2   21343

Crosskey, William Winslow
VRJC/WRIGHT LIBRARY

DEMCO

Po   on

"*We ask, not what this man meant, but what those words would mean in the mouth of a normal speaker of English, using them in the circumstances in which they were used.*"

OLIVER WENDELL HOLMES, JR.

Politics and the Constitution
in the History of the United States

VOLUME II (2)

Part V, Conclusion, Appendices, Notes, & Index

WILLIAM WINSLOW CROSSKEY

THE UNIVERSITY OF CHICAGO PRESS

CHICAGO & LONDON

The University of Chicago Press, Chicago 60637
The University of Chicago Press, Ltd., London

Copyright 1953 *by The University of Chicago*
All rights reserved. Published 1953 *in the*
United States and Canada. Midway Reprint 1978
Printed in the United States of America

ISBN: 0-226-12132-1
Library of Congress Catalog Card Number: 77-90070

Contents

PART IV

THE SUPREME COURT'S INTENDED PLACE IN THE CONSTITUTIONAL SYSTEM

PART V

THE SUPREME COURT AND THE CONSTITUTIONAL LIMITATIONS ON STATE GOVERNMENTAL AUTHORITY

IN CONCLUSION

APPENDICES

Contents

NOTES

INDEX

Part V

The Supreme Court and the Constitutional Limitations on State Governmental Authority

CHAPTER XXX

The Supreme Court's Destruction of the Constitutional Limitations on State Authority, Contained in the Original Constitution and Initial Amendments

1

THE task of the Supreme Court which John Rutledge described as that of "secur[ing] uniformity of Judgments" was that, of course, of acting as the nation's juridical head. The successive stages and present remarkable degree of the Court's declension in this capacity have already been treated in chapters xxiii–xxvi. The Court's two extensive failures "to secure the national rights" of Congress to legislate have also been noted: first, its indefensible fragmentation of Congress' power over commerce, and, second, its failure to recognize that body's general national legislative authority. There remains, however, one group of "national rights" that the Court has failed to "secure," about which comparatively little, thus far, has been said. These are the "rights" provided in the Constitution, that the states shall refrain from certain types of governmental action even though their action does not in any way conflict with action by the government of the nation.

The "national rights" of this kind are of two varieties: those that make some field, or fields, of national power, in whole or in part, exclusive; and those that interdict some type of governmental action considered to be inherently evil. The interdictions, in the tenth section of Article I, of state coinage of money, and state treaties and compacts, and the Contracts Clause, in the same section, if read in its actually intended sense, and not as the Court interprets it, are examples of the first of these two varieties; whereas the prohibitions, also in section 10, of state titles of nobility, state bills of attainder, and all retrospective state legislation are examples of the second. As might be expected, "the national rights" against the states, of the second variety, are in general paralleled by similar prohibitions upon the government of the nation; or, else, they are created by general provisions drawn to apply alike to both the nation and the states. This parallelism has not, however, been complete, at all times throughout our history; and, at present, the provision, in the Fourteenth Amendment, that "no State shall deny to any person within its jurisdiction the equal protection of the laws," is unparalleled by any similar prohibition directed to the government of the nation.

From the nature of these direct constitutional limitations on state authority, and the character of the two purposes they were meant to subserve, it can be seen that they are important elements in the total definition of state governmental power under the Constitution; and since these limitations, of both varieties, are much more numerous and extensive, and always have been, than is commonly supposed, a just understanding of their total number and extent provides further evidence of the restricted role in government that the states, under the Constitution, were to play; and of the great degree in which, even in this restricted role, they were intended to be subject to the control of the nation. The Supreme Court's failure, then, to "secure" and enforce these important "national rights" as they actually are written, constitutes further evidence of the pervasive trend, long observable in the Court's decisions, of favoring the state governments of the country, at the expense of the plainly provided "national rights" of Congress and the people; and, for that matter, at the expense—strange as it may seem—of the "national rights" of the Supreme Court itself as the intended general juridical head of the country.

Important as the history of what the Court has done in this field manifestly is in the foregoing connections, there is still another aspect in which it is even more important. For, while the trend of the Court's decisions during the first full century under the Constitution was, on the whole, quite consistently and unwarrantedly favorable to the states, a peculiar change set in at the end of that period, when Congress, in the Interstate Commerce Act of 1887, and, again, in the Sherman Act of 1890, at last sought to use its power of regulating commerce, which the Court, by that time, had so largely destroyed. With these first stirrings of Congress from a century-long lethargy, the Court began to see, in one of the limitations imposed on the states, by the Fourteenth Amendment, of 1868, a meaning it had never seen before,[1] and which, indeed, it had previously denied emphatically was there expressed.[2] This meaning had the effect of restoring, after a fashion, some parts, but by no means all, of the substance of the restrictions on state authority that the Court had earlier destroyed. But this effect followed in a very uncertain way, and only at the expense of subjecting all state governmental action to the Supreme Court's control, in a manner and degree, for which, it is certain, the Constitution does not provide. The most important consequence of this strange development was, however, that it laid a basis—quite sophistical, it is true; but, none the less, a basis—for the same kind and degree of Supreme Court control over Congress; and for this, it is equally certain, the Constitution does not provide, either. So, the history of what the Court has done with the direct constitutional limitations upon *state* authority is important, paradoxically, in completing the picture of what the Court has done, and how it has managed to do it, to the powers of the legislature of the nation.

The clause of the Fourteenth Amendment in which the Court suddenly saw the meaning that had all these extraordinary consequences was the so-called Due Process Clause, which provides as follows: "No State shall . . . deprive any person of life, liberty, or property, without due process of law." Although, by its plain terms, a simple guaranty of fair and appropriate legal procedure, or "process," in cases where life, liberty, or property is involved, the Supreme Court suddenly perceived, in this guaranty, a general roving commission, directed to itself, to review the essential reasonableness of all state laws, whether procedural in character or not. The fact that the Court's new vision occurred with respect to this particular part of the Fourteenth Amendment seems, at first thought, very odd. For the Equal Protection Clause of the same amendment, though not actually intended as a general roving commission to the Supreme Court either, was at least not merely procedural in its terms, and could therefore have been employed by the Court, in its crusade against the states, without quite such flagrant disregard of the words of the document as its use of the Due Process Clause compelled.[3] But there was this manifest difficulty: that there is no "equal-protection" guaranty in the Constitution, against Congress. So, the Court, it can be seen, was not completely free in its choice. The contentions of lawyers drove it in the direction it took; and movement in that direction was made easier than might be supposed, by earlier state-court holdings—unwarranted though these were—as to the meaning of similarly worded guaranties in state constitutions.

In the years that followed the Court's new insight, and especially in the period after 1900, a great mass of judicially created limitations upon state action was gradually worked out; particularly, in the legislative field. And because there was, in the Fifth Amendment, a Due Process Clause applying to Congress, all these limitations became, in potential effect, limitations on Congress, too. For the Court was careful to insist periodically, though not with complete consistency, that there was no difference in meaning between the two Due Process Clauses, in the Fifth and the Fourteenth Amendments.[4] So, the end result was that the Court at last managed to get into its hands a general discretionary control over all Congressional acts, not too different in substance, however different it may have been in theory, from the judicial veto over national legislation that the Federal Convention *four times* voted down.

The peculiarly broad terms in which the Court has conceived its imaginary commission against the states has had, moreover, a further peculiar consequence in the case of Congress. For, because the Court has thought of itself as commissioned to review the reasonableness of all state laws— or, as the "liberals" will have it, the question whether reasonable men could think the state laws reasonable—it has been possible for the Court to treat most of the express and specific limitations on state authority, which the Constitution contains, as categories of "unreasonableness," primary or secondary, which are forbidden, in general terms, by the "due-process" guaranty, too. In cases, therefore, which have involved state violations of the specific limitations, the Court has commonly intimated that the laws it overturns, are lacking, also, in what it calls "due process of law"; and, then, since the two Due Process Clauses are deemed by the Court, and correctly deemed, to mean the same thing, it has been able, with a superficial plausibility in other cases, to assert, *against Congress*, much of the substance of those specific limitations—the Contracts Clause of section 10 of Article I, and the Equal Protection Clause of the Fourteenth Amendment—which the Constitution actually expresses as limitations upon the states alone.[5] In the case of the Contracts Clause, this, to be sure, has merely meant, under the sense the Supreme Court gives it, that part of the destroyed meaning of the Ex-post-facto Clause of section 9 of Article I has been restored; but in the case of the Equal Protection Clause, no warrant for the Court's behavior can be found in the Constitution.

And in this connection, too, the Court's strange favoritism toward the states, as against Congress, comes to the surface in another way. For, whereas the Court has thus unhesitatingly asserted, against Congress, the substance of the foregoing limitations which, by the actual terms of the document, relate to the states only, it has denied, and still denies, that it is under any general duty to enforce, as against the states, the various specific guaranties relating to "process"—and "process," moreover, in the strict, literal sense—which the Constitution contains.[6] And the Court does this even though these guaranties, themselves in terms broad enough to apply to the states, were in the Constitution when the state Due Process Clause was adopted, and had, somewhat earlier, been held, by the Court, to create, as against Congress, constitutionally binding categories of propriety, or "dueness," in "process," in the particular phases of the subject they cover.[7] Yet, on elementary principles that every competent lawyer is supposed to know and understand, each and all of these specific "process" guaranties, in the circumstances stated, were made good against the states, by the adoption of the Fourteenth Amendment, extending to the states whatever were the standards of "due process of law" under the Constitution when the amendment was adopted. The situation is as simple as that. Yet so great is the muddle and confusion into which the Supreme Court has got this subject, that one of the members of the present Court can venture publicly to brand as "an eccentric," one of the ablest members of the Supreme Court since the Civil War, because, forsooth, as was his sworn duty, he took, and stubbornly maintained, this obviously correct position.[8]

By way of introduction, it need only be added that, although, during recent years, the "substantive" aspects of this thing called "due process" have fallen into disuse as against Congress, this, undoubtedly, is because the Court, as well as the Congress and the Presidency, has been, for some years now, under the domination of a single political party. For judicial review, in all its aspects, always tends to dwindle when this situation obtains. It is, moreover, completely certain that the Court's claim to general supervision over the states and Congress, in the name of "due process," has not been given up. Till recently, there was a strong minority on the present Court, that apparently was willing to take this step; but the majority Justices were, and presumably still are, unwilling to do this.[9] So, the situation remains potentially—and, against the states, actually[10]— what it long has been; since there is, as matters stand, no assurance at all that, if the national political situation should change, this wholly unwarranted power of general supervision over Congress would not again be used by the Court, in the future, in the ways it has in the past. The matter, then, is of continuing importance; and in this and the following two chapters, the history of the Court's extensive and extraordinary failure to enforce, as they are actually written, the various limitations upon state authority that the Constitution contains, will therefore be briefly reviewed.

2

Of the phases of this subject that have been treated earlier, the transformation of the prohibition of *all* state "ex-post-facto Laws," in section 10 of Artice I, into a prohibition of criminal "ex-post-facto Laws" only, was the earliest in date of occurrence. It took place in 1798. The probable original motive for this transformation, as we saw when the subject was treated, was a desire to free Congress' power of passing bankruptcy laws, from the civil phase of the Ex-post-facto Clause (in section 9 of the same article) which relates to national legislation. Consistently with this original purpose, the transformation, until after the death of Chief Justice Marshall, in 1835, worked little actual increase in the authority of the states within the field of contracts; for the Contracts Clause (also in the tenth section of Article I) was used, so far as the Court's theory of the clause permitted, to prevent such a result. The Contracts Clause was not, however, even during the days of the Marshall Court, a complete substitute for the civil phase of the state Ex-post-facto Clause which the Court so early destroyed. For the Contracts Clause could not well be made to operate where the element of contract was wholly absent; and the Court, for a long time, understandably felt that state validations, or "erections," of contracts, though accomplished retrospectively, could not be regarded as "impairments" of "the Obligation of Contracts" and, on this ground, void. In more modern times, with the advance of juristic science, this paradoxical result has, however, been achieved.[11]

An accurate brief summary of the effects of the Court's partial destruction of the state Ex-post-facto Clause is thus anything but easy to draw up. But it is clear, at least, that the Court's action, even in the early days, resulted in a considerable unconstitutional increase of state authority. Latterly, this effect has probably diminished in certain areas, and increased in others, because the Court, more and more, has tended to regard all "ex-post-facto Laws" which it fails to approve, as wanting in what it now calls "due process of law."[12] So, the state authority, nowadays, to "pass ex-post-facto Laws," contrary to the Constitution, is probably limited, in general, to those the Supreme Court approves as "wise," or "fair and reasonable"; or—in the so-called "liberal" formula—those it believes, "wise," "fair," and "reasonable" men might think were laws of that kind. And this means that, considered in relation to the Court's inflated modern theories of "due process of law," both the Ex-post-facto Clauses have come to be quite unnecessary and superfluous provisions of the Constitution.

Much the same sort of thing has happened, over the years, to the Contracts Clause, previously mentioned. Its judicial transformation, in 1827, from a sweeping prohibition of *"any* [state] Law impairing the Obligation of Contracts,"* to a prohibition of such "Laws," only in application to "Contracts [*previously formed*]," manifestly effected a tremendous unconstitutional increase in state legislative authority. In addition, it gave to the interstate theory of the commerce power of Congress, a plausibility that that theory could not otherwise have had; and it seems not too much to say that, without the Court's early partial destruction of the Contracts Clause, the interstate theory of the national commerce power would never even have been possible. So, the Court's destructive action in the case of the Contracts Clause was undoubtedly one of the great and disastrous victories over the Constitution, by the forces of "States' Rights"; a victory that manifestly has had much to do with the rise of that expensive, litigation-producing chaos in American commercial law which exists today. This effect began to develop almost immediately; but it was not until the accession of Chief Justice Taney, the successor of Marshall, that the practice began, of giving to the Contracts Clause, even in its retrospective phase (which was all the Court would recognize), no more than a "reasonable" enforcement. The Court's "reasonableness," in this respect, has grown amazingly since that time;[13] and since it is certain that what the Court does today, under the Contracts Clause, would be done by it, equally willingly, in the name of "due process," it appears that the Contracts Clause, too, has become, very largely, a supernumerary and superfluous part of the Constitution.[14]

The third of the direct limitations on state authority to which earlier chapters were devoted was the Imports and Exports Clause, also of the tenth section of Article I. This clause, the Court has never yet actually merged in "due process of law"; yet the course of its decisions thereunder has been, in many ways, similar to that under the other two clauses just considered. Thus, when the Court first transformed the clause, in 1868, from what it actually is, an express prohibition of *"any* [state] Imposts or Duties on Imports or Exports,"* to a prohibition of such state taxes "on [*foreign*] Imports and [*foreign*] Exports [only]," it simultaneously erected, within the interstate field, a substitute *implied* prohibition of state taxation of interstate commerce, to take the place of what it thus destroyed. This very interesting circumstance fully justifies the view earlier expressed, that the motivation behind this particular piece of "judicial statesmanship" was not originally "States' Rights." Yet there can be little doubt that, over the years, the motivation has altered; and since the original purpose is now quite forgotten, it seems safe to say that the Court's motive, today, is merely its usual one of tenderness toward the states. And from this inveterate tenderness, in this particular case, there has resulted a great unconstitutional increase in the authority of the states to tax—and to tax, moreover, in a particularly obnoxious, burdensome, and uneconomic way. For the Court's carefully provided substitute prohibition never has been more than "reasonably" enforced; and, as indicated earlier, the steady trend, for many years, has been for enforcement to become looser and looser, with the Court exercising the same kind of uncertain, unpredictable control over the subject, which, in other fields, it calls "due process of law." So, all three of these cases which were treated earlier have much in common.

About the same can be said of the Court's inadequate enforcement of the Full Faith and Credit Clause of Article IV, which has likewise been treated earlier, at several different points. For only in the field of judgments has anything like a "full Faith and Credit" been enforced; that is, the "Faith and Credit" required by the rules of "the conflict of laws," considering that subject to be what it was when the clause was drawn: a branch of the law of nations. As a matter of fact, the Court, in the field of judgments, actually has gone, in reliance on the Congressional act of 1790, somewhat beyond what the rules of the conflict of laws would require, though not so far as the act of Congress, reasonably read, would warrant. In the case of statutes, the Court has regarded the Full Faith and Credit Clause as requiring no more, in effect, than a "[reasonable] Faith and Credit" only; a "Faith and Credit," too, which has had little or nothing to do with the rules of the conflict of laws. And, as noted earlier, the Supreme Court's failure to understand the word "Records," in this clause, has produced a failure to enforce it, in the case of state decisional (or "common") law, which is substantially complete. So, it can be seen there are striking resemblances between what the Court has done under this clause, and what it has done under the other three clauses first considered above. For, under the Full Faith and Credit Clause, there has been a great unconstitutional extension of state authority; there has been a shift from the "*full* Faith and Credit" which the clause inexorably commands, to a "[*reasonable*] Faith and Credit" only; and this shift has necessarily given rise, once more, to an utterly unprovided discretionary authority in the Court. And besides these resemblances, there has even been, in the cases of recent decades, a marked tendency to merge the requirements of "full Faith and Credit," in what is nowadays known as "due process of law"; a tendency that is making the Full Faith and Credit Clause, also a very largely unnecessary and superfluous provision of the Constitution.[15]

The foregoing are the principal direct restrictions on state authority, to be found in the original Constitution, which the Court has failed to enforce as the restrictions are written. With the exception of the Ex-post-facto Clause, all of these have been of the first of the two varieties described at the beginning of this chapter; that is, they have been restrictions imposed upon the states to make certain phases of national power exclusive. The Supreme Court's destruction of these provisions, in their intended scope, has then been, over the years, a phase, in the main, of "States' Rights"; something entirely to be expected if the Court's steady hostility toward the governing powers of the nation, except in the very early days, is remembered. The situation with respect to the Ex-post-facto Clauses is, however, more or less of a special case growing originally out of what, undoubtedly, was a mistake in judgment by the Federal Convention, in not excepting the national bankruptcy power from the Ex-post-facto Clause that applies to Congress. And the later developments in the Supreme Court's decisions in regard to retrospective laws, as well as those in regard to the other matters covered by the clauses mentioned, have merely been a phase of the pronounced general tendency of the Court, since about 1890, to dissolve the Constitution, clause by clause, in a vast sea of Supreme Court discretion.

3

It might perhaps be supposed, by a reader unfamiliar with the Supreme Court's decisions, that its record must be very different in "secur[ing those] national rights" against the states, that were created to prevent governmental action of kinds considered to be inherently evil. This, however, is not the case. The Court, from an early day, has shown, and it still shows, the same marked favoritism toward the state governments, where limitations of this character are concerned, as it has, and does, in the case of those imposed to make some field of national power exclusive. Thus, the first eight amendments to the Constitution were all prohibitions of governmental acts that were deemed to be inherently evil; they are what is sometimes called a "bill of rights" of the American people; yet, since its decision in *Barron* v. *Baltimore*,[16] in 1833, the Court's position has been that none of the restrictions in these amendments is applicable to the states.[17] The Court's decision to this effect was announced by it, as if it were very obvious; but the fact is the decision was contrary to the considered opinion of good lawyers before that time, and it is not difficult to show that, in the scope in which the Court announced it, it was without any warrant at all.

The Court's general position in *Barron* v. *Baltimore* was correct, so far as the First Amendment was concerned. For the First Amendment reads as follows: "*Congress* shall make no law respecting an establishment of religion, or prohibiting the free exercise thereof; or abridging the freedom of speech, or of the press, or the right of the people peaceably to assemble, and to petition the Government for a redress of grievances." The explicit terms of these restrictions obviously preclude their application to the states. The history of their framing shows, too, in the plainest way, that the First Amendment was deliberately drawn to create a field, not only of exclusive, but of inviolable state power "respecting" religious establishments; for "*respecting*" these, Congress, it will be observed, was forbidden to legislate at all. In addition to this, Congress was forbidden *to "prohibit* the free exercise of religion"; or *to "abridge* the freedom of speech, or of the press"; or *to "abridge* the right of the people peaceably to assemble, and to petition the Government for a redress of grievances." The state powers of "prohibition" and "abridgment" with respect to all these matters were, then, likewise made exclusive by the First Amendment; but, unlike the state powers "respecting" religious establishments, they were not made inviolable. For Congress, plainly, was *not* prohibited *from prohibiting the states to "prohibit* the free exercise of religion," or *from prohibiting them to "abridge* the freedom of speech, or of the press," or "the right of the people peaceably to assemble, and to petition the Government for a redress of grievances." The power of Congress "respecting" these matters was, then, not blotted out; it was simply reduced to a negative supervisory power over the state governments; to a power, in other words, of securing the American people, in respect to these several matters, against any possible tyrannous action by the states. And if this seems a novel view to any reader, it should be observed that it is simply what the amendment says; and the history of its framing amply demonstrates that what it was to say was most deliberately and carefully determined.

Besides being correct with respect to the First Amendment, the doctrine of *Barron* v. *Baltimore* was also correct with respect to one clause of the Seventh; that is, the clause thereof which relates to appeals. This may be perceived at a glance; for the text of the Seventh Amendment runs, as a whole, as follows: "In suits at common law, where the value in controversy shall exceed twenty dollars, the right of trial by jury shall be preserved, and no fact tried by a jury shall be otherwise re-examined *in any Court of the United States*, than according to the rules of the common law."* The existence of an express limitation, in the

---

* It is perhaps worth noting that the Supreme Court, without apparent reason, gives "common law" one sense—"law," *whether statutory or customary*, as distinct from equity and admiralty—in its first use in the Seventh Amendment, and a different sense—"law," still as distinct from equity and admiralty, *but strictly customary*—in

"appeals" provision of this amendment, manifestly settles the correctness of *Barron* v. *Baltimore*, with respect to it; but it also emphasizes the otherwise obvious fact that the rest of the amendment, relating to trials, is comprehensive; comprehensive, that is, as between the courts of the nation and the courts of the states. So, unless we resort, once more, to the theory of blundering draftsmanship, which, we have seen, the Supreme Court's theories of the original Constitution so extensively compel, there is no way of accounting for the presence of the foregoing qualifying words in the "appeals" provision of the Seventh Amendment, except upon the basis that the First Congress, when it drew the amendment, understood and intended the first part of it to be general in application to both the nation and the states.

The situation is similar in the case of the First Amendment, considered in relation to all the other amendments (other than the "appeals" clause of the Seventh) now making up the first eight. For these amendments are all, in terms, literally general, too. The Fifth Amendment, the application of the last clause of which, to the states, was the precise point involved in *Barron* v. *Baltimore*, is typical of all of these. It reads as follows:

> No person shall be held to answer for a capital, or otherwise infamous crime, unless on a presentment or indictment of a Grand Jury, except in cases arising in the land or naval forces, or in the militia, when in actual service in time of War or public danger; nor shall any person be subject for the same offence to be twice put in jeopardy of life or limb; nor shall be compelled in any criminal case to be a witness against himself, nor be deprived of life, liberty, or property, without due process of law; nor shall private property be taken for public use, without just compensation.

Now, apart, once more, from the remote possibility of sheer negligence or want of skill, in the First Congress, when it drew these amendments —hypotheses, we shall see, which do not fit the facts—the only reasonable explanation for the variance in form thus existing between the First Amendment and all the others of the first eight is that the others were *intentionally* drawn in general terms, in order to apply both to the nation and to the states; whereas the First Amendment, though not precluding control of the states, by Congress, to the ends the amendment had in view (except in the case of "religious establishments"), was nevertheless drawn to apply, in respect of its restrictions, to Congress only. And if these were not the intentions of the First Congress, its draftsmanship of these amendments was bungling, in an extreme degree.

---

its second use therein. *Parsons* v. *Bedford*, 3 Pet. 433 (1830). The result of this inconsistent mode of interpreting the amendment is to restrain Congress absolutely from any reforms in the use of juries in civil cases, though the general opinion among lawyers, both today and in the eighteenth century, is that the use of juries in most civil litigation is not of real utility, and that the existence of a right to demand a jury in such cases is productive only of expense, trouble, and delay.

If we pass now from a consideration of the letter of these amendments (other than the First), to a consideration of their substance and the inherent probabilities as to what the men of the First Congress must have been likely to do in the case of amendments of their precise character, our conclusion—that they were intended, as they were written, to be general as between the nation and the states—will be very greatly fortified. For every one of the literally general prohibitions contained in these amendments relates to governmental action of a kind which, it is perfectly certain, was being forbidden because it was deemed to be inherently evil. It is therefore utterly impossible to suppose that, as to a single one of the matters the amendments cover, the true intention of the First Congress was to create sole and exclusive state powers to do the things forbidden.

Thus, by the clause of the Fifth Amendment which the case of *Barron v. Baltimore* involved, "private property" is forbidden to "be taken for public use, without just compensation." Surely, no good reason could exist for exempting the state governments from this requirement. And the same must certainly have been true of "the right of the people to be secure in their persons, houses, papers, and effects, against unreasonable searches and seizures," which the Fourth Amendment guaranties; also, of their right against the quartering of soldiers in their houses, protected by the Third Amendment; and of their "right to keep and bear Arms," covered by the Second. All the other provisions in these initial amendments have to do with the securing of fair and appropriate legal procedure, or "process," primarily in courts of law; a matter, surely, which it was quite as important to insure against denial by the states, as by the nation.

The provisions of the amendments with respect to this matter of legal process include, first of all, the general guaranty of fair and appropriate "process" in all cases involving "life, liberty, or property," which the Due Process Clause of the Fifth Amendment expresses. This is implemented, as to civil cases, by the "jury-trial" provision of the Seventh Amendment; and, as to criminal cases, by the requirement of "presentment or indictment [by] a Grand Jury," the provision against compelled self-incrimination, and that against double jeopardy, in the earlier clauses of the Fifth; by the right to jury trial, to confrontation by accusers, to compulsory process to obtain witnesses, and to the assistance of counsel, which the Sixth Amendment carefully stipulates; and by the provisions against excessive bail, excessive fines, and cruel and unusual punishments, which are covered in Amendment VIII. In addition to these, there is the matter of warrants, covered by the Fourth Amendment, which belongs under this head, too. If there was a single one of these guaranties which it was not quite as desirable to erect against the state governments, as against the nation, it is not easy to see why this should be; and since

VERNON REGIONAL
JUNIOR COLLEGE LIBRARY

all these guaranties were drawn, in literally general terms, in context with others drawn to apply to Congress only, the only reasonable inference is that they were meant to say what their words express.

Some might be inclined to urge, however, that there was equally good reason to extend against the states the rights which the First Amendment covers; that the First Congress, nevertheless, did not so extend them; and that any argument based upon the essential desirability of extending these other rights against the states, as well as the nation, is therefore illegitimate. But the fact is that what was done in the First Amendment was in accord with the inherent probabilities at the time. For it has to be remembered that, when these initial amendments were drawn, something very like religious establishments, and a certain degree of compulsion in religious matters, still survived in the New England states;* and it is certain, as we shall see presently, that the religious provisions of the First Amendment were drawn as they were, to meet the wishes of the New England men. As for the failure to blot out all governmental power, state as well as national, respecting the subjects of "free speech," "free press," and "free assembly," this is by no means difficult to understand if the fact is borne in mind that Shays' Rebellion, in Massachusetts, and other similar disturbances, in certain of the other states, were not very far in the past when these amendments were drafted. For the still fresh memory of these events probably produced a desire for some governmental control over the three modes of agitating that had underlain them. In these circumstances, state power over these matters, subject

---

* The Constitution of Massachusetts contained the following provision: "As the happiness of a people, and the good order and preservation of civil government, essentially depend upon piety, religion, and morality; and as these cannot be generally diffused through a community, but by the institution of the public worship of God, and of public instructions in piety, religion, and morality: Therefore, to promote their happiness, and to secure the good order and preservation of their government, the people of this commonwealth have a right to invest their legislature with power to authorise *and require,* and the legislature *shall,* from time to time, authorise and *require* the several towns, parishes, precincts, and other bodies-politic, or religious societies, *to make suitable provision,* at their own expence, *for the institution of the public worship of God,* and for the support and maintenance of public *protestant* teachers of piety, religion, and morality, *in all cases where such provision shall not be made voluntarily.* And the people of this commonwealth, have a right to, and do, invest their legislature with authority *to enjoin, upon all subjects,* an attendance upon the instructions of the public teachers as aforesaid, at stated times and seasons, if there be any on whose instructions they can conscientiously and conveniently attend. Provided, notwithstanding, that the several towns, parishes, precincts, and other bodies-politic, or religious societies, shall, at all times, have the exclusive right of electing their public teachers, and of contracting with them for their support and maintenance. And all monies paid by the subject to the support of public worship, and of the public teachers aforesaid, shall, if he require it, be uniformly applied to the support of the public teacher or teachers of his own religious sect or denomination, provided there be any on whose instructions he attends; *otherwise it may be paid towards the support of the teacher or teachers of the parish or precinct in which the said monies are raised.*" See, also, article 6 of the Bill of Rights, attached to the New Hampshire Constitution of the time.

to a negative control in Congress to prevent abuses by the states, was a natural compromise. The tenor of the First Amendment, then, is easily understandable in the conditions of the time; but it is not possible to understand why the nationalist First Congress should have been unwilling to extend to the states, the guaranties of life, liberty, and property, in the other amendments, which they were ready to erect against their new government of the nation. And since they cast these other amendments in terms that included the states, the rational conclusion is that they intended the amendments to mean what the amendments said.

Nor can it be contended there was not as much need to erect these amendments against the states as there was to erect them against the nation. As earlier pointed out, only about half the state constitutions of the time contained comprehensive bills of rights,[18] and because, as we saw in chapter xxvii, general judicial review was not a going institution in any of the states, in 1789, the state bills of rights, even where they existed, lacked the machinery of enforcement they have since acquired, and which, with the force of the nation behind it, would be made available in their support, as against the states, if a general bill of rights, against state as well as national action, was adopted. For, although, as we have seen, *general* judicial review was not provided in the Constitution against Congress, it was quite plainly provided there against the states. So, it must have been a great temptation to all believers in bills of rights, in states were they were lacking or were not enforced, to add a general bill to the Constitution and thus put all the rights it could be made to cover, on a firmer basis. And certainly the nationalists in the First Congress, even those who did not really believe in bills of rights, would not have objected to such a measure, as against the states, when they consented to it, as against the nation. The inherent probability, then, is that such action was taken. And when the further circumstance is brought to view, that at least one of the state ratifying conventions had seemed to desire the enactment of just such a *general* bill of rights, the probability of such action increases.

The state convention meant is that of Virginia. For the first of its recommendations for "Subsequent Amendments" was that "a Declaration, or Bill of Rights, asserting *and securing from encroachment* the essential and *unalienable* Rights *of the People*," be added to the Constitution, in "the mode prescribed in [Article V]." This, it was suggested, might well be done "in some such manner as" in a pattern declaration appended. That pattern declaration was a long and elaborate document, much too long for full quotation here. It seems sufficient to say of it, that it was modeled closely upon the Virginia bill of rights, of 1776, and that its style throughout was in the unrestrained general terms which, we have seen already, were employed in most of the first eight amendments afterwards adopted. The following excerpts are typical:

That in all capital and criminal prosecutions, a man hath a right to demand the cause and nature of his accusation.

That the people have a right peaceably to assemble together to consult for the common good.

That no freeman ought to be taken, imprisoned, or disseised of his franchises, or outlawed, or exiled, or in any manner destroyed, or deprived of his life, liberty, or property but by the law of the land.

In short, there was, in this pattern bill of rights that the Virginia convention submitted, not a single word, from beginning to end, that even remotely suggested it was anything other than what it seemed to be: a *general* bill of rights, meant to be binding upon the states, as well as the nation. And this view of it is fortified if its style is compared with that of the other amendments that the Virginia convention suggested; for these were all specific statements as to what "Congress" should do or should not do; as to what "the judicial Power of the United States" should do or should not do; or stipulations as to what "each State," notwithstanding the Constitution, should have power to do; or the like.[19]

Read straightforwardly, then, the sense of this first Virginia proposal seems clear. And when it is remembered, further, that the proposal was to add, *in gross,* this general and elaborate declaration of *"unalienable"* popular rights, to a document whose avowed purposes included that of "secur[ing] the Blessings of Liberty to ['the People of the United States'] and [their] Posterity"—a document, moreover, that purported to be, in all its parts, "the supreme Law of the Land," and to be "binding" on "the Judges in every State," "any Thing in the Constitution or Laws of any State to the Contrary notwithstanding"—when all this is considered, it is surely difficult to see what other sense could be attributed to this Virginia proposal, than that just suggested. Nor is it at all hard to believe that the convention of Virginia would recommend such a measure, if the desires of various of the state's leaders at the time, and the constitutional conditions then prevailing in the state, both of which matters have been considered previously in chapter xxvii, are recalled to mind.

For, in our earlier examination of these subjects, we learned that the Virginia constitution and bill of rights that were in effect in 1789, had originated as ordinary legislative enactments, subject, like any others, to alteration at any time by the state's legislature. Thomas Jefferson, we then saw, was of the opinion, in 1782, that the alterability of these documents, in this mode, had been quite definitely intended by the temporary ruling body that had enacted them; and he maintained that every successive legislature, from 1776 till the day he wrote, had passed acts inconsistent with these original basic enactments. The legislature, he said, exercised any kind of power it pleased; and there was no possibility that he could see, of opposing it, whether its acts comported with the state's constitution and bill of rights or not. And that he was right about this, at the time he wrote, the case of *Commonwealth* v. *Caton*, which we examined in chapter xxvii, demonstrates.

The Virginia constitution and bill of rights then in effect did eventually come to be looked upon as a "higher law" which the Virginia legislature was bound to observe; but as we saw in our earlier reference to the subject, this change had not yet occurred when the Constitution of the United States was adopted. This was indicated, partly, by Jefferson's continuing concern about the situation in Virginia, in letters he wrote from France, in 1785 and 1786; partly, by letters written to him in those same years, from Virginia; partly, by George Mason's remarks about the Virginia constitutional situation, in the Federal Convention; partly, by Mason's efforts, there, to obtain, in the Constitution, a bill of rights of the American people; and partly, by the uncontradicted statements made in the Virginia ratifying convention of 1788, that violations of the state's constitution and, more particularly, of its bill of rights had been continuous from 1776 up to that date. And Madison, who had been so greatly concerned, in the Federal Convention, to include in the Constitution provisions for "secur[ing] a good internal legislation and administration to the particular States," declared, in a letter to Jefferson, in the fall of 1788, that, in his experience in the Virginia legislature, he "ha[d] seen the [state's] bill of rights violated in every instance where it ha[d] been opposed to a popular current." More specifically, he said that, "notwithstanding the explicit provision in that instrument for the rights of conscience, it [was] well known a religious establishment w[oul]d have taken place in the state, if the Legislative majority had found, as they expected, a majority of the people in favor of the measure."[20] And that there still was, in 1788, no remedy for such violations, by judicial review, we saw from our examination of the so-called "Case of the Judges," wherein, just before the Virginia convention met, the judges of the state's Court of Appeals had "respectfully remonstrated" with the legislature, over the unconstitutionality of the enactments that the case involved. For, despite their "Respectful Remonstrance," the judges, it will be remembered, were forced, in the end, to give in to the legislature and accept that body's views on the point at issue.[21]

In the light, then, of all these facts, it does not seem at all improbable that there were, in the Virginia convention, many men who desired to use the opportunity that adoption of the Constitution presented, to put the rights declared in the Virginia bill of rights, upon a firmer basis. This would have been the consequence of declaring them, either originally or by amendment, in the Constitution of the United States. For the Virginia judges would then, not only be able, *but obliged*, to enforce the rights so declared upon the state's legislature, since the rights, thereafter, would be part of "the supreme Law of the Land" and, by express provision of the

Constitution, "binding" upon "the [Virginia] Judges," "any Thing in the Constitution or Laws of [the] State [of Virginia] to the Contrary notwithstanding." And to a proposal thus to declare these popular rights, the proponents of a bill of rights against Congress must have found it hard, indeed, to object. So, remembering that the first of the state's recommendations for amendments does seem very clearly to have been such a bill, there is, assuredly, little room for doubt that it was, in fact, what it appeared to be. And that makes reasonable the same conclusion in the case of those initial amendments to the Constitution that followed this form the Virginia convention had recommended.

It remains true, however, that the amendments in question, though undeniably general, are nevertheless not specific in their application to the states. They are, therefore, the kind of general words that, in proper circumstances, in the eighteenth century, were sometimes made the subject, under the rules of interpretation then in use, of equities of restraint. But such equities could arise only from some clear, strong evidence of a purpose narrower than that which the words to be restrained expressed. Such evidence, we learned in our earlier discussions, might consist of a deliberate statement of the purpose of a document in its preamble; it might consist in the relations observable between a document's several parts; or it might consist in the circumstances in which a document was written. But, in either case, as we learned, the evidence of purpose giving rise to such equities of restraint—or, for that matter, to equities of fulfilment—had to be strong and clear.

We have just finished examining the circumstances in which the initial amendments to the Constitution were written. Those circumstances, far from evincing, clearly and strongly, a purpose of the First Congress, narrower than that which its words expressed, rather indicate that its purpose was, in all probability, precisely that which they did express. We have seen, too, that a comparison of the First Amendment with the others drawn at the same time, and a comparison, likewise, of the expressly restrained "appeals" provision in the Seventh Amendment, with the unrestrained generality of all the other provisions in the amendments (other than the First), point to this conclusion, too. And on the basis, finally, of the general purposes stated in the document to which these amendments were about to be added, the same conclusion, undoubtedly, is warranted. For those purposes included the "secur[ing of] the Blessings of Liberty to ['the People of the United States']." And because this purpose was not one narrower, or other, than that which the amendments themselves appeared to envisage, but was, instead, one with which, in their strict literality, they exactly corresponded, it manifestly followed, under the eighteenth-century constructionary rules, that the words of the amendments would have to be given their full literal force; and this, even though their want of specificity in relation to the states could be regarded as in the nature of an ambiguity in them. For such a meaning for the amendments was required *if* "the Liberties" of the American people were to be *fully* "secured."

The one piece of evidence remaining (besides the history of the framing of the amendments, to be taken up in the next section) likewise fails to establish, strongly and clearly, any purpose narrower than that which the amendments literally express. This is the now almost forgotten preamble that preceded them when they were submitted to the states, by Congress.* This preamble began by reciting that "the Conventions of a Number of the States ha[d], at the Time of their adopting the Constitution, expressed a Desire, in order to prevent misconstruction or abuse of *its* Powers, that *further* declaratory and *restrictive Clauses* should be added." And it was then intimated that the amendments following were being submitted to the states, because, it was believed, "extending the Ground of Public Confidence in *the Government*, w[ould] best insure *the beneficent Ends of its Institution*."[22] This last indicates that the ultimate "objects" of the amendments, and those recited in the Preamble of the Constitution, were the same. And bearing in mind that "*the Constitution*" was, in fact, a scheme of "*Government*" through state "*Powers*" as well as national "*Powers*"; that some of the "Powers," of both these kinds, were express in the document, and some implied; that this was the theory of the merely declaratory amendment now the Tenth; and that "*its* Powers"—that is, the powers of the compound government provided in the Constitution—had originally been subjected, in many instances, to "*restrictive Clauses*" applying to the states—bearing in mind these things, it is difficult to see how the preamble to the amendments could be taken as *clear* evidence of a purpose, through the amendments, to impose further restrictions on the nation alone; evidence, that is, which would warrant an equitable restraint of this tenor, upon the plain letter of most of the prohibitions the amendments contain. And when, in addition, the further fact is brought to view, that "the Convention" of Virginia had seemed to ask "addition" of a *general* "Bill of Rights" to the Constitution, the impossibility of so taking the words of this unadopted preamble seems certain.

Its somewhat strange wording—possibly artful—may, however, have raised a question, when it first was read, and before the amendments themselves had been examined, as to what the amendments covered. But a preamble of doubtful meaning—one that merely raised questions to be resolved by a purview, rather than settled questions which a purview raised—was not the sort of preamble that would restrain general words in a purview, in the eighteenth century. And if the words it contained could be regarded as making doubtful the intended generality of the amendments that followed it, such doubts, like every other as to the meaning of

* The preamble to the amendments never became a part of the Constitution.

the Constitution, were to be resolved in the light of the clear preambular statement of purposes in the original document, of which the amendments, but not the preamble to the amendments, were about to be made a part. The result on this basis has already been indicated. So, however this subject be viewed, the going rules of 1789 would seem to have required the conclusion that the states were intended to be covered. And there is the further and final corroboration arising out of the one line of evidence still remaining to be examined; for, as we shall now see, this remaining line of evidence makes certain that the result compelled by the old constructionary rules is also the correct one, in fact. The evidence meant is the long-neglected history of the framing of the initial amendments, by the First Congress; a history that was recorded contemporaneously in the country's newspaper press and other publications of the time. And since these old records put all doubt at rest, they will be examined in detail, in the section of this chapter which follows.

4

As already recorded in chapter xxii, the first ten amendments originated in the House of Representatives, where they were presented in their initial form, on June 8, 1789, by James Madison. If the amendments had been adopted as Madison then presented them, the decision of the Supreme Court in *Barron* v. *Baltimore,* even as it related to the amendments cast in unrestrained general terms, would, in the main, have been correct. For, as Madison presented these amendments (or, at any rate, most of them), they were to be adopted *expressly for insertion in section 9 of Article I of the original Constitution;*[23] and in that particular section of the original document, there were already certain general prohibitions, the *intended* application of which, *to the nation only,* was nevertheless clearly indicated by other features of this particular part of the document.

These other features consisted of repetitions of certain of the literally general prohibitions of section 9, in section 10 of the same article, drawn, however, to apply, in terms, to the states only. Thus, with respect to "ex post facto Laws," it was provided, in section 9, that "no ex post facto Law sh[ould] be passed"; and, in section 10, it was provided that "no State sh[ould] pass any ex post facto Law." It can thus be seen that the contextual situation in this part of the original Constitution was almost the exact opposite of that in the initial amendments. For the First Amendment says, "Congress shall make no law respecting an establishment of religion"; whereas the Fifth Amendment and most of the others are in the form, "no person shall be deprived of life, liberty, or property, without due process of law." And those of the other initial amendments which are not in this form are in another equally general.* Hence, in the same way

* Those not in the unrestrained passive-voice form of the Fifth Amendment are in the form of the provision in the Fourth Amendment, that "no Warrants shall issue, but upon probable cause, &c."

that the First Amendment, and the single qualified provision in the Seventh Amendment, confirm the *intended general* sense of the unrestrained general provisions in the initial amendments generally, so the repetition with specific reference to the states, in section 10 of Article I, of various of the literally general prohibitions found in section 9, establishes that, *in that particular section of the Constitution*, the literal generality of certain of the prohibitions there to be found was *not* their *intended* sense. .Elsewhere in the original document, the mode of draftsmanship, we shall presently see, was different; as it also was, eventually, in the case of the first eight amendments. But under the mode of amending that Madison at first proposed, the intended sense of the general prohibitions already contained in the section to which his amendments were, in the main, proposed to be added, would have controlled their literal generality; and on this ground alone, *if* the amendments had been made as Madison proposed them, the Supreme Court's decision in *Barron* v. *Baltimore* would have been correct.

As Madison originally made his proposals, they included, moreover, still another feature that would have had this same effect. For Madison presented, along with various amendments cast in the passive voice with no actor, or agent, specified in them, one cast in the active voice, covering some of the same ground, but applying, by its express terms, to the states only. This amendment ran as follows: "No State shall violate the equal rights of conscience, or the freedom of the press or the trial by jury in criminal cases."[24] The situation, then, was that, in Madison's original proposals themselves, the relationship between the passives and the actives was the same as that between these same grammatical forms in sections 9 and 10 of Article I of the original Constitution. So, on this ground too, if the amendments had actually been adopted as Madison presented them, the Supreme Court's decision in *Barron* v. *Baltimore* would have been correct. But the amendments, as already indicated, were *not* so adopted, because Congress did not propose them in that form to the states; and the changes made in them by Congress, before it proposed them, plainly indicate that the sweeping doctrine of the Court, in the case just mentioned, was without any warrant at all.

Madison's proposals of the 8th of June were eventually handed over, to a select committee of the House of Representatives.[25] This committee, in a report made on the 28th of July, adhered to the *mode* of amending that Madison had suggested; that is, the committee proposed the making of the amendments by insertion, or deletion, or both, with respect to particular, named provisions of the original Constitution.[26] When the select committee's report was taken up in committee of the whole House, Roger Sherman, of Connecticut, on August 13th, objected to amending the Constitution in this manner. He proposed, instead, that the amendments be made in the mode which eventually was used, and which, since that time, has been uniformly used in all the amendments to the Constitution. He proposed, in other words, that the amendments be made in the form of independent propositions, clear, complete, and understandable in themselves, not depending for their meaning upon an intended relation to particular parts of the original document, to which, of course, if Madison's method had been followed, reference would have been necessary, in every case, to determine what the amendments meant. Sherman's proposal failed in the committee of the whole House;[27] but he renewed it, on the 19th or 20th of August, when the report of the committee was taken up by the House as such; and his proposal was then adopted.[28] That it was recognized this change in the mode of amending would affect the meaning of the proposed amendments and necessitate a rephrasing of practically all of them if their meaning was to be unaltered is certain; for Madison immediately urged this in objection to Sherman's proposal when that proposal first was made. It would "so far unhinge the business," he said, "as to occasion alterations in every article and clause of the report."[29]

In the report of the select committee, the first proposition suggested for insertion *in the ninth section of Article I* had read as follows: "No religion shall be established by law, nor shall the equal rights of conscience be infringed."[30] In committee of the whole House, on August 15th—that is, before Sherman's motion was adopted—this mode of expression was attacked as open to interpretation as applying to the states, even though, as just indicated, it was employed in an amendment which, at that date, was still being proposed *for insertion in the section just mentioned.* Huntington, of Connecticut, one of the objectors, explained to the men from other regions that "the ministers of the congregations to the Eastward were maintained by the contributions of those who belonged to their society; [that] the expense of building meeting-houses was contributed in the same manner; [and that] these things were regulated by by-laws." He feared, he said, that these arrangements "might be construed into a religious establishment"; that the proposed provision might therefore be held to apply to them; and that, should this occur, and "an action [be] brought before a federal court on any of [these] cases, the person who had neglected to perform his engagements could not be compelled to do it." It is noteworthy, too (though this is not recorded), that it was probably also an objection that the form of the foregoing proposed amendment did *not* preclude Congress from forbidding state "religious establishments" of the kind then still existing in the New England states, or from prohibiting the degree of compulsion in religious matters still practiced in some of those states, at the time. For, after some debate, it was agreed to alter the amendment to the following form, proposed by Livermore, of New Hampshire: "*Congress* shall make no laws *touching* religion, or infringing the rights of conscience."[31] It seems a certain inference from this transformation of this amendment to the active voice, with Congress specified as the subject, or actor, as it also does from the demand that such a change be made, that the obvious generality of the unrestrained passive-voice prohibitions now contained in the first eight amendments was perceived from the very first. And more evidence to this effect is provided by an attempt made—also in committee of the whole House—to limit the "double-jeopardy" prohibition now in the Fifth Amendment, by inserting, in it, the words "by any law of the United States." This attempt, however, was not successful.[32]

The adoption of Sherman's motion by the House, on August 19th, manifestly opened the door somewhat wider to the possibility of applying the unrestrained passive-voice prohibitions to the states. For, as the amendments thereafter stood, the one remaining thing that could have been taken to preclude such a result was the single repetitious active-voice prohibition mentioned above, which applied expressly to the states and forbade them to "violate the equal rights of conscience, or the freedom of the press, or the trial by jury in criminal cases." This had been opposed in committee of the whole House, but had nevertheless passed. A mere majority vote had been sufficient for this purpose in the committee; but in the House itself, one-third of the members plus one had power, under the Constitution, to defeat it.[33] It could not, then, have been at all certain that this single repetitious amendment applying to the states would pass; and if it did not, the sole surviving basis for inferring an exclusively national application for the various amendments drawn in unrestrained general terms would be destroyed, and all those amendments, by reason of their literal generality, would apply, not only to the nation, but to the states as well. In these circumstances, it might naturally be supposed, in view of what had passed before, that further efforts would have been made at this point to restrain, in some way, the various amendments that were cast in literally general terms, *if* it was *not* desired that they should apply to the states as well as the nation. No further efforts of the kind were, however, at this point, made; yet it is not improbable, in view of what afterwards occurred, that the members, of all shades of opinion, were merely marking time, till it was determined what was going to be done about the single repetitious amendment relating to "religious freedom," "free press," and "jury trial," which, in express terms, applied to the states.

That amendment passed the House on August 20th. The next day, Sherman, author of the motion the adoption of which had altered the *mode* of the amendments, presented a motion that the amendment which is now the Tenth be altered to read as follows: "The powers not delegated by this Constitution, *nor prohibited by it, to the government of the United States,* are reserved to the individuals of the* States respective-

* As noted earlier in chapter xxii, it is barely possible Sherman may have proposed that the "reservation" be made "to the individual States respectively." The record is not

ly."[34] The effect of the words in this motion that have been italicized was manifestly to accomplish in another way, substantially the same thing that the defeat of the single active-voice prohibition directed expressly to the states would have accomplished, had that defeat occurred. According to the *Gazette of the United States*, for August 22, 1789, Sherman's "motion was acceded to, and the clause then adopted." It is probable the *Gazette* was mistaken about the disposal of this motion; but if it was not, the action must, afterwards, have been rescinded; for, as the amendment now the Tenth was sent to the Senate, on August 24th, it was exactly as Madison had originally presented it.[35] Sherman's motion makes clear, none the less, that there was sentiment in the House, even at this early date, to extend to the states all the prohibitions which were laid on Congress; or all of them, at least, except those, probably, which related to "religious establishments." With this fact in mind, it becomes easier to understand what afterwards occurred in the Senate; and what the Congress as a whole eventually determined to submit to the states, in the way of proposed amendments.

In the Senate, the single active-voice amendment directed to the states, which forbade them to "violate the equal rights of conscience, or the freedom of the press, or the trial by jury in criminal cases," was voted down, on the 7th of September.[36] This, at first blush, may seem to evince that the majority in the Senate was against adding, at all, to the restrictions upon the states that the original Constitution contained. Such an inference would not, however, be warranted. For the Senate's voting-down of this amendment destroyed, it will not be forgotten, the sole surviving basis in the amendments, as they then existed, for inferring an intended application of their various literally general prohibitions, to the nation only. And that this effect of its vote was perceived by the Senate, and hence intended, except in so far as some contrary provision might otherwise be made, seems plain from the various other things which the Senate did to the amendments, and to which the House eventually agreed.

The amendments sent to the Senate by the House, on August 24th, had included only one active-voice prohibition addressed specifically to the nation. It read as follows, as the House eventually passed it: "Congress shall make no law establishing religion, or prohibiting the free exercise thereof . . . ."[37] It will be observed that, in this form in which this prohibition finally passed the House, legislation by Congress forbidding "religious establishments," and any kind of religious compulsion, in the states, had again become possible. It seems inferable, then, that there was a close division of opinion in the House, as to what, in this particular respect,

---

completely clear on this particular point; but for reasons set forth in chapter xxii, the version in the text seems the probable form of this Sherman proposal. This want of clarity in the extant record is, it will be observed, not relevant to the point under consideration at this point in the present chapter.

was desirable. Our main present interest is, however, that the negatory vote of the Senate, on September 7th, had no effect of extending this particular prohibition to the states; for the form of the provision precluded this. The amendment containing it went on, however: "nor shall the rights of conscience be infringed." And of this prohibition, since it was in the passive voice, with no particular agent, or actor, specified, and therefore general in its application, the reverse was true, unless its introduction by the conjunction "nor," and its inclusion in the same sentence with the "religious-establishments" prohibition applying to Congress only, would have saved it from being understood as applying to the states. In any event, it should be observed, it was one of the prohibitions the Senate had voted down, as against the states specifically, on September 7th.

With respect to "freedom of the press" and "jury trial in criminal cases,"[38] the other two matters covered by the prohibition voted down by the Senate, as against the states specifically, on September 7th, the situation was clear. For the proposed amendments relating to these subjects, that the House had sent, were in general terms; and if it was not desired that they apply to the states, something had to be done to preclude their being so understood. The amendments covering these matters read as follows:

> *The freedom* of speech, and *of the press*, and the right of the people peaceably to assemble, and consult for their common good, and to apply to the government for a redress of grievances, *shall not be infringed*.

> *The trial of all crimes* (except in cases of impeachment, and in cases arising in the land or naval forces, or in the militia when in actual service in time of war or public danger) *shall be by an impartial jury* of the vicinage, with the right of challenge and other accustomed requisites; and no person shall be held to answer for a capital or otherwise infamous crime, unless on a presentment or indictment by a grand jury; but if a crime be committed in a place in the possession of an enemy, or in which an insurrection may prevail, the indictment and trial may by law be authorized in some other place within the same state.[39]

The *differing* actions which, we shall now see, the Senate took with respect to the three foregoing literally general prohibitions relating to "rights of conscience," "jury trial," and "freedom of the press," taken with its total failure, despite its negatory vote of September 7th, to alter the literal generality of any of the other prohibitions which the House had sent, make sufficiently clear what the Senate was about.

Thus, the above amendment relating to "freedom of speech, press, and assembly" was changed, as a whole, on the 4th of September, to the active voice, with Congress specified as the grammatical subject, or actor. Later, on September 9th, the resulting amendment was combined with the "religious-freedom" amendment, *but with the "rights-of-conscience" provision wholly omitted*, to read, as a whole, as follows:

Congress shall make no law establishing articles of faith or a mode of worship, or prohibiting the free exercise of religion, or abridging the freedom of speech, or the press, or the right of the people peaceably to assemble, and petition the Government for the redress of grievances.[40]

Except that, in this form, power was still left to Congress to forbid "religious establishments" in the states, the foregoing is manifestly close to the amendment, now the First, as that was eventually proposed by Congress. And the inferences to be drawn from the Senate's change of the "free-speech," "free-press," and "free-assembly" elements of the antecedent amendment covering these matters, to the active voice, as they appear above, with Congress specified as the subject, or actor, seem plainly to be as follows: (1) that the Senate was fully aware of the effect of its negatory vote of September 7th, in destroying the sole pre-existing basis for restraining, to a merely national application, the literally general passive-voice amendments that had come from the House; (2) that, as to the particular subject of "freedom of the press," *one of the three subjects covered by the specific state prohibition voted down by the Senate, on September 7th,* and likewise as to the subjects of "freedom of speech and assembly" and, also, the subject of religion as a whole, a constitutional prohibition on the states, as distinct from the nation, was not desired; and (3) that the change of the prohibitions relating to the first three of these matters, to the active voice, with Congress specified as the subject, or actor, was therefore effected by the Senate to preclude such a result. This, after all, is the only conceivable reason there could have been for such a change as this which the Senate made. And that body's total omission of the literally general "rights-of-conscience" provision—*another of the subjects covered by the specific state prohibition that had been voted down, by the Senate, two days earlier*—manifestly fits into this interpretation, too.

So far as the prohibitions relating to religion are concerned, the Senate's motives for precluding their application to the states were, in all probability, similar to those, previously quoted, which Huntington, of Connecticut, had expressed, and in which other New Englanders had concurred, in committee of the whole House of Representatives, on August 15th. And in the case of the "free-speech," "free-press," and "free-assembly" prohibitions, the recency of Shays' Rebellion, in Massachusetts, and other similar disturbances, in certain of the other states, are the facts, as previously suggested, which should be borne in mind; for they and the religious conditions in the New England states undoubtedly supply the key to an understanding of what was done.

If, then, the Senate, *with the foregoing motives,* omitted the literally general "rights-of-conscience" provision and altered those relating to the rights of "free-speech," "free-press," and "free-assembly," to the active voice, with Congress specified as the subject, or actor—and certainly, it seems, it must have been with these precise motives that these changes were made—then the inference to be drawn from the Senate's *failure* similarly to transform the House amendment in reference to "jury trial in criminal cases"—*the third subject of the specific state prohibition that the Senate had voted down, on September 7th*—must be that it meant the prohibitions of that amendment to apply, in general,[41] not only to the nation, but to the states as well. And the inference to be drawn from the Senate's failure to make similar transformations in the case of all the other literally general amendments that the House had sent, and that the Senate's negatory vote of the 7th of September had likewise made applicable to the states, is the same. For, bearing in mind that the Senate's vote of the 7th destroyed the sole basis then still surviving for limiting *any* of the literally general amendments to the nation alone, its selective transformation of certain of these amendments to the active voice, with Congress specified as the subject, or actor, taken with its failure to transform, or in any other way limit, the other literally general amendments which it had before it, manifestly makes sense on no other basis.

It remains only to be added that the House eventually agreed to the Senate's alterations, subject to certain minor changes, most of which are not of any importance in the present discussion.[42] An exception, however, is the alteration made in the amendment which is now the First, insofar as it related to religion. As this had finally been passed in the Senate, after a good deal of trouble, and sent back to the House, it ran as follows:

Congress shall make no law establishing articles of faith or a mode of worship, or prohibiting the free exercise of religion. . . .[43]

Madison had originally proposed this amendment to read as follows:

The civil rights of none shall be abridged on account of religious belief or worship, nor shall any national religion be established, nor shall the full and equal rights of conscience be in any manner or on any pretext infringed.[44]

In the select committee's report made to the House, on the 28th of July, the amendment had read:

No religion shall be established by law, nor shall the equal rights of conscience be infringed.[45]

As earlier recorded, it was objected to this, on August 15th, in committee of the whole House, that it might be taken to apply to the states even though it was then expressly proposed for insertion in section 9 of Article I of the original Constitution. The amendment was thereupon changed, it will be remembered, on motion of Livermore, of New Hampshire, to read as follows:

Congress shall make no laws touching religion, or infringing the rights of conscience.[46]

This new phrasing, as before pointed out, forbade Congress to legislate on the subject of religion at all; and it was suggested earlier that the new phrasing probably meant that the original phrasing had also been considered objectionable by some of the New England men because it left Congress free to forbid state religious establishments and all state compulsion as to religious matters. The objectors—craftily, perhaps—did not apparently mention this objection when the amendment was first rephrased; and with reason, it would seem, since, in the House as such, before the amendment was sent to the Senate, it was changed again, this time to read as follows:

Congress shall make no law establishing religion, or prohibiting the free exercise thereof. . . .[47]

In this form in which this amendment had finally passed the House, Congressional supervision of the states on the subject of religion was, again, made plainly permissible; and though the amendment was changed by the Senate, reference to its version—the first one quoted above—will show that such supervision was possible thereunder, too. In the final form, to which both the House and the Senate agreed, the New Englanders, it appears, got *part*, however, of what they wanted. For the final version, now in the First Amendment, provided as follows:

Congress shall make no law respecting an establishment of religion, or prohibiting the free exercise thereof. . . .

So, in the end, there seems to have been a compromise on this subject of religion; and from the record of the vicissitudes the amendment went through,* and the remarks about it by Huntington, of Connecticut, heretofore quoted, certain inferences seem amply warranted.

In the first place, then, it can hardly be doubted that the foregoing changes, *back and forth upon this subject of religion,* must have been deemed significant. And if they were deemed significant, it must have been because Congress was understood to be possessed of power in the premises, to the extent that it was not restrained. Since, however, no power over the subject of religion is specifically enumerated in the Constitution, as belonging to Congress, this means that both by the New England men in the First Congress, who wished to forbid Congress to "touch" religion, and by their opponents there, who wished to leave Congress free to "secure Liberty" in the states on the subject, Congress was deemed possessed of *general legislative authority,* except in those areas, again, wherein it was in some way specifically restrained. And since all these changes, back and forth upon this subject of religion, took place *in spite of the fact* that an amendment had then been agreed to, corresponding in all material respects to the amendment now the Tenth,[48] these

* There were a number of other versions of the amendment unsuccessfully proposed in the Senate.

changes also mean that these men in the First Congress saw nothing in the amendment which is now the Tenth, that made any change in the Constitution, in this important respect. It can therefore readily be seen that the history of the framing of the First Amendment, as it relates to religion, provides highly cogent corroboration of the views as to the character of the powers of Congress, and the meaning of the Tenth Amendment, presented earlier in this book.

Besides the importance, in these respects, of this long-neglected episode in our early history, it can be seen that the many changes made in the First Amendment, as it related to religion, also establish, beyond the possibility of any doubt, that the initial amendments to the Constitution were most carefully drawn. It appears, too, from the history of the foregoing changes in the First Amendment, that the applicability to the states, of the amendments drawn unrestrainedly in the passive voice, with no actor, or agent, specified in them, was drawn to the attention of the House as early as August 15th. So, the House must have known what it was doing, when it finally agreed with the Senate to submit the amendments to the states in this general form—or, in certain cases, in another form equally general—*without any basis in them* to ground an inference that, despite their literally general scope, they were intended to apply only to the nation, and not to the governments of the states. The agreement by the House to extend to the states all the literally general prohibitions which the Senate had passed seems, moreover, to be quite easily credible in view of another fact recorded earlier in this section. For Roger Sherman's motion in the House, on August 21st, for altering the amendment which is now the Tenth, sufficiently shows that there must have been some sentiment in the House for such an extension, even before the Senate had acted. And the necessity for reaching agreement with the Senate, together with the essential reasonableness of what the Senate desired, apparently produced the necessary two-thirds vote in the House, in favor of the amendments as eventually proposed.

The obvious inference, then, is that the First Congress *intended* all the prohibitions in the initial amendments, that are cast in literally general terms, to apply to the states as well as the nation. There was, assuredly, nothing unreasonable in this, since the prohibitions in question were all for "securing Liberties" generally regarded as essential. Any man of the time who read the current newspaper accounts of Congress' proceedings must, then, certainly have concluded that the literal generality of these amendments was intended; and since it is reasonable to suppose the leaders—and, particularly, the anti-nationalist leaders—in the several states, read the accounts of Congress' proceedings religiously, the further inference follows that the legislatures of the states, when they ratified the first eight amendments, must have been aware that, within the scope of all those amendments, or parts thereof, which were expressed unrestrainedly in the passive voice, or in some other literally general form, they were ratifying limitations, not only on the nation, but on the state governments as well. So, it is not in any way strange that good lawyers in the early days—Justice William Johnson, speaking for the Supreme Court itself, in 1819, and for himself alone, in 1820;[49] the justices of the Supreme Court of New York, in that same year;[50] and the well-known law writers, William Rawle, of Philadelphia, and Joseph K. Angell, of Providence, in 1828 and 1829[51]—were of the opinion, before the Supreme Court's decision of *Barron* v. *Baltimore* had been handed down, that all such parts of the first eight amendments did apply, *in accordance with their plain letter*, to all governmental action, whether by the nation or by the separate states.

5

It appears, then, as well on the basis of the history of the initial amendments in the First Congress, as upon the basis of their literal import and the rule for their construction which the final "object" in the Preamble of the Constitution requires, that *Barron* v. *Baltimore* was incorrectly decided. Yet the Supreme Court, speaking through Chief Justice Marshall, announced its incorrect decision as if the correctness thereof were clear and certain, beyond the possibility of any doubt. The question presented in the case, the Chief Justice said, was considered by the Court to be "of great importance, but not of much difficulty." There was no dissent in the case; and since Justice Joseph Story was then on the Court, that distinguished judge—if we may believe his silence*—must have held this view, too. So, a brief look at the reasons adduced by the Court to support its decision seems in order.

Apart from certain implications from what he presented as the history of the period when the amendments were adopted—a history which, comparison with the preceding pages will show, was far, indeed, from being complete and accurate—the main argument of the Chief Justice was that, contrary to the views he had expressed in some of his more celebrated decisions,[52] the Constitution was to be taken as "ordained and established by the people of the United States for themselves, for their own government, and *not* for the government of the individual states." "Limitations on power," in the document, "if expressed in general terms," were therefore "naturally and necessarily applicable," he said, "to the government created by the instrument"; but "*not*" to the states, which the great Federalist Chief Justice actually described, in *this* opinion, as "distinct governments." Inspection of the original Constitution would show, he

---

* The inference is pretty strong from Story's *Commentaries*, apparently *written before Barron* v. *Baltimore* was decided, that Story was really of the contrary view. In what he had to say of the amendments, he cited Rawle throughout, with seeming approval. See, also, Story, III, 751.

added, that this had been the understanding of the framers. The contextual situation in sections 9 and 10, of Article I (already described), was "strong, if not conclusive," evidence of this. And, besides, if section 10 were inspected, it would be found that "the several limitations on the powers of the states which [were] contained [therein]" were "generally" restraints relating to "subjects intrusted to the government of the Union, in which all the states [were] interested. In these alone were the whole people concerned." In support of this view, the Chief Justice then set forth the various provisions of the section that actually were of the kind he described, *omitting all others.* "It would be tedious," he said, "to recapitulate [all of them]." So, bearing in mind the character of the first eight amendments (which related only to the unimportant subject of "securing Liberty"), and the fact (to quote his own words) that, "in *every* inhibition [in the original Constitution] *intended to act on state power,* words [were] employed which *directly express[ed]* that intent"— bearing in mind these things, or supposed things, "some strong reason" must be shown, the Chief Justice said, for taking the literally general, but unspecific, prohibitions in the various initial amendments, as applying to the states. "We search in vain for that reason," he observed in conclusion. "These amendments contain no expression indicating an intention to apply them to the state governments. This Court cannot so apply them."[53]

Now, remembering that the initial amendments were proposed as a group by the First Congress, two years after the original Constitution had been proposed by the Federal Convention; and remembering, further, that the amendments, in accord with the desire of Sherman, of Connecticut, had then been submitted in the form of clear and complete propositions, fully understandable in themselves, *without any necessity of referring to the Constitution to ascertain their meaning,* it seems a manifestly unlikely thing that many persons looked into the original Constitution, *to discover what the amendments meant.* And, in reading the amendments themselves, an American of 1789 would first have encountered a limited number of prohibitions "directly expressed" as applying to Congress only; and to a man of the time, the reasons why these particular prohibitions had been so "expressed," would have been entirely clear. Going on, he would next have encountered the Second Amendment, appertaining to *"the right of the people* to keep and bear Arms." And, here, he would have noted, not only that this seemed general in its terms, but that the protection of this "right of the people" was related, in the amendment, to the "necessity" of "a well regulated Militia" for "the security of a free State"; he would probably have reflected that "the security" of America had been confided, under the Constitution, to Congress; that "the Militia of the States" had been made therein an instrumentality of Congress, for use to that end; and he probably would have concluded, without much further thought, that, though the Second Amendment was general, in terms, it was nevertheless intended to apply *chiefly* to the states, in order to prevent them from impairing their "Militia" as an instrumentality of the nation. And the long series of general prohibitions in Amendments III–VIII, he would next have observed, had all to do with governmental acts generally considered to be inherently evil, because inimical to "the general Liberty"; and since the Constitution avowedly, and "the whole [American] people" certainly, were much "concerned" with "Liberty," *contrary to Marshall's strange words*, the American reader of these amendments, in 1789, could hardly have failed to conclude that the literal generality of most of their provisions had been intended, and that these amendments were meant to apply, in all such cases, both to the nation and to the states. The single "directly-expressed" exception in the Seventh Amendment would have confirmed him in this view; and he would, presumably, have felt still further confirmed when he came to Amendment IX. For that amendment plainly implied that the "rights" "enumerated" in the earlier amendments were *"retained* by the people"; and "the people" could not "retain" them, unless they were free of the authority, not only of the national government, but of the state governments as well. So, considering all these circumstances, it seems unlikely, in the highest degree, that many, if any, Americans, in 1789, looked into the original Constitution, to see what the amendments meant.

Yet, if we assume that some men did so, and that they observed there the contextual situation in sections 9 and 10 of Article I, which Chief Justice Marshall mentioned in the Barron case, it certainly would seem that they could only have felt still further confirmed by it, in the conclusions which the amendments, standing by themselves, compelled. For, as indicated earlier, the contextual situation in that particular part of the original document is almost the exact opposite of that in the initial amendments. It is almost the exact opposite because the literally general prohibitions in Article I are there used in context with prohibitions relating to the *same* subjects "directly expressed" as applying to *the states only*, whereas, in the initial amendments, the literally general prohibitions are used in context with others relating to *different* subjects "directly expressed" as applying *only to Congress*. So, the same mode of reasoning, *if applied with an even hand* to these two *different* contextual situations, results, very properly, in *different* conclusions regarding them; to wit, that the general prohibitions in Article I, despite their undeniable literal scope, were intended to apply to the nation only, but that those in the amendments were intended to apply, *as they were written,* to both the nation and the states. It therefore seems a certainty that, if any American of 1789 did observe the contextual situation in Article I, he could only have felt confirmed by it, in the view that Amendments II–VIII meant exactly what they said. And had such a reader observed, in addition, the character of the limitations, in Article I, which are there erected against *both* the nation and the states—the prohibitions, that is, upon titles of nobility, ex-post-facto laws, and bills of attainder—he would at once have perceived that they, like the literally general prohibitions in Amendments II–VIII, all have to do with matters considered to be inherently evil. So, again, he would certainly have concluded that Amendments II–VIII, subject to the single "directly-expressed" exception in the Seventh Amendment, applied to both the nation and the states.

Considering all this, it seems, then, to be perfectly clear that the reasons given by Chief Justice Marshall for the Court's strange decision in the Barron case—reasons in which Justice Joseph Story silently concurred—were reasons totally inadequate to justify the decision the Court was rendering. Remembering, too, the great abilities of Marshall and Story, it seems further to be certain that they must have known these reasons to be of this character when Marshall gave them. And if, on the basis of the considerations thus far adduced, there can be any doubt about this, there is one further aspect of the matter which should set such doubt at rest. For it is simply not true, as Chief Justice Marshall declared, in *Barron* v. *Baltimore*, that, "in *every* inhibition [in the original Constitution] *intended to act on state power*, words are employed which *directly express* that intent." No such words exist, for example, in the Full Faith and Credit Clause of Article IV. It commands, as we know, "full Faith and Credit" for every state's legislation, judicial precedents, and judgments—and therefore, of course, "inhibits" a denial thereof—"*in* each [of the other] State[s]." The clause, it will be observed, does *not* say "*by* each State." "State," in the phrase "*in* each State," is plainly a geographical expression, used to make the requirement of "full Faith and Credit," which the clause expresses, *general* in its application, both to state and national courts. It was in this wise, too, we have seen, that the First Congress interpreted this clause; for their act of 1790 prescribed the "faith and credit" for the "judicial proceedings" and "records" of the courts of the states, "*in every court within the United States.*" And the correctness of this interpretation has never been doubted. Yet, if the word "State," in the phrase "*in* each State," in the Full Faith and Credit Clause, is a geographical expression, the clause is undeniably one "intended to act *on state power*," *despite the want* of any "words [in the clause] which *directly express* that intent." And it follows that the intimation made by Chief Justice Marshall to support the decision in *Barron* v. *Baltimore* is not true in fact.

It may be supposed, however, that Marshall and, also, Story, who silently concurred in the Court's opinion, merely overlooked the Full Faith and Credit Clause of the Constitution. But there is another limitation in the document, quite as clearly of the character just described, which neither of these men could possibly have overlooked. This is the provision, in Article III, which subjects the courts of both the states and the nation, to the appellate jurisdiction of the Supreme Court of the United States, in certain of the cases within the categories of litigation which Article III describes. The provision is undeniably general in its terms; yet its application to the courts of the states is not "directly expressed"; indeed, it is not even indicated by the word "State" used geographically. And from the very beginning of the Government, "States' Rights" elements had urged, on the precise ground which Marshall's opinion in *Barron* v. *Baltimore* adopted, that the provision did *not* apply to the courts of the states.[54] This contention had come before the Supreme Court itself, in 1816, in the case of *Martin* v. *Hunter's Lessee*.[55] The contention was rejected in the Court's opinion by Justice Story, in no uncertain terms. Nevertheless, the contention was renewed, five years later, in *Cohens* v. *Virginia*,[56] and again rejected, this time in a Court opinion by Chief Justice Marshall. These cases, it should be remembered, were celebrated cases in the Court, even in the 1830's; and it is utterly impossible to suppose the issues in them were not still vivid to the two brilliant Supreme Court Justices who had written the opinions in them. Marshall and Story must, then, have been aware that there was, and could be, no general rule as to the intended sense of those general provisions in the Constitution, which are in terms broad enough to cover both the nation and the states, but whose application to the states is not "directly expressed." And if the inferences to be drawn from the ninth and tenth sections of Article I could not be applied, with justice—as, it is apparent, they could not—to the foregoing and other provisions of the original document, much less could they be so applied to the separately drawn and separately adopted initial amendments; and especially, for the purpose of defeating their plain literal sense. So, bearing in mind the ability of the two men concerned, the only tenable conclusion is that Marshall and Story knew full well that the Court's decision in *Barron* v. *Baltimore* was quite unjustified; that it was, in fact, just one more of the Court's many regrettable surrenders to the steady onslaughts of "States' Rights."

Nor does the fact that John Marshall wrote the opinion, and Joseph Story concurred in it, necessarily preclude this view. For we have Story's own word for it, in *Cary* v. *Curtis*,[57] in 1845, that it had long been his "habit to submit in silence to the judgment of the court where [he] happen[ed] to entertain an opinion different from [his] brethren." And Marshall, in *Bank of the United States* v. *Dandridge*,[58] in 1827, had said, that it was his "custom," too, "when [he] ha[d] the misfortune to differ from th[e] Court, [to] acquiesce silently in its opinion." The records of both men bear out their words; and the associate of both, Justice William Johnson, of South Carolina, said, in 1822, that, "in some Instances," Chief Justice Marshall delivered the opinions of the Court, "even when contrary to his own Judgement and Vote."[59] The motives of Marshall and Story, in pursuing such a course of behavior, were to minimize disagreement and personal ill-feeling in the Court; also, by consequence, to minimize, they hoped, the extent of the damage that some of their "States' Rights" brethren might do to the Constitution; and apparently there were times, too, when they wished to disguise from the country at large that the Constitution had, in fact, been flouted, in cases wherein, despite their efforts to prevent it, this occurred. Story's *Commentaries*, it has already been observed, were written according to this plan, too.[60]

Opinions today will probably vary, despite the conditions of constant danger to the Union, in which Marshall and Story worked, as to whether their policies, in these respects, were justified. There can, however, be no possible doubt that both men sincerely believed their course of action to be for the best interest of the country. And in the conditions of their time, it is not at all improbable that this was true. Yet, looking back from the point of view of later times, it is easy to see that Marshall's writing and delivering opinions he did not believe correct, and the practice which both he and Story followed, of concurring silently in decisions they believed to be wrong, have had, since their deaths, certain very unfortunate effects. For the great and deserved respect in which both these Justices have long been held has lent a peculiar authority to every opinion with which their names have been connected; and in consequence of this, many propositions of constitutional law found in such opinions have been unquestioningly accepted in modern times, which, there can be no reasonable doubt, Marshall and Story, themselves, must have regarded as utterly wrong when the opinions containing them were rendered.

That the doctrine of *Barron* v. *Baltimore* is an instance of this kind seems certain. For not one of the reasons for the doctrine, which Marshall gave, will bear examination. The opinion, like that of Justice Samuel Chase, in *Calder* v. *Bull*, earlier considered,[61] appears to have been a sham. And the decision of the Court, and the doctrine for which it stands, constitute, in fact, one of the most extensive and indefensible of all the various failures of the Court to enforce the Constitution against the states as the document is written.

And as for the whole body of restraints on state authority that the Constitution and its initial amendments contain, it is no doubt evident by now that virtually all of these were cut down drastically by the Court, at an early day, to a small fraction of what they had been intended to be. The general trend, then, of the Court's decisions within this field, during this relatively early period, perfectly coincides with the destructive trend of its decisions, during this same period, with respect to the national powers of government. The "rights," almost completely imaginary, of our separate states were plainly favored by the Supreme Court, prevailingly, over the plain and indubitable "national rights" of Congress; and these same imaginary "rights" of the states—that is, in effect, of the state governments—were also favored, prevailingly, over the plain limitations upon state authority which the Constitution and its initial amendments erected;

and this, whether these restraints on the states were set up "to secure the Blessings of Liberty," or to assure to "the People of the United States" "a more perfect Union" and a less expensive and less complicated form of government.

In more modern times, this favoritism toward the state governments, as against Congress and the people, has continued. Political pressures, it is true, have been such in the last half-century or so, that the Court has had to give way somewhat to the powers of Congress. But the powers the Court allows to Congress are still, as the discussion in preceding chapters has shown, far short of what Congress was intended to possess; and the powers of that body which the Court concedes are cluttered with a mass of technicalities that make their exercise by Congress difficult, expensive, and, in no small degree, ineffective. The states, on the other hand, are permitted by the Court to exercise powers they never were intended to have; and the Court still refuses to recognize that it is under a duty to enforce the first eight amendments against them.[62] The one qualification of these prevailing trends has been the Court's development, since about 1887, of its "substantive" theory of "due process of law." And this theory, though it has corrected, in spots, and in an uncertain way, some of the Court's long-standing laxness toward the state governments, has meant the development of a discretionary Supreme Court control over both the states and Congress, for which, as earlier intimated, the Constitution in neither case provides. The explanation of this strange development is, then, the remaining business of the present volume of this book; and, in the two chapters that follow, this last phase of the Court's long record, as the supreme and peculiar guardian of the Constitution, will therefore be taken up.

CHAPTER XXXI

The True Meaning of the Fourteenth Amendment*

1

THE Fourteenth Amendment to the Constitution of the United States, which became part of that document on July 27, 1868, provides, in its initial section—the section with which, in this chapter, we shall be principally concerned—as follows:

All persons born or naturalized in the United States, and subject to the jurisdiction thereof, are citizens of the United States and of the State wherein they reside. No State shall make or enforce any law which shall abridge the privileges or immunities of citizens of the United States; nor shall any State, deprive any person of life, liberty, or property, without due process of law; nor deny to any person within its jurisdiction the equal protection of the laws.

It is a fact universally recognized that the opening clause of the foregoing section of the Fourteenth Amendment was intended to nullify, as a proposition of constitutional law, the central doctrine of the famous case of *Dred Scott* v. *Sandford*,[1] decided by the Supreme Court, in 1857. This fact was freely conceded by the Court itself, in the *Slaughter-House Cases*,[2] of 1873, which were the first cases that came to it under this new amendment. The Court's decisions since that time have been consistent with this view; and to this limited extent, the true and intended meaning of the Fourteenth Amendment has undoubtedly been observed by the Court. The same, however, cannot be said of what that body has done under the remaining parts of the above-quoted first section: the Equal Protection Clause, the Due Process Clause, and the clause—generally known as the Privileges and Immunities Clause *of the amendment*—which prohibits all state "abridgments" of "the privileges [and] immunities of citizens of the United States."

According to the Supreme Court, in the *Slaughter-House Cases*, in 1873, the Dred Scott case, of sixteen years earlier, had decided "that a man of African descent, whether a slave or not, was not and could not be a citizen

---

* The matters dealt with in this and the following chapter are very simple and very obvious. Nevertheless, they are matters which still divide sharply the Justices of our highest court, as may readily be seen by reference to the recent case of *Adamson* v. *California*, 332 U.S. 46 (1947). And this being seen, the reasons for all the detailed explanation and analysis in this and the following chapter will no doubt be understandable to any reader who might otherwise wonder why such simple subjects are treated herein at such great length.

of a state or of the United States." It was this proposition which the Court recognized as nullified by the Fourteenth Amendment.[3] We shall see, eventually, that the Court's summation of what had been decided in the Dred Scott case was not precisely accurate; and the full purport of that case, flowing from the principles supposed to underlie it, was not explained by the Court, in the *Slaughter-House Cases*, at all. That purport was that no "man of African descent, whether a slave or not," could enjoy, under the Constitution of the United States, any right or protection whatsoever. All such men were left, by the principles of the Dred Scott case, to the absolute, unrestrained power of the separate states. This intended consequence of what was decided in that famous case was set forth therein, with the utmost particularity, in the Court's opinion, which the then Chief Justice, Roger Brooke Taney, of Maryland, delivered; and the propositions enunciated by Chief Justice Taney, in making clear this consequence, were still unoverruled, and, indeed, still wholly unqualified, when the Fourteenth Amendment was drawn and adopted. They were, therefore, a part of the standing "constitutional law" of that time; and we shall see, before we finish, that the propositions enunciated were such, and the words in which they were cast were such, that, when these factors are taken with the Court's earlier decision in *Barron* v. *Baltimore*, and with the very defective protection afforded against unequal state laws by the *Interstate* Privileges and Immunities Clause *of the original Constitution*, no doubt is possible as to what the whole first section of the Fourteenth Amendment was painstakingly and skilfully drawn to mean.

"The question," Chief Justice Taney said, early in the Court's opinion in the Dred Scott case, "is simply this: Can a negro, whose ancestors were imported into this country, and sold as slaves, become *a member of the political community* formed and brought into existence by the Constitution of the United States, and *as such* become entitled to all the *rights, and privileges, and immunities*, guarantied by that instrument to *the citizen?*" "The words *'people of the United States'* and *'citizens,'*" he also said, and truly said, "are synonymous terms and mean the same thing. They both describe the political body who, according to our republican institutions, form the sovereignty, and who hold the power and conduct the Government through their representatives. They are what we familiarly call the 'sovereign people,' *and every citizen is one of this people*, and a constituent member of this sovereignty."[4]

"Every *person*, and every class and description of *persons*," the Chief Justice further said, "who were at the time of the adoption of the Constitution recognized as citizens in the several States, became also *citizens of this new political body; but none other; it was formed by them, and for them and their posterity, but for no one else. And the personal rights and privileges* guarantied *to citizens of this new sovereignty* were intended to embrace those *only* who were then members of the several State communities, or *who should afterwards* by birthright or otherwise *become members, according to* the provisions of the Constitution, and *the principles on which it was founded.*" "The question before [the Court]," the Chief Justice then repeated, "[was], whether the class of *persons* [to which Dred Scott belonged] compose[d] a portion of *this people* [*of the United States*], and [were] constituent members of *this* [*national*] *sovereignty?*" And having thus propounded, for a second time, the question the Court was to decide, the Chief Justice forthwith announced the Court's decision: that "persons" of Dred Scott's "class" were *not* "a portion of the [American] people and constituent members of this national sovereignty"; that "they [were] *not* included, and were not intended to be included, under the word 'citizens' in the Constitution, and c[ould] therefore claim none of the *rights and privileges* which that instrument provides for and secures *to citizens of the United States*"; or, to use the term he had just said was synonymous, *to "the people"* of the American Union.[5]

An examination of the Constitution and its initial amendments discloses that there are to be found therein certain "privileges" and "immunities" which, in express terms, are dealt with as those of "Citizens *of the United States*"; certain others which, in express terms, are dealt with as those of "Citizens *of the States*"; and still others which, in express terms, are described as belonging to "*the people.*" Besides these, there are some other "privileges" and "immunities," chiefly in the Fifth Amendment, which are treated, in terms, as those of all "*persons*"; and there are, in the original Constitution, as well as in the amendments, many which are dealt with, without any express indication as to who are the holders thereof.

Of the three types of provision mentioned first in the foregoing paragraph, the first type is exemplified in those parts of Articles I and II of the original Constitution, which confine the "privileges" of serving as President, as Senator, and as Representative, to such "Citizens of the United States" as meet certain other qualifications there set up. The second type is exemplified in the previously mentioned Interstate Privileges and Immunities Clause of Article IV of the original Constitution, by which it is stipulated that "*the Citizens of each State* shall be entitled to all Privileges and Immunities of Citizens in the several States." And in Article III of the original Constitution, the "privilege" of suing in the courts of the United States, under certain of the mandatory "party" categories there set forth—particularly, in the interstate diverse-citizenship cases—is also given, in express terms, to "*Citizens of the States.*" As for the third type of provision first mentioned above, it is to be found in certain of the first eight amendments. Thus, the First Amendment forbids Congressional legislation "abridging *the right of the people* peaceably to assemble, and to petition the Government for a redress of grievances." The Second forbids "infringements" of "*the right of the people* to keep and bear Arms." And the Fourth Amendment, after alluding to "*the right of the people* to be secure in their persons, houses, papers, and effects, against unreasonable searches and seizures," declares that such "searches and seizures" shall not take place.

Now, bearing in mind the view of the Court in the Dred Scott case—a view which seems unquestionably to have been correct—that "the people" and "citizens of the United States" are, in general, synonymous expressions in the Constitution, it seems sufficiently clear that the unavailability, to "persons" of Dred Scott's "class," of all the foregoing "privileges" and "immunities" given in terms to "the people," in the First, Second, and Fourth Amendments, was within the principle of the Dred Scott decision. It is likewise clear that the same is true of all "privileges" and "immunities" given by the Constitution, in terms, to "Citizens of the United States." The situation, however, as to those "privileges" and "immunities" which the Constitution gives, in terms, to "citizens of the states," is somewhat more complicated and requires some further explanation. This is true, likewise, of those which the Constitution gives without specification as to the identity of the intended beneficiaries; and it is true, too, of the rights given in the Fifth Amendment, in express terms, to "persons."

The precise decision in the Dred Scott case—at any rate, the precise decision with which we are at this point concerned—was that "persons" of Dred Scott's "class" were not entitled to the "privilege" of suing in the courts of the United States, under the interstate diverse-citizenship jurisdiction. This "privilege," as already noted, is given, in terms, in Article III, to "Citizens *of the States*." But to a proper understanding of the constitutional significance of the Dred Scott case, it is essential to observe that this "privilege" was denied to Scott because the Court considered it to be one of the "rights, and privileges, and immunities, guarantied by" the Constitution, to "citizens *of the United States*," *only*. There can be no doubt about this, because the Court, immediately after referring generally to such "rights, and privileges, and immunities," declared, in so many words, that "*one of [these] rights* [was] the privilege of suing in a court of the United States in the cases specified in the Constitution."[6] And that the Court desired the principle of its decision to be understood as excluding Dred Scott and his "class," *on this same ground*, from the limited right of equality "in the several States," which the Interstate Privileges and Immunities Clause confers, in terms, upon "*the Citizens of each State*," is likewise certain from other things the Court had to say.

Thus, for one thing, the Court took the position that the various states, under the Constitution, could still, if they chose, confer upon "persons" of Dred Scott's "class," the rights and privileges of "*citizenship*" *within themselves respectively*. And the possibility of such state action made necessary, the Court said, that "the rights of citizenship which a State m[ight thus] confer *within its own limits*, and the rights of citizenship *as a member of the Union*" be "not confound[ed]." "It d[id] not by any means follow, because [a 'person' like Scott] ha[d] all the rights and privileges of a *citizen of a State*, that he must be *a citizen of the United States*. He m[ight] have all the rights and privileges of the *citizen of a State*, and yet *not* be entitled *to the rights and privileges of a citizen* in any other State."[7] That the Court was here converting the "privileges and immunities" given by the Interstate Privileges and Immunities Clause to "the Citizens *of each State*," into "privileges and immunities of citizens *of the United States*," and was denying, contrary to the plain letter of the clause, that "*the Citizens of each State* [were] entitled to all Privileges and Immunities of Citizens in the several States," seems perfectly plain and certain.

But the Chief Justice, apparently, was fearful he would not be understood. So, he repeated that, although "each State" might still confer "*the character of citizen*" upon "any one it th[ought] proper," still such a "citizen" would "*not* be . . . *entitled* to sue as such in one of [the nation's] courts, nor *to the privileges and immunities of a citizen in the other States*." And he wound up by declaring that to put the "citizen" of any given state, "in every other State, upon *a perfect equality with* [*such other state's*] *own citizens* as to rights of person and property"—as the Interstate Privileges and Immunities Clause did—was, in effect, to "*ma[k]e him a citizen of the United States*."[8] And since the Court held that "persons" of Dred Scott's "class" could not be "citizens of the United States," it of course followed that they could not have the benefit of the clause in question. In short, having recognized—without real warrant—that there could be "citizens of the states" who were *not* "citizens of the United States," the Court proceeded to restrain the plain letter of the constitutional provisions relating to "citizens of the states," in a way to make their benefits available only to the supposedly smaller class of "citizens of the United States."

As we have seen, the Court justified its restraint of the letter of these provisions, by declaring that the Constitution had been "formed by [citizens of the United States], *and for them[selves] and their posterity, but for no one else*." In support of this view, the declaration in the Preamble was cited, that "*the People of the United States*, in order to form a more perfect Union, establish Justice, insure domestic Tranquility, provide for the common Defence, promote the general Welfare, and secure the Blessings of Liberty to [*them*]*selves and* [*their*] *Posterity*, [had] ordain[ed] and establish[ed] th[e] Constitution *for the United States of America*."[9] Considering the terms in which the Preamble thus is cast, and the manifest good sense of the Court's view on this particular point on other grounds, there can be no doubt that, for many purposes, this view of the Supreme Court in the Dred Scott case is correct. The Constitution was made by Americans, for Americans. Yet it is, on the face of the matter, highly questionable that this indubitable purpose of those who established our government should be taken to exclude from each and every "privilege" or "immunity" under the Constitution, all "persons" who are not "citizens of the United States." And granting, for the sake of argument, the correctness of the Supreme Court's view, that there could be "citizens of the states" who were *not* "citizens of the United States," it seems, in particular, to have been completely unwarranted, to restrain the "strong" words of those particular provisions which give "privileges" or "immunities" to "Citizens *of the States*," in such a way as to make the rights they confer available only to the theoretically smaller class of "citizens *of the United States*." But however unjustified such a restraint may have been, there can be no doubt that such was the tenor and purport of the Dred Scott decision.

And blinking, once more, the totally unwarranted character of the doctrine that the Court thus announced, it also seems clear that that doctrine applied, and by much the stronger reason, to all "privileges" and "immunities" under the Constitution, which are dealt with therein, *without specification* as to the character of those entitled to enjoy them. For, if the doctrine applied to restrain, as above, the "strong" words, "Citizens of the States," it certainly applied to restrain in a similar way the provisions from which these "strong" words were absent. And the doctrine applied, too—and, again, it would seem, by stronger reason—to those "privileges" and "immunities" under the Fifth Amendment which are therein made available, in terms, to "persons." For the word "persons," being a colorless term and less specific than "Citizens of the States," was not so "strong" against the Supreme Court's doctrine as the phrase "Citizens of the States." So, merely on the basis of these logical considerations, it would undoubtedly be inferable that *every* "privilege" and "immunity" under the Constitution and its various amendments was to be regarded, under the principles of the Dred Scott case, *as* a "privilege" or "immunity" of "citizens *of the United States*," *only*. This, after all, is no more than the plain meaning of the Court's insistence that the Constitution "was formed by ['citizens of the United States'], for them[selves] and their posterity, *but for no one else*." But the Court did not leave this sweeping consequence of its momentous decision to inference; for, in what it had to say of the power of Congress over the technical "territories of the United States," it went out of its way to make specifically clear that this was exactly what it meant.

The power of Congress over the "territories," the Court declared, could "never be a mere discretionary power under [the American] Constitution and form of Government. [For] the powers of the Government, *and the rights and privileges of the citizen [were] regulated and plainly defined by the Constitution itself*." Then, after some further preliminary discussion, it was added that "a reference to a few of the provisions of the Constitution w[ould] illustrate this"; and thereupon, in an elaborate way, the Court made such a reference to various provisions of the document and its several amendments, which were deemed by it to be definitive of "rights and privileges of the citizen." The rights of religious freedom, and freedom of speech and the press, which are protected by the First Amendment, *without specification* as to who are intended to enjoy these rights, were mentioned first. Then came the right of free assembly and petition, and the right to keep and bear arms, which the First and Second Amendments, respectively, describe as *"rights of the people."* The limitation on "forfeitures" in punishments for treason, under Article III of the original Constitution, was next in order; and then the right against the quartering of soldiers, the right that "private property shall not be taken for public use without just compensation," and the right to trial by jury, each of which is protected, *without specification* as to the identity of the holders of these rights, by the Third, the Fifth, and the Sixth and Seventh Amendments, respectively. And, then, finally, the "due-process" guaranty and certain other provisions of the Fifth Amendment were included, though the protection afforded by all of these is, in terms, made available to all *"persons."* All these provisions, regardless of their different terms, the Court treated indifferently as creating "rights and privileges *of the citizen.*"[10]

In view, then, of this elaborate exemplification by the Court, as to what it meant by "rights and privileges"—or, as it sometimes said, "rights, and privileges, and immunities," or at others, "privileges and immunities"—"of citizens of the United States," no doubt seems possible that it was intended, *by the principles* of the Dred Scott case, to restrain the availability of *all* "privileges" and "immunities" under the Constitution and its various amendments, to *"citizens of the United States," only.* And bearing in mind that the Court was holding that all "men of African descent, whether slaves or not," were absolutely debarred from becoming "citizens of the United States," this plainly means, as was stated at the beginning, that the full and true purport of the Dred Scott case was that all "men of African descent, whether slaves or not," were to be bereft thereafter of all rights and protection, *under the Constitution of the United States,* whatsoever. This, to the present-day mind, seems an unbelievable decision; but to those familiar with the political demands of the South of the time when the decision was rendered, such a tenor in the Court's holding will not be difficult to credit. For it was exactly what the South, for a long time, had been demanding.

2

The foregoing, then, was the general doctrine concocted in the Dred Scott case which it was one of the chief aims of the Fourteenth Amendment to undo. That undoing was accomplished, and fully and completely accomplished, by the initial provision of the amendment (which, in the actual drafting, appears, somewhat strangely, to have been an after-thought) that "all persons born or naturalized in the United States, and subject to the jurisdiction thereof, are citizens of the United States and of the State wherein they reside." This, for the single purpose of making available to Negroes, *exactly as they were available to others,* all "privileges and immunities of citizens of the United States," was all that was required. Yet, for the full attainment of the ends the framers of the amendment had in view, this result was insufficient.

It was insufficient because there were two ways in which, even in the case of white men, the "privileges and immunities of citizens of the United States" had long been imperfectly secured. One of these was the result, in the main, of the Supreme Court's decision in *Barron* v. *Baltimore,*[11] in 1833. For the Court had then held, as we know, that none of the "privileges" and "immunities" under the first eight amendments was available and valid, as against the states. This doctrine, unsatisfactory even where the rights of white men were concerned, would, if unchanged, have left the nation's new Negro citizens wholly unprotected against various state acts that could very easily have been employed, by a state so disposed, to nullify and defeat much that the Fourteenth Amendment was framed to accomplish. So, the framers of the amendment, apparently accepting, as part of the practical standing "law," the foregoing doctrine of the Dred Scott case, that all "privileges and immunities" under the Constitution were those "of citizens of the United States," and of no others, went on to provide, *using the language which the Court itself had used,* that thenceforth "no State sh[ould] make or enforce any law abridging *the privileges or immunities of citizens of the United States.*"

As the states antecedently, according to the Court, had been free to abridge, in any degree they thought proper, any and all those rights to which the first eight amendments related, the conclusion seems an easy and natural one, that a total extinguishment of this antecedent state power was the precise end to which this particular clause of the Fourteenth Amendment was directed.* And reflection will show that there was, as a matter of fact, nothing else, not merely nugatory, for the clause to mean. For the Supremacy Clause of Article VI had always taken care of all "privileges" and "immunities," both under the Constitution and the laws of Congress, which the Court deemed directed against the states; and the "privileges" and "immunities," covered by the first eight amendments, which, it had held, were not directed against the states, were the only other "privileges and immunities of citizens of the United States" (except

---

* It ought, perhaps, to be noted at this point that the Ninth Amendment rather bears out the above doctrine of the Dred Scott case as to the character of the various rights created by the Constitution. It says: "The enumeration in the Constitution, of certain rights, shall not be construed to deny or disparage others retained"—not "reserved," be it noted—"*by the people.*"

for a few similar "privileges and immunities" in the original document) which there were *under the standing law*. The whole iniquitous doctrine of *Barron* v. *Baltimore* was, then, apparently intended to be wiped out, both as to the First Amendment, in reference to which, we have seen, the doctrine was justified, and as to all the others of the first eight amendments, in reference to which, we have also seen, it was not. So, the whole "Bill of Rights"—as it is sometimes called—was made valid, and available, by this clause of the amendment, *in favor of all* "citizens," as against the states.

This, as suggested, seems a plain, straightforward, and obvious conclusion. Yet it has been contended seriously, by writers looked upon as experts in the field, that this is not true at all.[12] The best known of these writers has argued that the language of the Privileges and Immunities Clause is hopelessly inadequate to make the first eight amendments good against the states, because, he says, it does not even purport to create any new "privileges or immunities" against them; yet he argues, at the same time, that the language of the clause, taken literally, is so sweeping, in its effects, as practically to preclude all state legislation whatsoever.[13] There seems, on the mere face of the thing, to be some slight inconsistency between these two positions; but the essay in which these views are advanced is one of a group on constitutional law, selected, not many years ago, by the Association of American Law Schools, as "of permanent value."[14] So, it would be wrong to conclude too hastily that this is the case.

In support of his second argument—that, taken literally, the Privileges and Immunities Clause would wipe out the possibility of state legislation, and that it was, therefore, "by no means easy" for the Supreme Court to prevent it from having this effect—the writer just mentioned maintains that, "*read naturally,*" the clause "seems to say that any privilege or immunity whatsoever enjoyed by one who is a citizen of the United States shall not be abridged by a state." He accordingly argues that, "if under [any state's] law at the time the amendment went into effect a citizen of the United States residing in [such state] might there lawfully sell intoxicating liquor, no subsequent State prohibition statute could abridge this privilege." The same, he thinks, would be true of every other right enjoyed by any citizen under any state law in effect when the amendment was adopted. And the consequence, he says, is that "no readjustment [by state law] of relative rights, not even moderately ameliorating social legislation," would have been a possibility under the Privileges and Immunities Clause of the Fourteenth Amendment, had not the Supreme Court, "in a statesmanlike manner," and—it may be added—in a manner contrary to a well-settled elementary rule of construction, "found an interpretation that render[ed] the clause innocuous." "[For, otherwise,] whatever a citizen might lawfully have done on July 27, 1868"—the date when the amendment took effect—"would have become," so this learned writer avers, "a fixed privilege . . . beyond the power of the States to curtail."[15]

Now, the first thing that strikes the mind in considering this "natural reading" of the Privileges and Immunities Clause is that prohibiting the states to "abridge the privileges or immunities of citizens of the United States" is a very *un*natural way of saying that "all state legislative powers shall henceforth cease." It seems *un*natural, too, to identify "the privileges and immunities of citizens of the United States," mentioned in a new provision of national law, not with those existing under the standing law of the United States when the provision was adopted, but with those existing—and existing, manifestly, in a very different sense—under the standing law, at that time, of the separate states. And especially does this seem an *un*natural thing to do, when it is considered that the effect of this procedure is to make "the privileges and immunities of citizens of the United States," different in every state; for this seems to rob the new provision of national law, of its national character. But the most *un*natural-seeming thing of all is for this particular writer to take the Privileges and Immunities Clause as creating, against the states, all these new and previously unheard-of "privileges" and "immunities" against action by the states, when, in the other branch of his argument, as already intimated, he maintains stoutly that the language of the clause is hopelessly inadequate to create, against the states, any new "privilege" or "immunity" whatever. So, taking all these factors into account, it seems a fair conclusion that this "natural reading" of the Privileges and Immunities Clause is not, in fact, a "natural reading," at all.

Turning now, to the other branch of this writer's argument, he contends thereunder that the Privileges and Immunities Clause merely forbids the states to "abridge"—that is, to diminish, or impair—"the privileges or immunities of [American] citizens" which already existed when the amendment was passed, or which were, at the same time, or subsequently, somehow *otherwise* created. And because the "privileges" and "immunities" under the first eight amendments had existed antecedently, he says, against the nation only, the Privileges and Immunities Clause could mean, as to all of these, only that the states were not to "abridge" these rights *as they existed against the nation*. "The[se] old immunities," he goes on to explain, "[were] only exemptions from certain kinds of acts emanating from the central government"; and hence, he reasons, "the only possible way a State could invade one of them would be *in some unknown manner* to force or induce the central government to do one of the proscribed acts." It is thus evident that this branch of his argument makes the Privileges and Immunities Clause ridiculous. Nor does he deny this. Rather, he insists upon it; for he considers the absurdity in his result to be the fault of those who drafted the clause, and not of himself. The failure of the clause formally to create new "privileges or immunities" against the states—a failure which does not seem to trouble him under the other branch of his argument—is, he insists, a fatal defect. For how can a state be guilty of "abridging" rights which have never been created?[16]

To perceive how really fantastic this writer's whole argument is, it is well to note in just what sense the first eight amendments appertain to rights in the nature of "privileges" and "immunities." The two words, it is to be observed, are not actually used in these initial amendments, though some of the amendments do use terms that are equivalent. Thus, the First Amendment speaks of *"the right of the people peaceably to assemble, and to petition* the Government for a redress of grievances"; and the Fourth Amendment speaks of *"the right of the people to be secure* in their persons, houses, papers, and effects, against unreasonable searches and seizures." There are some other instances of this mode of speech; but these are enough for our purpose. For the First Amendment illustrates the apparent sense of the word "privileges" as applied to the amendments: it was used to designate *affirmative, or active,* liberties; *"rights,"* that is, *"to do"* certain things, such as "assemble and petition" *without governmental restraint.* And the Fourth Amendment illustrates the sense in which the word "immunities" was used: to designate *mere negative, or passive, liberties; that is, "rights" simply "to be secure"—* or "to be immune"— from certain types of governmental action, such as "unreasonable searches and seizures." And, here, it is pertinent to remark that the affirmative liberties all comprehend "immunities," or negative liberties, for their protection. *"The right of the people peaceably to assemble"* comprehends, for example, *"the right to be secure* from governmental interferences with such assembling." So, the word "immunities," it would seem, could have been used alone, in the Fourteenth Amendment, to cover all the rights to which the first eight amendments appertain. And "privileges," likewise, could have been used alone for this purpose; since, in its ordinary legal sense, it comprehends "immunities" as one type of "privilege." It need only be added that the generic term "rights" could also have been used alone, in place of both "privileges" and "immunities," without in any way altering the essential meaning.

Inspection will show that not all the first eight amendments are as explicit as the First and Fourth in their reference to "the rights" they cover. Many are in the form of the Due Process Clause of the Fifth Amendment, which simply says that "no person shall be deprived of life, liberty, or property, without due process of law." *"The right to be secure"* from the deprivations thus proscribed is, nevertheless, the "right" to which this guaranty obviously relates; and inspection will show that all the others of the first eight amendments, whether they mention particular "rights" explicitly or not, do have to do, in the same way, with "rights," either "to be secure" from something, or, else, "to do" something with security, such as have just been described.

Inspection of the amendments also will show that what is essentially the same mode of prohibition as that employed in the Privileges and Immunities Clause of the Fourteenth Amendment is employed in many others of them, also. Among the first eight amendments, it is found in the First, Second, and Fourth; and it also appears in the Fifteenth and Nineteenth Amendments, of more recent adoption. For our purposes, it is enough to examine the First Amendment, which is the most similar, in mode of expression, to the Privileges and Immunities Clause of the Fourteenth. It provides, in part, that—

Congress shall make no law . . . abridging . . . the right of the people peaceably to assemble, and to petition the Government for a redress of grievances.*

Here, it will be observed, no language is used *directly creative* of the "right," or "privilege," forbidden to be "abridged"; for there is no declaration that "the people *shall have the right* of free assembly and petition." And that "right," or "privilege," it is absolutely certain, did not exist previously against Congress, though it had been provided antecedently, in *some* of the state constitutions, as against the governments of certain states.[17] Yet, in spite of these facts, the "right" is plainly treated, in the First Amendment, *as an already existing "right,"* in exactly the way that the Fourteenth Amendment treats "the privileges or immunities of citizens of the United States" as *existing* "privileges and immunities." For the command to Congress, to "make no law abridging the right," or "privilege," of "free assembly and petition" is in almost the exact words which the Privileges and Immunities Clause of the Fourteenth Amendment uses. So, if that clause in the Fourteenth Amendment is ineffective in form, it is hard to see why the First Amendment, as it relates to "free assembly and petition," is not ineffective, also. Yet this has never been supposed.

The foregoing prohibition in the First Amendment, and those in similar form in certain of the others, show sufficiently that it is no very extraordinary thing to forbid the "abridging," or the "infringing," or the "violating," of a "right" not previously existing against the agency forbidden, and not *formally* created against it in the prohibition itself. It appears, too, from the fact that the various amendments cast in this form have been effective, that such a mode of expression cannot be so hopelessly deficient as the writer above quoted would have his readers

---

* In some of the other instances, the verbs "deny," "infringe," and "violate" are used, rather than "abridge"; but this is an inconsequential difference. For, if you cannot "abridge" a right before it is created, presumably you cannot "deny," "infringe," or "violate" it, before its creation, either.

believe. Nor does this seem strange. For, after all, it is a commonplace that, although, in practice, "rights" do invariably exist against some particular person or governmental agency, men constantly speak about them *in gross;* and of rights deemed fundamental, or "unalienable," like those to which the first eight amendments relate, such a mode of speaking is particularly common.

So, the utter hopelessness of the mode of expression used in the Privileges and Immunities Clause of the Fourteenth Amendment is something pretty hard to see. For, as already noted, that mode of expression is virtually identical with the mode employed in the First Amendment as it relates to "free assembly and petition," and very similar to that employed in various of the other amendments, as above stated. In the First Amendment, the particular "right"—or "privilege"—to which that amendment relates, is identified *directly* as that of "free assembly and petition"; and the same direct mode of identification is followed, also, in the Second, Fourth, Fifteenth, and Nineteenth Amendments. In the Fourteenth Amendment, on the other hand, the "privileges or immunities" to which it relates, are identified *indirectly* as those "of citizens of the United States." What these had been held by the Supreme Court to be, when the Fourteenth Amendment was drawn, we have seen from our examination of the Dred Scott case. There can, therefore, be no reasonable doubt as to what "privileges" and "immunities" were meant. And when it is borne in mind that, in the First Amendment, one of these very "rights"—the "right," or "privilege," of "free assembly and petition" —not previously existing against the Government of the United States, and not formally created against it by the First Amendment, was, nevertheless, effectively secured by it, against the United States, through a mere declaration that "Congress sh[ould] make no law abridging th[at] right," it surely is very difficult to see why the general declaration, in the Fourteenth Amendment, that "no State shall make or enforce any law which shall abridge the privileges or immunities of citizens of the United States," should not be equally effective to secure this "right," or "privilege," as one of "the privileges or immunities of citizens of the United States," against the governments of the states. For, except that one of these prohibitions is general where the other is particular, the parallel between the two seems complete. And of course the same considerations apply to all the other "rights," or "privileges," or "immunities," to which the first eight amendments relate. So, the just conclusion undoubtedly is that the profound metaphysical argument we have just been considering is nonsense. And no other argument against taking the Privileges and Immunities Clause in what seems to be its obvious, natural, and sensible sense, ever has been conceived.

3

As suggested at the beginning of the last section, there was one other peril, besides that intended to be remedied by the Privileges and Immunities Clause, to which, at the date of the drawing of the Fourteenth Amendment, the rights of American citizens, as against the states, had long been exposed. This second peril—a serious matter even in the case of white men—was, without any doubt, far more serious in the case of the newly liberated Negroes, whether "citizens of the United States," or not. The peril in question grew from the peculiar terms in which one of the rights, under the original Constitution, had been stated; the right, that is, which the so-called *Interstate* Privileges and Immunities Clause *of Article IV of the original document* confers. That clause, it will be remembered, reads as follows:

The Citizens of each State shall be entitled to all Privileges and Immunities of Citizens in the several States.

As Chief Justice Taney had indicated in the Dred Scott case, this clause gave to the "citizens of each state" an "*equality* in rights of person and property," in each of the other states, *with such other state's own citizens*.[18] This view of the clause was likewise expressed in the Dred Scott case, by one of the dissenting Justices, Benjamin R. Curtis, of Massachusetts;[19] and though there was another view of this clause (to be noticed hereafter) which had for some time had many adherents when the Fourteenth Amendment was drawn, this other view was not, in any sense, a part of the standing "law" of the country, and was, moreover, not what, it appears quite certain, the Interstate Privileges and Immunities Clause had been intended to mean.

Under the more orthodox view, taken by the two above-named Justices in the Dred Scott case, the theoretically primitive power of each of the states to create inequalities in rights among its own citizens, or among them and outsiders who were *not* citizens of any other of the United States, was deemed to survive, under the Interstate Privileges and Immunities Clause, *completely*. Each state had the power, too, according to this more orthodox view, to create inequalities in rights, even as against citizens of other American states, provided only it did not deny to these any privilege or immunity that it accorded to its own citizens *generally*. For the right to "equality" under the Interstate Privileges and Immunities Clause was deemed to confer a right merely to that minimum of privileges and immunities which each particular state, in the exercise of its power to create special privileges and immunities, might choose to accord to its own citizens as a group. The "Citizens of [other] States" were *not*, in other words, considered to be entitled, under the clause in question, to the special "privileges and immunities" which a state might choose to confer upon more favored members of its own citizenry, or, presumably (if this should occur), upon favored Americans of other states or favored foreigners. And as Chief Justice Taney pointed out, in the Dred Scott case, even this imperfect right was lost by any "person who, being the citizen of a State, migrate[d] to another State." "For, then, as he explained, "[such a person] bec[a]me subject to the laws of the [latter] State in which he live[d], and [was] no longer a citizen of the State from which he [had] removed." The rights given under the Interstate Privileges and Immunities Clause were "confined," the Chief Justice said, "to citizens of a State, who"—being, of course, also citizens of the United States—"[were] temporarily in another State *without taking up their residence*." For, if they took up their residence and became domiciled within the state, they at once became *completely* subject to the state's jurisdiction to discriminate in favor of other individuals, or groups of individuals, and against them; that is, to deny them the rights the state accorded to its other citizens as a group.[20]

This, then, was the second of the pre-existing infirmities in "the privileges and immunities of citizens of the United States" which the framers of the Fourteenth Amendment apparently desired to cure. Such a cure, they undoubtedly believed, was desirable even for the protection of white men; for, against the notorious New York steamboat monopoly in the early years of the century, and against many other unequal state acts after that time, the Interstate Privileges and Immunities Clause had proved a totally inadequate protection.[21] And if the newly liberated Negroes of the Southern states, whether "citizens" or not, were to be secure, under the Constitution, from discrimination by the states, especially by those "wherein they reside[d]," this power of the states to discriminate between person and person, had obviously to be brought to an end. So, a third clause was added to the amendment: the clause which provides that "no state shall deny to *any person within its jurisdiction* the equal protection of the laws." Read in the light of the prior law, these words seem perfectly plain in intention: they were intended to supplement the old, inadequate Interstate Privileges and Immunities Clause of Article IV, by destroying utterly the state power which had survived thereunder, of discriminating between "persons" *in the predicament which this Equal Protection Clause describes;* that is, "person[s] within [a state's] jurisdiction." For, in the light of the prior law, it seems certain these words were not intended as words of limitation; they were, instead, precautionary words of emphasis, inserted to remove all possible doubt that the right to "equal protection" which the clause conferred, was to belong to all "persons" *even though* they should be, in the fullest possible sense, "within [the] jurisdiction" of the state concerned. And if "equality in protection" were accorded to these, it would have likewise to be accorded to all other "citizens," also, under the Interstate Privileges and Immunities Clause of the original Constitution.

As to just what the words of the Equal Protection Clause import in the way of rights against the states, it seems plain that they relate, at any rate primarily, to the defensive activities that states carry on, *in behalf of individuals* molested in any of their interests, by other individuals in society. In its application to such activities, the Equal Protection Clause differs markedly from most of the other restraints and limitations that the Constitution contains; for these, in general, restrain and limit the punitive and regulative powers of government *as against individuals*. It would seem to follow, then, that the Equal Protection Clause was meant, primarily, to give to each individual within each state— whether there permanently or not—a right that the sanctions of the state's tort law and criminal law, in particular, should be as freely and completely available, both legislatively and administratively, in defense of his interests, as in defense of those of any other individual within the state. A similar right as to the equal availability of a state's contract law was undoubtedly also intended; indeed, a similar right was meant with respect to each state's entire system of jurisprudence. And since it is not to be denied that state-created monopolies in all ordinary callings consist essentially, and solely, in a state's "protecting" particular, favored individuals from the free competition of others, in ways that individuals generally are not "protected," it is clear that the Equal Protection Clause also made illegal all existing, as well as all future, state-created monopolies of this kind. For if the words of the clause did not demand this result, it is not easy to see why. And, last of all, it would seem the Equal Protection Clause likewise required that a state act equally, when proceeding *against individuals*, whether in a punitive or a regulatory way, because "equal protection of the laws" manifestly comprehends the right to be "equally protected" from the acts of state officers, as well as the acts of individuals unconnected with a state's government.

The foregoing, then, seems the general nature of the protection the Equal Protection Clause was meant to require; but it is equally important to a true understanding of the clause, to see clearly what it was *not* meant to require. And it seems certain it was not meant to require "equal," or just, state laws *in general;* or, to put the matter in another way, it was not intended to end *all* unjust discrimination within the separate states. Instead, the clause was aimed at a very special and particular kind of unjust discrimination, or injustice: it was aimed at inequalities, or discriminations, in law, *as between "persons."* This certainly is the plain meaning of "deny[ing] to any person the equal protection of the laws"; for these words import that "the protection of the laws" has been made *"unequal" as between some "person" and other "persons."* And to a sound interpretation of the clause, it is essential to see just what such interpersonal legal inequality, or discrimination, is; and just what it imports, in a negative way, as a limitation upon the guaranty against the states which the clause in question expresses.

Concretely, "equal protection of the laws" *as between "person" and "person"* implies, in a negative way, that a state law discriminating, *even in the most arbitrary way*, between, let us say, farmers and others would nevertheless not lie within the guaranty for which the Equal Protection Clause provides. For to say that a law discriminates between farmers and others is really to say that it discriminates between agriculture and other employments. Such a law would, therefore, involve no inequality *as between "persons"*; for, as to *all* "persons" *engaging in agriculture*—that is, all those indulging in a certain type of behavior—it would apply in the same way. Such a law, whether just *or unjust*, wise *or unwise*, constitutional *or unconstitutional on some other ground*, would, therefore, involve only an inequality *as between types of behavior, or conduct*. All law involves such inequality and could not exist otherwise. The Equal Protection Clause cannot, therefore, reasonably be taken as relating thereto. For the clause certainly was not meant to outlaw all state law, or—what is the same thing—the type of inequality which is essential to it. And neither, it seems certain, was the clause meant to make reviewable by the Supreme Court of the United States, the question whether all state laws involving such inequality—that is, of necessity, *all* state laws—are "wise," or "fair and reasonable"; or even the question whether "wise," or "fair and reasonable," men might think they were laws of that kind.

It follows, then, that, if, in any particular instance asserted to fall within the ambit of the Equal Protection Clause, the claimed inequality as between "persons" can be restated as an inequality between types of behavior only, it is proof positive that the inequality is not of the kind the clause in question forbids. This is the essential criterion for keeping the administration of this clause within the true limits of what the clause was intended to cover. For, while there are, no doubt, other criteria necessary to a full working-out of the true meaning of the clause, this one alone, if kept in mind and consistently applied, would be enough to save the clause from misconstruction as what, we shall see, it has, apparently, sometimes been thought to be: a general roving Supreme Court commission to review the reasonableness of *the classifications of behavior* involved in all state acts of legislation.[22] In addition, the foregoing criterion, as to the true limits of the Equal Protection Clause, is an important help in comprehending the over-all scheme of the whole first section of the Fourteenth Amendment, and, also, the true relationship between its several parts. And by making these things clear, the criterion helps to indicate the appropriate answer to the only question as to the general meaning of the first section of the amendment, which can be considered to be *not* immediately clear in the light of the prior law.

The question meant is whether one of the necessary effects of the Equal Protection Clause is not to make available to all aliens, *as against the states*, all "the privileges and immunities of citizens of the United States." Superficially, there appears to be a certain difficulty in returning a negative answer to this question; and this, although, even on the face of the matter, it is not very likely that a constitutional "right to keep and bear arms" was meant to be conferred on aliens, even as against the states only; or that the same "right of free assembly," and "freedom of speech and the press," was meant to be given them, which American citizens enjoy. On the other hand, "aliens" and "citizens" are both "persons"; every "person within [a state's] jurisdiction" is entitled, as against the state, to "equal protection of the laws"; and the question is how an alien can be considered to be "equally protected" if he does not enjoy, as against the state, all "the privileges and immunities" to which, as against it, "citizens of the United States" are entitled. The true answer to this question (which becomes pressing once the Privileges and Immunities Clause of the Fourteenth Amendment is understood) is made apparent by remembering the foregoing criterion of the nature of the "equal protection" which the amendment commands, and by remembering, also, that the "denial" of "equal protection" which the amendment forbids, is a "denial" by the separate "States," and not by the government of the nation.

Citizenship, it is further important to bear in mind, is a status; that is, it is a state of having certain rights and owing certain duties, which differ from those which an alien owes and has. The words of the Fourteenth Amendment certainly imply that this status and that of alien, also, were intended to continue, even as against the states. For "all persons born or naturalized in the United States, and subject to the jurisdiction thereof," who, of course, are less than *all* "persons," are declared, by the initial clause of the amendment, to possess the status of citizen; and then, in ensuing clauses, what seem to be differing directions to the states, as to the rights of "citizens," on the one hand, and of all "persons," on the other, are given. And, here, it needs further to be remarked that the laws of naturalization, which enable aliens, under certain restrictions, to acquire the status of citizen, are made by Congress, not by the states. For Congress, in making these laws, is not bound to refrain from purely "personal" discriminations as between aliens; and if any such discriminations appear in our naturalization laws, the resultant inequality in rights *as between* "*persons*," though, without doubt, a "denial" of complete interpersonal legal equality, is, nevertheless, not unconstitutional, because it is a denial thereof by Congress, not by the states. So, bearing in mind the legal essence of citizenship as above set forth, it is clear that to take the Equal Protection Clause as requiring the states to extend to aliens, as against themselves, all "the privileges and immunities of citizens of the United States," would be, in effect, to take it as requiring them to treat aliens as, *to that extent*, naturalized, contrary to the laws of Congress. This certainly would be an anomalous result, inconsistent with Congress' power over the subject, and inconsistent, too, with what seems to be the plain over-all implication of the Fourteenth Amendment itself. So, it appears unquestionable that the Equal Protection Clause cannot justifiably be so taken.

But this leaves us with the question, what was intended by making the guaranty in the Equal Protection Clause available to aliens as well as citizens. And it is here that a clear perception of the true nature of that guaranty is useful; for it makes immediately clear what was meant. It was meant to forbid, *to the separate states*, all legal discrimination between alien and alien; between alien and citizen; or, for that matter, between citizen and citizen, as *"persons"*; that is to say, between any of these *on a purely personal basis*. Inequalities in rights established by the states, which depend upon skin color or any other purely personal characteristic; which depend upon the fact that a man is the particular "person" he happens to be; or which depend upon the fact that others are favorites of those in authority are examples of the kind of thing which the Equal Protection Clause forbids, and which it forbids in favor of alien and citizen alike. But despite the fact that aliens are entitled to this purely interpersonal legal equality which the clause commands, they are not otherwise made equal with the citizen, by this clause, even as against the states.

This conclusion, it will at once be seen, accords with the superficial probability, pointed out above, which arises out of the nature of certain of the constitutional "privileges and immunities of citizens of the United States." In addition, it accords with what, we shall now see, are the absolute constructional necessities of the situation, growing out of the presence, in the initial section of the Fourteenth Amendment, of the one clause thereof which has not yet been considered. That clause, the so-called Due Process Clause, provides that "no State shall deprive any person of life, liberty, or property, without due process of law." The "privilege," or "immunity," to which this clause relates, was, we have seen, one of "the [pre-existing] privileges and immunities *of citizens of the United States,*" according to the doctrine of the Dred Scott case; and according to the doctrine of *Barron* v. *Baltimore,* it was one of the rights of citizens which the states could freely abridge. So, if, by virtue of the Equal Protection Clause, added to the Privileges and Immunities Clause, of the Fourteenth Amendment, this particular "privilege," or "immunity," "of citizens of the United States," was made available, as against the states, to all aliens, as well as citizens, "within [the] jurisdiction" of each of the states, the Due Process Clause of the same Amendment was, and is, a quite unnecessary provision.

It is true, it may seem, upon a casual comparison of the Equal Protection Clause and the Due Process Clause, that this is not clearly the situation that exists; for the words "within its jurisdiction," in the Equal Protection Clause, are not found in the clause relating to "due process," and it may accordingly seem that the latter clause may have been included to make its guaranty available to all "persons," whether "within [a state's] jurisdiction" or not.[23] But the briefest consideration will show that this cannot really have been the case; for the notion of a state's "depriv[ing a] person of [either] life [or] liberty"—that is, of executing a person, or imprisoning a person—who is *not* "within its jurisdiction," is absurd on a physical basis. Some slight application for the clause, in reference to the "property" of "persons [not] within [a state's] jurisdiction," is no doubt imaginable; but the utter impossibility of any application with respect either to the "life" or the "liberty" of "persons [not] within [a state's] jurisdiction," is enough to show that the Due Process Clause could not have been inserted for their benefit. And because these parts of the clause would be made completely meaningless if the Equal Protection Clause made "due process of law" available to all "persons"—aliens, as well as citizens—"within [the] jurisdiction" of any state, it is evidently necessary, in accord with an elementary rule, to take the Equal Protection Clause as *not* having this effect. When this is done, the elementary rule is satisfied, that the parts of a writing are to be so construed that all of them have some effect; the Equal Protection Clause is then taken, too, in accord with what seems to be its full, plain, literal sense; and the whole first section of the Fourteenth Amendment falls into good order as a careful, skilful, and consistent example of the drafting art. And all this being true, it seems certain that the Equal Protection Clause ought to be taken in the manner that has just been described.

4

There remains the question of the intended meaning of the Due Process Clause of the Fourteenth Amendment. And with respect to this, the most relevant consideration undoubtedly is that the clause is, in every respect but one, identical in terms with the similar clause of the Fifth Amendment, adopted in 1791. The one difference between the two is that the clause in the Fourteenth Amendment, unlike that in the Fifth, is in the active voice and explicit in its intended application to the states only. In this single difference, there is, however, nothing that should vary the meaning of the new clause, from that of the old, except, of course, that the new clause cannot be taken as applying to the nation. And since the Due Process Clause of the Fifth Amendment was in the Constitution when the similar clause of the Fourteenth was adopted, the natural conclusion is that the latter clause was intended to make good, as against the states, everything that the Due Process Clause of the Fifth Amendment comprehended. This is the conclusion, too, which is required by orthodox elementary rules of construction. And since the Due Process Clause of the Fourteenth Amendment is expressed as a guaranty to all "persons" *and is a clause in addition to the Privileges and Immunities Clause,* which made "due process," *as a right of citizens,* good against the states, the conclusion seems inevitable, in spite of the unoverruled restraining principle of the Dred Scott case, that the things the clause made good against the states were made good by it, *in favor of alien and citizen alike.*

Our primary inquiry, then, must be what was comprehended by the "due-process" guaranty in the Fifth Amendment of 1791. In 1786, before either this amendment or the Constitution itself had been drawn up, Alexander Hamilton observed of the phrase "the law of the land," in the thirteenth article of the constitution of New York then in effect,* that "the best commentators" explained this phrase as "mean[ing] *due process of law; that is,*" he said, "*by indictment or presentment of good and lawful men,†* and trial and conviction in consequence."[24] Hamilton had gotten this idea from the writings of the famous English legal commentator, Sir Edward Coke, one of "the best commentators" he mentioned. It is today generally recognized, however, that Coke's identification of "due process of law" with the phrase "law of the land" in Magna Carta, and his definition of both phrases as having the signification that Hamilton quoted, were merely two among a great many other twistings of fact, of which Coke was guilty in his writings. Actually, there appears to be little or no likelihood that "law of the land" in Magna Carta had the concrete meaning Coke suggested; and "law," in the phrase "due process of law," in certain later historical instances which Coke also mentioned, had undoubtedly been used to include acts of Parliament. The whole phrase "*due* process of law" therefore meant, in these historical instances, "the process *required* by law"—that is, the whole law, consisting of the Common Law and the amendatory acts, if any, of Parliament. The requirement, then, was not a requirement that any particular "process" be followed; it was simply a requirement that the "process" of the courts, in the cases covered, be that "required," or "appropriate," under "the law"—that is, the whole law, common and statutory, as it existed at any particular time. Or, to put the matter in another way, the requirement was, historically, an admonition to the King and his agencies, the courts of justice, not to indulge, in the cases

---

* The thirteenth article provided "that no member of th[e] state sh[ould] be disfranchised, or deprived of any of the rights or privileges secured to the subjects of th[e] state, by th[e] constitution, unless by the law of the land, or the judgment of his peers."

† Hamilton's italics.

covered, in any innovations of "process" which were *not* authorized by acts of Parliament.[25]

This meaning of "due process of law" is manifestly in accord with the plain letter of the phrase, even at the present day; for all dictionaries, without exception, define "due" as meaning "appropriate," or "required." There can also be no doubt that "due" was in common use, in this sense, in 1789–91, when the Fifth Amendment was drawn up and adopted. It is, then, an undeniably probable thing that the Due Process Clause of the Fifth Amendment was understood in the foregoing sense, by some men at least, at that time. Yet it is to be observed that, with this meaning, the clause must have seemed rather superfluous, in view of the careful provisions in the Constitution for complete Congressional supremacy, and the Presidential and judicial oaths of office. The language of the clause is, moreover, completely general as to the agencies of government it is intended to control; and it seems, accordingly, to be the reasonable view that the clause was intended, and that it was, in all probability, read by most persons at the time it was adopted, as in some way limiting government generally, including the legislature, as to the kind of "process" to be followed in the cases the clause covers. These considerations pretty clearly exclude for the phrase what would otherwise be its most obvious meaning; the meaning, that is, which the phrase actually had in the English historical instances above mentioned.

Another possibility is that Sir Edward Coke's narrow, concrete sense of "due process of law"—as meaning "indictment and presentment of good and lawful men, and trial and conviction in consequence"—is what was intended by the phrase in the Fifth Amendment; and, hence, that the Due Process Clause thereof simply made mandatory upon all agencies of government, including Congress, this particular "process of law." And remembering that Coke's view was repeated by Blackstone, and that Blackstone, in the America of 1789, was well and widely known, it can hardly be denied that there is a high probability the Due Process Clause of the Fifth Amendment was casually read by many persons, in this sense, when the amendment was adopted.[26] But here, again, there would have been this insuperable difficulty for any reflecting man: that Coke's narrow, concrete sense of "due process of law" would make specifically superfluous the antecedent requirement, *in the Fifth Amendment itself*, of "presentment or indictment by a Grand Jury" in the case of "all capital or otherwise infamous crimes." So, some other meaning for "due process of law" seems mandatorily required by its immediate *and inseparable** context in the Fifth Amendment.

In seeking for some other meaning, one other possibility is that the "process of law" the amendment requires, is the whole "process," in

---

* Inseparable, that is, because the state legislatures had to ratify or reject the Fifth Amendment as a whole.

a more inclusive sense than that mentioned by Sir Edward Coke, which was "required," or "appropriate," under the national standing "law"—that is, the Common Law—when the Fifth Amendment was adopted. And here, it will be observed, there is a certain similarity in the situation under this "due-process" guaranty of the Fifth Amendment, and that under the requirement, in Article IV of the original Constitution, of "full Faith and Credit." For, though the language of these two provisions is very different, the meaning of both undoubtedly is that what is "appropriate" *shall* be done; and, as we have seen, the applicable standard of "propriety," under the clause in Article IV, undoubtedly is, and was, the standard of the Common Law. There is one important difference, however, between the two cases; for, whereas the Full Faith and Credit Clause contains a comprehensive express permission to Congress to legislate within the field it covers,[27] there is no such explicit and comprehensive permissive provision in the Due Process Clause of the Fifth Amendment. So, if "due process" meant comprehensively the entire "process" "required," or "appropriate," under the Common Law, the result would be to preclude Congress from any legislative change whatever within the field. On the face of the thing, it seems improbable that this would be comprehensively provided; and a little reflection upon the Constitutional context will convince that, in fact, no such provision was made. For, if the Due Process Clause had been meant as a general guaranty of all the elements of the "process" "required," or "appropriate," under the Common Law, there would manifestly have been no reason at all for the specific guaranty, *in that same amendment*, of any *particular* element of Common Law "process," such as the guaranty, previously mentioned, of "presentment or indictment by a Grand Jury" in the case of all "infamous crimes." So, we seem to be brought mandatorily, again, by the inseparable context of the clause, in the Fifth Amendment, to the one remaining possibility: that the phrase "due process of law" therein simply means "the appropriate process of law" *in a general way* and contemplates various sub-categories of "propriety" thereunder.

This possibility, so far as the letter of the phrase "due process of law" is concerned, is fully justified by the ordinary usage of the English words of which it is composed. The meaning fits, too, with the other more particular "process" guaranties contained in the Fifth Amendment. For it is perfectly understandable that the framers of the amendment might wish to set up precise Constitutional categories of "propriety" as to the particular phases of legal "process" that those particular "process" guaranties cover, whilst, at the same time, they left other phases of the subject to more general tests of "propriety" (the nature of which will be considered presently) under the general guaranty which the Due Process Clause expresses. And in much the same way, it is understandable that the First Congress, in framing the initial amendments, might have thought it desirable *to make possible* an even more extensive Constitutional implementation of the phrase "due process of law," by submitting simultaneously, but separately, to the legislatures of the states—as they did in the case of the amendments now the Fourth, Sixth, Seventh, and Eighth —various specific guaranties as to other particular phases of the subject to which the Due Process Clause, in a general way, relates. So, there can be no doubt that to take the Due Process Clause of the Fifth Amendment as commanding, in a general way, various sub-categories of "appropriate" legal process is the one interpretation that completely fits the entire documentary context. And, this being true, it would seem that this is what the "due-process" guaranty truly means.

The most obvious of the sub-categories of "appropriate" legal process which the Due Process Clause comprehends is that comprising all those elements of "process" that are specifically covered, and enjoined upon the Government, by the various particular "process" guaranties in the Fourth, Sixth, Seventh, and Eighth Amendments, and in the other clauses of the Fifth. For, manifestly, nothing else than what they enjoin can possibly be "appropriate," or "due," "process," under the Constitution, with respect to the particular phases of the subject they cover; and it is certain that the phases they cover in a specific way fall within the general language of the Due Process Clause, as well. These considerations, then, settle inescapably the nature of the first sub-category of "propriety" in "process" under the general "due-process" guaranty of the Fifth Amendment; and the nature of the particular "process" guaranties, it is also easy and important to see, *absolutely* settles the nature of the other sub-categories of "propriety," or "dueness," in "process" under the general guaranty, as well.

For the particular "process" guaranties of the Constitution are of two kinds: those that prescribe particular elements of Common Law "process"; and those that enjoin modes of "process," as to particular matters, which the framers of the amendments regarded as desirable, even though the Common Law did *not* require them.[28] And since all these more particular guaranties fall short of covering the subject of "process" with absolute completeness, it is evident that all those elements of Common Law "process" which were not outlawed by the Constitution as amended, even though they were not commanded by it, were nevertheless considered to be "appropriate," or "due," "process of law"; for, if they had not been so regarded, they would presumably have been outlawed, as other phases of Common Law "process" were, in the initial amendments or the original Constitution. But though such *un*forbidden, *un*prescribed elements of Common Law "process" are, unquestionably, "due," or "appropriate," "process," under a just construction of the Due Process Clause of the Fifth Amendment, read in its *complete* Constitutional context, it also follows, merely because such elements of Common Law "process" are *un*prescribed, that legislative innovations with respect to them are possible. So, we reach the final question: what is the test of "dueness," or "propriety," in the case of such procedural innovations? And the only possible answer is that they must, in their nature, be "reasonable" and "fair." For, if this is not the case, the Due Process Clause might as well have been omitted, since the Constitutionally prescribed phases of "process" are covered by the specific "process" guaranties, and the unprescribed and unforbidden phases of Common Law "process" would have been permissible anyhow, even if the Due Process Clause had been omitted. And because all dictionaries record the usage of "due" to cover what is "appropriate" as morally fit, this interpretation is justified by the plain letter of the clause, as well.

The foregoing seems to be the *whole* meaning of the Due Process Clause of the Fifth Amendment. It is, in short, a general guaranty of "due," or "appropriate," "process" in all cases where "life, liberty, or property" is at stake; and the three tests of "dueness," or "propriety," in "process" under it are, first, whether the "process" at issue in a particular case is one *un*forbidden by the Constitution; second, whether, being so *un*forbidden, it is supported by "applicable" precedents at Common Law; and, third, whether, if *not* so supported at Common Law, such a Constitutionally *un*forbidden "process" is, nevertheless, in its nature, essentially "reasonable" and "fair." We have seen, in the foregoing, that adherence to these three standards of "propriety" under the Due Process Clause is, by the plain terms of the clause and of the specific guaranties also, the duty of every department of the Government; but it is especially the duty of the courts, and of the Supreme Court in particular, because the subject of "appropriate legal process" relates directly and especially to the proper discharge of the judicial functions. So, the clause, it is clear, is one of those comprehended within the limited type of judicial review explained in chapter xxviii.

It is important to observe, however, that, although this is true, the Supreme Court's discretion, under the Due Process Clause, *justly* interpreted, is not unlimited. Thus, the Court is invested, first of all, with discretion, to mark out the just limits of the various particular "process" guaranties that the Constitution and its amendments contain. This discretion, as to some of these guaranties, such, for example, as those under Amendment VIII, is broad within the scope of the guaranties concerned; but it is, as to none of the specific guaranties, an unguided discretion and, as to most of them, is narrow indeed. The Court is invested, second, with discretion to determine whether any unforbidden, unprescribed "process" is supported by Common Law precedents "applicable to American conditions" at the time when the Fifth Amendment was adopted; that is, 1789–91. This, in the main, is an historical inquiry, difficult in some phases perhaps, but not impossible. And, last of all, the Court has discretion—and, in this case, a completely free discretion—to pass on the "reasonableness" and essential "fairness" of any legislative innovations on Common Law "process" that are not specifically forbidden by the Constitution. Cases involving such innovations within the criminal field are not, because of the number and character of the specific "process" guaranties, of very frequent occurrence; they are more frequent within the civil field; yet it is clear that the Supreme Court, under this Due Process Clause, enjoys something less than a general unguided discretion to review the "fairness" and "reasonableness" of all Congressional acts, *even within the procedural field.* And if the words of the clause are heeded, there is, of course, no right to review the substantive acts of Congress at all.

The conclusions thus far reached are all inferable with certainty from the words of the Due Process Clause of the Fifth Amendment, read in their actual context; a context made up, we have seen, of the remainder of the Fifth Amendment itself, of the other initial amendments, and of the original Constitution. And this being true, it would seem to follow inescapably that these conclusions must represent the truth. They can, however, easily be corroborated by evidence of other kinds; and, in particular, by the Supreme Court's own first decision under the clause in question, so far as that decision went. The decision meant is that in *Murray's Lessee* v. *Hoboken Land and Improvement Company*, in 1855.[29] The opinion in the case was written by Justice Benjamin R. Curtis, of Massachusetts, one of the small number of really brilliant lawyers, besides Marshall and Story, who have sat upon the Court; it was rendered in a case that seems to have been completely free of distorting political pressures; and it commanded the unqualified assent of the entire Court membership of the time.

The plaintiff in the case contended that the "process" enacted by Congress which was there in issue would "deprive" him of his "property without due process of law." "To what principle," Justice Curtis asked, in considering this contention, "are we to resort to ascertain whether [any particular] process, enacted by Congress, is due process?" "*We must examine the Constitution,*" he unhesitatingly replied, "*to see whether th[e] process is in conflict with any of its provisions.*"[30] It is thus past contention that, to the Supreme Court of 1855, the first and paramount test of "dueness," or "propriety," in "process," under the "due-process" guaranty of the Fifth Amendment, was whether a given "process" measured up to the standards set by the various specific "process" guaranties in the Fourth, Sixth, Seventh, and Eighth Amendments; in the other clauses of the Fifth Amendment; and in the original Constitution. This sensible judicial view was, then, incontestably a part of the standing law, as to what "due process" meant under the Constitution, when the Fourteenth Amendment was adopted. It will be important to bear this fact in mind in what follows.

Justice Curtis also went on to say that, if a particular "process" enacted by Congress was found, upon examination, to be one *not* specifically forbidden in the Constitution, the next criterion of its "dueness" was its correspondence with "those settled usages and modes of proceeding existing in the common and statute law of England before the emigration of our ancestors, and which [were] shown not to have been unsuited to their civil and political condition by having been acted on by them after the settlement of this country."[31] Thus, the Court of 1855 also recognized the second of the sub-categories of "dueness," or "propriety," in "process" under the Due Process Clause, herein set forth. Beyond these two, however, Justice Curtis and the Court of 1855 did not go. They did not need to go beyond them, because the "process enacted by Congress" that was at issue in the Hoboken case was a "process," not forbidden by the Constitution, which had been followed at Common Law in England and was in widespread use in America when the Fifth Amendment was adopted. So, the opinion in the case proceeded, without more, to hold that the "process" was "*due* process of law."

This first case in the Court under the Due Process Clause of the Fifth Amendment thus falls short of completely corroborating the view of the meaning of the clause here presented; but it does definitely corroborate that view, so far as it goes. Considering, then, that the things the case says are plainly inferable from the context of this "due-process" guaranty in the initial amendments and the original Constitution, and that the rest of what has here been said is also inferable on that same basis, the conclusion appears to be fully warranted that the meaning of "due process of law," under the Constitution as it existed in 1866–68, when the Fourteenth Amendment was drawn and adopted, was that already set forth. And it follows, under an elementary rule, that the phrase, in the Due Process Clause of the Fourteenth Amendment, had this same meaning, too.[32] So, the first effect of the clause in the later amendment was to make good in favor of all "persons," including aliens, as against the states, all those particular "process" guaranties which the Fourth, Sixth, Seventh, and Eighth Amendments, and the other clauses of the Fifth Amendment contain. And the clause in the later amendment also meant, for the same reason, that, as against all "persons," including aliens, each state was required to keep its legal "process," in other respects, in accord with the Common Law; or, in any of these other respects wherein it might desire to depart from the Common Law, to keep its innovations upon that law "reasonable" and "fair." And this, it would seem, is a sensible result. For, as we have seen, all the foregoing rights, general and particular, were made available to citizens, as against the states, by the Privileges and Immunities Clause of the Fourteenth Amendment; and no good reason appears why all these guaranties, general and particular, relating, as they all do, under a just construction, merely to the character of the "process" to be followed, primarily in courts of law, should not be available to aliens, too.

5

The foregoing considerations pretty well dispose of the meaning of the Due Process Clauses of the Fifth and Fourteenth Amendments if the words of those clauses are read as meaningful English words taken in the sense they seem to have had for centuries. For it seems a safe assertion that, in all their uses, both in the Constitution and elsewhere, the words "due process of law" have always meant one and the same thing; that is, "required," or "appropriate," legal procedure. The standards of "propriety" that have been intended have no doubt varied from instance to instance in which the words have been used; but the words themselves pretty certainly have borne a constant sense, and the only real problem is to discern, in any given instance, what the standards of "propriety," or "dueness," in "process" are, which, in that particular instance, the words comprehend. In the Constitution of the United States, the singularly rich context of particular "process" guaranties makes such a determination easy and certain; and there seems proportionately little excuse for the Supreme Court in having gotten so far astray. Nevertheless, the Court long has been far astray and still remains so; for it still maintains that the two Due Process Clauses of the Constitution invest it with a general unguided discretion to review the essential fairness and reasonableness, of all laws which either the state legislatures or Congress may pass.[33] So, a complete treatment of our subject requires the consideration of this further question: whether, in spite of the plain meaning of the "due-process" guaranty read in its actual Constitutional context, there is any evidence at all, in the case either of the Fifth Amendment or the Fourteenth Amendment, that the clause was intended, or understood, when adopted, to invest the Supreme Court with such a discretionary reviewing power.

We have seen what Alexander Hamilton thought about the subject of "due process of law," in 1786, before the Constitution had been put together. In the years 1789–91, when the initial amendments were pending, discussions of these proposed changes were few; and none is known, which related to the Due Process Clause of the Fifth Amendment. Supreme Court decisions under the clause did not begin, we have seen, until 1855; and the only direct evidence there is, of the earlier understanding of the clause, is that to be found in the very casual comments upon it, made by the early American legal commentators, James Kent, William Rawle, and Joseph Story, in the 1820's and 1830's. The comments of none of these writers will bear up under a strict examination. For they apparently all assumed, without a close examination of the Constitutional text and context, that the "due-process" guaranty in the Fifth Amendment was merely one relating to procedure in criminal cases; and because the subject of criminal "process" was so nearly completely covered by the particular "process" guaranties that the Constitution contains, they tended to regard the general "due-process" guaranty of the Fifth Amendment as not of much importance. This explains the extreme casualness of their views; but it also establishes beyond any doubt that they did not even dream of the meaning the Supreme Court gives to the "due-process" guaranties today.

Just how completely the subject of criminal "process" is covered by the particular "process" guaranties in the initial amendments may be seen by reviewing briefly just what they comprehend. Thus, the Fourth Amendment covers the preliminary subject of search warrants and unreasonable searches and seizures. The earlier clauses of the Fifth Amendment provide that all prosecutions for capital or otherwise infamous crimes shall be begun by presentment or indictment by a grand jury; that no person shall be subject for the same offense to be twice put in jeopardy of life or limb; and that no one shall be compelled in any criminal case to be a witness against himself. The Sixth Amendment requires, in all criminal cases, a speedy trial by an impartial jury of the locality in which the crime is charged to have been committed; it requires that the accused shall be informed of the nature and cause of the accusation against him, and that he shall be confronted with the witnesses against him; and it allows him compulsory process for obtaining witnesses in his favor, and gives him a right to the assistance of counsel in his defense. The Eighth Amendment adds to the foregoing a stipulation that excessive bail shall not be required; that excessive fines shall not be imposed; and that cruel and unusual punishments shall not be inflicted. It is thus evident that the whole "process" of criminal prosecution, from beginning to end, is pretty well covered by these particular guaranties; and if one believed, as Kent and Rawle and Story did, that the "due-process" guaranty in the Fifth Amendment was one relating to criminal "process" only, it is easy to see that that guaranty might be viewed as one adding very little to the particular guaranties and, hence, as not a guaranty of much importance.

That the "due-process" guaranty cannot, however, be limited to criminal cases seems clear. In the first place, the processes of imprisonment and sequestration of chattels were used, when the guaranty was drawn, and still are used, as coercive "processes" in equity. At that date, too, imprisonment for debt was widely practiced; and exemplary, or punitive, damages are, and always have been, plain deprivations of the property of him who has to pay them. It seems evident, too, that even compensatory damages are of this same character; for the execution of a judgment for such damages involves, necessarily, a deprivation of property for the judgment debtor. There remain, it is true, a few civil cases to which the language of the Due Process Clause does not well apply; cases, that is, in which a plaintiff sues to recover property belonging to him which his defendant detains. But these cases are exceptional; they are within the reason for applying the provision to all the other cases, both civil and criminal; and under an equitable interpretation, of the kind deemed proper when the Fifth Amendment was adopted, the provision ought, it would seem, to be regarded as covering these, as well as all other cases involving life, liberty, or property, whether criminal in character or not. Kent and Rawle and Story, had their minds been directed to this problem, would probably have agreed with this view. But they were used to meeting the subject of "due process of law" in criminal contexts; the clause in the Fifth Amendment had not yet been in litigation at the time they wrote; and because the earlier clauses of the amendment all related to criminal matters, they appear not to have noticed that the qualification "in any criminal case," contained therein, did not carry through to the guaranty of "due process of law." This oversight shows the casualness with which they must have viewed this clause; and this, again, indicates they did not even dream of the Supreme Court's view of the clause today.

Of the three commentators just mentioned, Rawle, one of the leaders of the bar of his time, in Philadelphia, may be considered first; for his views are the clearest and, despite too great narrowness in the respect just indicated, are, of the three, the nearest to the truth. In his *View of the Constitution*, of 1828, Rawle treated the Due Process Clause as a general guaranty of fair proceedings, and trial according to law, in criminal cases. "The protection of the individual against all severity, in the prosecution of justice," he says—and by "the *prosecution* of justice," Rawle, it is clear, meant "criminal justice"—"characterize[d]," he went on, "the greatest part of the fifth,* and the whole of the [sixth† and] eighth amendment[s]." Indicating his view that the restrictions in these amendments applied to the legislative, as well as to the judicial authority, Rawle observed, however, that, with respect to the legislature, such a restriction as that in the Eighth Amendment, against "excessive fines," involving, as it did, the exercise of discretion, was "rather to be considered in the light of a recommendation than as a condition on which the constitutionality of the law depend[ed]." "[For] the judicial authority," Rawle believed, "would not undertake to pronounce a law

---

* The exception he had in mind was the final clause of the Fifth Amendment, that "private property shall not be taken for public use, without just compensation."

† Rawle had dealt with the Sixth Amendment as having this character, immediately before this particular statement was made.

void, because the fine it imposed appeared *to them* excessive; and, therefore, if the legislature should commit, and persist in, gross errors in this
respect, the ultimate remedy must be sought among the checks on the
legislative power, which w[ould]," he said, "[t]hereafter be brought
into view." From his subsequent discussion, it appears he meant the
popular right, direct and indirect, of electing Congress. As he expressed
similar views in respect to other Constitutional restraints that left room
for discretion, it can be seen how slowly the modern notions of the
Supreme Court's reviewing power must have developed.

After Rawle had reviewed all the various particular restrictions on
criminal proceedings which the Fifth, Sixth, and Eighth Amendments
contain, his final comment was that "it follow[ed] from all [these par-
ticular] precautions that *no one c[ould] be deprived of life, liberty or
property, without due process of law;** and [that] the repetition of this
declaration [in the Fifth Amendment, was] *only valuable*, as it exhibit[ed]
the summary of the whole, and the anxiety that it should never be forgotten."[34] It can thus be seen that, to Rawle, as to the Supreme Court
nearly thirty years later, the primary test of "propriety," or "dueness,"
in "process," under the "due-process" guaranty, was what was required
by the other more particular "process" guaranties of the Constitution
itself. If he meant, however, by "only valuable," that the Due Process
Clause did not import any further guaranty of "fairness" and "reasonableness," as to any phase of "process" which the more specific guaranties
omitted, it was, of course, too narrow a view to take. It is not very likely
that Rawle meant to say this; but whether he did or did not, it is clear
he had no idea that the Due Process Clause was a general, unguided
commission to the Supreme Court of the United States, to review the
wisdom and reasonableness of all the legislation of Congress.

In his *Commentaries on American Law*, in 1827, the famous James
Kent, previously chief justice, and then chancellor, in the state of New
York, had taken a view of the Due Process Clause, which, though in
some respects similar, seems rather to have depended upon a casual
acceptance of the narrow, concrete understanding of "due process of
law" which Alexander Hamilton had expressed in 1786. Kent's view is,
therefore, quite certainly impossible if the Due Process Clause of the
Fifth Amendment is read in context; but his view helps, nevertheless,
to show how slightly this clause was regarded by good lawyers in the
early days, and how utterly unsuspected by them the meaning was,
which the Supreme Court gives to the clause today. Thus, after reviewing various particular restrictions on criminal proceedings which "ha[d]
been transcribed," he said, "into [the national and most of the state con-
stitutions] from *magna carta*, and other fundamental acts of the English
Parliament," Kent concluded by declaring that, in the United States

---

* Rawle's italics to indicate quotation in substance.

generally, "no person c[ould] be taken, or imprisoned, or disseised of his freehold, or liberties, or estate, or exiled, or condemned, or deprived of life, liberty, or property, unless by the law of the land, or the judgment of his peers." "The words, *by the law of the land*, as used in *magna carta*, [were] understood to mean," he explained, "*due process of law*, that is," he said, "*by indictment or presentment of good and lawful men*."[35] This, of course, is not quite an explicit statement that "due process of law," in the Fifth Amendment, had the narrow, concrete meaning that Hamilton had given to the phrase, in 1786. But this seems implied; and although such a view of the meaning of the phrase in the Fifth Amendment is quite impossible, it at least makes clear that James Kent, in the 1820's, saw no general, roving Supreme Court commission, in the Due Process Clause of the Fifth Amendment, to review the wisdom, or reasonableness, of all the acts that the Congress of the United States might pass.

The same complete innocence of this strange view is observable, also, in the *Commentaries on the Constitution* which Justice Joseph Story, of the United States Supreme Court, published in 1833. Like Kent and Rawle, Story treated the Due Process Clause as appertaining solely to criminal prosecutions. For, after commenting upon the more particular, antecedent criminal provisions of the Fifth Amendment, and upon the other restrictions on criminal procedure which the original Constitution and others of the amendments contain, Story's comment was that the Due Process Clause of the Fifth Amendment was "but an enlargement of the language of magna carta, '*nec super eum ibimus, nec super eum mittimus, nisi per legale judicium parium suorum, vel per legem terrae,*' neither will we [the King] pass upon him, or condemn him, but by the lawful judgment of his peers, or by the law of the land." "[For] these latter words, *per legem terrae*, (by the law of the land,) mean[t] *by due process of law*," he explained; "that is," he went on, "*without due presentment or indictment, and being brought in to answer thereto by the due process of the common law*." "So that this clause in effect affirms the right of trial," he at length concluded, "according to the process and proceedings *of the common law*."[36] That Story meant, by this, "trial in *criminal* cases" is manifest from the context. So, the "enlargement" he spoke of must have consisted in the more extended application of the Due Process Clause to all departments of government, whereas the provision in Magna Carta, under the construction Story was following, had applied to the King and his courts alone. This view of the clause, as absolutely guarantying all phases of Common Law process, is a view, we have seen, which cannot be maintained. So, Story, too, must have been giving this clause only slight attention; but that does not alter the fact that the meaning the Supreme Court now gives to the clause was something he did not even remotely suspect.

We have seen, to be sure, that Story's *Commentaries* cannot, in all instances, be unquestioningly accepted as evidence of their author's true views. But, in this instance, Story is corroborated by Rawle and Kent; and Kent, at least, would certainly not have failed to speak out on this particular subject. A staunch advocate of judicial review, his record on the New York courts precludes the possibility that he would not have announced the view of "due process of law" that the Supreme Court takes today *if* he had ever heard of it. It is to be observed, too, in this instance, that the view of Kent and Rawle and Story—that the "due-process" guaranty is merely procedural—is in accord with its actual words. For it is only when its words, as meaningful English words, are disregarded, that any other view is possible. So, we may safely conclude—and, indeed, it is regarded, among legal scholars, as a commonplace—that the Due Process Clause of the Fifth Amendment was not originally intended to mean, and was not, for over a hundred years, even held by the Supreme Court to mean, what the Court insists that it means today. And considering the identity in terms between the two Due Process Clauses of the Constitution, it seems a certainty the same statement, as to the intended meaning of the Due Process Clause in the Fourteenth Amendment, can be quite safely made. Yet the contrary has sometimes been contended.

Such contentions have been based partly upon the fact that the process of judicially distorting "due process of law" into "due substance of law" had been begun by the state courts of New York, under their state constitution, in 1856, ten years before the Fourteenth Amendment was even drafted.[37] In additon to this, the majority Justices of the Supreme Court, in the following year, had, to a certain extent, fallen in with this New York heresy, in the case of *Dred Scott* v. *Sandford*. This occurred when they held the Missouri Compromise of 1820 unconstitutional under the Due Process Clause of the Fifth Amendment.[38] The Dred Scott decision, as well as the New York decision that preceded it, were rather remote, however, from the Supreme Court's modern theory of "substantive due process of law"; at most, they were first steps in that direction. So, even if the Due Process Clause of the Fourteenth Amendment were taken as comprehending the doctrine of the Dred Scott decision in this respect, it would not go far toward validating the Supreme Court's modern doctrine. But there are good reasons for not taking the clause in the sense in question.

In the first place, the Dred Scott case was not only wrong; it was also, though not overruled, a thoroughly discredited case when the Fourteenth Amendment was adopted. Much the same was true, too, of the New York case it had emulated. For not only was *Wynehamer* v. *The People*[39] the subject, at the time, of widespread disapproval in New York itself;[40] its doctrine had, in addition, excited unfavorable comment, rather than emulation, in the other states.[41] In these circumstances, it is obviously unlikely that these cases were relied upon, by the draftsmen of the Fourteenth Amendment, to give to the words of the "due-process" guaranty in it, a "substantive," as well as a "procedural," scope. For, after all, the words "due process," which the amendment employs, do mean "due *process*"; they cannot certainly, without the most violent distortion, be taken to signify the customarily contrasted legal category of "substance." So, remembering that the first beginnings of the "substantive" view were a discredited heresy, rather than an accepted tenet, when the Fourteenth Amendment was drawn, it does seem that, if "due substance" was meant, the framers of the amendment would have said so plainly. And this they did not do.

If these considerations seem insufficient with the Dred Scott case still unoverruled, there is one other circumstance which settles absolutely that the Due Process Clause of the Fourteenth Amendment was not intended, and cannot justifiably be taken, in a substantive sense. This is the presence, in the amendment, of the Equal Protection Clause. For, if the Due Process Clause had been intended in a substantive sense— that is, if it had been intended as a general national guaranty of "fair and just *substance*" in all state laws—the Equal Protection Clause would not have been needed. It would not have been needed, because, of all types of "injustice," or "unfairness," in law, a purely interpersonal inequality under the law is undoubtedly the clearest and most obvious. And this, it appears, is the opinion of the Supreme Court itself.[42] The rule, then, which forbids interpretations that make any part of a deliberately drawn document meaningless, plainly requires that the Due Process Clause of the Fourteenth Amendment be *not* substantively taken; for the Equal Protection Clause proves the draftsmen of the amendment were aware that their Due Process Clause, in accord with its plain, literal terms, was a guaranty of appropriate "process" only.

6

With this conclusion, we come to the end of our consideration of what the first section of the Fourteenth Amendment, considered as a rational whole, should be held to mean. The conclusions presented have all been reached in the same way as the other, earlier conclusions in this book: by a straightforward acceptance of what the words of the amendment say; especially, when read in the light of the antecedent provisions of the Constitution, and the Supreme Court's theories, when the Fourteenth Amendment was drawn, as to what those antecedent provisions meant. So read, *and read as a whole*, the first section of the Fourteenth Amendment seems crystal clear; and since it has long been established that the framers of the amendment *intended* it to mean all these things which, we have seen, it plainly does,[43] it is difficult to see how the Supreme Court can possibly have failed to understand the amendment, five years after its adoption, when the first cases under it arose. For the framers' intentions as to the meaning of their amendment had been declared by them in Congress;[44] the Supreme Court, at the date of these first cases, must surely have been—or, at the very least, it could and should have been—familiar with these suggestive speeches; and it was, assuredly, not too much to ask, in addition, that the Justices have some familiarity with the earlier decisions of their own Court. So, one's wonder must be great at what, we shall soon see, the Supreme Court has done.

But the basis for appraising the Court's record in this respect is not, even yet, complete. For it is difficult to see, even if the Justices had been totally ignorant of their own Court's earlier decisions, and ignorant, also, of the framers' explanations of their amendment in Congress, how they could, even then, have failed to reach the conclusions as to the meaning of the first section of the amendment, which have been set forth herein. For, to start with the Due Process Clause, any rational reader, even a layman, would surely have supposed, if he read that clause with the antecedent clause of the same kind in the Fifth Amendment, that it was intended to forbid, by the clause in the Fourteenth, as to all "persons," and as against the states *specifically*, what was already forbidden, *more generally*, in the same terms, in the Fifth Amendment. Such a reader might not have had the slightest idea what "due process" was, or why such an added provision was necessary; but whether he had or had not, he would still surely have concluded that the meaning of the phrase, in the Fifth and Fourteenth Amendments, must be the same. And that would have been all he needed to know, in order to comprehend essentially what was being done by this particular clause of the amendment.

And passing, next, to the Equal Protection Clause, its words also, if read with the slightest reflection, are clear; and while its words alone do not disclose the need for the clause, a perception of the general nature of what the clause forbids is certainly quite possible without the least understanding of the need. And the initial clause of the amendment, giving citizenship to "all persons born or naturalized in the United States, and subject to the jurisdiction thereof," is likewise immediately clear in meaning, except the condition about "jurisdiction," which does, undoubtedly, require some professional knowledge for its comprehension.[45] So, there is, of the whole first section, only the clause forbidding state "abridgments" of "privileges or immunities of citizens of the United States" that could, by any stretch of the imagination, give any essential trouble; and with the assistance to be derived from the rest of the Constitution and its amendments, and from an ordinary English dictionary, its meaning, also, could very easily have been made sufficiently clear.

For, if any reader, puzzled as to what "privileges" and "immunities" were, had consulted an ordinary dictionary, he would have learned that an "immunity," in legal usage, is a "freedom," or an "exemption," from something onerous in law or government; and he would have found that a "privilege," in its most common sense, is "a right, advantage, *or immunity,*" enjoyed by a person, or by a class of persons, "beyond the rights, advantages, and *immunities of others.*" And had such a reader looked through the Constitution and its various amendments, he would have found, as we know, many provisions appertaining to rights, presumably to be enjoyed by all "citizens," if not by others, which, he would at once have seen, fully answer to the foregoing dictionary definitions. In particular, he would have found, in the first eight amendments, a long series of such rights, plainly in the nature of "freedoms," or "immunities"; some given in terms to "the people"; some to "persons," and some, as we know, without specification as to who is to hold them, but which, nevertheless, no rational reader could possibly doubt, were at least to be enjoyed by "citizens." The Privileges and Immunities Clause would then, at this point, have been clear in its general import: "no State" was thenceforth to "make or enforce any law abridging" any of these "freedoms," or "immunities," whether enjoyed peculiarly by "citizens of the United States," or by them in common with others. Such a reader might not have had any knowledge at all of the need for this new and seemingly sensible prohibition; but whether he had or had not, he would, again, surely have felt no doubt that the states were being forbidden to deny, or impair, any of these "freedoms," or "immunities," to which the first eight amendments appertained, or, for that matter, any of those which are given anywhere else in the Constitution. And a reader who understood so much would have understood the whole essential meaning of the entire first section of the Fourteenth Amendment. So, what the Supreme Court has done, under this lucidly drawn provision of the document it is sworn to uphold, seems remarkable in the highest degree.

CHAPTER XXXII

The Supreme Court's Transformation of the Fourteenth Amendment

1

THE first of the things the Supreme Court has done to the initial section of the Fourteenth Amendment is to make its Privileges and Immunities Clause completely nugatory and useless. For, with the exception of a single case to which the clause was plainly misapplied in 1935[1]—a case, it may be added, which has since been overruled[2]—the Court has consistently refused, throughout the entire eighty-two years the amendment has been in force, to give to the clause any application at all. The modern Supreme Court freely admits this fact;[3] and if the four dissenting Justices in the *Slaughter-House Cases*,[4] of 1873, can be believed, the Court majority had then already determined to take the extraordinary step of nullifying this new provision of the Constitution, a scant five years after it had been adopted. The evidence indicates that the dissenting Justices were fully justified in this serious charge they made against the Court majority; but to perceive the truth of this, it is necessary to go rather at large into the facts and issues which the *Slaughter-House Cases* presented.

The state act there under attack had been passed by the "carpet-bag" legislature of Louisiana, under "a shallow pretence," as Justice Stephen J. Field, of California, put it in his dissenting opinion, of enacting "sanitary regulations" for the protection of the meat supply of the city of New Orleans. In actual fact, the act was one to incorporate seventeen favored citizens as the Crescent City Live-Stock Landing and Slaughter-House Company and to grant to them, in the corporate capacity thus conferred, a twenty-five-year monopoly of the business of maintaining stock-landings, stock-yards, and slaughter-houses, within an area of some twelve hundred square miles in and around the city in question. The sanitary regulations consisted merely of a stock-inspection provision and certain restrictions as to the areas in which the new company's facilities might be erected; but if the company could conduct its business subject to these simple regulations with safety to the public health, there was, as Justice Field persuasively observed, no reason why the individual butchers compelled by the act to hire the facilities of the defendants could not, with safety to the public, do the same. So, the sanitary excuse was a pretty transparent cover for a state-created monopoly; and because every such monopoly consists essentially in a giving to the monopolist of a special protection which is denied to others, the fact that the Louisiana act was in plain violation of the Equal Protection Clause of the new amendment, under anything like a literal and straightforward reading, cannot very well be denied. In that sense, then, the act "abridged" an "immunity" belonging to the whole class of "citizens of the United States" and was, accordingly, in violation, technically, of the Privileges and Immunities Clause of the amendment, as well.

The Court majority did not deny that a violation of the Equal Protection Clause, or any other provision of the Constitution giving rights to citizens as against the states, would be a violation of the Privileges and Immunities Clause of the amendment. What they did deny was that the Equal Protection Clause, or any other provision of the Constitution applying to the states, had been violated. The other point they conceded.[5] And it was with reference to their concession upon this point that the minority made their accusation that the Privileges and Immunities Clause of the new amendment was actually being destroyed. For they charged the majority with intending to give to the clause no other meaning than that just indicated; and, as Justice Field pointed out, if it had no other application and related only to privileges and immunities otherwise "specially designated" as against the states, or "necessarily implied" against them in the Constitution, "it was a vain and idle enactment, which accomplished nothing, and most unnecessarily excited Congress and the people on its passage." "[For] with privileges and immunities thus designated or implied no State could ever have interfered by its laws, and no new constitutional provision," he quite correctly said, "was required to inhibit such interference. The supremacy of the Constitution and the laws of the United States [had] always controlled any State legislation of that character."[6]

It will be observed that these remarks by Justice Field made perfectly clear to the Court majority the nature of the minority's charge against them; and certain other remarks by Justice Joseph Bradley, of New Jersey, another of the dissenters, brought out another important phase of the matter, upon which Justice Field had not touched. For, although Justice Bradley, like the other dissenters, was unwilling to limit "the privileges and immunities of citizens of the United States," under the Fourteenth Amendment, to those actually enumerated in the Constitution, he did nevertheless explicitly insist that "some of the most important" of these were enumerated there. "The States," he agreed, "were merely prohibited from passing bills of attainder, *ex post facto* laws, laws impairing the obligation of contracts, and perhaps one or two more. But other privileges and immunities of the greatest consequence were enumerated, although they were only secured in express terms, from invasion by the Federal government; such as the right of *habeas corpus*, the right of trial by jury, of free exercise of religious worship, the right of free speech and a free press, the right peaceably to assemble for the discussion of public measures, the right to be secure against unreasonable searches and seizures, and above all, *and including almost all the rest*, the right of *not being deprived of life, liberty, or property, without due process of law*."* "These, and still others [were] specified," the Justice said, "in the original Constitution, or in the early amendments of it, as among the privileges and immunities of citizens of the United States, or, what," he considered, "[was] still stronger for the force of [his] argument, the rights of all persons, whether citizens or not."⁷ And certainly, he intimated, the Privileges and Immunities Clause of the new amendment forbade, for the future, state "abridgments" of all these definitely enumerated rights.

It is thus past all doubt that the meaning of the Privileges and Immunities Clause set forth in the last chapter was drawn to the attention of the Court majority when the *Slaughter-House Cases* were decided. And considering this fact, it would certainly seem that, if the majority had not, in fact, been guilty of the unlawful purpose the minority charged, they would have said so plainly and cleared themselves of guilt. For this they could very easily have done by indicating their willingness to take the clause in dispute, in the sense just indicated; that is, as making good against the states every privilege and immunity which the Constitution and its amendments enumerated, including those which the Court had antecedently held to be "abridgable" by the states. Had the Court majority done this, they would have refuted completely the minority's charge against them, whilst, at the same time, they would have avoided committing themselves, and the Court, to the extreme and unjustified view which the minority wished to take; that is, that the Privileges and Immunities Clause forbade the states to "abridge" any of an indeterminate number of vague and indefinite "privileges and immunities which of right belong[ed]," so the minority said, "to the citizens of all free governments."⁸ And all this being true, the fact that the majority chose, as we shall see, rather to be ambiguous and evasive upon this point, strongly suggests that the minority Justices knew whereof they spoke; a conclusion well confirmed by other evidence.

The opportunity for the evasiveness that the majority displayed, arose directly from the extreme position the minority advocated. That position, despite its complete impossibility under a rational view of the clause in dispute, was undoubtedly urged by the minority in entire good faith. For it is clear from a reading of their opinions that the minority Justices were sincerely convinced of the rectitude of their views. This, considering the character of those views, seems somewhat remarkable; but the apparent

---

* Justice Bradley's italics.

explanation is that they were confused by the similar words—"privileges" and "immunities"—in the Privileges and Immunities Clause of the Fourteenth Amendment, and the Interstate Privileges and Immunities Clause of the original Constitution.

It appears that the minority must have been aware that some cure for the long-standing imperfections of the Interstate Privileges and Immunities Clause of the original document had been intended. Apparently, too, they perceived that the case before them was of the type of iniquity which the old clause had long allowed. And though two, at least, of them saw, and desired to hold, that the case before them was covered by the Equal Protection Clause, they all appeared to be unable to see that it was that clause, and not the Privileges and Immunities Clause of the amendment, which had been employed to remedy the deficiencies in the Interstate Privileges and Immunities Clause of the original Constitution. It was this, apparently, that led them to seek a meaning for the Privileges and Immunities Clause of the amendment that would make the state act before them a violation of that clause, too; and this, quite apart from any denial of "equal protection" that the act might involve.

The meaning they fixed upon was that already indicated; a meaning which took the clause of the amendment as providing what, in the years just before the Civil War, it had been very widely urged, was the true meaning of the Interstate Privileges and Immunities Clause of the original Constitution. Justice Bradley, indeed, desired actually to hold that this old clause, not yet authoritatively interpreted to the contrary when the *Slaughter-House Cases* arose, itself had the meaning in question. "It [was] true," he conceded, "the courts* ha[d] usually regarded [it] as securing only an equality of privileges with the citizens of the State in which the parties [were] found." But "the language"—

The Citizens of each State shall be entitled to all Privileges and Immunities of Citizens *in* the several States—

was "fairly susceptible of a broader interpretation." And Justice Bradley accordingly declared it his view that "it [was] the privileges and immunities *of citizens*, that is, *of citizens as such*," which the clause had been intended to cover. These, he said, were "the privileges and immunities, which [were], in their nature, fundamental; which belong[ed], of right, to the citizens of all free governments."[9]

Justice Noah H. Swayne, of Ohio, another of the dissenters, agreed with these views; but the other two dissenters—Chief Justice Salmon Portland Chase, also of Ohio, and Justice Field—did not. Their view, in which Justices Bradley and Swayne concurred, was that already indicated: that the Privileges and Immunities Clause of the new amendment was intended to make good the deficiencies of the similarly named clause of the original document, and that it did this by providing what Justices Swayne and

---

* That is, state courts and inferior national courts.

Bradley desired also to hold was the true meaning of the clause of the original Constitution. The opinion of Justice Field dealt with this phase of the dissent; and it is in what he had to say in reference thereto that the basis of the confusion in the minds of the dissenters most clearly appears.

"The terms, privileges and immunities, [were] not new in the amendment," Justice Field observed, "[but] were in the Constitution before the amendment was adopted. They [were] found in the second section of the fourth article [quoting it], and [had] been the subject of frequent consideration in judicial decisions." These had treated the words as denoting "the privileges and immunities, which of right belong[ed] to the citizens of all free governments"; and had held that "the citizens of each State," by the terms of the old clause, were entitled to enjoy all such rights "in the several States upon the same terms and conditions as they [were] enjoyed by the citizens of the latter States." "[And] what th[at] clause [of the original Constitution had done] for *the protection* of the citizens of one State against hostile and discriminating legislation of other States, the Fourteenth Amendment d[id] for *the protection* of every citizen of the United States . . . , *whether they reside[d] in the same [State] or [not]*."[10]

Standing alone, the foregoing statements, with their talk of state "residence" and "protection," could perhaps be taken to refer to the Equal Protection Clause of the amendment. It appears, however, that this was not what Justice Field intended; for he went immediately on to say that, "if under the fourth article of the Constitution equality of *privileges and immunities* [was] secured between citizens of different States, *under the fourteenth amendment the same equality* [was] secured *between citizens of the United States.*" And that the Privileges and Immunities Clause of the amendment (to which, in fact, his whole opinion was devoted) was the clause he had in mind in these remarks is likewise shown, by his insistence, a little further on, that "what the clause [in the original Constitution had done] for the protection of citizens of one State against the creation of monopolies in favor of citizens of other States, the fourteenth amendment d[id] for the protection of every citizen of the United States against the creation of any monopoly whatever. [For] *the privileges and immunities of citizens of the United States, of every one of them,* [was] secured against *abridgment* in any form by any State."[11]

That the strange and almost incredible confusion appearing in these passages was a thoroughly honest one, in the case, at least, of Justice Field, and that he was striving, in the *Slaughter-House Cases*, faithfully to perform, and not to repudiate, the duties of the judicial office, are facts which seem quite amply proved by his own eventual confession of error in this matter, nearly twenty years later. This occurred in the case of *O'Neil* v. *Vermont*,[12] in 1892, after it had been argued unsuccessfully in *Spies* v. *Illinois*,[13] five years earlier, that the true intent of the Privileges and Immunities Clause of the Fourteenth Amendment was that set forth in the preceding chapter of this book. "After much reflection," Justice Field confessed, in dissent from the Court's decision, "I think the definition given at one time before this court by a distinguished advocate—John Randolph Tucker, of Virginia—is correct, that the privileges and immunities of citizens of the United States are such as have their recognition in or guaranty from the Constitution of the United States." And thereupon, after a review of the situation that had resulted from the Court's decision in *Barron* v. *Baltimore*, in 1833, he announced this conclusion: that "the Fourteenth Amendment, as to all such rights [as those covered in the first eight amendments], place[d] a limit upon state power by ordaining that no State sh[ould] make or enforce any law which sh[ould] abridge them."[14] So, in the end, Justice Field, the only one of the dissenters in the *Slaughter-House Cases* still surviving in 1892, did come around to the just and proper view. And this view also was taken, in *O'Neil* v. *Vermont*, by Justice John Marshall Harlan, of Kentucky, a newer member of the Court, of whom more hereafter.[15]

As already indicated, the view of the Interstate Privileges and Immunities Clause which Justices Bradley and Swayne desired to take in the *Slaughter-House Cases*, and which all four of the dissenters therein believed had been written into the Constitution by the Privileges and Immunities Clause of the Fourteenth Amendment, was a view of the earlier clause which had become rather common in the years just before the Civil War. It had been then urged, on occasion, in behalf both of slavery[16] and anti-slavery interests;[17] and there can be little doubt it was an outgrowth of the Court's unfortunate decision in *Barron* v. *Baltimore*. For, taken with the earlier partial destruction of the Ex-post-facto Clause and the Contracts Clause, that decision brought to an end nearly all the intended Constitutional protection against the states. And the Interstate Privileges and Immunities Clause being still, at that time, not yet authoritatively interpreted to the contrary, it probably seemed to advocates of this more extended view of this clause, that it afforded another opportunity to obtain what the Court's earlier decisions had destroyed.

The mere language of the Interstate Privileges and Immunities Clause, standing alone, could no doubt bear the broader interpretation; and it is easy to understand that, after the decision of the Supreme Court in *Barron* v. *Baltimore*, the broader meaning probably seemed to fulfil a very genuine need. But the plausibility of the broader view arising from this need was a plausibility that had not existed when the clause was drawn; and that arising from its words disappears if it is compared with the clause in the Articles from which it originated. For the clause in the Articles explicitly indicated that an interstate equality in rights *under the laws of each state* was what was intended; and comparison will show that the clause in the Constitution is no more than a simplified and condensed version of the clause in the Articles. Besides this, it is inherently improbable that any such vague, indefinite, and essentially unlimited limitation on state authority was intended. So, it cannot be doubted that the view of the Interstate Privileges and Immunities Clause which Justices Bradley and Swayne desired to take was, in reality, a quite unjustified view.*

It remains to be shown why the dissenters in the *Slaughter-House Cases* were likewise not warranted in the broad view they desired to take of the similarly named clause in the Fourteenth Amendment. In support of that view, they cited certain remarks about the earlier clause which had been made by Justice Bushrod Washington, in the circuit-court case of *Corfield v. Coryell*,[18] in 1823. "We cannot [agree]," Justice Washington had then said, "that, under this [clause], the citizens of the several States are permitted to participate in all the rights which belong exclusively to the citizens of any other particular state, *merely* upon the ground that they are enjoyed by those citizens." "What are the privileges and immunities of citizens *in* the several states?" he had then inquired. And in answer to his own question, he had gone on to say that he and the local judge "fe[lt] no hesitation in confining these expressions to those privileges and immunities which [were], in their nature, fundamental; which belong[ed] of right, to the citizens of all free governments; and which ha[d], at all times been enjoyed by the citizens of the several States which compose[d] th[e] union, from the time of their becoming free, independent, and sovereign." The Justice then proceeded to indicate what he thought these rights were. Reference to his opinion will show that they covered a great deal of ground; but he nevertheless concluded that the right in issue in the case before him was not "fundamental."

Reading the opinion as a whole, it is perfectly clear that Justice Washington and his associate in this Corfield case meant only to hold that the right of equality given by the Interstate Privileges and Immunities Clause was *limited* by their vague and fanciful doctrine of "fundamental privileges and immunities." It was a little meaningless rhetoric to excuse their failure to apply the clause strictly as the clause was written. Nevertheless, if their limiting doctrine had actually been settled "law" when the Fourteenth Amendment was adopted; that is, if there had been Supreme Court decisions that there was a body of "fundamental privileges and immunities," to which alone the clause referred, "which belong[ed], of right, to the citizens of all free governments," then, since the Government of the

---

* The clause in the Articles reads as follows: "The better to secure and perpetuate mutual friendship and intercourse among the people of the different states in this union, the free inhabitants of each of these states, paupers, vagbonds and fugitives from justice excepted, shall be entitled to all privileges and immunities of free citizens in the several states; and the people of each state shall have free ingress and regress to and from any other state, and shall enjoy therein all the privileges of trade and commerce, subject to the same duties, impositions and restrictions *as the inhabitants thereof respectively*, provided that such restrictions shall not extend so far as to prevent the removal of property imported into any state, to any other state, of which the owner is an inhabitant; provided also that no imposition, duties or restriction shall be laid by any state, on the property of the United States, or either of them."

United States is such a government, the prohibition to the states, in the Fourteenth Amendment, against the "mak[ing] or enforc[ing of] any law which sh[ould] abridge the privileges or immunities of citizens of the United States," might, with some show of plausibility, have been argued to have the scope the dissenters in the *Slaughter-House Cases* wished to give it. This, at any rate, is the best that can be said for their position.

But the difficulty is that the decision in the Corfield case was merely one by a single Supreme Court Justice, acting on circuit, with the concurrence, apparently, of the local district judge. And when the Fourteenth Amendment was drawn, there was no basis at all for belief that the Supreme Court had approved, or would approve, the views expressed in the Corfield decision. For only one case under the Interstate Privileges and Immunities Clause had, at that time, reached the Supreme Court, the case of *Conner* v. *Elliott*,[19] in 1855; and in that case, Justice Curtis, speaking for a unanimous Court, had expressly declined, in rejecting the claim of constitutional privilege in the particular case, to define what "the privileges and immunities" covered by the clause, in general, were. And the remarks about the clause which this same Justice and Chief Justice Taney had made in the Dred Scott case, in the year following, were equally devoid of suggestion that Justice Washington's views had been, or would be, adopted.[20] So, it is certain his talk about "privileges and immunities, which belong[ed], of right, to the citizens of all free governments," in the Corfield case, was not a part of the standing "constitutional law" of the country, in 1866–68, when the Fourteenth Amendment was drawn and adopted. And it follows that there was, and is, no basis for reading that talk into the Fourteenth Amendment.[21]

The majority in the *Slaughter-House Cases* were, then, undoubtedly correct in rejecting this extreme view that the minority Justices wished to take. Nevertheless, it is significant of what was going on, and of the state of mind of the Court majority, that they felt it necessary to misquote, in their opinion, both the Interstate Privileges and Immunities Clause of the original Constitution, and what Justice Washington had had to say about it in the Corfield case. The clause was quoted in the Court's opinion as follows: "The citizens of each State shall be entitled to all privileges and immunities of citizens *of* the several States." And Justice Washington was quoted as inquiring "what [were] the privileges and immunities of citizens *of* the several States." These misquotations made somewhat easier the conclusions the Court majority desired to reach: (1) that the Interstate Privileges and Immunities Clause related to privileges and immunities "of" *state* citizenship; (2) that Justice Washington, "throughout his opinion," had spoken of the rights under that clause "as rights belonging to the individual as a citizen *of a State*"; and (3) that the rights the clause covered, were, therefore, not comprehended by the words "privileges or immunities *of* citizens *of the United States*."[22]

Justice Bradley, in his dissent, called attention to this double misquotation in the majority opinion. "It is pertinent to observe," he tartly remarked, "that both the [Interstate Privileges and Immunities Clause of the original Constitution], and Justice Washington in his comment on it, speak of the privileges and immunities of citizens *in** a State; not of citizens *of** a State."[23] And since it can hardly be supposed the Court's double misquotation, so favorable to the conclusion it wished to reach, was inadvertent, the necessary conclusion would seem to be that these petty misquotations were deliberate; a device adopted to give to the majority opinion, rapidly read, an added plausibility.

The Court opinion in the *Slaughter-House Cases* was written by Justice Samuel Freeman Miller, of Iowa, the same Justice who had engineered, for the Court, the destruction of the interstate phase of the Imports and Exports Clause, in *Woodruff* v. *Parham*,[24] in 1868. A careful study of the opinions in these two cases will show that, in point of technique employed, they have much in common. And in the *Slaughter-House Cases*, the misquotations that Justice Bradley pointed out were not the only evidence of what was there going on. For even more significant were the ambiguity and evasiveness, earlier mentioned, which the majority displayed in meeting the serious charge that the minority made against them: that they were bent on robbing the Privileges and Immunities Clause of the Fourteenth Amendment, of all effective meaning whatsoever.

Justice Miller turned his attention to this phase of the case after he had held, with complete correctness, that the clause in question could apply only to those "privileges and immunities of citizens of the United States" which "owe[d] their existence to the Federal Government, its National character, *its Constitution*, or its laws." "Lest it should be said," he added, "that no such privileges and immunities [of citizens of the United States were] to be found, [the Court would] venture to suggest some." The Court's "suggestions" ran as follows:

One [such right] is well described in the case of *Crandall* v. *Nevada*. It is said to be the right of the citizen of this great country, protected by implied guarantees of its Constitution, "to come to the seat of government to assert any claim he may have upon that government, to transact any business he may have with it, *to seek its protection*, to share its offices, to engage in administering its functions. He has the right of free access to its seaports, through which all operations of foreign commerce are conducted, to the subtreasuries, land offices, and courts of justice in the several States." And quoting from the language of Chief Justice Taney in another case, it is said "that for all the great purposes for which the Federal government was established, we are one people, with one common country, we are all citizens of the United States"; and it is, as such citizens, that their rights are supported in this court in *Crandall* v. *Nevada*.

* Justice Bradley's italics.

Another privilege of a citizen of the United States is to demand the care and protection of the Federal government over his life, liberty, and property when on the high seas or within the jurisdiction of a foreign government. Of this there can be no doubt, nor that the right depends upon his character as a citizen of the United States. *The right to peaceably assemble and petition for redress of grievances, the privilege of the writ of* habeas corpus, *are rights of the citizen guaranteed by the Federal Constitution.* The right to use the navigable waters of the United States, however they may penetrate the territory of the several States, all rights secured to our citizens by treaties with foreign nations, are dependent upon citizenship of the United States, and not citizenship of a State. One of these privileges is conferred by the very article under consideration. It is that a citizen of the United States can, of his own volition, become a citizen of any State of the Union by a *bona fide* residence therein, with the same rights as other citizens of that State. To these may be added the rights secured by the thirteenth and fifteenth articles of amendment, and by the other clause of the fourteenth, next to be considered.[25]

Now, as it has many times since been pointed out, *Crandall* v. *Nevada*[26] was decided by the Supreme Court *before* the Fourteenth Amendment was adopted; and, so, if the Privileges and Immunities Clause of the new amendment referred only to rights of the precise kind the Crandall case exemplified, the dissenters in the *Slaughter-House Cases* were clearly correct in their charge, that the majority were robbing this new Constitutional provision of all real meaning whatsoever. For, if such, in fact, was its only reference—or, more accurately, the only reference the Court majority would recognize—then, as Justice Field pointed out, the Clause would not affect the course of the Court's decisions at all; and it might, then, just as well have been omitted from the Constitution. And all the rights, *save two*, that Justice Miller "suggested," were *clearly* rights of the precise kind involved in the Crandall case; that is, they were rights that would have been enforced upon the states, whether there had been any Privileges and Immunities Clause in the Fourteenth Amendment or not.

The two exceptions were the right of "free assembly and petition," and "the privilege of the writ of *habeas corpus*," which rights, it may have been observed, were buried by Justice Miller, in accord with an old practice often used in the drawing of brokers' circulars and similar documents, in the midst of all the other "suggestions" his opinion contained. One of these rights, that of "free assembly and petition," is one of those covered by the first eight amendments. The Justice's "suggestion" of this right was, then, susceptible of being taken as an indication that *all* the rights covered by the first eight amendments had been made good against the states; and so taken, it would have been a complete refutation of the charge the minority made. But, on the other hand, the right was also susceptible of being taken, and was, in fact, afterwards taken by the Court,[27] as relating only to "assembling" for the consideration of matters of concern to the nation, and to "petition[ing] the [national] Government" for relief. And so taken, it was, of course, but one more example of rights of the kind the Crandall case had involved; indeed, it would seem that, as a "seek[ing of the national government's] protection," it would have been directly within the language from the Crandall case that Justice Miller quoted.

The "suggestion," then, of this particular right was plainly ambiguous, and evasive, with respect to the serious charge the minority Justices had made; and since it was the *only* right covered by the first eight amendments that had this convenient character, it is not to be doubted it was most carefully selected for its peculiar function in the Court majority's opinion. For its "suggestion" made possible, without a loss of face, the taking of the Privileges and Immunities Clause, in future cases, as making good against the states, *all* the privileges and immunities under the first eight amendments, *if* the reaction to the *Slaughter-House Cases* should be of a kind to make this unwelcome course seem necessary. At the same time, the peculiar character of this right, and the careful overweighting of the Court's "suggestions" in favor of the meaningless meaning "suggested" by the Crandall case made the future total destruction of the clause very easy, *if* this seemed safe.

The situation with respect to "the privilege of the writ of *habeas corpus*" was similar. For, although, by the terms of the original Constitution, the writ was guarantied against suspension "unless when in Cases of Rebellion or Invasion the public Safety m[ight] require it," the guaranty was one of those in section 9 of Article I, which, for reasons already explained in chapter xxx, had always been held as a whole—and, it would seem, correctly held—not to be directed against the states. The guaranty against suspension of the writ had, therefore, never been regarded as forbidding its suspension by state law, in the courts of the states;[28] but the writ was available, nevertheless, in the national courts, to obtain the discharge of any person held in custody by a state, in violation of the Constitution, the laws, or the treaties, of the United States.[29] The Court's "suggestion" of this privilege as one of those "of citizens of the United States," to which the Fourteenth Amendment related, was, thus, again, ambiguous and evasive, with respect to the minority's charge. For the "suggestion" could be taken, either as one that the guaranty against suspension was now operative against the states in their own courts, or as one that the right to the writ against the states, in the national courts, under the circumstances stated, was one the states could not "abridge." If only the latter was meant, the Privileges and Immunities Clause of the amendment was again, in reality, being given no effect at all; but if the former was meant, it was being given its true and intended force. And from the Court's opinion in the *Slaughter-House Cases*, it is utterly impossible to tell which of these two very different things was meant, although the careful overweighting of the Court's "suggestions" in favor of the meaningless meaning of the Privileges and Immunities Clause, and the ambiguous character of the two rights just discussed, can certainly leave little doubt as to what the majority intended to do if they dared.

So, the Court's opinion in the *Slaughter-House Cases* was, undoubtedly, most craftily written; written so as to enable the Court, with a good face, in future cases, to jump either way: to observe the intended meaning of the Privileges and Immunities Clause if that seemed unavoidable, or, in the alternative, to destroy the clause utterly if this seemed safe. And the fact that this elaborate preparation was made also means that the majority Justices saw and fully comprehended the possibility of the intermediate, plain, and sensible meaning of the Privileges and Immunities Clause here expounded, to which, indeed, Justice Bradley called attention, in his dissenting opinion. So, the majority must, as the minority charged, already have determined, *if* they dared, to destroy this new provision of the Constitution completely.

2

The first clear evidence that the Supreme Court did, in fact, mean to destroy the Privileges and Immunities Clause of the Fourteenth Amendment was provided in the case of *Walker* v. *Sauvinet*,[30] three years later. The right to jury trial covered by the Seventh Amendment was there claimed by the appellant, as one of the "privileges and immunities of citizens of the United States," which, by the plain terms of the Fourteenth Amendment, no state could longer "abridge." The Supreme Court replied that the Seventh Amendment, "as ha[d] been many times decided, relate[d] only to trials in courts of the United States"; and that "a trial by jury in suits at common law pending in the State courts [was] not, therefore, a privilege or immunity of national citizenship, which the States [were] forbidden by the Fourteenth Amendment to abridge." No further explanation was given. Justice Field and one of the majority Justices in the *Slaughter-House Cases* dissented.

This was the beginning. Similar contentions as to others of the "privileges and immunities" covered by the first eight amendments soon followed and met a similar fate, in each case without any real explanation by the Court.[31] And thus the situation continued for nearly a quarter of a century. The only other fact about this period that it seems necessary to note is that one of the rights thus summarily disposed of was "the right to keep and bear Arms," which, it will be remembered, the Second Amendment describes as a "right *of the people*." This was in *Presser* v. *Illinois*,[32] in 1886.

Such, then, was the general situation when it was urged upon the Court, in *Maxwell* v. *Dow*,[33] at the turn of the century, that the requirement in the Fifth Amendment as to indictment or presentment in the case of capital and otherwise infamous crimes, and that in the Sixth Amendment as to jury trial in all criminal prosecutions, had been made good in favor of all citizens, as against the states, by the Privileges and Immunities Clause of the Fourteenth Amendment. The Court denied this contention and, in its opinion, at last attempted an explanation and justification of the general position it had theretofore silently assumed. The decision of twenty-four years earlier, in *Walker* v. *Sauvinet*, denying the right of jury trial covered by the Seventh Amendment, was first cited by the Court; and the question then asked, whether "any one of the rights secured to the individual by the Fifth or by the Sixth Amendment [was] any more a privilege or immunity of a citizen of the United States, than [were] those secured by the Seventh." "In none," the Court said, "[were] they privileges or immunities granted and belonging to the individual *as* a citizen of the United States"; they were, instead, "secured to all persons as against the Federal Government, entirely irrespective of such citizenship." From the nature of this statement, it is clear the Court, by the date of *Maxwell* v. *Dow*, had completely forgotten the contrary doctrine of the Dred Scott case, that all "privileges and immunities" under the Constitution were those "of citizens of the United States" only. So, it was able confidently, and with a good face, to conclude that "it [was] not correct or reasonable to say that [the Privileges and Immunities Clause of the Fourteenth Amendment] cover[ed] and extend[ed] to certain rights which [the citizen] d[id] not enjoy *by reason* of his citizenship, but simply because those rights exist[ed] in favor of all individuals as against Federal governmental powers."[34]

These statements of the Court, in *Maxwell* v. *Dow*, might, if they were considered in isolation, quite well be taken as a recognition that those rights to which the First, Second, and Fourth Amendments refer as "rights of the people" *were* made good, as against the states, by the Privileges and Immunities Clause of the Fourteenth Amendment. For, as Chief Justice Taney had correctly declared, in the Dred Scott case, "the people," and "the citizens," of the United States are, in the Constitution, synonymous expressions. But the Court of 1900 seems to have overlooked this fact, and it had apparently forgotten this phase, also, of the Dred Scott decision. For, despite the character of its above-quoted statements, the Court, in *Maxwell* v. *Dow*, cited its earlier decision, in *Presser* v. *Illinois*, with approval: that "the right *of the people* to keep and bear Arms" was still, even after the Fourteenth Amendment had been adopted, a right *not* available to citizens, as against the states. And it concluded obscurely that it had shown, by its various citations, that "the privileges and immunities of citizens of the United States d[id] not *necessarily* include *all* the rights protected by the first eight amendments." By this, it apparently meant to say, though hardly in very clear fashion that the terms in question did not *"necessarily"* include *any* of the rights under those initial amendments. And since the terms did not, in the Court's opinion, *"neces-*

sarily" include these rights, the Court seemed to feel at liberty to deny the appellant's contention.[35]

The utterly unwarranted character of the Court's act in doing this becomes apparent when the recited "objects" of the Constitution are remembered. For one of those "objects," as we know, is the "secur[ing of] the Blessings of Liberty to ['the People']"—that is, "to the Citizens"—"['of the United States'] and [their] Posterity"; and even if the Court had been correct that the meaning of the Privileges and Immunities Clause for which the appellant contended was one merely possible, and not "necessary," it still would have been its duty to take the clause in the sense favorable to the appellant, because that sense, manifestly, was the sense that best comported with, and best promoted, this end, or "object," which the Preamble of the Constitution states. The point, we have seen, is an elementary one in the art of documentary interpretation; but, as the reader has doubtless by now observed, it is not a point to which the Supreme Court has ever paid much attention where the Constitution of the United States is concerned.

The utterly confused character of the Court's opinion in *Maxwell* v. *Dow* (in which all the Justices, save the sensible and forthright John Harlan, fully concurred*) is further demonstrated by the Court's attitude toward the attempt made by appellant's counsel, to induce it to consider what really was the historic and intended meaning of the Privileges and Immunities Clause of the Fourteenth Amendment. The speeches in Congress, by the framers of the amendment, in which they had explained what they conceived their proposal to mean, were cited to the Court. Its answer was that "the question whether the amendment express[ed] the meaning which those who spoke in its favor may have assumed that it did, [was] one to be determined by the language actually therein used and not by the speeches made regarding it." This, of course, was completely correct; and so was the Court's further statement that "the safe way [was] to read [the] language [of the amendment] in connection with the known condition of affairs out of which the occasion for its adoption [had] arisen, and then construe it, if there [were] therein any doubtful expressions, in a way so far as [was] reasonably possible, to forward the known purpose or object for which the amendment [had been] adopted."[36] Yet, despite this unimpeachable orthodoxy in the Court's general attitude, it manifestly did not do, along these lines, what even a layman could easily have done with an ordinary English dictionary, and much less did it do what might, with reason, have been expected from the nation's highest court, staffed, presumably, with men expert and learned in the "constitutional law," not only of their own particular time, but also of all those previous times when, as in 1866–68, the Constitution had been amended.

---

* Justice Field, who, would no doubt, have agreed with Justice Harlan had died three years before.

For, if the Court of 1900 had been thus learned in the standing "law" of the time when the Fourteenth Amendment was adopted, it could hardly have failed to see that what it was doing in *Maxwell* v. *Dow* did not measure up, at all, to the standards it announced, of what was right and proper.

In view of this manifest weakness and confusion in the Court's opinion in *Maxwell* v. *Dow*, it is by no means strange the case did not put at rest the important constitutional question it dealt with. So, after a decent interval and the accession of three new Justices to the Court,[37] the point was urged again, in 1908, in the case of *Twining* v. *New Jersey*.[38] It has been truly observed, by one of the present members of the Court, that "decisions of [that learned body] do not have equal intrinsic authority."[39] And, from this point of view, *Twining* v. *New Jersey* is surely a case ranking very low on the list; for the Court unquestionably appeared in that case at its worst. The important questions that the case involved were presented, on behalf of the appellants, by one of the ablest lawyers who ever appeared before the Court: the late John G. Johnson, of Philadelphia. And considering the known ability of this great lawyer, it cannot possibly be doubted that he presented his correct contention cogently: that the Privileges and Immunities Clause of the Fourteenth Amendment had been intended to make good, and did by its plain words make good, in favor of all "citizens," as against the states, the various "privileges and immunities" which the first eight amendments covered, and, among others, the "immunity" from compelled self-incrimination that the Twining case involved. And this being true, the "long deliberation" that followed, between the argument of the case, and the Court's decision of it— from March 20, to November 9, 1908—is not very hard to understand; for, considering the nature of the Court's eventual decision, there hardly can be a doubt that the question debated was whether that august tribunal, the Supreme Court of the United States, should confess its own past errors and, for the future, abide by the Constitution, or whether, instead, it should preserve a false dignity and continue, as in the past, to flout that document. And the Constitution unfortunately lost out; for the determination apparently was that it was now "too late," as one of the participating Justices, twenty years later, expressed it, to observe the Fourteenth Amendment to the Constitution.[40] Justice Harlan, alone, dissented, in one of his characteristically forthright and vigorous opinions.

So far as the majority opinion in the Twining case relates to the Privileges and Immunities Clause, it is not only actually, but quite openly, a simple refusal to consider what the appellants had to say. The view that the clause had made the first eight amendments good against the states "ha[d] been, at different times, expressed," the Court noted, "by justices of th[e] court." "Mr. Justice Field in *O'Neil* v. *Vermont*, 144 U.S. 323, 361; [and] Mr. Justice Harlan in the same case, 370, and in *Maxwell* v.

Dow, 176 U.S. 606, 617," were mentioned; and others of the Justices might have been—notably, Justice Bradley, who, it will not be forgotten, had clearly explained, in the *Slaughter-House Cases*, within five years after the Fourteenth Amendment had been adopted, the effect of its Privileges and Immunities Clause in wiping out the Court's old error in *Barron* v. *Baltimore*. The Court also conceded, in this Twining case, that such a view of the effect of the clause had "undoubtedly" been "entertained by some* of those who framed the Amendment." "[Yet] it [was] not profitable," the Court declared, "to examine the weighty arguments in its favor, for the question [was] no longer open in th[e] court." "The discussion in [*Maxwell* v. *Dow*]," the Court also said, and with a certain truth, "ought not to be repeated. All the arguments for the other view [had been] considered [in that case] and answered"—as, after a fashion, they had—"the authorities [had been] examined and analyzed, and the decision rested upon the ground that this clause of the Fourteenth Amendment did not forbid the States to abridge the personal rights enumerated in the first eight Amendments, because those rights were not within the meaning of the clause 'privileges and immunities of citizens of the United States,'"[41] This not very accurate summary of the not very accurate statement in *Maxwell* v. *Dow* completed what the Court, in the Twining case, had to say about the Privileges and Immunities Clause of the Fourteenth Amendment as an attempted correction of the Court's old error in *Barron* v. *Baltimore;* and it seems perfectly clear the Court simply refused, once more, to be corrected. For all it decided was that its former decisions, *whether right or wrong*, were "the law" and would in the future, as in the past, be followed. But, at least, this extraordinary attitude of the Supreme Court of the United States, toward the document it was sworn to uphold, was made clear.

3

The systematic clarifying effect of the decision in *Twining* v. *New Jersey* was not limited to the Privileges and Immunities Clause of the Fourteenth Amendment. For it was likewise argued in the case that the "immunity" claimed, since it was one of those specific "process" guaranties that the earlier clauses of the Fifth Amendment, and the Fourth, Sixth, and Eighth Amendments, as a whole, contain, was made good in favor of all "persons," whether aliens or citizens, against the states, by the Due Process Clause of the amendment in question; and this contention, the Court, in the Twining case, likewise systematically denied. The argument in support of this part of the decision is long and involved; but it is not difficult to perceive that, in this phase also, the Twining case was simply a

---

* There is no known evidence that any of the framers of the amendment held a contrary view, though some did think it accomplished more than a simple correction of the Court's past error in *Barron* v. *Baltimore*.

determination by the Court to adhere to its earlier decisions, *whether these were warranted or not*. To perceive this, it is necessary, however, to go back, once more, to the *Slaughter-House Cases*, and to review briefly the course of the Court's subsequent decisions under the Due Process Clause of the Fourteenth Amendment, before the Twining case came up for decision.

In what had been said of the Due Process Clause in the *Slaughter-House Cases*, the Court majority had been on firm ground. Justices Bradley and Swayne, of the minority, had been desirous of taking a position upon this clause that would have amounted to affirming the view of "due process of law" that had been implicit in the Dred Scott decision; that is, they wished to take a position that would have amounted to an avowal of the constitutional heresy nowadays known as "substantive due process of law." For what they wished to hold was that a law prohibiting the plaintiffs from using certain properties of theirs for stock-landings, stock-yards, and slaughter-houses, as they had theretofore been accustomed to do, "deprived" them of their "property without due process of law."[42] This position, the majority clearly, and indignantly, refused to take.

The guaranty of due process, the majority said, was not new in the Fourteenth Amendment; it had been in the Fifth Amendment, as a restraint on the national power, practically from the beginning of the Government; and it had been in the constitutions of nearly all the states, as a restraint upon the power of the states, for as long or, in some cases, for longer. Precedents, therefore, were available, as to what the words of this guaranty meant. "And it [was] sufficient to say that under no construction of [its words] that [the majority] ha[d] ever seen, or any that [they] deem[ed] admissible, c[ould] the restraint imposed by the State of Louisiana upon the exercise of their trade by the butchers of New Orleans be held to be a deprivation of property within the meaning of that provision."[43] This is all that was said; and it must be confessed it was all there was any need to say in the case before the Court. Yet it did leave uncertain whether the Court meant to give the Due Process Clause a just construction, as making good, in favor of all "persons," as against the states, the various particular "process" guaranties that the first eight amendments covered; and considering the determination which, we have just seen, the Court majority had then already reached as to what they meant to do to the Privileges and Immunities Clause, there surely was good ground for fear as to what further illegal action they contemplated. For they obviously could not deny to "citizens," as against the states, the various particular "process" guaranties in the first eight amendments, constituting most of what those initial amendments covered, if they recognized the Due Process Clause of the Fourteenth Amendment, as validating all these "process" guaranties against the states, in favor of all "persons" whatsoever.

It was, once more, not long, however, before evidence began to accumulate as to what the Supreme Court meant to do; and as in the case of the Privileges and Immunities Clause, the first hint came in the case of *Walker* v. *Sauvinet*,[44] in 1876. For, in that case, besides denying the contention of the appellant under the Privileges and Immunities Clause, the Court went out of its way to say that, although "a State c[ould] not deprive a person of his property without due process of law," yet "this d[id] not necessarily imply that all trials in the State Courts affecting the property of persons must be by jury." Other similar decisions soon followed;[45] and in *Hurtado* v. *California*,[46] in 1884, the Court held that the Due Process Clause of the Fourteenth Amendment did not even require "indictment or presentment by a Grand Jury," in a prosecution by a state for murder. The amazing character of this holding will at once be apparent if some of the facts set forth in chapter xxxi are recalled to mind. For Coke and Blackstone, we saw, had treated "indictment or presentment by good and lawful men" as the very essence of "due process of law" in their writings; Alexander Hamilton had expressed a similar view of the meaning of the phrase in 1786; and Rawle and Kent and Story, writing in the 1820's and 1830's, had all also recognized that "indictment or presentment by a Grand Jury" was a part of the content of the phrase "due process of law," as employed in the Fifth Amendment.

The foregoing facts will indicate at once why the opinion in the Hurtado case was long and labored; for, after all, it is not easy to prove what is not true. But there were other reasons why the opinion-writer's difficulties in the case were great. One was the fact, which the Court could not well deny, that the meaning of the "due-process" guaranty in the Fifth and Fourteenth Amendments was the same. The appellant, moreover, insisted upon this fact and cited to the Court its own first opinion under the Fifth Amendment, which, he maintained, established the right for which he contended, as a necessary element of "due"—or "appropriate"—"process of law" under the Constitution. The case he cited was *Murray's Lessee* v. *Hoboken Land and Improvement Company*,[47] which, it will be remembered, had been decided, in 1855, only a few years before the Fourteenth Amendment was adopted. And in 1866–68, when the amendment was adopted, the views it expressed were still unqualifiedly the views of the Supreme Court. They were, then, indisputably, a part of the standing constitutional law of that time; and, as such, they were among the presuppositions upon which the draftsmen of the Fourteenth Amendment were entitled to rely in deciding how they should say what they desired their new amendment to provide. There can be no doubt about this; for it is elementary law which the Supreme Court itself had then, as it has since, in other connections, many times affirmed.[48]

It is important, further, to note that the part of the Hoboken opinion that was cited to the Court in the Hurtado case was the part wherein

Justice Curtis had explained how the "propriety," or "dueness," or "process" under the Constitution was to be determined. "To what principle," he had asked, "are we to resort to ascertain whether [any particular] process, enacted by Congress, is *due* process?" "We must examine the Constitution," was his answer, "to see whether th[e] process is in conflict with any of its provisions."[49] So, one part of the standing law upon which the draftsmen of the Fourteenth Amendment were entitled to count; upon which, it is clear, they did actually count; and upon which, certainly, they would have been compelled to count, had they desired their new "due-process" guaranty to be something different, was that the general guaranty of "due process of law," in the Fifth Amendment, was, *first of all*, "a summary of the whole," as William Rawle had expressed it, in 1828,[50] of all the specific "process" guaranties that the Constitution and its amendments contained.

And the slightest reflection will show that this was necessarily true. For the phases of "process" covered by the specific "process" guaranties were within the words of the general guaranty, and the specific guaranties fixed what was "appropriate," or "due, process of law," *under the Constitution*, as to the phases of "process" they covered. The general guaranty was, however, something more than a mere summary of the specific guaranties; and, so, Justice Curtis had gone on to say, that, if a particular "process" enacted by Congress was found *not* to be specifically forbidden by the Constitution, the next test of its "dueness," or "propriety," was whether it was supported by English Common Law or statutory precedents that had been received into American practice before the "due-process" guaranty in the Fifth Amendment had been adopted. Beyond this, as noted in our first mention of this case, Justice Curtis and the Court of 1855 had not gone, because the "process" in issue in the case before them was easily shown to be "appropriate," or "due, process of law" by this second test. And the Court, accordingly, so held.[51]

Now, the real relevancy of the Hoboken precedent to the Hurtado case arose from the fact that proceeding in a capital case, on a mere information by a state district attorney, as the state of California had done in the Hurtado case, was one of the modes of criminal "process" that were specifically outlawed by the Constitution. For, by the initial clause of the Fifth Amendment, it was provided, subject to a single exception not relevant to the Hurtado case, that "no person sh[ould] be held to answer for a capital, or otherwise infamous crime, unless on a presentment or indictment of a Grand Jury." And from this fact, it necessarily followed, under Justice Curtis' first test in the Hoboken case, that proceeding, in a murder case, without such a "presentment or indictment," could not be "due," or "appropriate," "process of law" under the Fifth Amendment. Since, moreover, the Fourteenth Amendment was part of the same instrument as the Fifth, and the ordinary presumption of continuity in meaning of terms within a single document was in no way rebutted, it further followed that, for a state to proceed in a murder case, without a "presentment or indictment of a Grand Jury," could not be "due," or "appropriate," "process" under the Fourteenth Amendment, either. A plainer case, under elementary principles of construction—principles the Supreme Court had repeatedly avowed[52]—could not, then, well have been imagined. So, it can be seen the opinion-writers' difficulties in the Hurtado case were very great indeed. And the way out of his difficulties that the opinion-writer, Justice Stanley Matthews, took, and that the Court majority in the case accepted, is, beyond doubt, another example of the Supreme Court at its worst.

The appellant's counsel in the Hurtado case made the mistake of arguing that the Court, in the Hoboken case, had adopted the Common Law test of "dueness" in "process" absolutely; that no innovations by the states upon Common Law "process" were, therefore, possible; and that, since "presentment or indictment by a Grand Jury" was required at Common Law, in capital cases, it was required in such cases under the Fourteenth Amendment. This unsound argument provided Justice Matthews with a way out of his very great difficulties; and it cannot be denied that he used it most adroitly. He began by quoting Justice Curtis' *two* tests of "dueness" exactly, and *in the order* in which they have just been stated here. He then commented that "*this*, it [was] argued, furnish[ed] an indispensable test of what constitutes 'due process of law'; that any proceeding otherwise authorized by law, which [was] not thus sanctioned by usage, or which supersede[d] and displace[d] one that [was], c[ould] not be regarded as due process of law." These remarks, of course, could have reference only to Justice Curtis' *second* test of "dueness" in "process"; and thus the mind of the reader was guided deftly away from his *first* test which would have decided the Hurtado case in the appellant's favor.

"The real syllabus" of Justice Curtis' remarks in the Hoboken case, Justice Matthews went on, was "that a process of law, which [was] not *otherwise* forbidden"—this "otherwise," of course, was a veiled reference to Justice Curtis' *first* test of "dueness"—"must be taken to be due process of law, if it c[ould] show the sanction of settled usage both in England and in this country; but it by no means follow[ed] that nothing else c[ould] be due process of law." The complete correctness of this last proposition cannot, of course, be gainsaid; but its relevancy to the case before the Court was another matter. "To hold that such a characteristic [was] essential to due process of law," the opinion went on, "would be to deny every quality of the law but its age, and [thus] to render it incapable of progress or improvement. It would be to stamp upon our jurisprudence the unchangeableness attributed to the laws of the Medes and Persians."[53] In this way, the Court began, in its Hurtado opinion, a side-trail some five or six pages long; began it with a "red herring," all redolent of "liberalism" and everything "progressive" and "forward-looking" in the law; and it is immensely interesting to note that, after a lapse of over sixty years, the scent still lingers, in sufficient strength, to confuse the "liberal" mind.[54]

The Court's long side-trail in the Hurtado case was adorned, along the way, with many impressive citations and much learned discussion, calculated—or, at any rate, certain—to mislead the unwary reader. But the Court finally got back to conceding, six pages away from Justice Curtis' embarrassing views, its absolute duty to "construe ['due process'] in the Fourteenth Amendment by," what it called, "the *usus loquendi* of the Constitution." "The same words," it said, "[were] contained in the Fifth Amendment"; yet that amendment "ma[d]e specific and express provision for perpetuating the institution of the grand jury," in "capital and otherwise infamous" cases. The Court could not "assume, without clear reason, that any part of this most important amendment"—the Fifth—"was superfluous. The natural and obvious inference [was], that in the sense of the Constitution, 'due process of law' was not meant or intended to include, *ex vi termini*,* the institution and procedure of a grand jury in any case. The conclusion [was] equally irresistible, that when the same phrase was employed in the Fourteenth Amendment to restrain the action of the States, it was used in the same sense and with no greater extent." And, so, the Court concluded, a state's trying men for murder and other infamous crimes, without an "indictment or presentment of a Grand Jury," was not interdicted by the Due Process Clause of the Fourteenth Amendment.[55] Justice Harlan, as was to be expected of that able and forthright man, dissented from this preposterous decision.†

Now, it is perfectly obvious that the Court, in the Hurtado case, under a show of interpreting "due process of law" in its actual context in the Constitution, really interpreted it *in vacuo; that is, in no context at all.* It is obvious, too, that, whilst insisting that "due process of law" meant the same thing in the Fifth and Fourteenth Amendments, the Court nevertheless held to be "due"—or "appropriate"—"process" under the Fourteenth Amendment, a "process" by a state which it could not possibly have held, and which it is absolutely certain it would not have held, to be constitutionally "appropriate"—that is to say, "due"—"process of law" if it had been required by an act of Congress. And the Court did these things in the very face of its own earlier decision, of 1855, in which, with respect to the Fifth Amendment, the Constitutionally fixed primary content of "due process of law" had been unhesitatingly recognized by a unanimous

---

* It should be observed how very necessary this interpolated Latin phrase is to prevent, even a casual reader, from perceiving, at this point, the correct conclusion.

† Justice Field did not participate in the Hurtado case; but in view of his dissents in *Walker* v. *Sauvinet*, 92 U.S. 90 (1876), and *O'Neil* v. *Vermont*, 144 U.S. 323, 361 (1891), he would, no doubt, have agreed with Justice Harlan, had he done so.

Court. Considering, then, the character of the opinion and decision in the Hurtado case—the manner in which the Court scampered quickly away from Justice Curtis' plain and sensible views, mouthing the while its own "forward-looking," "liberal," and "progressive" doctrines— and considering, too, the factors of established earlier usage which, entirely apart from the Constitutional context and the Hoboken case, demanded a conclusion contrary to that which the Supreme Court reached, it is certainly difficult to believe that the error of the case was unconscious, or that the opinion written to justify that error was not a deliberate trick.

Whether the true situation was, in fact, as just suggested, or whether, instead, the Court's strong wishes simply misled it, may seem difficult to say. But there were certain aspects of the situation in 1884 that cannot, in this connection, be put out of view. The first was the Supreme Court's known purpose, existing from the date of the *Slaughter-House Cases*, of 1873, to make completely meaningless the Privileges and Immunities Clause of the Fourteenth Amendment. A second was the utter impossibility of the Court's accomplishing this in more than a merely formal way, with respect to the many particular "process" guaranties in the first eight amendments, if the ordinary, orthodox rule of interpretation were followed, and the Due Process Clause of the Fourteenth Amendment were recognized to make good against the states, in favor of all "persons," both aliens and "citizens," the various particular "process" guaranties just mentioned. And a third factor was that this manifest difficulty in which the Court was involved, was fully, if sophistically, met by the paradoxical principle of the Hurtado case: that every element of "process" that was prescribed in the Constitution was to be excluded as an element of "due"— that is to say, "appropriate"—"process of law" thereunder.

So, granting that, on the whole, the Court of the 1880's was a mediocre Court, it still is difficult to believe that the decision in the Hurtado case was a mere inadvertent blunder. And there is, in addition to all the foregoing considerations bearing against this indulgent view, the further fact, that the destructiveness of the principle of the Hurtado case—its specific effect of robbing the Due Process Clause of *all* its most definitely intended meaning—was carefully pointed out, by Justice Harlan, in his dissent. If "presentment or indictment by a Grand Jury" was excluded, he said, from the meaning of "due process of law" under the Constitution, by its separate specific guaranty in the Fifth Amendment, then "inexorable logic" required that jury trial in criminal cases, that immunity from double jeopardy and compelled self-incrimination, and that all the other particular "processes" guarantied specifically by the Constitution be considered to be excluded, too. "I do no injustice to my brethren," Justice Harlan said, "by this illustration of the principles of the[ir] opinion."[56] And various cases that the Court decided after the Hurtado case show that he spoke the truth.[57] So, it seems impossible to conclude that the Supreme Court in the Hurtado case made a mere inadvertent blunder. And this means that the decision was a deliberate and conscious violation of the Constitution.

4

Such, then, was the character of the second of the Supreme Court's established doctrines that were under attack in 1908, in *Twining* v. *New Jersey;* and considering the character of the doctrine, it surely is not a matter for wonder, that the attack was made. Upon this basis, too, it is not to be doubted, if the ability of the man who argued the case is remembered, that the utterly unconstitutional character of the Hurtado doctrine was made perfectly clear to the Court. For the Twining case, it will be remembered, involved the privilege against compelled self-incrimination, which is one of the particular "process" guaranties that the Fifth Amendment, in one of its earlier clauses, covers. The privilege, therefore, was made good against the states by the Due Process Clause of the Fourteenth Amendment; but the appellants in the Twining case could not enjoy the privilege, unless the perverse doctrine of the Hurtado case was in some way repelled. So, it is not to be doubted that the unconstitutional character of the Hurtado doctrine was made completely clear to the Court. But, again, as in the case of the Privileges and Immunities Clause, the Court's final determination apparently was that it was "too late" to observe this definitely intended meaning of the Fourteenth Amendment. The "convenient vagueness" which the Court had contrived to give to the phrase, "due process of law," in the Hurtado case, by tearing it from its context and interpreting it *in vacuo*, was therefore not forsworn; instead, every effort was made—and, beyond question, deliberately made—to add to it. So, in this second aspect too, the Twining case undoubtedly discloses the Supreme Court at its worst.

The opinion in the case begins by presenting "due process of law" as something almost mystical in its nature. There are "few phrases of the law," the opinion explains, "[which] are so elusive of exact apprehension." The true essence of "the conception" the Court seemed to think almost indefinable. And, accordingly, it "ha[d] always preferred [that the] full meaning [of the phrase] should be gradually ascertained by the process"— which we have met before—"of judicial inclusion and exclusion." Nevertheless, there were "certain general principles" from which important conclusions had been drawn in earlier cases. The first of these, based upon the circumstance that "the conception" went back to Magna Carta, was that "what [was] due process of law m[ight] be ascertained by an examination of those settled usages and modes of proceeding existing in the common and statute law of England before the emigration of our ancestors, and shown not to have been unsuited to their civil and political condition by having been acted on by them after the settlement of this country."

"*This test,*" the Court then coolly observed, "*was adopted by the court, speaking through Mr. Justice Curtis, in* Murray *v.* Hoboken Land Co. . . . Of course, the part of the Constitution then before the court was the Fifth Amendment. If any different meaning of the same words, as they are used in the Fourteenth Amendment, can be conceived, none has yet appeared in judicial decision. 'A process of law,' said Mr. Justice Matthews, commenting on this statement of Mr. Justice Curtis, 'which is not otherwise forbidden, must be taken to be due process of law, if it can show the sanction of settled usage both in England and this country.' *Hurtado* v. *California,* 110 U.S. 516, 528."[58]

In this wise, then, did the Court begin in the Twining case; and in the manner evident in the above quotation, did it get rid of that troublesome, clear-headed fellow, Benjamin R. Curtis. It avoided quoting him; instead, actually misrepresented him in the statement printed in italics above;* and, then, covered its misrepresentation, very subordinately, indirectly, and unobtrusively, with the quotation from the Hurtado case which follows. That this was a vast improvement over the Hurtado technique of dealing with Justice Curtis cannot be denied. For the Justice's real view, which was the view, also, of the Court of 1855, for whom he spoke, that the primary test of the "dueness" of "process" under the Constitution is whether the particular "process" is anywhere forbidden *therein,* was completely excluded from the opinion. And it was so faintly suggested in what followed as scarcely to attract attention at all. That this great improvement over the Hurtado technique was unconsciously wrought is hard to believe; for it is too consummate an example of a certain type of lawyer's art. And, besides, there is too much else in the Court's opinion in the Twining case, of an essentially similar kind.

Thus, the next effort of the Court was to repeat all the irrelevant arguments of the Hurtado case about the illiberality of an absolute Common Law standard of "dueness" in "process of law." But the arguments were not merely repeated; they were embellished and enriched in a high degree. To adopt Justice Curtis' standard of the Hoboken case absolutely, would,

---

* The sort of misrepresentation involved in the above-quoted passages from the Twining opinion—that is, misrepresentation by omitting to state any fact necessary to make any stated fact which, in itself, is true, not misleading—is actionable, both civilly and criminally, in the case of transactions in securities, under the Securities Act of 1933. 48 U.S. Stat. 74, secs. 11, 12, 17, and 24. It is so, also, in England, *Rex* v. *Kylsant,* L.R. [1932] 1 K.B. 442. It certainly does seem that the Supreme Court of the United States should be above these tactics which, in other walks of life, carry civil liability and heavy criminal penalties. One can imagine the righteous indignation the Court would display if counsel were to attempt such a thing in argument. It should be added that the present Supreme Court is, of course, not directly chargeable with the tactics pursued by its predecessors in the cases discussed in the text; but the majority of the present Court insists upon adhering to the doctrines established by these very questionable methods, and one member of the Court praises the decisions which employed these methods as "great" decisions, and the Justices who employed them as "among the greatest in the history of the Court." 332 U.S. 46, 59, 62, 65 (1947).

the Court said, be to fasten "the procedure of *the first half* of the *seventeenth* century upon American jurisprudence like a strait jacket, only to be unloosed by constitutional amendment."[59] Reference to the Hoboken case will show that, although Justice Curtis did speak of "those settled usages and modes of proceeding existing in the common and statute law of England *before the emigration of our ancestors*," and although he did also speak, somewhat vaguely, of proof of suitability to American conditions by the actions of "our ancestors," in following these English practices "after the settlement of this country," his actual procedure was to prove that the practice before him had been in use in England at the ancient day he mentioned, and then to prove its suitability to American conditions by statutory examples drawn from the practice in Massachusetts, Connecticut, Pennsylvania, South Carolina, New York, and other states *just before the Fifth Amendment was adopted*. So, the standard Justice Curtis actually applied in the Hoboken case was that of the *late eighteenth* century, not "*the first half of the seventeenth*."[60] Such were the facts. But the Court in the Twining case did not care for facts; there had to be room for growth.

Nevertheless, the Court went on, if Justice Curtis' views, "as elucidated in *Hurtado* v. *California*," were adopted for the purposes of the Twining case, "that alone [would] almost be decisive," because "the practice of compulsory self-incrimination" had certainly "existed for four hundred years after the granting of Magna Carta," and "was not entirely omitted at trials in England until the eighteenth century." Besides this, it had been "acted on" in America, in "the trial, in 1637, of Ann Hutchinson (which resulted in [her] banishment [from Massachusetts]), for holding and encouraging certain theological views."[61] There was thus no possible room for doubt that compulsory self-incrimination was sanctioned by the Common Law, and, in addition, it had manifestly been part of American criminal "procedure in the first half of the seventeenth century." So, it was plainly within Justice Curtis' views, "as elucidated in [*Twining* v. *New Jersey*]"; and therefore, of course, by his antiquated test, so "elucidated," it was "due process of law."

But the Court in the Twining case, being a very "liberal" Court, was understandably unwilling to rest its decision on the infamous precedent of Ann Hutchinson's persecution. It "preferred," it said, without rejecting the inference to be drawn from "English" law, to rest its decision on "broader grounds." Was the immunity from compelled self-incrimination "of such a nature that it must be included in the conception of due process of law"? Was it "a fundamental principle of liberty and justice which inheres in the very idea of free government"? And, here, it was to be remembered that, "in our peculiar dual form of government," nothing is more "fundamental" than "the full power of the State to order its own affairs and govern its own people." The Court had no authority to interfere in such matters and "pass upon the expediency, wisdom or justice of the laws of the States." Such a thing was unheard of. Its only power was "to determine [the] conformity [of state laws] with the Constitution," including, of course, their conformity with that "elusive" requirement, "due process of law," which was so hard to "apprehend." The question before the Court was thus manifestly very difficult. "[But] one aid to [a] solution [was] to inquire how the right [against compelled self-incrimination] was rated during the time when the meaning of due process was in a formative state and *before* it was incorporated into American constitutional law. Did those who then were formulating and insisting upon the rights of the people entertain the view that the right was so fundamental that there could be no due process without it?"[62]

In seeking an answer to this question, the Court again went back to Magna Carta; came down through many things of equally little relevance subsequent thereto; and finally wound up with "the history of the incorporation of the privilege in an amendment to the National Constitution." This history, the Court quite correctly said, was "full of significance" for the purpose in hand. "The nine States requisite to put the Constitution in operation [had] ratified it without a suggestion of incorporating this privilege."[63] The Court did not add that, in most of these states, bills of rights—"paper checks," as they were contemptuously called—were considered not only to be useless, but harmful, and wholly out of place in republican governments. It also did not observe that the most relevant evidence, in view of this fact, was what was finally put into the so-called national "bill of rights" when it was at length agreed, reluctantly by many, to add such a thing to the Constitution. These seem strange omissions; yet, in reality, they were of little moment, because of what the Supreme Court, in the Twining case, was trying to do.

For the Court, in that case, was accepting, and seeking further "evidence" to support, the perverse view of the Hurtado case: the view that all the particular "process" guaranties in the Fourth, Sixth, Seventh, and Eighth Amendments, and in the other clauses of the Fifth, were enumerated therein, not because they were regarded by "those who then were formulating and insisting upon the rights of the people," as "so fundamental that there could be no due"—or "appropriate"—"process without [them]," but because they were not regarded by these persons as essential to "appropriate," or "due, process of law" at all. Indeed, the whole purpose of the Court, in referring to the events leading up to the framing of the first ten amendments, was to bring out the fact that only four of the thirteen states, during the ratification campaign, had demanded an amendment forbidding compulsory self-incrimination, and that these four states had "separately and simultaneously" asked that a general guaranty of "due process of law" also be added to the Constitution. This proved, the Court perversely averred, that "the privilege was not conceived to be inherent in due process of law, but on the other hand a right separate, independent and outside of due process.[64] So, the Court's omission of the evidence in the so-called national "bill of rights" was of no moment at all; for, even if the Court had gone into that evidence, it would have reasoned perversely from it.

Such, then, was the celebrated case of *Twining* v. *New Jersey*, a case which one of the members of the present Court has strangely described as disclosing "the judicial process [of the Supreme Court] at its best."[65] If that be true, it is a severe indictment; for all the Court did in the Twining case was to adhere to its own earlier decisions, whether these were warranted by the Constitution or not. This was done candidly enough in the case of the Privileges and Immunities Clause; for, as to it, we have seen, the Court simply refused to consider the appellant's arguments, at the same time conceding that those arguments were "weighty" and in accord with what the framers of the Fourteenth Amendment had intended. In the case of the Due Process Clause, the Court was less straightforward. But what it did, nevertheless, was to adhere to the iniquitous doctrine of the Hurtado case; re-doing all that the Hurtado opinion had attempted to do to disguise the true character of the doctrine; burying the plain and sensible views of Benjamin R. Curtis and the Court of 1855, a little more deeply in the past; misrepresenting those views; and arguing from the evidence of the ratification campaign, in the same perverse way that the Court in the Hurtado case had argued from the evidence in the Fifth Amendment. Small wonder, then, that Justice Harlan, who had protested the Court's unconstitutional behavior, in respect to these matters, on every other occasion since his appointment to the Court, felt impelled again to dissent. He considered it his "duty," he said—and he might well have said "his sworn duty"—to protest.[66] And it is for this, his signal devotion to the Constitution and his judicial oath, that this distinguished and able man was recently branded "an eccentric" by one of the members of the present Court.[67] But, as the reader will doubtless by now perceive, there is a sense in which the epithet is merited; and in the sense in which it is merited, it is an accolade.

With the decision of the Twining case, the Court's destruction of the Privileges and Immunities Clause of the Fourteenth Amendment, and its perversion of the Due Process Clause thereof, even within its proper field of procedure, were clear and complete. Yet, despite this fact, the bar has never been able fully and finally to accept these consequences of the Twining decision; and the arguments the case rejected have therefore since been repeatedly re-urged.[68] But to no effect; for the Court has never budged from the position it then took. The first-mentioned clause it stubbornly treats as completely meaningless and nugatory, and the latter it treats as investing it with an absolutely discretionary right of unguided judicial review.[69] In the exercise of this wholly imaginary right, the Court, it is true, has enforced upon the states, since the Twining case, *some* of the particular "process" guaranties covered by the first eight amendments, and *some parts* of some others.[70] It has done this, however, not because these guaranties, *as definitely prescribed parts of "due process of law" under the Constitution when the Fourteenth Amendment was adopted*, are *necessarily* included in the general "due-process" guaranty contained in that amendment; "but"—as the Court, in the Twining case, insisted would be true if such things should ever be done—"because [the rights so enforced] are of such a nature that they are included in th[at] *conception*"—"so elusive of exact apprehension"—"due process of law."[71] The difference is important; for the Court's theory, divested of all tall talk, simply means that the Court enforces, as against the states, such only of the particular "process" guaranties, or parts thereof, as the Court majority, over the years, has desired.

5

The Supreme Court's arbitrary selection of certain of the specific "process" guaranties as those it will enforce against the states is but one phase, and a distinctly minor one, of its exercise, under the Due Process Clause of the Fourteenth Amendment, of a general discretionary control over all state legislation, both substantive and procedural, in the name of "due process of law." That the text of the Due Process Clause does not justify the Court in its exercise of this control is a commonplace among those conversant with the subject. Yet, despite this fact, it is paradoxically true that the original development of "substantive due process," unlike the Court's systematic nullifying of the Privileges and Immunities Clause, and unlike its refusal to enforce the specific "process" guaranties as part of the "process of law" that is "due," or "required," under the Fourteenth Amendment, was not, apparently, in the case of some of the participating Justices at least, a deliberate violation of the Constitution.

Cogent assurance of the truth of this arises from the fact that Justice John Marshall Harlan, who stood out so valiantly against the Court's unconstitutional behavior in these other two respects, was nevertheless one of the leaders in the development of "substantive due process of law." A good deal of a moderate in applying the doctrine, Justice Harlan seems, in spite of its unwarranted character, to have been a thorough believer in its general Constitutional propriety; and that his was a thoroughly sincere belief, none will doubt who are familiar with his great devotion to the Constitution; his general record as a Justice of the Court; and, more particularly, with his vibrantly honest dissenting opinions in connection with the Court's two indefensible actions above mentioned. The fact seems certain that Justice Harlan would never have concurred in the doctrine of "substantive due process of law," unless he had sincerely believed it to be justified by the Constitution. So, considering the real character of the doctrine, his belief in its Constitutional propriety, which, it is reasonable to suppose, other Justices of his time probably shared, manifestly presents something of a problem.

The answer to this problem undoubtedly lies, in part, in the character of the doctrine of "substantive due process of law"; in part, in the ideas lying behind the doctrine; and in part, in the way the doctrine developed. But it also undoubtedly lies, to a considerable extent, in the character of Justice Harlan himself. For, although he was, through the years of his tenure, the outstanding judge of the Court of his time, it is perfectly clear that he lacked those acute powers of analysis which Justices like Story and Marshall possessed, and which, had they been added to his other qualities, would have made Justice Harlan a judge of the very first rank. His lack in this respect is, in fact, nowhere more conspicuous than in his dissents in the Hurtado and Twining cases, and in the case of *Maxwell* v. *Dow*. For, while his eminent good sense informed him at once that any interpretation of the Privileges and Immunities Clause which made that clause effectively meaningless could not be correct, and condemned for him, out of hand, a principle so highly and obviously destructive as that of the Hurtado case, it must be confessed that, apart from his vigorous insistence on these aspects of those cases, he did not make very clear just why the actions of the Court majority in them were in conflict with the Constitution. And the want of analytical power which produced this failure undoubtedly is what made possible his sincere concurrence in the Court's other unwarranted doctrine of "substantive due process of law." For the results of that doctrine—which probably seemed to Justice Harlan only a preventing of the legislatures from doing evil—did not shock his sense of what was right and proper; and his want of analytical power saved him from difficulty with the actual text of the Constitution. And since, as already remarked, he was the outstanding judge of the Court of his time, it is reasonable to suppose that others of the Justices of that same time were similarly free from intellectual discomfort, where "substantive due process" was concerned.

As already suggested, the way the doctrine developed had a good deal to do with making this outcome possible. For the first applications of the "due-process" guaranty outside the strictly procedural field were to cases of a very special kind. The previously mentioned case of *Wynehamer* v. *The People*,[12] decided in New York, in 1856, was typical of these early substantive applications. In it, the New York Court of Appeals held unconstitutional a very drastic prohibition act which the legislature of the state had passed. The act, subject to certain unimportant exceptions, had made it unlawful to keep liquor, including liquor owned when the act was passed, for a single instant after it took effect, in any place other than a dwelling-house; to do so was made a crime; any

VERMON REGIONAL
JUNIOR COLLEGE LIBRARY

liquor so kept was declared a public nuisance and made liable to destruction as such; and all legal protection to it, as property, was withdrawn. The court considered that these provisions left many liquor-owners no real alternative, but to destroy their own property or else idly await the destruction of it by the state, and the criminal penalties that the new law prescribed for such inaction. In view of these features, the court held the act to be, from the moment it took effect, a deprivation of property in all pre-existing liquors without due process of law. The provisions of the act for carrying out its already-imposed sentence, by forms of legal process entirely usual and lawful in other connections, could not alter the unconstitutional character of the act, the Court of Appeals said.

Now, it is surely not hard to see that application of the local New York "due-process" guaranty, to the foregoing act, had a good deal of plausibility. And that cases of this kind were regarded by many as in a special class is pretty well indicated by Justice Samuel Freeman Miller's attitude toward them. For, although, as we have seen, he had roundly condemned what is now called "substantive due process," in the *Slaughter-House Cases*, of 1873, he nevertheless indicated, in a prohibition case from Iowa, in the year immediately following, that, if the Iowa act had applied to liquors lawfully owned when the act was passed, the question of its propriety, under the Due Process Clause of the Fourteenth Amendment, would have been a very grave question, indeed.[73] It is to be noted, nevertheless, that the New York legislature had not, by the act involved in the Wynehamer case, actually taken away from their owners, the liquors in application to which the act was held unconstitutional; it had merely changed very drastically and detrimentally the state's rules of law as to what uses of such liquors were lawful. It is clear, too, that the legislature had not made absolutely impossible the continued retention of previously owned liquors by the owners thereof; it had merely made such retention very difficult without offense to the new law. The Wynehamer case therefore involved a new departure in the judicial interpretation of the "due-process" guaranty; for it treated the highly detrimental change in the rules of property in liquors, which the case involved, as the equivalent of a physical taking-away of the liquors; that is, as a "depriving" of the liquor-owners, of their "property without due process of law." It would be hard to deny that a legislative extinguishment of *all* rights in a piece of property would be the practical equivalent of a physical taking of the property; for, in such a case, the absence of a physical taking would make no difference whatever to the owner. But such cases do not commonly arise; the Wynehamer case was not such a case, though it was, no doubt, a rather close approach to such a case; and, as a precedent, it consequently implied that the courts were entitled to pass judgment on all legislative alterations

VERNON REGIONAL
JUNIOR COLLEGE LIBRARY

in the rules of property, as to whether they were so drastically detrimental as to amount, in the court's opinion, to an unconstitutional "deprivation of property" in the thing concerned.

The importance of the Wynehamer case and of others like it, which, after a time, began to accumulate, was in starting this practice going; for, in consequence of the habit of lawyers, in arguing, and of courts, in deciding, of matching case with a case, it was not long before courts were reviewing, under the "due-process" guaranties, every legislative act affecting property rights adversely. The result was to transform the import of the phrase, "to deprive of property," from that of a physical taking, to that of a mere detrimental alteration in the rules of property; and since the word "property" was taken in a very inclusive sense comprehending the right to pursue accustomed occupations and to contract freely for the sale of one's services, the transformation effected was very extensive. A somewhat similar development likewise took place, by an easy contagion, with respect to the phrase "to deprive of liberty."[74] The word "liberty" in the "due-process" guaranties had originally been understood as denoting "liberty of the person"; and the guaranties, as they related to "liberty," had accordingly been understood as mere prohibitions of imprisonments without a proper trial.[75] But, gradually, the word came to be interpreted as signifying, also, "liberty of conduct," particularly "liberty of contract"; and just as detrimental changes in the rules of property were treated as "deprivations of property," so changes of a detrimental kind, in the rules of conduct, particularly in the rules as to the making of contracts, came to be treated by the courts, as "deprivations of liberty," which, when sufficiently drastic, were declared to be unconstitutional. In this process of expansive interpretation, the word "life," in the "due-process" guaranties, never became involved. Yet, in the end, the triad, "life, liberty, and property," came to stand for all the interests of men which are subject to government;[76] and virtually any legislative alteration of existing rules of law became reviewable in the courts under the guaranties of "due process of law."

It is impossible to deny that, there are, in the writings of the period immediately preceding 1789–91, when the "due-process" guaranty first came into the Constitution of the United States, many instances of the use of the triad, "life, liberty, and property," in this extensive sense; indeed, the word "property" alone was, at that period, still sometimes so used. The fact remains, nevertheless, that, when the triad, "life, liberty, and property," was used with the verb "deprive," and in context with the phrase "due process of law," its sense was less extensive; for the whole of such contexts—that is, these "due-process" guaranties—were understood merely as guaranties against capital and other sanguinary* punishments, against imprisonments, and against the physical taking-away of property by way of punishment or, if the context was not exclusively criminal, in the course—though much less certainly—of the administration of civil justice.[77] The meaning of the triad, then, was fixed in the particular context wherein it appeared in these guaranties, in a special sense; very much as we have seen, in an earlier chapter, the word "commerce" was fixed in meaning, in the eighteenth century, in the phrase "to regulate commerce," or as the word "animal" is fixed in meaning, in the phrase "animal kingdom" today. And just as it would be entirely unwarranted to take "animal kingdom" as meaning "the kingdom of beasts," unless this were in some clear way indicated as the intended meaning in a particular context, so the extended meaning which the courts gradually gave to "life, liberty, and property," in the "due-process" guaranties, was a meaning of the triad unwarranted in that context, for an exactly similar reason. But the reason, though sound, was too subtle to restrain judges, otherwise convinced of the rectitude of their course of action, when it was undeniable that "life, liberty, and property" could, without violence to the English language, be given the interpretation they gave it, in developing "substantive due process of law."

Thus much of the development of this doctrine is, then, not too hard to understand, or too hard to accept as having taken place without any calculated violation of the Constitution. There remains, however, a much greater difficulty growing out of the fact that, in their administration of the "due-process" guaranties, the courts approved hosts of legislative alterations in the rules of property and conduct, plainly detrimental to the interests of the persons complaining thereof, in which, nevertheless, the actual "process" of enforcement was indistinguishable from that in cases of other acts of legislation which they condemned as "deprivations of liberty, or property, *without due process of law.*" The problem, then, is how the judges who first did these things can have supposed that what they did was warranted by the text of the "due-process" guaranties of the various constitutions, state and national, as some of them undoubtedly did suppose.

The answer grows out of another proposition that became involved in the "due-process" cases at an early date, which the Wynehamer case, in New York, had rejected as unnecessary to be considered in that decision.[78] This was the proposition that all legislative power, under our American system of government, is limited power. Legislative power was limited, the courts maintained, not only because it was legislative power and, hence, not power to do executive and judicial acts, but, also, because it was a power to act, even legislatively, for a certain

---

* The sanguinary punishments, less than capital, were deemed to be "deprivations of life" *pro tanto*.

end, or certain ends, only. Thus, the courts sometimes said that legislative power was power to make rules for the promotion of "the common good"; at others, they spoke of the power of the legislatures as a "police power," a power to make rules to promote "the public health, safety, morals, and welfare."[79] But in whichever of these ways the legislative power was described, the courts maintained that, if the act passed by the legislature was not in fact—that is, not in the Court's judgment—promotive of "the common good" or "the public health, safety, morals, or welfare," it was in excess of the legislature's power and, so, void and not a "law." And however "due" a particular "process" of enforcement might be in the case of a valid legislative act, the same "process" used to enforce an invalid act was not, the courts maintained, "due process of law." The gist of such judgments, though never explicit, was plainly this: that the "process" involved, though it might be "due process of" something or other, could not be "due process of *law*," because what was being enforced by the "process" was not "law."

It is thus evident that the subsumption of "substantive due process" under the "due-process" guaranties depended upon a shifted emphasis in interpretation, from "*due process* of law," to "due process *of law*." If this shifted emphasis had been pointed out, to the Justices who effected it, as something unwarranted by the Constitutional text, they would probably have replied that "law" in the "due-process" guaranties must mean "valid law," because it would not be "law" otherwise. A plausible-seeming answer, no doubt; but one which proves so much that it proves its own impropriety. For if "law" means necessarily "valid law," then "process of law," by the same token, must necessarily mean "valid process of law." And why, then, say "*due* process"? Why not merely forbid deprivations of life, liberty, and property, "without process of law"? The answer of course is that no competent draftsman would ever suppose that, by a prohibition so worded, he had made clear the necessity that the "process" must meet certain standards of "propriety." The addition of "due" to modify "process" indicates that necessity; and if it also had been intended, in the "due-process" guaranties, that the substantive "law" to which a "due process" might relate, should also meet certain standards of "propriety," it is surely clear that the adjective "valid," or some equivalent word, would have been employed in the guaranties to modify "law." The shift in emphasis which "substantive due process" involves is thus one clearly unwarranted by the Constitutional text; but the basis of objection to it, if we may judge from the behavior of Justice Harlan and, no doubt, some others of those who participated with him in the development of this doctrine, was too subtle to be perceived by judges who were convinced they were merely preventing the legislatures from doing evil, and who, in addition, were not accustomed to reflect very closely on the meaning of statutes and other documents.

And, here, it should be remembered that the world is still full of people, seemingly otherwise intelligent, who believe their own judgments of what is for "the common good" to be objective determinations of fact. The Justices responsible for "substantive due process" appear to have been, in the main, men of this persuasion. It should be remembered, too, that the process of expansive interpretation of the "due-process" guaranties, which has just been sketched, began when these Justices were very young men; it began, moreover, in cases to which application of the guaranty had a considerable, though false, plausibility; and it was, finally, one of those much-admired "gradual processes of judicial inclusion and exclusion," by matching case with case. The effect of all these factors, taken together, was to detach "due process of law" completely from its constitutional context, in both the state and the national constitutions. In consequence of this, "due process of law" became a "concept"; a "concept," as the Court explained in *Twining v. New Jersey,* which was very "elusive of exact apprehension."[80] And anything and everything became possible.

How far all this had proceeded before "substantive due process" actually found its way into the Supreme Court's decisions may be gauged, moreover, from this circumstance: that Justice Stanley Matthews, in the Hurtado case, in 1884—six years before the Court's first "substantive" application of "due process of law," in 1890[81]—was able to say, without, apparently, any very obvious absurdity, that the limitations imposed by the Due Process Clause of the Fourteenth Amendment consisted of "those fundamental principles of liberty and justice which lie at the base of all our civil and political institutions."[82] Just how these "fundamental principles" would differ from the "fundamental privileges and immunities, which," according to Justice Field and the other dissenters in the *Slaughter-House Cases,* "belong[ed], of right, to the citizens of all free governments" and, hence, to "citizens of the United States,"[83] under the Privileges and Immunities Clause of this same amendment, would be a nice question, indeed. Yet Justice Miller, who had so indignantly rejected this view of the dissenters in the *Slaughter-House Cases,* accepted Justice Matthews' equally vague and open-ended definition of "due process of law," in the Hurtado case, without even a murmur of dissent.

In the case of *Twining* v. *New Jersey,* twenty-four years later, Justice Matthews' definition of "due process of law" became, in the hands of Justice Moody, the opinion-writer in the Twining case, "the *fundamental principle[s] of liberty and justice which inhere . . . in the very idea of free government* and [are] *the inalienable right[s] of a citizen of such a government.*"[84] This, surely, is the exact, obvious, and undeniable equivalent of the vague and confessedly incorrect idea of the meaning of the Privileges and Immunities Clause which Justice Field had unsuccessfully urged in the *Slaughter-House Cases*. Yet, so great is the muddle and confusion into which the Supreme Court's decisions have got this subject that the interesting spectacle may be observed, in a recent case, of a Justice of the present Court fairly shuddering over "the mischievous uses to which [the Privileges and Immunities Clause of the Fourteenth Amendment] would lend itself if its scope were not confined [as the *Slaughter-House Cases* first 'confined' it]," whilst, *at the same time*, he praises most extravagantly the Twining case, wherein the Court adopted, as the meaning of the Due Process Clause *of the selfsame amendment*, the foregoing plain equivalent of Justice Field's confessedly incorrect original interpretation of the Privileges and Immunities Clause—the vaguest and most open-ended interpretation of the clause ever suggested—which the *Slaughter-House Cases* rejected![85] If this is not a case of tweedledum and tweedledee, it would be hard, indeed, to imagine a case that would be.

Further evidence of the confusing effect which trying to interpret "due process" as a "concept" existing *in vacuo* is bound to have may be seen, too, in certain other remarks by this same Justice, in this same recent case. For he protests vigorously therein that it would outrage the English language to take the Due Process Clause of the Fourteenth Amendment as making good against the states, in all cases involving the "life, liberty, or property" of any "person," every element of legal "process" which was "required," or "due," by the terms of the Constitution, as against the nation,* when the Fourteenth Amendment was adopted. This, he thinks, would be a meaning beyond "the common understanding." He suggests, instead, that "due process of law" means "ultimate decency in a civilized society."[86] But—to turn his own words against him—"those reading the English language with the meaning which it ordinarily conveys . . . would hardly recognize [the Due Process Clause of] the Fourteenth Amendment as a cover for the" type of *unguided* Supreme Court review of all state legislative acts which this Justice really means by "ultimate decency in a civilized society"; and this, moreover, would undoubtedly be true even if it were known beforehand that "ultimate decency in a civilized society" were deemed to require such review.

That the notion of "due process of law" as a "concept" existing *in vacuo* is what lies at the base of this Justice's imperceptions may be seen, too, from his repeated insistence in his writings, before his elevation to the Court, that the Equal Protection Clause and Due Process Clause of the Fourteenth Amendment, and the Due Process Clause of the Fifth,

---

* It will not be forgotten that the Fifth Amendment is not actually so limited. *Cf.*, chapter xxx hereof.

are "expressed in words so undefined, either by their intrinsic meaning, or by history, or by tradition, that they leave the individual Justice free, if indeed they do not actually compel him, to fill in the vacuum with his own controlling notions of economic, social, and industrial facts with reference to which they are invoked."[87] For, as we have seen in chapter xxxi, such statements are without foundation if the words of the foregoing provisions are read in their Constitutional context, as meaningful English words, taken in accord with certain elementary rules of interpretation upon which the draftsmen of these provisions were entitled to rely; upon which, it is clear, they did rely; and which the Supreme Court would unhesitatingly apply, and has applied, in all other connections.[88] It is only when the central phrases of these provisions are torn from their context and read as abracadabras, in total disregard of all ordinary rules of documentary interpretation, that the "convenient vagueness" which this Justice thinks these phrases have, appears. So, the fact seems clear that this is how he reads them; and what he does, it is needless to add, many others do, also.

The gross impropriety of thus reading these provisions of the Constitution of the United States, out of context, cannot possibly be denied; and neither can the fact that these provisions, when properly read, are simple and lucid provisions. Yet, it is only necessary to recur to the indignant opinion this same Justice rendered in the same recent case, to perceive that he is utterly unaware that his way of reading "due process of law," and the other phrases he mentions, is improper; and to see too, that he is utterly unsuspicious that the various beliefs he so passionately holds are impossible to reconcile with Constitution, or even, as we have seen, with each other. So, it is beyond doubt that very obviously wrong beliefs about very simple matters may be sincerely entertained by a Supreme Court Justice, in consequence of the Court's various "gradual processes of judicial inclusion and exclusion." And since the development of "substantive due process"—unlike the Court's original nullification of the Privileges and Immunities Clause, and unlike its refusal to enforce the specific "process" guaranties, as against the states, under the Due Process Clause—was very clearly one of these gradual, inclusionary and exclusionary processes, it does not seem too hard to see how Justices, like John Marshall Harlan, could concur in this development and yet entertain a sincere belief that they were abiding faithfully by the Constitution. It is the much-admired gradualness of the judicial process, and the decisional technique of comparing case with case, rather than with the relevant Constitutional provisions *read in context*, which make these strange things possible. And it is precisely because the Court's other two before-mentioned abuses under the Fourteenth Amendment were *not* gradual, but catastrophic, in their onset, that the opposite view of their nature only is possible: they were deliberate and calculated nullifications of the Constitution.

The fact nevertheless remains that the whole doctrine of "substantive due process" is without justification in the actual words of the document, as against either Congress or the states. But although this is unqualifiedly true, the paradox remains that a good deal of what the Court has done in the name of "substantive due process," against the states, is not unconstitutional. This is true because so much of what it has done in the name of this doctrine consists of things it ought to have done under some substantive limitation upon the states which it has either destroyed, partially or totally, or else merged in its all-inclusive doctrine of "substantive due process of law." These merged or destroyed clauses of a substantive, or partially substantive, kind, include, as we have already seen, the Ex-post-facto, Contracts, and Full Faith and Credit Clauses of the original Constitution; they include all the literally general substantive prohibitions in the initial amendments of 1791; and they include the Privileges and Immunities Clause, and the Equal Protection Clause, of Amendment XIV, of 1868. So, when account is taken of all these clauses, the objection to "substantive due process," as against the states, is seen to be logical, rather than substantial, over a very considerable area, indeed.

The situation is different against Congress. This is true, not only because there is, in the Constitution, no "equal-protection" guaranty applying to Congress; and not only because Congress is empowered to legislate, under the Full Faith and Credit Clause, in the precise areas wherein the states are restrained; it is true, likewise, because, more generally, there is, as against Congress, no general right, in the Supreme Court, of judicial review. The Due Process Clause of the Fifth Amendment is, it is true, one of those provisions falling within the limited type of judicial review, described in chapter xxviii, for which, as against Congress, the document does, indeed, seem to provide; but this is true of the clause, only in its just, and intended, procedural scope. The whole of "substantive due process" falls outside this limited type of judicial review. It is, then, unwarranted on this ground, as against Congress, in addition to being unwarranted as an interpretation of the "due-process" guaranty itself. And being thus doubly unwarranted against Congress, there can be no possible doubt the doctrine ought to be given up.

6

To complete our survey of what the Supreme Court has done to the initial section of the Fourteenth Amendment, we have yet to inquire into the course of the Court's decisions under the Equal Protection Clause thereof. Here, though there is not much to relate, it is necessary to go back, once more, to the *Slaughter-House Cases,* of 1873; and to recall to mind that those cases had involved, in thinly disguised form, a state-created monopoly of the business of maintaining stock-landings, stock-yards, and slaughter-houses, in and around the city of New Orleans, which the "carpet-bag" legislature of Louisiana had enacted for the benefit of seventeen specially favored citizens. For, as Justice Bradley, one of the dissenters, observed, ten years later, in a related case, "if it [was] not a denial of equal protection of the laws to grant to one man, or set of men, the privilege of following an ordinary calling in a large community, and to deny it to all others, it [would be] difficult to understand what would come within th[is] prohibition."[89]

Yet the Court majority in the *Slaughter-House Cases* denied this simple and obvious fact, that the Equal Protection Clause of the Fourteenth Amendment was violated by the state act before them. That clause, they said, was "so clearly" a provision for "the [negro] race and [the] emergency [arising from their emancipation], that a strong case would be necessary for its application to any other." And they went on to declare that they "doubt[ed] very much whether any action of a State not directed by way of discrimination against the negroes as a class, or on account of their race, w[ould] ever be held to come within the purview of [the clause in question]."[90] So, in the *Slaughter-House Cases,* the unjustified technique of the Dred Scott case, which had denied to Negroes the benefit of constitutional rights not restricted to white men,[91] was once more applied, though with reverse effect, so as to restrain to Negroes only, rights which were plainly given by the fundamental law, to every "person," white or black, or red or yellow, who was "within [the] jurisdiction" of any of the states of the Union. On the face of the thing, this was rather a daring thing to do. So, it is not surprising to find the Court adding obscurely that, "as it [was] a State that [had] to be dealt with, and not alone the validity of its laws, [the Court might] safely leave th[e] matter until Congress sh[ould] have exercised its power";[92] that is, its power to "enforce" the Fourteenth Amendment, which was specifically given by the fifth section thereof.* Yet, if the "carpet-bag" character of the Louisiana legislature is remembered, the complete safety of the Court's thus remitting its unwarranted decision to correction by Congress, as then constituted, will no doubt be quite obvious. And when Congress did exercise its power under the amendment, as to other phases of the subject of "equal protection of the laws," the Court, with Justice Miller concurring, held the act of Congress to be unconstitutional and void. Justice Harlan alone dissented.[93]

The Court's treatment of the Equal Protection Clause, in the *Slaughter-*

---

* The fifth section of the Fourteenth Amendment reads as follows: "The Congress shall have power to enforce, by appropriate legislation, the provisions of this article [that is, the Fourteenth Amendment]."

House Cases, within five years of the date when the Fourteenth Amendment was adopted, was, then, essentially similar to its treatment, therein, of the clauses of the amendment which those cases did not, in actuality, involve. And that it was the settled intention of the Court, as of the date of the *Slaughter-House Cases,* to make the Equal Protection Clause, also, a meaningless and nugatory clause, except in the one application the Court's opinion mentioned, cannot very well be doubted. This determination, however, was one to which the Court did not long adhere; for, by 1886, it had applied the clause in protection of the rights of Chinese against purely interpersonal state discriminations.[94] Even before this, indeed, the nature of the guaranty had been explained for the Court, by Justice Field, substantially as it has been explained in the preceding chapter of this book;[95] and though some phrases were then used, which, since that time, have been employed in other contexts in a way tending to blur what the Equal Protection Clause really means, there were no cases of this kind, in the 1880's.

Another development, the true significance of which has often been misconceived, is the Court's holding, at about the date of the Chinese case above mentioned, that corporations are "persons" within the Equal Protection Clause of the Fourteenth Amendment.[96] Considering the purely interpersonal character of the guaranty expressed by this clause; considering, too, the fact that the clause had been used to repair the defect in the Interstate Privileges and Immunities Clause of the original Constitution; and considering, finally, the fact that the latter clause had been held inapplicable to corporations, it would obviously be impossible to defend this position, taken in what, no doubt, is its apparent sense, of requiring the states to treat corporations in the same fashion as individuals. For that would mean that the states would be restrained from discriminating between the behavior of men individually, and their behavior in organized groups. The tempting possibilities in the Court's dictum with respect to corporations, taken in this apparent sense, seem immediately to have been perceived by the corporation lawyers of the period; and a large number of cases involving claims by corporations under the Equal Protection Clause resulted. None of these cases seems, however, to have been successful in obtaining for corporations equality in treatment with individuals. Instead, the Court, speaking, again, through Justice Field, explained the rights of corporations, under the clause, in a mode which reduced them to mere equivalence with the rights of the natural persons composing a corporation, to carry on their particular activities, in corporate form, with the same legal protection that is accorded to other natural persons carrying on similar activities, in the same form—an application of the Equal Protection Clause which is manifestly quite right and proper.[97]

For the purposes of this book, this completes what it seems necessary to say of the Court's decisions under the Equal Protection Clause of the Fourteenth Amendment. For, in the years after 1887, when "substantive due process" began to develop, the conception of "equal protection of the laws" ceased rapidly to have a distinguishable and separate history. Rights under the clause became substantially merged in "substantive due process of law"; and though decisions have sometimes occurred which appear to take the Equal Protection Clause as being itself a general roving commission to the Court, to review the reasonableness of all state laws,[98] the clause, in general, like the many others mentioned in chapter xxx, has undoubtedly become, in reference to the Supreme Court's modern theories, a quite unnecessary and superfluous part of the Constitution. And such, it seems clear, will be the condition of the clause, so long as "substantive due process" continues.

In Conclusion

CHAPTER XXXIII

Solutions and Problems

THE matters treated in the last three chapters complete the detail of what it seems necessary to say of the Supreme Court's record as the special and peculiar guardian of the Constitution. Viewing that record as a whole, it is apparent the Justices, over the years since 1789, have very generally done things they ought not to have done, and, quite as generally, left undone the things they ought to have done; and, further to pursue the language of the Book of Common Prayer, it does truly seem that, in their discharge of this important function, there has been no health in them. Such a view of the Supreme Court's services within this field is no doubt somewhat unusual; but the facts upon which this view is based have been set forth in detail, in preceding chapters, and judged on the basis of that detail, and with reference to what it was expected the Supreme Court would do, there cannot be a doubt that the Court's long record has been one, pervasively, of failure.

The causes of this failure, it is perfectly clear, have been multiplex and highly complicated. Simple instances of deliberate, wilful distortion by the Justices, to facilitate accomplishment of desired political ends, have undoubtedly occurred; and, equally certainly, there have been, at times, weak yieldings to pressure to adopt particular meanings of the Constitution, whether warranted by its words or not. But by no means all the Court has done can be explained so simply. For many of its misconstructions plainly rest upon factors of honest misapprehension that have been exceedingly complicated in their genesis. The accepted interstate theory of the power of Congress under the Commerce Clause is a case in point. Originally a deliberate, politically motivated distortion, the theory eventually was buttressed by changes in the prevailing usage of the key-words, "Commerce," "regulate," and "States," in the clause, from what was usual when these words were used by the Federal Convention, in 1787. These changes in usage had no relation at all to politics; they were not even generally recognized to have occurred; they were simply chance factors that supervened to obscure and complicate the true Constitutional situation. And to them, rather than politics, the continuing general belief today, in the correctness of the interstate theory, undoubtedly is due; and this, even though such belief has not been enough to prevent the Supreme Court from yielding to current political pressures and allowing Congress to legislate very much as if the supposed interstate limitation upon its power over commerce did not exist; as, of course, in fact, it does not on a straightforward documentary basis.

The situation is basically similar as to various other important provisions of the Constitution; and notably so, in the case of the Full Faith and Credit Clause of Article IV; the Election-of-Electors Clause of Article II; and the Time, Place, and Manner Clause, the Imports and Exports Clause, and the two Ex-post-facto Clauses, of Article I. Besides these instances in the original document, there is the fundamentally important Tenth Amendment, as to which the situation is much the same. In the case of all these provisions, the accepted present-day view of what was meant thereby depends, in one way or another, upon changed usage, since the date of drafting and adoption, of some key-word or words which the particular provision contains. And though, in the case of the phrase, "ex post facto Laws," its changed sense in modern American legal usage is undoubtedly a result of the Supreme Court's deliberate, politically motivated distortion of the two Ex-post-facto Clauses, in 1798,[1] the altered usage in all the other cases took place without any discernible relation to politics at all. These changes, then, are like the changed usage of the words of the Commerce Clause: they are accidental factors that have supervened to lend a false plausibility, and seeming historicity, to the accepted pseudo-orthodox theories of all the foregoing clauses as their actually intended meanings.

The complex factors that have operated to produce these results have been considered in detail in preceding chapters and need no recapitulation here. But it is important to note that, for all these changed word-meanings to operate in the manner they have, a common predisposing cause was necessary. Thus, in the case of the Commerce Clause, if the power of Congress thereunder had been actively used in the early days, as originally was expected, the question of the true scope of the power would repeatedly have come up; the original view of it would, in many different ways, undoubtedly have been recorded; and a later misconception of the power, based upon changed meanings of certain of the words in which it is given, would not, it seems certain, have been possible. To the rise and acceptance of the interstate theory, it was, then, plainly prerequisite that the original understanding of the Commerce Clause should have been imperfectly recorded; or, else, scantily recorded; or recorded in some not readily accessible way. And for any of these things to have been true, the power in question, during the period when the key word-meanings were changing, had to be in disuse. The long inactivity of Congress before the Civil War was thus absolutely essential as a predisposing cause to the particular misinterpretation of this power which has occurred; and reference to earlier chapters will show that similar factors of long disuse were likewise operative, in the case or all the other clauses whose accepted pseudo-orthodox interpretations depend today, in whole or in part, upon supervening changes in the usage of words employed in them.

The long inactivity of Congress in the period before the Civil War was important, also, in another way. For, besides allowing time for destructive changes in word-meanings to occur, it likewise allowed time for various of the legal and political ideas of 1787 to pass into the limbo of forgotten things and be replaced by new ideas, which were anachronistically imputed to the men of 1787, although it is certain they had, in some cases, never even heard of such ideas and, in others, having heard of them, disapproved them heartily. These changes, moreover, were of a kind that affected systematically the accepted views of the Constitution as a whole. So, the importance of the long pre–Civil War inactivity of Congress, as the predisposing cause of the modern theories of our government, can hardly be exaggerated.

Of the legal and political ideas that have changed without general recognition of the fact, since 1787, one that, we have seen, has had a most profound effect upon accepted theories of the Constitution is the passing of the eighteenth-century modes of documentary interpretation and legal draftsmanship. It is certain no group of lawyers of today, intending what the Federal Convention intended in the Constitution, would express that intention as the Convention expressed it. There would not, today, be any reliance on a preambular statement of the general purposes for which the Government was formed; the peculiar relationships between general and particular propositions which appear in the Constitution again and again would not be found in a modern document; and certainly no modern draftsman would rely on necessary negative implications arising from such relationships to express important parts of his intention. Yet it is certain the Federal Convention did these things, because it is only when we assume that they did, and apply to what they did, the accepted eighteenth-century constructionary rules, that the Constitution *as a whole* makes sense. So, the passing of the eighteenth-century rules and drafting practices, coupled with the general unawareness of intervening change in these matters, has, beyond all doubt, been a factor of great importance in producing the particular body of constitutional theory that today is considered orthodox.

Similar effects arose from the passing, during the pre–Civil War period, of the mode of thinking about government which divided the subject into the two "capital heads" of "police" (or "polity") and "policy"; which regarded "war" and "commerce" as the "heads" of "policy"; and which understood "police" (or "polity") to be made up of "domestic Tranquility," or "public peace," and the subject of "establish[ing] Justice." For the obsolescence of this mode of thought, and the almost complete forgetting of the categories in which it had been carried on, made completely unintelligible much that was written about the Constitution during the ratification campaign. In addition, these factors obscured the important fact that the Preamble of the document was a technical and exact provision, carefully drawn with an eye to the antecedent Confederation and the then existing constitutions of the states, and intended to give clear notice that the "heads" of government previously claimed as the exclusive preserves of the states were being added to the "objects" that had belonged to the nation under the Articles, in order to make the new government under the Constitution, a national government in the fullest sense. The obscuring of this purpose, there can be little doubt, was an important contributory cause of what occurred after the Civil War, when, at last, the national governing powers, as powers to be used, began to be considered.

It is important to remember, too, that the constitutional decisions in the pre-war years had had to do, in the main, with the validity of state governmental acts, rather than with the validity of governmental acts of the nation. John Marshall, it is true, managed to make certain of the early attacks upon state acts, into occasions for extensive disquisitions—as nationalistic as, in the circumstances, he could make them—upon the nature and scope of the governing powers of the nation. But this sort of thing ceased with Marshall's death. The emphasis in the decisions of the Taney Court is upon the scope and nature of the powers of the states. And as already observed in earlier chapters, the great "States' Rights" Chief Justice claimed for the states, in *The License Cases*,[2] of 1847, a police power that was, in fact, a power of complete and very largely inviolable intrastate sovereignty. The tremendous change from the ideas of 1787 which this claim involved may be seen from these considerations: (1) that "police" had no such extensive signification when the Constitution was drawn; (2) that the exclusion of the nation from the field of "police," even in its proper sense, was ridiculous, in view of the plain terms of the Preamble; (3) that, under the original Constitution, there were, in fact, no paramount "States' Rights" of any kind, except in reference to the election of Presidential electors and, in a very technical and limited sense, in reference to certain matters relating to the militia; and (4) that, by the initial amendments of 1791, no such "rights" were intended to be created, except in the limited areas covered by the First Amendment, and even in these, the states were left subject to Congressional control in favor of "Liberty," save in the case of "religious establishments."

In view, then, of the profundity of the change involved in the coming into currency of the foregoing inflated notion of the position and "rights" of the states, the importance of the long inactivity of Congress prior to the Civil War, as a predisposing cause of what occurred thereafter, seems manifest. And the rise of this false notion of the "rights" of the states made plausible another profound change from the ideas current in 1787. For, if the "rights" of the states were as extensive as the new theory of the states' police powers made them, and if, by consequence, the legislative rights of Congress were a few artificially limited powers, then some agency manifestly was required to hold Congress within these powers and so protect the "rights" of the states from violation. And since the old ideas of legislative supremacy and judicial obedience had, by the date of the Civil War, very largely given place, in the states, to judicial review of legislation, the Supreme Court of the United States was, not unnaturally, regarded as the body intended, under the Constitution, to discharge this imaginary function. So, the body which had been attacked by the "States'-Righters" of 1787 and 1788, as the great, insidious "engine of consolidation,"[3] and which, there can be no doubt, was, in fact, set up "to secure the *national* rights and uniformity of judgments" *against the states*,[4] at last came to be regarded, in the years after the Civil War, as the supreme and peculiar guardian of a great mass of wholly imaginary "rights" *of the states against Congress*. And that this strange and anomalous development could never have taken place without the long inactivity of Congress before the Civil War seems certain.

The foregoing false ideas, all of them natural enough in view of the circumstance that the states had, in fact, done nearly all the governing before the Civil War, manifestly could not fail to have a very great impairing effect upon the powers of Congress when, at last, after nearly a century, those powers came to be considered as powers to be used in the internal government of the nation. Clear as this is, and profound as the destructive effects of the various foregoing new views undoubtedly were, there was one other unperceived change in accepted ideas, by the date of the Civil War, which there can be no possible doubt was far more destructive of the powers of Congress than all the foregoing ideas put together. This was the unquestioning acceptance, by that date, both by the Court and by the legal profession generally, of the utterly unfounded notion that the various branches of the Common Law, and the British statutes in amendment thereof, had *not* been regarded as "Laws of the United States," to the extent of their applicability to American conditions, when the Constitution of the United States was adopted.

The Supreme Court's docile acceptance of this false premise—originally, as we have seen, a mere part of "the party line" of Jeffersonism, around 1800—not only narrowed greatly the important second category of "the judicial Power" in Article III; destroyed, or helped to destroy, the Supreme Court's general juridical supremacy; and obscured the scope of Congress' judicial-rule-making power; in addition, it foreclosed completely any true understanding of the enumeration of Congressional powers that the Constitution contains. For, as the discussion in earlier chapters has shown, there is, quite literally, no possibility of understanding this important matter, except upon the assumption—fully warranted by its perfect fit and its rationalizing effect upon a great multitude of otherwise unruly facts—that, to the extent of their applicability to American conditions, the various branches of the Common Law, and the British statutes in amendment thereof, were deemed to be "Laws of the United States" when the Constitution was drawn and adopted. And since the grant, to Congress, of a general national legislative power was bound to seem incredible, unless the enumeration could be perceived to be consistent with such a grant, the unquestioning acceptance, by the date of the Civil War, of the contrary, false and confusing notion about the Common Law was undoubtedly basic to the Court's false doctrines as to the extent of the powers of Congress; and, it may be added, as to many another subject, as well.

Thus, the incapacity of the Court to understand the enumeration, which resulted directly from its taking the foregoing piece of political propaganda for a proposition of fact, strongly predisposed it, especially after various relevant word-meanings had passed out of use, to misread the fundamentally important Tenth Amendment. And once that amendment was misread, the misunderstanding of the powers of Congress was very greatly strengthened. For the view of Madison, at least, that the Tenth Amendment was not intended to make any change from the original Constitution, was not unknown; and this seemed to corroborate the view, already entertained, that the enumeration of Congressional powers, contained in Article I, had actually been made to secure the powers there enumerated, as against the states. And this view was still further confirmed—or, at least, it seemed to be—by Madison's notes on the Federal Convention, when those notes at last were published. So, for a long time, the "States' Rights" (or Southern, anti-nationalist) theory of the Constitution has undoubtedly been sincerely and widely viewed as the true and orthodox theory of the subject.

And given the Court's complete misconception of the purpose of the enumeration in Article I, and its belief that the Tenth Amendment and the records of the Convention confirmed the "States' Rights" view of Congress' powers, it is not hard to see, in a general way, how the Court's other main errors—politics apart—came about. For, if the enumeration of Congressional powers could not be understood, except as a device for making clear the powers which Congress was to have, and the powers which it was not to have, as against the states, the Common Defence and General Welfare Clause simply had to have some other meaning than what it seemed to say. The purposive, or "spending-power," theory of this clause acquired, in these circumstances, a very natural, if spurious, plausibility; a plausibility, moreover, that was greatly increased if the actual spending power, in Article IV, was conveniently forgotten, as of course it was. And the same imperious necessity, growing out of what seemed to be the only possible theory of Congress' enumerated powers, likewise produced the Court's complete forgetfulness of "the powers of the [whole] Government" in "the sweeping clause"; it disposed the Court to read "all" as "only" in the initial section of Article I; and it goes far to account for the Court's view that the Preamble is an empty verbal flourish, totally irrelevant to what the Constitution truly means. These matters, there can be no doubt, came gradually to seem, to the Court, minor details in the Constitution, by comparison with the one major, ineluctable fact of the long and detailed enumeration of Congressional powers which the Court was totally unable to account for, if Congress had general legislative authority. So, it is apparent the major errors of the Supreme Court all hang together: they all depend, in very great degree, upon the Court's incapacity to understand the enumeration; and that incapacity has depended, in turn, upon the Court's naïve acceptance of the foregoing piece of barefaced Jeffersonian propaganda as a fact.

The destructive and falsifying effects of this false premise, which the Justices, for well over a century, have not deemed it necessary even to question, have extended, moreover, to still other important phases of the constitutional theories the Court entertains. This is notably true, for example, in the case of its long-standing misconstruction of the Commerce Clause. For, as will probably be remembered from earlier chapters, there is, in the eighth section of Article I, immediately following the power given Congress "to regulate Commerce," an enumeration of other, more specific powers which are also undeniably of a commercial character. These more specific commercial powers include, among others, the powers of Congress "to coin Money, regulate the Value thereof, and of foreign Coin, and fix the Standard of Weights and Measures"; "to establish post Offices and post Roads"; and "to establish uniform Laws on the Subject of Bankruptcies, throughout the United States." The presence of these and certain other powers in the Congressional catalogue is, manifestly, as utterly impossible to account for, on a "States' Rights" basis, *if* the Commerce Clause is comprehensive, as the whole enumeration is, upon such a basis, *if* the Common Defence and General Welfare Clause is literally taken. And this being true, the Court's false belief about the Common Law, and its consequent incapacity to understand the enumeration, have naturally predisposed it to take some view of the national power over commerce which would make the enumeration of these particular commercial powers comprehensible under the "States' Rights" theories. The interstate interpretation of Congress' general commercial power, despite its unidiomatic and unnatural character, has met the Court's needs in this particular. For, if the general power of Congress "to regulate Commerce" is subject, in its internal phase, to an interstate limitation, the presence of these particular commercial powers in Article I is seemingly easy to account for, consistently with the "States' Rights" view: being nation-wide in scope—that is, being free of an interstate limitation—they had to be enumerated, upon the assumption stated, *if* they were to be possessed by Congress in their *full* latitude. So, without minimizing the part that politics and other factors have played in the long-standing misconstruction of the Commerce Clause, it is perfectly clear that the Court's acceptance of Jefferson's false postulate about the Common Law has had a profoundly confusing and falsifying effect with respect to this matter, too.

Still another such effect of Jefferson's false premise may be discerned in the conventional, pseudo-orthodox view of the Supremacy Clause of Article VI. For acceptance of Jefferson's false dogma about the Common Law inevitably precluded the Court from perceiving what was undoubtedly the most important of "the Laws of the United States [in 1787] which [were *not* to be] made in Pursuance of [the new Constitution]." The Common Law, it needs to be remembered, was not only, at that time, by far the most extensive of all such "Laws," it was, in addition, the only such "Law" that was at all likely to be of permanent importance. The "legislative acts" of the old Congress were, after all, comparatively few; they were of passing interest; and were sure, in a little while, to be forgotten. So, excluding the Common Law as a "Law of the United States" was certain, sooner or later, to make the "in-Pursuance" branch of the Supremacy Clause seem utterly meaningless and nugatory, unless, indeed, the words, "in Pursuance of [the new Constitution]," were taken to mean "in strict conformity with its provisions." And this being true, it is in no way remarkable that this branch of the Supremacy Clause has long been taken in this sense which, for well over a hundred years, has been the only sense it seemingly could have, and which, according to the accepted pseudo-orthodox theories, establishes the constitutionality of judicial review against Congress. The discussion in chapter xxviii has shown that this last is an illegitimate inference even when the "in-Pursuance" branch of the Supremacy Clause is taken in the sense just indicated; yet the inference is undeniably more plausible when the words, "which shall be made in Pursuance of [the new Constitution]," are so taken than it is when their true intent and meaning are understood. And since Jefferson's false postulate about the Common Law obscured all this, it can be seen, again, how utterly confusing and destructive his false postulate has been.

And to all the foregoing effects of Jefferson's false tenet—a tenet established in the Supreme Court's decisions in the disgraceful fashion earlier recounted—there is one other to be added. This is the theory entertained by the present-day Court that, with respect to all questions of Common Law, the national courts, including itself, are courts inferior to the courts, even the lowest, of the respective states. The theory is one, it is true, that the Court could not possibly hold if the Judiciary Article of the Constitution were read and understood; yet, as we saw in chapter xxvi, the theory is, nevertheless, very largely a consequence of the Court's uncritical acceptance of Jefferson's false postulate, that "there is," in the words of the late Justice Brandeis, "no federal general common law";[5] that the Common Law, as Justice Holmes insisted, "is always the law of some State."[6] So, considering that this dogma has thus been operative, after the lapse of more than a hundred years, to produce this completely new destruction of the Constitution; and considering, also, that it has had all the other destructive effects outlined above, it would seem unquestionable that acceptance of this dogma has, by all odds, been the most fundamental and far-reaching error the Supreme Court has ever made.

In general, what has occurred, then, is this: the Constitution, a carefully drawn legal document of the late eighteenth century, has been interpreted in accord with word-meanings, and legal and political ideas, current, not when the instrument was drawn, but nearly a full century later. That the Constitution, so interpreted, should seem, in certain respects, crazily inadequate to the needs of good government; that its commercial provisions, to take one example, should seem, when so interpreted, to have been carefully drawn to make impossible the legal uniformity in the commercial field which has so long been desired; and that its judiciary provisions, to take another example, should appear, under such an interpretation, to have been deliberately calculated "to establish" chaos and uncertainty, rather than the "Justice" of which the Preamble speaks: these things, surely, fantastic as they are, are not surprising as results of such an unheard-of mode of interpretation. For, after all, word-meanings, over a century's time, cannot possibly be supposed to have changed in consonance with the needs of government. To read the Constitution in accord with modern word-meanings, where word-meanings have altered, is, then, certain to give arbitrary results. And of the unperceived changes in legal and political thought which have supervened since 1787, most of these, like Jefferson's false postulate about the Common Law, were, in their beginnings, carefully calculated sophistries having for their precise object the destruction of the governing powers of the nation. So, to accept these changed ideas as a basis of interpretation is even more certain, than accepting the altered word-meanings, to give fantastically inadequate results. Yet it is in accord with such sophistries, mostly Jeffersonian, and in accord with word-meanings arbitrarily altered since the instrument was drawn, that the Constitution usually is interpreted.

If the character of the politics of the pre–Civil War period is remembered, together with the nearly complete inactivity which the politics of the period long had enforced on Congress, and if, in addition, the antinational reaction and *laissez-faire* politics, after the war, are borne in mind, it can hardly be considered surprising that the Constitution was interpreted, during the 1870's and 1880's, in the manner it was against Congress. But beginning with the passage of the Interstate Commerce Act, in 1887, the politics of the country, and the pressures therefrom arising, have been increasingly favorable to a recognition of the national governing powers for which the Constitution actually provides. This is clear from the well-marked tendency of the Supreme Court itself—most noticeable since "the Roosevelt Court Fight," of 1937, but going back for upwards of at least thirty years before that date[7]—to uphold various acts of Congress, especially under the power over commerce, which, upon any straightforward application of the Court's constitutional theories, have been beyond Congress' authority. Yet, in spite of this marked and notorious tendency in the Court's decisions, its fantastically incorrect theories of the Constitution have persisted; indeed, as we saw in chapter xxvi, these theories, in the judiciary field, have actually grown and proliferated, in recent years, in a manner plainly contrary to the political trends of the times, and to the manifest needs of the country. And these phenomena, manifestly inexplicable on the basis of politics merely, do seem rather extraordinary. For, with the actual provisions of the Constitution, and the pressures of politics, in coincidence, the normal expectation would surely be that the Court's theories would tend gradually to shift back to a rational congruence with the document it is sworn to uphold.

That this has not occurred is undoubtedly to be explained by the poverty of scholarship in the field, and the consequent miseducation that Americans, and particularly lawyers, have long received in the subject. Thus, of all the misconstructions noticed in the foregoing pages, only those relating to the Fourteenth Amendment, and not always all of these, are commonly recognized and treated, in the conventional scholarly literature on constitutional law. There have been, it is true, one or two surmises that the Ex-post-facto Clauses may perhaps originally have been understood in the sense suggested in chapter xi;[8] but the evidential bases of these surmises have been too limited to ground any certain inference to this effect, and the revealing implications which the true meaning of the Ex-post-facto Clauses has for other parts of the Constitution have never been developed. Of the remaining problems covered in these pages, the only other that is ever even touched upon, in the conventional scholarly literature of the subject, is judicial review against Congress. Usually, it is supported. And while there have been some angry attacks, these have not perceived and presented the true and intended meaning of the "in-Pursuance" branch of the Supremacy Clause; they have been, accordingly, attempts, in essence, to make that branch of the Supremacy Clause meaningless; and they have—perhaps in consequence and, at any rate, in view of this fact, quite justly—failed.

The situation, then, is that the scholarship in the field has, not only, on the whole, supported the Supreme Court's unfounded claim to a general right of judicial review against Congress, it has given its support, likewise, to virtually all the unwarranted theories of the Constitution (other than "substantive due process of law") which the Court, in the exercise of its supposed right of judicial review against Congress, has developed. The correctness of the Court's interstate interpretation of the Commerce Clause has, for example, never really been questioned;[9] its false dogma that the national government is a government of specifically enumerated particular powers has gone virtually unchallenged;[10] and the theory the Court took over from Jefferson, that the Common Law was not one of "the Laws of the United States" when the Constitution was drawn, has been accepted without even a murmur of dissent. The scholarship in the field has thus failed completely to afford any assistance to the Court, through constructive criticism of its more important and basic theories. Far from affording assistance, indeed, the legal scholarship of the country actually helped to mislead the Court into that great mass of new errors, in the judiciary field, of which the Court, since 1938, has been guilty. And the latest contribution from the legal learned world is an elaborate attempt to justify the Supreme Court's continued flouting of the plain and simple provisions of the Fourteenth Amendment.[11]

But though there has been this almost total failure, on the part of the academic branch of the legal profession, and, indeed, on the part of historians and political scientists, to offer any constructive criticism of the Court's various theories, there has been no dearth of urgings from these scholarly groups, that the Court must not allow its theories, however correct these may be, to interfere with needed legislation by Congress. The Constitution, these men solemnly affirm, is "a living document"; and the plain duty of the Court, they say, is to keep the powers of Congress "abreast of the needs of the times." The actual provisions of the historic document relating to Congress' powers, which this book treats, are deemed by these learned men to be without importance, except as the mere starting point of a magnificent development, still going on, with which the Court, though truly invested (as they believe) with the general right of judicial review against Congress, ought by no means to interfere, but, rather, promote by every means that lies within—or, indeed, without—its power. For it would be wrong that the Congress of today should be in any way trammeled by our antiquated and outmoded Constitution.

The intellectual difficulties involved in the foregoing theory of the Supreme Court's function are pretty obvious, even for judges flatteringly described as "judicial statesmen." Nevertheless, since the political pressures for Congressional action in fields forbidden under any straightforward application of the Supreme Court's paralyzing theories have been very great, the Court has actually done, increasingly, what the "liberal" chorus of academic lawyers, historians, and political scientists has urged. Mouthing at all times, carefully, its main traditional theories of the Constitution, the Court, through a series of highly sophistical applications of various of its subsidiary theories, has actually permitted Congress to legislate, over an increasingly broad field, very much as if its main theories had been repudiated. As already indicated, however, these main theories have not been repudiated. In consequence, even in the field of commercial regulation, where the ideas of the "living-document" school have been most extensively applied, the power of Congress is still incomplete; its laws, accordingly, have still to be fragmentary and complicated in their incidence; and a never ending process of jurisdictional litigation must still be carried on, in their enforcement. And besides all this, uniform law, though so long desired in the commercical field, is still, as a practical matter, unattainable. So, the ideas of the "living-document" school, it is perfectly clear, have not provided a pragmatically satisfactory solution; and, in addition, they are, quite obviously, not intellectually respectable.

The ideas—or, rather, the sophistries of this advanced school of thought are manifestly a product of intense wish operating under conditions of profound and unquestioning certitude, not inferior to that of the Supreme Court itself, that the Court's traditional theories of the Constitution are historically correct and accurate. Yet the evidence presented in preceding chapters—much of it within easy reach of the lawyer's hand, and all of it readily available among the materials upon which history, supposedly, is based—conclusively shows that the Court's theories lack the historic character which the learned world has indolently conceded to them. For, when the words of the historic document are read in the senses we have seen they had when the document was drawn; when all distorting legal and political ideas that have since arisen are rejected; and when, in addition, the Constitution is interpreted as a rational whole, and not as an agglomeration of unrelated parts, the scheme of government for which it provides is at once seen to be one very different from that which the Supreme Court's complicated theories describe. The scheme of the Constitution is simple and flexible: general national power, subject only to a few simple limitations, with the state powers, in the main, continuing for any desired local legislation. So, if the Constitution were allowed to operate as the instrument was drawn, the American people could, through Congress, deal with any subject they wished, on a simple, straightforward, nation-wide basis; and all other subjects, they could, in general, leave to the states to handle as the states might desire.

That such a simple and flexible scheme of government, for which, it is clear, the Constitution actually provides, is much to be preferred to the complicated technicalities of the Supreme Court's theories, even when these are eked out with the "liberalizing" sophistries of the "living-document" school, can surely not admit of any doubt. For, under the scheme of the Constitution, the laws of Congress need not, any longer, be complicated and fragmentary in their incidence; the incessant jurisdictional litigation that now goes on, over the powers of the nation, and the powers of the states, would be a thing of the past; and, in general, all those expensive and paralyzing complexities in our government, which the opening chapters of this book described as resulting from the Supreme Court's theories, would be forever and completely at an end. And with these things accomplished, the Court itself, as in the early days, could, with great benefit to the American people, devote itself undistractedly to its own truly intended function as the nation's juridical head.

The considerations brought together in the foregoing chapters point the way, then, for accomplishing these very desirable ends under the Constitution. This means that solutions have been found within the four corners of the historic document, for the various evils of complexity, expensiveness, and inefficiency, in our government, which are usually attributed to its ancient and supposedly outmoded provisions. And the Constitutional soundness of these solutions is fully warranted by the perfect fit that exists between the theories on which they depend, and the actual provisions of the Constitution. For, unlike the accepted pseudo-orthodox views, the theories of the Constitution here presented involve no manhandling of the historic document and require no disregard of any of its provisions. And these things being true, the first part of the program of this book, as sketched out in its opening chapter—our proposed inquiry into the true and intended meaning of the Constitution, and our then promised exposition of the complete adequacy of its scheme of power to the governmental needs of the present day—has now been accomplished.

But though solutions have thus been found within the actual, historic Constitution for the various problems of government suggested in the opening chapters, these solutions, as then predicted, raise problems in another field. They do this because the solutions found depend upon views of the Constitution which it is utterly impossible to reconcile with much that has long been accepted as true constitutional history. Such history, it is clear from considerations already presented, is a history written, in its early parts, to account for the drawing and adoption of a constitution of the United States that, in fact, *never* was drawn and adopted; and it is a history written, in its later parts, to account for the development of the present government of the United States, from the inadequate beginnings supposed to have been provided in this wholly imaginary constitution. That a history written under such fundamentally false assumptions should have little relation to historic fact is only to be expected. And, hence, it results that a true understanding of the Constitution raises many questions of an historical kind, to which no answers can be found in conventional histories.

Thus, to begin with, there is the undeniable general fact that the Constitution, as here presented, seems like a bolt from the blue, when considered as issuing out of its antecedents as these are described in standard histories: the pre-Revolutionary dispute with England, the American Revolution, the Articles of Conferation, the co-existing state constitutions, and the campaign for increasing the powers of the old Congress, in the middle 1780's. For, if the view of the Constitution here presented is true—and the perfection of its fit with the document gives full warrant that it is—then the conventional accounts of these antecedent matters necessarily become, in very large degree, incredible. And the question arises, what these antecedents of the Constitution really were, under a true view of them.

In the foregoing pages, some few isolated aspects of the question just propounded have been incidentally considered; and, at various points, some suggestions appear, of the way in which the events and institutions antecedent to the Constitution have been unconsciously distorted, in history, into an enforced consistency with the later theories of "States' Rights." But though such suggestions may be found in the foregoing pages, the task of putting the Constitution, rightly understood, into context with the events and institutions which preceded it, has not yet been attempted and accordingly remains as one of the chief subjects to be dealt with in subsequent volumes of this book.

A somewhat similar general question arises when the Constitution is considered in relation to the long disuse of the national powers thereunder, in the period before the Civil War. For, if, during this long period, extending back almost to the beginning of the Government, the political conditions were such that the powers under the Constitution could not be used, how are we to account for the fact that a constitution providing for such extensive powers was drawn up by the Federal Convention, and, after extensive discussion, ratified by the American people? More concretely, how are we to suppose the states of the South, which, so early in the nation's history, opposed every the slightest power sought to be exercised, except in the military field, were ever induced to ratify the Constitution containing what, we have seen, it did in fact contain?

Some parts of the answers to these questions, too, have been suggested at various earlier points in the present volumes; but a complete and thoroughly convincing answer to the problems indicated has not been attempted, because such an answer is possible only on the basis of various matters still to be considered. These include various forgotten phases of the politics of the late 1780's: the politics that made the Federal Convention, and the Constitution, possible. They include an account of what really went on in the Federal Convention and in the ratification campaign. And they include various unexpected events during the early years of the Government, and the failure, then, of certain other, expected events which had been confidently counted upon when the Constitution was formed. For it was the changed politics arising out of these new conditions that so quickly supervened, which prevented the new scheme of government from ever actually being put into operation. And, as suggested earlier, it was the consequent long disuse of the national powers, which extended up to, and beyond, the Civil War, which was the essential predisposing cause of all that great mass of interconnected misconstructions of the Constitution which constitute our constitutional law of today.

These, then, in their most general terms, are the problems that remain, of those set out in the opening chapter as constituting the program of this book; and it is the expectation of the author to offer, at some future time, a consideration of these remaining problems in full detail. The effort then will be to put the Constitution, as here presented, into context with the actual events, institutions, and politics, which preceded it; and into context, also, with the events and politics, and the many politically motivated misconstructions, which followed in the years after the Constitution was adopted. And when, on the basis of the actual evidence, a true view of all these matters has been built up, it will be found that weight, not doubt, has been added to the conclusions, as to the true view of the Constitution itself, which have been presented in the foregoing pages.

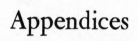

Appendices

The professions of disinterested patriotism we made, when we engaged in the cause of liberty, and appeared in vindication of the rights of humanity; the wisdom and fortitude we displayed through an arduous conflict, and the singular advantages we were, and even now are under, gave mankind every reason to expect we should have made essential improvements in the science of government; recovered it out of its depressed situation; restored it to its original purity, and established a system in such perfection as to excite the emulation of other nations. Notwithstanding this, we have suffered the most amazing weakness and absurdity to assume the place of energy and consistency; have rendered our political interests perplexed; exhibited a striking proof of the fallibility of human wisdom, and inconstancy of human nature, and rendered our federal government a matter of surprise to all mankind.

Some of the most material errors and defects of our political institutions[1] I will attempt to point out; but previously it will be necessary to observe something of the nature and design of government in general.

The general object of government is the security and promotion of the temporal interest and happiness of mankind, and its establishment is occasioned by the evil dispositions of man, (the only source of human misery) for were they suitably disposed to observe the rules of justice, the principles of humanity, and the dictates of conscience, civil government would be unnecessary; but as this is a state of perfection, this world never has, since the apostacy, and probably never will enjoy, human authority became necessary to restrain the turbulent passions of mankind, dispense justice, and support order and regulation in society. This undoubtedly, was the only object government had in view, at the time of its first introduction into the world. But as people multiplied, and societies increased, malicious designs and attempts arose beween them, which extended its views and purposes to national security and defence; Besides these, the great dependencies which naturally subsist between mankind universally, rendering friendly and commercial intercourses between nations not only necessary but advantageous, suggested the utility of national agreements and treaties, whereby such communications could be promoted with safety, and to mutual benefit. Wherefore commerce became an object of government. These constitute the capital distinctions of government with respect to its ends.[2] The first relates to the internal police of civil society, which, as it does not immediately affect my present design, I shall dismiss for the present.—The others are political, and chiefly relate to foreign powers;[3] and may be considered under the articles of war, and of friendship and trade.

[From *The New-Haven Gazette and Connecticut Magazine*, May 17, 1787.]

The article of War comprehends every thing relative to the safety and defence of a nation, not only at a time of open and actual hostilities, but in times of peace; which is always necessary to be improved, in making the best preparations for defence; otherwise a nation would be continually exposed to the ambitious views, and malicious designs of other powers. Nothing will preserve the tranquility of the public so effectually as being in a constant preparation for defensive operations. It therefore necessarily comprehends and extends to a great variety of subsequent and dependent objects; such as forming treaties

1. The original 1784 edition says "civil and political institutions."
2. The words "with respect to its ends" did not appear in the 1784 edition.
3. The exception to this statement, as pointed out at pages 151–52 of the text of this book, was "internal commerce." Cf., pages 1182–84, 1193–94, and 1204 *infra*.

of alliance, raising armies, directing their operations, regulating and ordering the militia, building and equipping fleets, erecting fortifications, establishing and supplying magazines, detecting and punishing high-treason; also to foreign embassies, foreign aids, national revenue, and in short, to every particular and minute circumstance, with which the safety and honour of a nation may be any way connected, or, on which they may in any respect be dependent.

Commerce, as an object of government, comprises every thing relating to the interest and wealth of a nation in general; and therefore extends to every particular interest and property, which may be affected or influenced by trade. —The productions of a country by agriculture and manufacture, is the source of national wealth, and basis of commerce; The husbandman furnishes the means of subsistence, and the raw material for fabrication and manufacture; The manufacturer and mechanic prepare those raw materials for use, and the merchant, by commerce, renders the superfluous productions of a country valuable, which otherwise would be of little worth, and by an exchange of commodities, supplies the people with such articles of foreign produce and manufacture, as are not furnished among themselves, and which may be necessary for carrying on their various branches of business, or for the comfort and convenience of the people. In promoting these general interests, by carrying on an (almost) endless variety of business, necessarily derived from them, the learned, the ingenious, the seaman, artificer, and day-labourer, find employment and support. On the mutual aid and support of the whole of these, depends the advancement and prosperity of each, and on this also, depends the opulence of a nation; and therefore, equally requires the encouragement and protection of government.[4]

Agriculture and manufactures are of such consequence to a nation, that either to destroy, or injure, or not encourage them, would be as preposterous, as it would be for a farmer to neglect the cultivation of his lands, and sell them occasionally by the piece to buy bread. The importation of every article of produce and manufacture from foreign nations, which a country affords, should therefore be prohibited; even admitting that they could be imported of a better quality and at a cheaper rate; for by the encouragement of having a certain market, people are induced to exert themselves in making improvements, which is the only method by which one nation can be made to excel another, in the quality and cheapness of their commodities. In this country, for instance, iron, beef, pork, butter, cheese, cyder, beer, soap, candles, hats,

4. This paragraph read as follows in the 1784 edition:
"Commerce, as an object of government, comprises every thing relating to the interest and wealth of a nation in general; and therefore, extends to every particular interest and property, which may be affected or influenced by trade.—The productions of a country by agriculture and manufacture, is the source of national wealth, and basis of commerce; which consists in exchanging commodities, by giving such as a nation has a superfluity of, for those they really want. In effecting this exchange, merchants become useful and important in a community. By them the superfluous productions of a country are rendered valuable, which otherwise would be of no worth, by them the people are supplied with such articles of foreign produce as they need for consumption, and for carrying on their several branches of business, and by them the seaman, artificer and labourer find employment and support. On the mutual aid and support of these professions and branches of business, depend the advancement and prosperity of each and on the prosperity of the whole depends the opulence of a nation; and therefore, should be equally protected, and encouraged by government."

saddles, shoes, and cloaths ready made, can all be produced and made, in sufficient quantities (at least for the use of the country)—and therefore to admit their free importation from other nations would be essentially injurious to an important part of the community, a fatal impediment in the way of improvement, and in effect destroy the natural advantages we have to promote the interest of the public.—And not only those articles of produce and manufacture, which are commonly made and produced, should be thus encouraged, but those also a country is naturally adapted to, by, not only laying a proper restraint on their importation, but at the same time giving certain bounties, which will gradually increase their production, and lessen the necessity of importation; by which means an easy change may be made without sensible injury. The articles of silk and hemp in particular, might be cultivated to as great perfection in this country, as in any whatever, and in quantities, not only sufficient for home consumption, but for exportation. In like manner should those manufactures be encouraged, the materials of which are imported from other nations; for instance, cordage—however necessary it may be to import hemp, cordage should be prohibited.—Furthermore, shipbuilding, freighting, and seamen, are of great national consideration, a very considerable part of the inhabitants of trading nations, depend on these for support; and in the great circle of mercantile business, the merchants find their interest immediately connected therewith. And besides, all maritime powers have found their strength consists in a great measure, in the number and ability of their seamen. Wherefore, as shipbuilding is a great and important branch of business in this country, the building or purchasing of ships abroad should be prohibited; neither should an inhabitant be permitted to freight a foreign ship; nor should our own ships be navigated by foreign seamen.

The great advantages resulting from trade, have always excited the envy, jealousy and ambition of trading nations, who have made it their most capital stroke of policy to forestall and engross partial and exclusive benefits. But as commercial intercourses are mutually beneficial, and all nations have an equal claim to the advantages of their own trade, their interests cannot be accommodated any other way, but by a reciprocity; giving the same privileges that are given; which is a rule founded in perfect justice and utility, and the only one that can be admitted without injury either to the one or the other. This principle being just, the forming and supporting commercial treaties by government, is absolutely necessary; for in an unlimited, undefined intercourse, an equality in advantages can never be maintained, nor many inconveniences and real prejudices be prevented. And whenever two nations carry on a trade upon general principles, and general terms, (as is sometimes the case) without extending their agreement to minutiae, it is requisite for government to establish such particular regulations as will render such a commerce uniform, safe and beneficial, according to the particular situation and circumstances of the respective nations.

But commerce is an object of government for other reasons.—Nations often are under such circumstances, that an embargo on several articles of trade, such as provisions in a time of general scarcity, and naval and military stores in time of war, are indispensibly necessary.—And further, the experience of all nations evinces, that trade is the best foundation on which a revenue can be established; because, by being judiciously laid on particular articles of luxury, and superfluity, it will operate with propriety and equality, and may be collected with facility and certainty.

These are some of the reasons why commerce is and ought to be an object of government.[5]—However necessary and advantageous a free trade, or a trade established on liberal principles, may be to a nation, it should not be a licentious one. The great object of trade is to promote the interest of the community in general, and so long as that end can be answered, it is no matter how free and extensive it is, the more so the better; but when the interest of the public is injured by trade in any particular instance, every reason would justify a restraint. It is therefore essentially necessary, for the interest of individuals, as well as that of the whole, that trade should be systematically settled by government, and regulated in such a manner as that the various particular interests of a nation may mutually assist each other; and that the foreign nations engross no unequal advantage.*

Under these denominations, of War; or that in which the peace and safety of a nation consists;—and of Commerce; or the correspondence and connections of a nation with other nations, and with one another, the whole political interest of a nation may be included and considered. And, as they are of general and equal concern to the community,—extend to a great variety of subordinate interests and concerns—and are extremely intricate and complicated in their operations and influences; so, for these reasons, it is absolutely necessary that such a system should be established, as will promote, secure, and regulate those interests, by the unanimous aid and concurrence of the whole nation; for, to this end, it is frequently necessary to call the united strength of a nation into exercise, for its defence.—A proportion of private property is always necessary to be contributed for the purpose of securing the more important interest of the public, and a due observation of national treaties, and internal[6] regulations, is indispensible, to promote the general weal and render advantages among the people equal. And in the formation of a political system, to render it complete, and in any measure adequate to the interests and necessities of the people, the institution of an ultimate, decisive counsel and authority, is essentially necessary; for without this, it will be impossible to prevent a great variety of evils and perplexities; much more to render a nation flourishing and happy.

The variety of sentiments, interests and views of individuals hath always laid society under the necessity of fixing some rule, whereby their aggregate

---

* It is a doctrine advanced by many, and probably true, that for the benefit of mankind in general, trade should be free as air. But, any one nation in the great circle of universal correspondence, interrupting that freedom, lays every other nation under a necessity of adopting similar measures; for disadvantages cannot be prevented, nor an equal share of advantages secured in any other way.

5. It will be observed that what has gone before was not intended by the author of *The Political Establishments* as an exhaustive discussion of "the regulation of commerce." Like most of the writers of the 1780's, the focus of his attention was foreign commerce, since it was deemed that the general "commercial languor" of the moment stemmed from maladjustments in this field; but he none the less makes perfectly clear that a power "to regulate commerce" would include complete power over internal business as well. *Cf.*, his two statements as to the nature of "commerce, *as an object of government*," *supra*, page 1182 and footnote; also, his further summarizing statement upon this subject to be found in the paragraph of his pamphlet immediately following that to which this note is appended.

6. The word "internal" is not included in the 1784 edition. This emendation by the author of the pamphlet no doubt reflects the general insistence, which arose subsequent to the original publication of his pamphlet, that full internal, as well as external, commercial power was necessary for Congress.

opinion could be determined, without which public proceedings would be impracticable; so, notwithstanding the power of individuals, naturally are equal; yet the unanimity and decision of national acts are so essential to the existence and welfare of communities, that it is of equal necessity, that the authority of the whole should be reduced to one point; or, the power of the nation deposited in such a manner, as to govern the whole with unanimity, efficacy and dispatch. It is impossible there should be a political body without a head, or without some institution invested with powers as extensive as the objects of legislation or the interests of the people; for, all matters of government are so complicated, interwoven and dependent, that an interruption in the operation of one act, would disconcert and render nugatory the best devised plan that ever was formed; and a division of power destroy the foundation of government itself. Suppose in an army, the several divisions and subordinate officers should take it upon them to debate the necessity and propriety of general orders, and determine their conduct according to their several inclinations and opinions; what would be the consequence? Again, suppose the planetary system was (for once) put under the direction of as many supreme powers, what confusion and destruction would ensue! Just so, where the people are under no supreme authority, and are ultimately determined by individual opinions and resolutions; anarchy and confusion must necessarily be the fatal consequence.

The perfection of government consists in such an unanimity, as that the body politic can act together without dissension, being animated by one spirit, originating in an undivided source of power; so that were it practicable for governments to be administered by one man, who was under the invariable influence of justice and good policy, in whom the people could confide without reserve, it would undoubtedly be the best and most perfect; and therefore a deviation from such a form, renders government in a greater or lesser degree imperfect; for every division of power, whether equal or subordinate, does, in proportion to the nature and extent of such divisions, divide the political interest of the people, and naturally tends to create parties and introduce faction. Of all the various forms of government established in the world, an absolute monarchy has the preference on several accounts; because it is capable of securing the most perfect union, can render the execution of resolutions more speedy and efficacious, the burdens and advantages of government more equal, and political views and measures more consistent; but, considering the state of human nature, and the great temptations an absolute monarch is continually under, to abuse his trust, and tyrannise over the people, it is a dangerous government, and sufficiently justifies the people in guarding against those evils, by establishing such subordinate institutions as will more effectually secure their liberties. Such institutions however, cannot be considered as perfections in government, but as a matter of necessity, either to check the arbitrary stretches of sovereign power, or to assist in administration. On these principles all arrangements in government should be regulated.

[From *The New-Haven Gazette and Connecticut Magazine*, May 24, 1787.]

Having premised thus much, I will proceed to observe some of the most essential errors and defects in our political establishments, and

First, they are not capable of preserving a union of views and measures; nor of rendering the burthens and advantages of government among the people equal.—The first principle of our national existence is the sovereignty and independence of the several states, which in fact, makes us so many separate and distinct nations; for, thirteen sovereign and independent powers, will have thirteen separate and independent interests to promote and secure, and for that purpose, will establish as many different systems of policy.— In this state of division we were at first settled, and when our late contest with Great Britain commenced, we had no leisure (had we been ever so much inclined) to deliberate on and settle a constitution for the government of the whole: yet, being involved in one general calamity, and unanimously determined to make a vigorous defence, saw the necessity of forming some plan of union, whereby our efforts might be rendered the more efficacious and successful; wherefore, a congress of delegates from the several (then) colonies, was appointed to direct and advise, in all matters relating to the whole, so far as respected the war; which was probably all that was intended at the time of that appointment; for the powers they were invested with, were confined to that object.[7] However, Congress, to remedy the apparent defects in their institution, render it perpetual and competent to the purposes of national policy, formed the articles of confederation and perpetual union, whereby, they became invested with certain powers, which, however ample they were intended, were by no means answerable to the proposed end; being circumscribed with regard to their objects, in some instances merely recommendatory, in others implied, and in but very few determinate.—Here it is worthy of notice, that the union which took place at the beginning of our late contest, was founded on an occasional friendship, resulting from our being involved in a common calamity, and the necessity we were under, of uniting in means and measures, for our mutual defence and deliverance; which occasion being removed, the friendship and union founded upon it must necessarily dissolve.

The union which existed between the states at that time, having so much of the appearance of a permanency, was probably the occasion of leading the people into an error, by building their expectations too much on it, and in neglecting such measures as were necessary to confirm and consolidate it. But, if the states wish to become perfectly united, it is evident, it must be done on other principles, from more extensive views, and by other means than those which produced our first union. The most permanent bond by which individuals or communities can become united, is interest; or the uniting the interest of the whole in such a manner, as will the better and more effectually promote and secure the interest of individuals. And it is unquestionably true, that the more numerous the people, the more extensive their interests, and the greater their property, which are included in a union, (so that a nation be not too burdensome and unwieldy) their peace and safety is the better secured, and their interests the better advanced. But were we to judge of the present professed union of the states, by the nature of the union of their interests, we must conclude that they are in fact not united; and, remaining in the same situation, never can be united; For the civil and the political interests of the public are completely divided, formed and established in each of the states, and are respectively considered their primary and fundamental objects. The general interests and concerns therefore of the confederation, which are either matters of burden or advantage, become objects of subordinate consideration, and matters of variance. This division

7. The evidence to be presented in a later volume of this book indicates that the author of *The Political Establishments* was not accurately informed upon this point.

in our political system, forms the governing principle, by which the views and measures of the states are directed; which, so far from constituting a real, permanent union, sets up thirteen interests in opposition to one another, fixes the ultimate powers of government in each of the states, and renders the institution of Congress entirely subordinate, or rather, useless. For if Congress can be capable of answering any good purposes to the states, it must be by investing that body with such powers, as are fully adequate to the purposes of the institution. But if we consider the nature and extent of the powers of Congress in some particular cases, we shall see to what they amount.

In case of a war, congress have a right to declare war, raise and commission armies, and direct their operations, but here their power ceases. They can neither levy money, cloathing nor provisions, nor can they order out the militia on any emergency; without which, those primary acts would be altogether trifling.

The subsequent supports necessary to render such a resolution effectual, depend on the approbation and concurrence of the states, on which there can be no certain dependence, for it would be with that, as with every other subject, wherein the particular states were involved. They would take into consideration the propriety and necessity of the measure, and according to its agreement, or disagreement with their interest, would determine; therefore, to suppose there would be a unanimity in this case, would be to suppose their interests[8] affected by it; which, though it may happen, is not to be depended on; for besides the many supposeable cases which might be mentioned, to shew wherein the particular interests of the states, may be differently affected by a war, the most effectual measure an invader could take to render his attempts successful, would be to detatch particular parts from the general concern. How far public men, and public bodies of men can be influenced by improper motives, I will not pretend to determine; how[ev]er, be this as it may, one thing needs no proof, that the concurrence of the states in case of a war, is dependent on their interest being equally concerned in it, and on this concurrence the efficacy of the power of Congress depends, which (logically) is no power at all.—Several things may be urged here, as, that the right of Congress to direct every measure with decisive authority, necessary for the prosecution of a war, is implied in the general article whereby they are empowered to make war.—The states viewing themselves sovereign and independent, would of course undertake to determine, how far they would be bound by an implied authority; and therefore it would be needless to say anything further upon it.—It may again be said the honor of the states is engaged for their mutual support.—Whatever opinion some may have of the public honour, for my own part, I have no idea of it, where interest is in the question. I have often read of the evasion of, even, public solemn engagements, for the sake of promoting or securing an interest; but never heard of a nation, insuring, or sacrificing their interest to their honor. But had we no historical instances of this nature, the conduct and disposition of the states on several occasions, are sufficient to teach us that public honor alone is but a mere phantom.—But further, it may be said, that the articles of confederation &c. oblige us to a unanimity in every national measure.—I am sensible it is said there shall be a perpetual union between the states; I know also, in treaties of peace, it is said there shall be a perpetual peace,

8. Four words of the 1784 edition, which seem necessary to the sense of this passage, are missing (probably as a result of a typographical error) at this point, from the New Haven reprint. The words are "must necessarily be equally."

and in treaties of alliance, that there shall be a perpetual friendship &c. between the contracting parties; all of which are equally binding, for they are
all founded on public interest and political motives, and so long as those
interests remain the same, the agreements founded upon them will undoubtedly
be observed, but no longer. The articles of confederation, by which the states
are united, are of the nature and force of a treaty of alliance only; which,
considering the variety of public interests in opposition,—and the spirit of
selfishness so prevalent through the continent, we cannot rationally expect
will be sufficient to preserve the unanimity, so essentially necessary to the
welfare, and even the existence of a nation.—Upon the whole therefore, the
concurrence of the states in case of a war, would be an event rather to be
hoped than expected.

Again—In case of commerce.—Most of what hath been said in the foregoing
case, may be applied in this; the sovereignty of the several states will substantially supercede the authority of Congress, and the spirit of emulation
and rivalry, which prevails among the several divisions of the people, effectually
prevent any general regulations from taking place from mere recommendation. By the articles of confederation, Congress are empowered to settle
treaties of friendship and trade with foreign nations; but they cannot establish
a custom house on the continent for the purpose of collecting a stipulated
duty, neither can they prevent the states charging foreigners with an additional impost. They cannot prohibit the importation of any one article of
foreign produce and manufacture, however prejudicial to the interest of
the public, nor lay an embargo in any instance,—In short, the power of Congress respecting trade, is so very contracted and deficient, the sovereignty of
the states so unlimited and so undefined, and their views so various, that
so long as we remain in our present political situation, our commerce, which
might be improved to great and general advantage, will be a confused
ruinous affair.

Furthermore—in the case of a national revenue. This is an object of the
highest importance to a nation, in which the interest and honor, the safety
and happiness of the public, and the property of individuals are deeply
interested. It is what has embarrassed all our public proceedings, and involved
us in difficulties not easily surmounted.—However necessary it is there should
be a unanimity, punctuality and equality in the support of government, and
discharge of public obligations, under our present circumstances, it is
evidently impracticable to accomplish these purposes.—In order to render
the burdens of the public equal among the people, it is first necessary to
ascertain the just proportion due from each state; but this cannot be done,
because no just ratio can be established, whereby the comparative value of
the states can be determined.—Congress, after considering the subject for
a long time, can form no satisfactory judgment; they first fixed on the
quantity of land, improvements &c. which was found inadequate; after which,
they proposed a calculation of the number of inhabitants, but this will give
no more light on the subject than they would have had without it; the truth
is, there can be no truth nor certainty in either.

[From *The New-Haven Gazette and Connecticut Magazine*, May 31, 1787.]

There is no way to determine the worth of a nation, or state but by the
revenue it is able to produce, without affecting[9] its real worth of property;

9. Probably a misprint for "assessing," which resembles "affecting" in eighteenth-
century script. The word, however, is the same in the 1784 edition of the pamphlet.

which depends, in a great measure, on a variety of incidental or local circumstances, that can never be fairly accounted for; and therefore, were it possible to ascertain the real value of each of the states, and charge the national expenditures on them, on that principle, it would at least be unequal, if not unjust; because, the ways and means they may have to raise their proportionate quotas, may be essentially different. Two of our states may, in the opinion of well informed judicious men, be of equal real value, and yet, one be able to raise twice as much as the other, and with as little prejudice to its real interest; merely (it may be) on account of its being so situated, as to accumulate a greater share of national, external advantages, which advantages, of what kind soever, being promoted and secured at the joint expence of the United States should therefore, be improved for, and applied to the equal benefit of the whole.

Admitting however, that a just proportion, according to the real value of the states could be ascertained: yet, the same difficulties will arise among their respective inhabitants. To charge the necessary annual quotas on the people in the usual method, would inevitably ruin the greatest part of the inhabitants. For some years past they have paid to the extent of their abilities, and yet have fell short more than three fourths of the requisite amount.*

Many, very many, whose bills of taxable estate amount to a very considerable sum, are, with all their industry and frugality, scarcely able to keep the bailiffs from the door. To distress and even ruin such, while the same proportion does not affect the rich and opulent, is a most oppressive mode of supporting the public, and an effectual means of introducing an aristocracy. To levy a tax on real property, has indeed the appearance of justice and equality, because, it supposes a man worth a thousand pounds will pay ten times as much, as him, who is worth but an hundred, but in its operation, nothing can be more oppressive. The principle is wrong, and no nation existing can be supported on it.†

* A Gentleman of consideration, and property (I presume) in the State of Connecticut, hath in his late publications, stated the amount of taxes, which he suggests, has been paid by the State, in the course of the last six years; which including the impost and excise amounts, if I remember right, to near 1,800,000.—This sum is supposed to be greater, than any other nation (in proportion to the number of inhabitants in Connecticut) ever hath, or can pay.

As I am not in a capacity to say much, with respect to the revenue of the State of Connecticut, with accuracy and certainty, shall only observe here, that when we consider, that the tax on continental Bills, is computed to have been paid in at a depreciation of forty for one, but that in fact, the depreciation was, at that time, from seventy two, to one hundred and eight for one, and the tax paid at those rates.—When we consider, that the principal amount of all the other taxes, was payable in public securities, of various denominations, and at various rates of depreciation.—And when we consider, that there are large balances still due on those taxes, we have reason to suppose, so much money in specie, or specie value, hath not in reality, been paid by the inhabitants of the State. It is evident however, that in the present mode of taxation, no more could have been collected. But if so much money hath really been collected from the people, a question of some considerable consequence arises in the minds of the people, what is become of it? For they have no account of any public debts being paid; nor do they find themselves any way exonerated, by the payment of so large a sum.

† The Gentleman before quoted, strenuously urges the excellency of the mode of taxation in Connecticut, and the preference it hath, to all other modes of raising a revenue, on account of its equality.—To which I would observe, that if the inhabitants

Some kinds of property of equal prime value with others, will produce a much greater profit; and a man worth a hundred pounds estate, comparatively with the utmost prudence and industry cannot support a family with decency, while the man of a thousand pounds property, may, not only support his family affluently, but add a hundred pounds to his estate annually; such a man therefore, can pay a hundred pounds to the public as easy as the other nothing.

The most eligible method by which a nation can be supported; or, the purpose of the States answered, is by a tax on trade, which the experience of all nations have proved to a demonstration. Of all the other modes of taxation it has the preference, because it requires money from those who have it, and who in this way would pay it with freedom. It should not therefore, be laid indiscriminately on all kind of goods, for that would destroy one of its most essential purposes.—Articles of importation may be classed under three denominations viz. articles of luxury and superfluity, those of common and general use, and such as are of real and universal necessity.—The first of which, should be charged with a high duty, because those only, who are of abilities will, or, ought to make use of them. The great and unrestrained consumption of such

---

were possessed of property equally alike, it would, indisputably, operate with perfect equality. Before the war, the expences of the State were so trifling, that whether it was equal, or not, no person felt it; but since the expences of the public are large, and felt by every person, and since all persons do not possess property alike, the equality of the rule can be determined *only*, by the effects it hath in its operation, on the people, in their different circumstances. By this we find, that the *opulent* can pay their taxes, and support their families, some decently, some affluently, and some luxuriously; and besides this, increase their property annually. But that the *poor* farmer, day labourer, and mechanic, who might just make out a living, without any extraordinary burden, are by this mode, reduced to great necessities in the article of living, and are necessitated to let their property be taken from them, and sold for trifling considerations, to pay their taxes; and finally, many of them are obliged to go out of the state, to seek a place where they can enjoy the fruits of their labour in a greater degree, than they could here. In addition to this, the great advantages given to Collectors by law, over the property of the people, greatly augments the oppression. If such instances of hardship and inconvenience were few, and rarely known, they would be scarcely worthy of notice. We might in such a case, conclude the rule or mode of taxation was good. But, when we consider the long list of names, with which all the News-papers in the State, are weekly crowded, for three years past, notifying, that so much of their lands, would be sold at public vendue, as would pay their taxes, and charges arising thereon; we have every reason to conclude, that there is essential defect, with regard to the equality of supplying the treasury. And therefore, untill I see so much of the lands, of the *wealthy* men of the State, advertised for sale at vendue, as will pay *their* taxes &c. I shall continue to think, that however equal the mode may be, as it respects *property*, it is extremely unequal, as it respects *individuals*. It is possible, some material amendment might be made, with respect to this mode. But, if *such* an amendment cannot be made, as will draw the principal part of the money the public requires, from the wealthy, and in a great measure free the *poor* and *industrious* part of the community, from the burthen of taxation, I see no way to prevent a very considerable part of the people being ruined, their little property falling into the hands of the rich, and consequently, the introduction and establishment of an aristocracy.

All nations have found it impracticable to raise as much money, by a tax on real property, as they have found necessary to answer their purposes, at many times, if not always; and therefore, they have had recourse to external taxation, or a tax on the importation of foreign commodities. In doing this they have generally two objects in view, the one, to put it out of the power of the people, in general, to make use of for-articles in the time of the war, when they were at enormous prices, prove that people will gratify their taste, (at least) as far as their purses will admit.—The second should be taxed, yet, so as not to prevent their general use; but the third should be freed from duties—And with regard to exports, I can see no reason, why they should in all cases be exempt from a duty, though small, it would be an auxiliary aid, and very justly chargeable on those foreigners, (especially) who in like manner, charge our trade with a duty. I admit however our own merchants should be an exception.

[From *The New-Haven Gazette and Connecticut Magazine*, June 7, 1787.]

But whatever essential purposes, a judicious, well established impost might answer, yet, so long as the States hold themselves absolutely sovereign and independent, it will be impracticable, without a miracle, to establish a general impost at all, by their unanimous consent. The resolves of the States upon this, and most other national questions, have hitherto been, and probably always will be, so various and essentially different that we have no reason ever to expect any proposed measures *being* refered to the States, for their concurrence, (how-

---

eign productions, and lay them under the necessity of supplying their wants, by their own industry; and the other to draw money from the opulent, who can make use of foreign superfluities and luxuries, at advanced prices, without a sensible injury to their personal interests; And for the same reason, they have often laid heavy duties on superfluous property. By such methods, they have either directly, or eventually raised large sums from the opulent, which it would have been impracticable to have done, by the mode of taxation, adopted in most of the States, in the state of Connecticut in particular.

The debts of the United States are great, and the payment of them must, in the most easy and eligible methods, be burdensome to the people. And I conceive it to be a matter of great consequence to the happiness of the people, that the most easy methods should be devised and adopted, for the support of government, and the payment of the public debt; and a strict rule of economy observed in the public expenditures.

I do not pretend to be so well acquainted with the subject, as to give a positive opinion, with respect to the best methods of discharging the public debt, But I have thought, whether, if any impost was granted to Congress, (to be managed as circumstances might require) together with all the unlocated lands, they would not be a sufficient deposit for the security of all the public debts, *foreign* and *domestic,* were they funded together. If it should be found that they were sufficient, and the public debts funded accordingly, I apprehend, that all the creditors of the United States, would be perfectly satisfied, the states relieved from many perplexities, and the people freed from many burdens.

There is one special reason, which appears to me to be a conclusive one, why the unlocated lands should be considered as continental property, and not the property of individual States; which is, that they are an *acquisition,* by the joint efforts, and at the joint expence of *all* the States. No man can claim a property upon fairer pretensions, nor upon more legal grounds; and therefore, I can see no reason, why they should not be given up to the United States, and applied to the payment of their debts. Whether these lands, together with an impost would be sufficient, to fund all the Continental debts, I cannot determine; So far as I am capable of judging, I should suppose they would, and indeed much more; For, with respect to the lands, it is manifest, if a federal government was once established, and the frontiers well secured, they would rise in value, at a rapid rate; and it is obvious to all, that an impost, may be judiciously laid, without being, intolerably burdensome. So that on the whole, it appears to me, that the continental debts might be sufficiently funded, and finally paid, in methods more easy and eligible, than any which have, as yet, been adopted.

ever important and beneficial) will be adopted and rendered effectual. Neither, (under this circumstance) would a general impost operate with justice and equality: for, the national debt being proportioned and charged to the respective states, the collections by impost would necessarily be credited to the state, where such collections were made: The greatest importations of goods are confined to particular states, yet, their consumption is nearly equal through, the whole, in proportion to the number of inhabitants; therefore, the duties being paid by the importer, and charged accordingly on his goods, the non-importing state, which consume them, would in fact pay the duty, while the importing state had the benefit of it. This is a perplexing circumstance in the policy of the nation, is unequal and unjust, and will not admit of a remedy, while in *one* nation, we have *fourteen* interests to promote and secure. Were it necessary, other cases might be mentioned, but these will be sufficient to demonstrate what I proposed, that the powers of Congress are insufficient to maintain a unanimity and consistency, in national views and measures; and that the sovereignty and partiality of the states, will prevent their agreement to any measure, necessary to promote the general interest; or to support the fundamental principles of government. Which I presume will be allowed a defect.

Second: Our civil and political establishments are essentially defective, as they are not founded on the free and unanimous choice of the people. A right in the people, to chuse what form of government they think will best promote their publick interests; or, in other words, what form they please, is founded in nature, and cannot be legally superceeded, nor vacated; consequently, any form of government set up among a free people upon any other foundation, or, by whatever other means is an usurpation and illegal. I am aware it may be objected, that at the declaration of independence, constitutions were formed, and consented to by the people in many of the states; and in others, their governments were previously settled in like manner.

To which I would observe, that in those states whose governments were new modeled, all the propositions refered to the people for their approbation;[10] also, the silence of the other states upon this point, were all grounded on a presumption, that our separate state governments were unalterable, and must necessarily be retained, which put the matter upon a very unfair and illegal footing, because, it left the people without a choice. Have the people ever had an opportunity of considering and debating the subject, and of making a deliberate choice? certainly they have not; and no man to this day, knows what form of government is most agreeable to their wishes; only, it is presumed they would not prefer a Kingly government because, a King once attempted to bind us in all cases whatsoever. Tho' by the way, there is no impossibility in a people's being as effectually shackled without a King, as with one.

Since by our joint efforts, we have obtained a complete emancipation from British thraldom, have entirely changed our political circumstances, are become jointly concerned in our national interests, and at liberty to choose what form of government we please; the first question in the order of things to be determined, is, what form of government is most suitably adapted to our present situation? and after that, whether we will establish such a form, for the government of the American nation? This would settle the whole matter upon its proper basis. But to attempt to conform a plan of government, (originally

10. It should be remembered that there was no such "reference to the people" in most cases.

calculated for, and intended to keep us divided[11]) to our present circumstances, principally, because we happened to be originally settled in such a state of division, and have become habitually attached to it; especially, when we have it in our power, to choose and establish a government, suitably adapted to the present circumstances of the States, may justly be esteemed, an extraordinary instance of prejudice and prepossession.

It may be further urged, that the articles of confederation, by which the institution of Congress, and the sovereignty of the States were confirmed, was by the choice and consent of the people. They were certainly established by the *consent* of the people; but that consent was not the result of their free and deliberate *choice*, by themselves, or their delegates, for that purpose appointed. Those articles, when proposed to the people for their acceptance,[12] were grounded, like all other propositions at that time, on the presumption, that the sovereignty of the States was like the laws of the *Medes* and *Persians*, unalterably fixed; and therefore, were adopted as a matter of necessity, being accompanied with no alternative. But it is worthy of notice, that, at that time, the exigency of public affairs, rendered speedy resolutions necessary, and the confusion of the times, put it out of the power of the people, to pay that attention to the subject, its nature and importance required; which affords a sufficient reason and ground for after consideration. For had they, under such circumstances, adopted the best and wisest measures, it would have been strange indeed.

To close this general observation, we will suppose the present inhabitants of America, had now emigrated from foreign countries, and collected on the continent, being under no kind of government, they would naturally adopt some method, whereby the sense of the whole could be taken, a choice made, and a form established: At a convention appointed for that purpose, would they propose the institution of thirteen sovereign and independent powers, as the best method they could devise to cement a union, and promote their common interests; and over these, to institute a political legislative authority, invested with very few powers, all of which in their operation, ultimately depend on the unanimous concurrence of the other powers? There is such an absurdity in the proposition, that it would be impossible ever to reconcile it in idea with common sense.

Third, another defect in our institutions, is, the division of the civil and political powers. Whatever powers Congress is invested with, are entirely of a political nature; which, if they were complete; as they undoubtedly should be, upon the principles, or spirit of the federal system, it would leave the powers of the respective States entirely civil. But, even if this were the case, there would be an imperfection in it; for there is a necessary connection and dependence, between every kind of public interest, and an intimate correspondence, between all acts of legislation. When the powers of government are divided, in such a manner, there will be many things, closely connected with the political interest of the nation, which Congress cannot take cognizance of; others, of a civil nature, will fail of a completion, for the want of a more extensive power, than the states respectively can have, and some matters may

11. The 1784 edition says "to keep us divided and subject to another power." This view of the imperial system of separate colonies was common in 1776.

12. It should be remembered that, except in New Hampshire and Massachusetts, the Articles of Confederation were "proposed to the people" only in the sense of being proposed to the several state legislatures.

arise, wherein it may be questionable, whether they come within the jurisdiction of either of the states, or of Congress. So that notwithstanding a complete division of power, on this principle, would render the system more perfect than it now is; yet, still there would be an imperfection in it.[13]

To sum up the state of our political establishments, the amount appears to be this. The states are so many greater divisions of the people, whose political interests are separated and opposed to one another, whose objects are different and measures various; and being sovereign and independent cannot be controlled. And Congress, in whom we have any semblance of a union, considering the nature and extent of their powers, the design of the institution, and the little regard paid, to their recommendations, and resolutions, by the states, is a burlesque on government, and a most severe satire on the wisdom of the people. On the whole, viewing the aggregate state of our governments, they appear to be founded on no established principle, are aiming at no certain end, and have not union enough to prosecute any one particular purpose to effect, nor, to give a sufficient weight and dignity to national resolutions;[14] And therefore, like every ill formed government, naturally tends to the introduction of all kinds of licentiousness, confusion and perplexity whereby the people suffer many present inconveniencies, and are exposed to many future real evils. Some of which I will mention.

First;—The people, for the want of an efficient federal government, suffer many inconveniences, respecting their commerce; *foreign* and *domestic*. The commercial nations in Europe, knowing our weakness in this respect,

13. This paragraph reads as follows in the 1784 edition:
"Third: another defect in our institutions arises from the division of our civil and political powers. The general idea is, that Congress superintends the political interest of the whole, while the authority of the states is confined to the civil interests of their respective inhabitants. But so perfect a division cannot be made here, as may at first be imagined; for, there is a necessary connection and dependence between every kind of public interest, and an intimate correspondence between all acts of legislation. —When the powers of government therefore, are divided, as in the present case, there will be many things closely connected with the political interest of the nation, which Congress cannot take cognizance of; others, merely of a civil nature will fail of their accomplishment for the want of a more extensive authority than the states respectively have, and some rights there are, claimed by the civil powers, which are of general concern.—An instance in each.—The detecting and punishing high treason is entirely of a political nature, yet, Congress, who ought to be the guardian of our common and political interests, cannot take cognizance of such a crime; for all judicial proceedings, originate in the states.—The security of literary property, has always been thought reasonable and necessary for the encouragement of learning and the promotion of the liberal arts, yet, what advantage would it be to an author, to have his works secured to him in one state, while all the others were at liberty to republish and sell them?—The admission of inhabitants and granting the rights of citizenship to foreigners, is an object of general concern; for whether there are advantages, or disadvantages resulting from it, the whole will be affected; yet, it is a right claimed by each state, and every town, to admit what description of persons, or characters they please, as inhabitants and subjects.—However reasonable this might be before our independence, at this time it is necessary that the authority of the whole should determine, what characters are proper to be admitted as subjects."

14. In the 1784 edition of *The Political Establishments*, the author insisted once more at this point that the then existing state governments, and the Articles as well, "ha[d] not the sanction of general choice, [but were] formed by an unhappy concurrence of occasional and accidental circumstances, and [were] incapable of promoting and securing the interest, honor and happiness of the people."

take great liberties with the trade and navigation of this country; by regulating and controlling it in such a manner, as to render the commerce of the United States, wholly subservient [to] their interest; by which means, our navigation is suppressed, and theirs, in that proportion increased. And under the specious pretence, of supporting their navigation laws, the property of the citizens of America, is wantonly taken from them, on trifling pretences, and proceeded against to final confiscation. Look into our Ports!—*There* we see crouds of British Vessels, which find protection, indulgence, complaisance and full freights.—There we see (almost daily) Vessels advertised for sale, recommended by this peculiar and advantageous circumstance, with a note of emphasis, that they are *really* British built, and *there* we see American Vessels, *lying by* useless, stripped, with brooms at masthead. Go to the British Islands in the West-Indies, and what do we see there? An American Vessel fired at, if within reach of a Fort. Taken if within reach of a man of war,—Seized, condemned and sold, if within reach of a Custom-House officer,—And an *American*, treated with imperious contempt, stripped, and sent naked away. Behold the contrast! had the States a well constituted federal government, would these things be so?

The same cause also, is productive of a variety of inconveniencies and perplexities, respecting the commercial connections and intercourses, of the respective states. *One* state will receive gold at one rate, *another* at another rate. In *one* state, paper money passes at *one* rate, and is more stable,—In *another*, it passes at *another* rate, and is more unstable,—In *one* paper money is a tender in all payments,—In *another* it is no tender.[15] *Some* states, will free the productions and manufactures of the United States from a duty, *others*, charge a duty on them as foreign, and all the States, charge a duty on a foreign commodity, imported from another State, where it had been entered, and duty paid; so, that transporting it from one State to another, the whole would be swallowed up in an impost,—moreover,

The laws of the respective States are so various, and essentially different with respect to their foreign trade, that *some* States are singularly benefited, while *others* are laid under singular disadvantages. *Some* States, shut their ports entirely to British Vessels; *others*, open their ports freely to all nations, without discrimination,—*Some* States, charge *one* duty on foreign Vessels; *Others* charge *another*, and *some* charge an American, and a foreign Vessel alike. *Some* States, charge *one* duty on foreign merchandize, imported in a foreign Vessel, *Others* charge *another*,—And others again, make no difference between goods imported in a foreign and American Vessel,—*Some* States charge *one* duty on foreign merchandize imported in an American Vessel, *others* charge *another*,—And while *some* States prohibit the importation of certain foreign articles, *others* admit of them freely. So that on the whole, it must appear evident to every one, that the navigation and trade of the States, are in a confused, perplexed situation.

The great object of the respective States, relative to trade, appears to be, to rival one another,—To obtain partial advantages, and to raise money from it, in some way or another, no matter how; without any view to a national system, without paying any regard to the effects, or influence their jargon

15. The reader will note that the references to paper money and tender laws in this paragraph sufficiently indicate that the phrase "commercial connections and intercourses, of the *respective* states," earlier in the paragraph, and the phrase "domestic commerce," in the paragraph before, are *not* to be taken as referring *only* to what we now call "interstate commerce."

of commercial laws, have on the interest of particular States,—on the property of individuals, on agriculture and manufactures, and consequently, on the wealth of the nation on which its power depends, and in which its safety and defence consists.

It is certainly the highest folly, for the States to think of establishing a system of trade, independent of one another. The local situation, together with the natural, and unavoidable connections and dependencies, which subsist between them, renders such a scheme wholly impracticable, without doing great violence to the natural order of things, and great injury to one another.

Did we rightly consider, and fully comprehend the intimate connection there is between the interest of individual States, and the States unitedly. Between individuals and the public,—That the promotion of the one, promotes the other, and that it is impossible to injure the one, without injuring the other, it would have a tendency to destroy that narrow policy, which hath hitherto governed the States; and eradicate those contracted ideas which terminate in *self*, and which is the governing principle, of many of the *Bell-Weathers* of the flock.

[From *The New-Haven Gazette and Connecticut Magazine*, June 21, 1787.]

Secondly; Another inconvenience the people suffer, arises from the misapplication of the ways and means, the United States are in the possession of, for raising a national Revenue. As I have said something considerable on this point, shall add but little here. It is a doctrine which will forever remain true, and which should be established as a principle in all government, that a people, who are subjected to all national burdens, should be entitled to a participation of all national benefits and advantages; Therefore, as the expences of the United States are intended to be equally born by them—and as the revenue of the States must arise, in a great measure, from an Impost; so all the States ought to participate in all the advantages, which may be derived from that source. It is manifest however, that they *now* do not. *Philadelphia*, and *New-York* import the principal part of the goods consumed in *Connecticut*, *New-Jersey* and *Delaware*, who consequently pay the duty on them; but *Pennsylvania* and *New-York* enjoy the benefits of it. So that this way and means of raising public monies, which ought to be applied to the benefit of the whole, becomes partial.

Third: Another inconvenience which the people suffer, is the expence of supporting so many complete governments. The obligations the United States are under—The importance of supporting a national credit, and the incompetency of their resources affords reason sufficient, for observing a strict rule of Oeconomy, and keeping public expences within the bounds of moderation and necessity. And therefore, unless there be some special reason (not applicable to any other nation) for supporting so many governments in *one* nation, the people ought to be released from such a burden.

Fourth: By the establishment of such a number of sovereign and independent powers, the States are placed on the same footing, with respect to one another, with the different nations in Europe, and (more than possible) will be under the same necessity, as *they* are, of maintaining a balance of power, and standing armies for their security and defence, against one another. It is true, this may not happen; But, besides those causes of contention, which occasionally take place between neighbouring nations, in the course of events, there are many other matters, lying between the States, which might soon be wrought up into high dispute.

The apparent friendship which now prevails through the States, may incline us to think, it will never be otherwise; But, the experience of past ages, gives us reason to fear, this may not always be the case; and therefore, points out the propriety, of timely taking measures, to prevent such an event. Some few ages back, six Kings, (if I remember right) reigned at one time, on the Island of Great-Britain; and in a later period of time, two powerful competitors claimed the Crown. The consequences of which were, that the Island for a great length of time, was deluged in blood, and the people suffered every other kind of Calamity, which could result from civil discord.

The same pride and ambition, the same lust for power and dominion, and the same spirit of selfishness, possesses the minds of people in *these* days, as did in *those*. We have therefore, every reason to conclude, that the same effects will follow, according to the natural order of things.

Fifth: Another evil, to which the States are exposed, in their present situation, is, that some petulant, ambitious spirit may be stirred up, to attempt a revolution by force. Such an event is almost a never failing consequence, of a weak and disordered government. At a time when a general uneasiness prevails among the people, an enterprising, subtle genius, would not find it extremely difficult; to secure a party, capable of accomplishing such a purpose.

As *all* countries have produced such men, and *most* nations have experienced violent revolutions, the States can have no particular reason, for making an exception of themselves.

Sixth: The political division of the States, exposes us to the insults of other nations. Our territories are encroached on, by the *English* in the north, and by the *Spaniards* in the South,—Our flag insulted on the seas, Our property sported with, and considered as common plunder, and in short, the dignity of the States, as a nation, held in contempt. The reason of all this, undoubtedly, is, that the States have no respectable government; that the strength is divided, and that they are unable to resent an indignity; or, retaliate an injury.

I once observed to an English Gentleman, that the Americans would, undoubtedly, take measures, to counteract the designs of Great Britain, respecting our trade. *Pish!* says the Gentleman, what can the Americans do? They have neither government nor power. Great Britain could shut up all their ports, so that an American Vessel would not dare to stir out of their harbours: and burn all their Towns on the Sea-Coasts into the bargain. *America* take measures against *Great-Britain* indeed!—Now, a man who knows nothing of such insults, but by hearsay, feels them not, nor cares any thing about them; but, a man who frequently sees, hears and feels the effects of them, must feel extreme pain and mortification.

Besides those indignities and insults, to which we are exposed, we are exposed to an invasion. The weakness of a nation (which all Europe supposes is the case with the States,) always attracts the notice of other nations, and often stimulates some to make an invasion, in expectation of an easy conquest. The security of the States against such an event, hath hitherto consisted, in the present state of European politics; particularly, of the maritime powers. France supported our independence, because, it tended to diminish the strength, of the only maritime power that nation had reason to fear; But the same system of policy among those powers, may not always prevail. Circumstances may take place, which may make it the interest of all *those* powers, who have possessions this side the Atlantic, to confederate, for the purpose of suppressing the rising power of these States. Besides this, when we consider, that altho' Great Britain recognized our independence; yet, it is possible she has not lost sight of us. That our navigation, interferes with the navigation, of most of the formidable, commercial powers in Europe; That we are bounded on either side by an ambitious, encroaching nation, and that those nations, who have loaned the States money, may become clamourous for payment, or to have their debts well funded; we have reason to conclude, that there are causes enough in embryo, to produce a rupture in some future period; perhaps sooner than we are aware. Let the event be as it may, these circumstances, point out the propriety, of consolidating the strength of the nation, and making the best preparation for the worst events.

Considering the defects and incompetency of our government, which would be the most prudent and adviseable, either to proceed in this state of confusion and uncertainty; or, to attempt a reformation? This is a question of important consideration, and requires a candid unprejudiced determination.— The right and privilege of choosing, and finally establishing what form of government we thought proper, a government that would better promote and secure our temporal happiness, was the only motive we could have for engaging in an unequal war.—It was that, which animated our soldiery in all the distressing scenes of hunger, cold and toil, and inspired them with fortitude and resolution in the day of severe trial.—It was that, which allayed the anguish of the disconsolate widow, and composed the spirit of the bereaved parent, it was that, in short which raised, and supported that unbounded spirit of patriotism through the whole, which trampled under foot with indignation & contempt, the tempting proffers of pecuniary considerations, combated the power of contagion in dungeons, and triumphed in pillars of smoke over conflagrated towns.—And, after a success equal to our highest hopes, to be disappointed in that alone which could reward us, that only, which we contended for, to have a government established, incapable of securing our invaluable civil and political interests, and of promoting our highest temporal happiness. How distressing to the liberal soul!—How mortifying to the patriot spirit!—Far better would it have been, by all the loss of property we have sustained, the sacrifice of friends, and the misery we have suffered, had we remained as we were, subjected to another power.

If therefore, our government is defective, (which every candid observer must acknowledge,) why not reform? In all cases of error and defect, a thorough reformation and amendment, hath always obtained the sanction of general approbation and preference. And if, in cases of lesser moment, a reformation is necessary, the reasons are rendered proportionably more forcible and conclusive, in cases of magnitude and importance, as is the present. Even admitting, our establishments had been the general choice of the people, and confirmed in the most binding manner, it would certainly be a greater proof of wisdom to reform their errors, than to obstinately persist in them. An inflexibility, may be consistent in a bigot, and fanatic, but constitutes no part of the character of a wise man. To set out in government on right principles, and in a right manner, is that on which, the interest and happiness, of a great and growing people now depends, and is as necessary to promote that purpose, as it is in any business in life to insure success; to do otherwise in both cases, creates perplexities and embarrassments, and commonly ends in destruction.—The principles on which our government is founded, we have already found by experience to be totally wrong, have rendered administration weak, if not contemptible, introduced perplexity and disorder, and the further we proceed, the more we shall be involved in difficulties. And without a reform, it does not require the spirit of prophecy to foretell a dissolution, and the succession of a perfect aristocracy; which always rises on the ruins of a monarchy, or springs out of the weakness of democracy. Every reason therefore, and every motive which can be adduced in any case, urges a political reformation.

[From *The New-Haven Gazette and Connecticut Magazine*, July 5, 1787.]

Here it will naturally be enquired, what reformation can be proposed? To which I will answer; that I conceive that no reformation or amendment can answer any effectually good purpose, short of the abolishment of our state governments, and the forming a constitution, whereby the whole nation can be united in one government. Enlarging the powers of Congress, (which might be done) will not answer the purpose because, so long as the sovereignty of each state exists, the source of all our political evils remains the same.* I am aware such a proposal will meet with a powerful opposition. Habit, attachment, and custom, together with private interest and views will all conspire against it.—But certainly we are rational, and propose some end by all our actions, and would at least be thought to prefer the best methods to accomplish our purposes. Our temporal felicity, as a nation, is undoubtedly the end we propose by government, and it would not be amiss to enquire with candour how that can be best promoted? In the course of such an enquiry it must appear, that without an union there can be no nation; consequently among a people disunited, their political views, purposes and designs must fail of accomplishment;—that without a supreme head or original source of power, there can be no union—and where there are thirteen sovereign, independent powers established among a people, there can be no head—the title therefore which we have assumed, viz. *The UNITED States*, is perfectly unmeaning—How far then this proposal is a dictate of wisdom, I will leave to the candid and impartial to determine. But the interested and ambitious will find their feelings too much affected by such a reformation to acquiesce in it. Interested motives are the appendages of human nature, they are interwoven in the constitution, and it is a matter of no surprise that they often predominate; nothing less is to be expected therefore than a strenuous vindication of a system so admirably calculated to make *a great many* GREAT MEN. But is it reasonable that the interest and happiness of the people should be injured, for the sake of gratifying the

* Although I still think, it would be much to the interest and happiness of the people, could they be persuaded to throw all the states into one grand republic, yet I apprehend such a measure would not obtain their approbation at this day, and therefore it may be supposed a revisal of the federal system will extend no farther than an enlargement of the powers of Congress. In this case I conceive a just line should be drawn between the civil and political power of the nation. That Congress should be vested with full powers in all national concerns, even to their remotest and most extensive objects; and, that the power of the respective states should be reduced to civil administration. For a national government to be invested with less powers than these, is trifling, temporizing and sporting, with the most important interests of the nation.

Such a division of power would be productive of one good consequence, besides rendering the government otherwise more perfect, which is, that it would prevent disputes which might otherwise arise hereafter, respecting territory; for in this case it would be of little consequence whether the dominion of individual states were enlarged or circumscribed.

views of individuals, however laudable? Or, would it not be much more to the lasting honor of men of influence and abilities, to be the first in promoting the general weal, rather than from partial motives, to keep the people divided, and obstruct the most effectual measures for the public good? The memory of a well known illustrious character, will live with veneration and applause, long after a dignified ambitious and selfish man will be forgotten; and that, not merely on account of his conspicuous situation, but the distinterestedness of his motives, his zeal for the public good, and fidelity in the discharge of his important trust. May all our public men "go and do likewise!"

The particular objections which may be made to such a proposal I cannot foretell; however, I will suppose some few,—as, that revolutions and alterations in government are dangerous—They often are so, especially when they rise from party faction; but as the people are the original of power, they have a right to establish what form they please, of reconsidering their constitutions, and making such amendments and alterations as they think will better conduce to the accomplishment of their purposes—There can therefore, be no danger in a unanimous agreement, without which such a proposal cannot take effect—At the same time, I will freely acknowledge, that no alteration should be made without an absolute necessity; for frequent change, renders government unstable, and endangers both public and private interest.

Again: It may be objected that the liberties of the people might be affected by such an alteration.—Much hath been said on the subject of civil liberty, and from what hath been said; or, whatever (I can conceive) can be said upon it, I cannot believe, it consists in a plurality of equal supreme powers; especially, the several governments of the states; for, besides, the novelties and singularities which distinguish some, the matter of prerogative and privilege, in many, if not all, are left wholly undefined and unlimited, so that neither the people know the extent of their privileges, nor the legislature, the bounds of their power; and where there is no rule established for public procedure, there can be no stability nor certainty. Neither do I believe, liberty consists in an over abundant representation.—When the various interests of a people can be fairly represented by one hundred men, 'tis much better, than to add nine hundred more, provided they be men of abilities and integrity; for experience proves that great bodies retard proceedings, and that the wisdom of measures does not always bear an exact proportion to numbers.—Nor do I think liberty consists in, or can be better secured by supernumerary offices and officers. There is a fitness in the several parts of governments, as necessary to be observed for the completion and perfection of the whole, as in any constructure whatever.—Nor, further, does liberty consist in licentiousness: for one great design of government is to regulate the conduct of mankind.—But, liberty consists in the right and privilege of the people, to choose what government they please, and to elect their legislative authority. This is the whole.* Should the legislature pass

* When I say, the liberties of a people consist in their right, to chuse and establish what form of government they please, and to elect their legislative authority, I would not be understood to mean, that the people are not entitled to any other civil right. But I have along, gone upon this principle, that all the rights, liberties &c. of the people; together with the power of government, in all its branches should be defined, stated, and constitutionally settled. This being done, I apprehend, the people have nothing to do, but to elect their legislative and executive authority; whose power being stated, and fixed, like the boundaries of the ocean, "Hitherto shalt thou come, but no further," every act of theirs therefore, which breaks over these bounds, would

an act subversive of their subsequent rights (which it is supposed would be defined in their constitution) it would necessarily be null; and besides, they have always the power of obtaining redress, in their right of changing their representatives.–This position therefore, is so far from injuring the liberties of the people, that it is the only method whereby they can be effectually secured. But

Further: It may be objected, that it would be impracticable to settle all our interests and concerns so as to unite them in one government.–To descend to particulars here, would exceed my designed brevity, as the subject is extensive; however, I can see no greater difficulty, in adjusting and settling all those interests, and reducing them to one joint concern; than there would be for so many merchants to settle their private affairs and unite their interests in one common stock, for the purpose of trade. But, again.

Some may object; that one legislative body could not particularly attend to the more minute circumstances of many interests and concerns, dispersed among a people so extensively situated, as the citizens of America are.

When its considered, that there are nations as extensive as ours, with seven or eight times as many inhabitants,–who are under one government only, we may rationally conclude it is not impracticable–However, I would not be understood as rejecting every other kind of institution; subordinate institutions, it is possible may be established with great propriety, and[16] necessary for purposes.

But the greatest objection that can be made, I apprehend, arises from this circumstance;–The customs and manners of the people, of the respective states are different,–In some respects essentially different,–and are accommodated, and provided for, by their civil establishments and codes of law, more agreeably, than perhaps they could be by any other system, that could be devised.– Men of liberal sentiments, however, who were disposed to harmonize, might, easily remove such an obstacle, and accommodate themselves to any judicious system, calculated to promote the general happiness of the community. But to men of contracted minds, and prepossessed in favour of their own customs, manners, laws and modes of administration, such an objection would prove an insuperable bar, in the way of uniting the civil interests of the states. The prevailing disposition of the citizens of America, with respect to this particular, must be refered to time for decision.[17]

[From *The New-Haven Gazette and Connecticut Magazine*, July 12, 1787.]

Whether this proposal is the most eligible that can be made; or, whether such a reformation can ever be effected, I will not pretend to assert positively; to me however, it appears the only measure that can be adopted, to relieve us from

---

in its own nature, be void–might justly be opposed, and could be remedied, by a change of representatives, and civil officers.

A government settled in this manner, I imagine would have a happy tendency, to destroy that spirit of jealousy, which is so apt to prevail in popular governments; for if people, understand what rights, liberties and privileges they, are entitled to, and are satisfied they are sufficient.–If they know what powers government is armed with,– if they are satisfied that those powers are necessary to be exercised, for the good of the community,–that they are just, and not exorbitant, and cannot be exceeded, I can hardly be persuaded, that any cause of jealousy could exist.

16. The words "to answer useful and" appear in the 1784 edition at this point. As they seem necessary to the sense, their omission from the New Haven reprint was undoubtedly a typographical error.

17. This paragraph was not in the 1784 edition.

our present difficulties, to promote the welfare of the present age, and lay a solid foundation for the prosperity of future generations; but should a better be propounded, I give this up, as freely as I made it.

It is undoubtedly the desire of every individual on the continent, that a cordial unanimity and harmony, should be promoted among the people, their rights, liberties and privileges secured in the most effectual manner, the blessings of foreign and domestic peace prolonged, a weight and dignity stamped on all our national measures, and government in every branch duly supported; And under reconsideration of this subject, the question will naturally arise, whether our present political establishments, are capable of answering those desireable and important purposes? and from what hath here been observed, as well as what might be farther urged, I think it must appear evident to every impartial mind, that they are not; if so, the question will then remain, whether it be the best and wisest measure, to let our political and general interests take their own course, and run the hazard of a violent revolution, and an uncertain administration; or, to settle, by deliberate council and choice, a form of government, while we have it in our power; before our prejudices become too deep rooted to be removed, and our separate jarring interests too firmly established to be united; and which may serve, not only for the present day, but a hundred years hence; when it is probable, America will be the greatest nation in the world?—Let impartial, unbiassed reason determine.

That our government in its present state, can be of long continuance, appears to me impracticable; either, the states will renounce all pretentions to a union, and set up for themselves absolutely independent, or, an aristocracy take place, established on the various interests of the people at large; or, party feuds bring about a revolution; or, (what is most advisable) a reformation, and more permanent and competent institutions established, by the unanimous consent of the citizens; for a people never did, nor ever will rest satisfied under a government, either too oppressive; or, too weak, and inadequate to their views and necessities; they will by some means or another effect an alteration, but whether for the better or worse depends on the disposition of the people, and views of leading men.—Before it be long, we shall be able to determine, what kind of spirit prevails through this continent.

With regard to a form of government, I will only observe, that a democracy appears to be the most agreeable to the present views of the Citizens of America, and is probably the best calculated to promote the equal good of the people; yet as it is the most difficult to frame, easily disordered, and not readily rectified; so, on these accounts, there are none requires a foundation so judiciously laid.—It is a form, which novelties and refinements injure; its materials should be calculated to answer their particular purposes, not for ornament but real use—The more simple its construction, (so it be competent to its purposes) the more secure. The dignity which is thought to be so essential in government, in this form, does not consist in the splendors of a Court nor terrors of an army, but in the excellency of its constitution, wisdom of its political measures, justice of its laws, and abilities and fidelity of its executive authority. Whenever a democratical government is established, and exercised on the principle of justice and sound policy, it is undoubtedly the best form that can be instituted, because it makes the laws, and not men supreme, and the equal good of the people its object. Is, by being thus founded, in no danger of falling into contempt, and always sure of the best support a government can have, viz. the approbation, and mutual aid of the people.

To the great body of the citizens of America, I refer what I have observed on this subject; and so far as I have been guided by truth and reason, I shall hope for the candour and attention the importance of the subject justly demands, but no further, it is a case of such consequence, that we certainly ought to attend to it and divest ourselves of prejudice, in our enquiries and determinations respecting it, and,

To complete what I had in view, I will make this further proposal; that a competent number of men of approved abilities, experience and integrity, be elected by the people throughout the states, to convene at a certain time and place, with full powers to form a constitution for the government of the American nation, on the principles of a solid union, and equal benefits.

Should this measure be adopted, I have not the least doubt, but such a convention would form a constitution, whereby all our public interests might be united, the liberties and privileges of the people more effectually secured, and a weight and dignity stamped on all our national proceedings, which would obtain general approbation, and render the nation great and happy.*

* I cannot avoid expressing the satisfaction I feel, on account of the proposal being made by Congress, for a convention to be held in Philadelphia, for the express purpose of revising the federal system—That so many of the most respectable States, so rapidly acquiesced in the proposal, and have chosen men for their delegates, who are the boast and ornament of their country, and, I think every one who wishes the prosperity of the United States, must be highly pleased also.

We have every reason to expect from such a measure, the most important benefits; for it cannot be doubted, but that a plan of government will be devised, suitably adapted to the situation and circumstances of the states, and adequate to the wants and necessities of the people. In this case the only remaining difficulty (if any) would be to have it adopted, as the free choice of the people. And on this account we should have nothing to apprehend, were it not, that some people, for some reason or another, have stated objections, to giving any power out of their own hands, as they term it, lest the liberties of the people should be endangered. It hath, unhappily, been the case, when measures have been proposed, in the assemblies of the states, evidently calculated, for the benefit of individual, or confederate states, for some to mount the political *hobby-horse*, and set up the cry of liberty. On these occasions, we frequently hear of our forefathers coming to this howling wilderness for liberty,—and if we grant money or power to congress, our liberties will be in danger,—that congress is profuse &c.

It is, undoubtedly the duty of a free people to be tenacious of their liberties, and guard against encroachment; but it does not from thence follow, that we should be suspicious of every public measure, or public character. A people ought to be able to distinguish between such measures, as have a natural tendency to injure them in this respect, and those which are calculated to promote their welfare.—The suggestions that it would be dangerous to grant money or power to congress; or to establish a federal government adequate to the national purposes, are manifestly unmanly and unreasonable; yet they have their effect on minds naturally suspicious and timid, and those unenlarged; whereby many men of illiberal sentiments, base and selfish views, and also of weak intellects, draw a train after them like a comet.—In the insinuations which are frequently made use of, there is not only, a great share of illiberality, but also, a great degree of puerility.—Let me have your knife, says *Tommy* to *Billy;* no I won't says *Billy* you will cut your fingers if I do, and I can make a whistle as well again as you can.—Whether there is more reason in one case than in the other I submit.

In case it should finally be proposed, that congress should be established as the federal head of the states, invested with ample powers (for it is perfect nonsense to talk about government, without adequate power) let us briefly enquire whether we should have any special reason, to suspect our liberties would be endangered. The result of such an enquiry, will shew us what foundation there is for those jealousies, which are said to possess the minds of many; and, perhaps, point out the place, from which they originate.

If a foreign prince should come into this country, with a force sufficient to force the submission of the people, and set himself up as king, without a previous agreement, or compact, the people would have just reason to fear their liberties would be encroached on, if not totally destroyed. But this is not the case with Congress—Congress is, and will be (if the federal system undergoes a revisal) instituted by the free suffrages of a free people. The members of that body, are annually elected; are equally intrusted[18] in public measures, with the rest of the people, and annually return to the rank of common citizenship. Besides, I recollect no instance, wherein Congress ever attempted to extend its powers, beyond the limits prescribed, by the articles of confederation.

These things being so, I can see no just reason to suspect, that the liberties of the people would be in danger of abridgement by investing that body with every necessary power. And when I consider, that the people do, without hesitation grant more extensive, or at least more undefined powers, to the respective assemblies (composed of men on the same footing, and elected on the same principles, with the members of congress) I cannot believe that the jealousies which are said to exist among us, originated in the great body of the people; but in some little ambitious soul, who aspires to an inch height above his fellow-citizen; or a mercenary one, whose views are pointed to some little pecuniary place. Both of whom might think themselves in danger of failing in their views, by parting with money or power, or by making any alteration in the federal system. For my own part, I should be much more afraid of such men, notwithstanding the apparent distress they are in about our liberties, than I should of granting competent powers to a federal government. But let us consider this matter a little further.

Suppose, that congress should be invested with ample powers with respect to security and defence, the navigation and commerce of the nation, in their most extensive connected and dependent objects; what would there be in this, of which we should have reason to apprehend any evil consequences? It would be granting no new, or extraordinary powers. These are powers which the assemblies of the states, have always held and exercised, all the difference would be, that the power is lodged in a different place; and the advantage would be that the measures would be more uniform, consistent and efficacious; whereas they are at present neither. In the one case, there would be a harmony; in the other, endless confusion. There would therefore be no extraordinary reason for fear by such an alteration in our federal government, except from the maladministration of those in places of trust. If this should be objected, I shall only observe, that it is impossible to constitute any government whatever, to which such an objection may not be applied. In our present situation, it may be urged with as much force, as in any state whatever.—If a nation furnishes no men, worthy of public confidence, it is a most unhappy and unfortunate nation indeed.

The idea which is generally entertained, that by the institution of government, the people *give up* some part of their liberty and property, for the security of the remainder, appears to me, not to be strictly just. It rather appears, that upon democratical principles, it is simply *uniting* the power and wealth of the people, to be exercised and improved, in the most easy, eligible and effectual methods, for the mutual benefit and advantage of the whole; and for the express purpose of securing to themselves, the full enjoyment of their liberties, without abridgment.—Again,

Suppose Congress should be fully empowered with respect to national revenue, and be enabled to fund the national debts?—The right of granting money, naturally and unalienably belongs to every man, and should be sacredly held as such. But as a community cannot exist without a government, and government cannot be supported nor national purposes accomplished, without expences; so, the people are under a necessary obligation, (founded on the reason and nature of things) to make provision for the payment of those expences. And, as it is found impracticable to do this, by the contributions or donations of the people, nor by their individual determinations;

18. Apparently a typographical error for "interested."

nor yet, by collecting the majority of voices, from the whole body of the people; so, for their convenience and the accomplishment of this purpose, there appears to be a propriety, and indeed, a necessity of the people's granting full power to a representative body, to apply the public advantages the nation may be possessed of, to the purpose of raising public money; and to lay an equal tax, according to the exigencies and necessities of government. By this means the people maintain their natural right, of granting money by their consent only, and at the same time answer the purposes of government. Such a power, the citizens of the United States may grant, with equal safety, either to Congress; or, to the respective assemblies, they being equally, the representatives of the people. Congress can have no greater reasons, nor stronger motives, for exercising despotic controul over the property of the people than the assemblies of the states have; nor, is it possible to invest Congress with powers, in this particular, more extensive and unlimited, than the assemblies at present exercise. So that I can see no reason, or cause, for withholding from Congress, a power to raise such sums of money, as may be necessary, for the purposes of the United States; provided there is a sufficient reason for granting such a power to a federal government, instead of the assemblies of the States,—To which, little need be said,— The United States, are, professedly, one nation,—have national interests and concerns—are under national obligations—and have national resources.—What institution then, have the states, or can they have so properly adapted to these circumstances, as Congress; which is composed of representatives of all the States? Especially, when we consider, that from experience, we can expect no unanimity, nor conformity, in the resolves of several assemblies, on any national question or proposition—Furthermore,

Suppose the governours of the respective states, as Captain-Generals of the militia, and Vice Admirals of the navy, should derive their authority from Congress. Could any material objection be made to such an establishment? Unquestionably, the strength of the nation would be better united, and could be applied with greater efficacy and dispatch, and in a better conformity, to the principal operations in a time of war. It would, at least, establish (not an improper) subordination, and consequently, render the union more perfect. Nature in all its works, its established order and operations, demonstrates that without an original power, and due subordination, it is impossible, either in nature, or art, to maintain, or even constitute, an active union. This principle must be adopted in the final settlement of our government; or, to render ourselves consistent, we must renounce all pretensions to a union.

THE END

APPENDIX B

The Observator

[From *The New-Haven* (Conn.) *Gazette*, August 25, 1785.]

THE OBSERVATOR. NO. I.

There was probably no nation, or people, so advantageously circumstanced both by nature and providence, as the inhabitants of America are; and yet, none perhaps, ever neglected to improve their advantages in a greater degree, nor none ever embarrassed themselves more rapidly, and effectually, through bad policy, than we have done.

The difficulties which we experience at this time, and which are every day encreasing, arise from a variety of particular causes—one of which is the peculiar state of our government.

It requires nothing more than what hath ever been the result of experience, to prove, that the political interest of a nation, can never be promoted and secured, without the most unequivocal and perfect union; for no measures, however well adapted to promote the interests of the whole, will operate with efficacy among a people, whose common interests are partially united; and therefore, it can never be expected that a system of policy which establishes so many separate and independent interests, as ours does, can maintain a unanimity in views and measures; nor render any general act of government efficacious.— Circumstanced, as we at present are, with respect to government, it would be as impracticable to confine the views of the different states, or unite them in any one consistent plan of measures, as it would be to unite all the streams of water on the continent, and confine them in one channel. The consequence of this is, our public, political interests, and with them individual interests (for they will stand or fall together) cannot be promoted, but must be neglected, and in the end inevitably ruined.

Our separate state governments, (each sovereign and independent) which forms the basis of our political system, I never could think, would serve the interests of the public; but on the contrary, that innumerable evils would necessarily flow from them, and such as would be highly prejudicial to the interests and welfare of the people; and this opinion, I think, must appear to be just, by what we experience every day; yet our prejudices are so many and strong, that a sacrifice of this favourite Hobby-Horse would be an event scarcely to be hoped for at this time; and therefore a remedy for our political evils is not to be expected from that quarter. We might however remedy many, if not most of them, by entrusting our common interest in the hands of Congress; and without that much, at least, it is in vain we pretend to a union; for without some institution, invested with powers as extensive as our political concerns are—powers free from impediment or controul—powers capable of preserving a consistency and unanimity, government will forever remain in a state of confusion and perplexity: The act of one part will eternally counteract and destroy the efficacy of the act of another.

Our present want of an efficient government, is severely felt in all our political interests, especially in our commerce. Foreigners avail themselves of this advantage, and will continue to injure us more and more, even to a total overthrow of our trade, if our measures are not altered. This evil every one sees; yet such is the variety of our supposed interests, and our views in consequence of it, that no agreement can take place, in the measures necessary to check its progress. The furthest any proposal has extended in this case, is, to invest Congress with a power to regulate our trade; but even in this, there does not appear to be a unanimity: however, should the states agree in this, it would fall short of what is necessary; for every political interest of a nation is so blended together, and dependent on one another, that, unless there be a sovereign power sufficient to govern them all, the end of public measures will be lost, by an interruption in some of their more remote and extensive operations; and therefore, if the states should not invest congress with full powers in all their common interests, their granting them powers respecting trade only, would be but a mere temporizing, and fail of answering its purposes fully.

It is a matter of the utmost surprise to all people of understanding, that the Americans, who are in general the most enlightened in the principles of government of any nation, perhaps, in the world, should institute a Congress, to superintend their political interests—by whom alone those interests can, at present be promoted, and in whom only they can have any pretensions to a union; and yet deny or neglect to give them the powers, necessary to answer the purposes of their institution. The reason of this preposterous conduct cannot, perhaps, be readily given, or explained; but one of the most popular objections, I have ever heard, to granting ample powers to congress, is, that the ambition of men in power is unbounded; so that should congress have a liberal grant, there would be danger in time, of their assuming powers incompatible with the liberties of the people; but surely a wise people—a people, who are in every sense free and unembarrassed, could so frame a constitution, and establish a government in such a manner, as most effectually to guard against despotism, and at the same time answer all its most essential purposes. This objection, if it be the true reason for not granting congress sufficient powers, must appear to be extremely weak, and the effect of a most unreasonable jealousy. Should some foreigner come into this country, claiming regal and despotic powers, there would be great reason in opposing his ambitious views; or, were the appointment of the members of congress for life, or made hereditary, there would be just occasion for watching their steps with a jealous eye; but so long as we maintain that fundamental part of our constitution—that great palladium of civil liberty, *Annual Elections*, no nation can have less to fear from ambitious views, or despotic measures; for every year, every man who fills the most important stations, and by whom alone the people can be injured in their civil rights, may be divested of every mark of distinction, and returned to the rank of common citizenship, and become an equal sharer in the consequences of public measures, with their fellow citizens. The liberty of a people does not consist in, or depend on the withholding power, where power ought to be given; but principally on the establishment of a government on a good foundation, on a constitution, which provides for all possible cases of public necessity, which at the same time, shuts up all the avenues of corruption and maladministration, and which clearly defines and recognizes both liberties of the people, and prerogatives of government. When a government is thus settled, every man in power, knows the length of his tether, and every citizen knows the extent of his liberties, and what they consist in:—this gives security and creates confidence—and such a government, a wise and brave people can always guard and defend; but when a national administration is dependent on occasional circumstances—on the caprice of men in power, and on the ambition of men of opulence, there can be neither stability, security, nor confidence.

If our political interests—if an efficient national government, are matters of indifference, nothing need be said, or done about it,—but, if the very existence of a nation, ultimately depend, on the establishment of a sovereign power, then surely, the reasons for the United States, investing in some body, powers, co-extensive with national concerns, must appear to be powerful and conclusive. And as we have adopted the plan of conducting our political affairs, by a Congress, annually elected by the several States, it is but right,—it is but what sound policy would dictate, to grant to that body full and ample powers (constitutionally settled) to conduct the public concerns of the nation, without impediment. If there be reason for distrust in doing this, I cannot conceive it possible to establish any political, or civil institution, wherein full confidence can be placed.

But, perhaps, our distrust does not arise so much from the nature of the institution, as from the character, or conduct of those who have, or do compose the Congress.—Whether there be any just cause of complaint on this ground, I will not pretend to say; but, if there are no men of abilities and integrity among us, it is our misfortune; if there are, and we do not prefer them, it is our folly. However, if we view the measures of Congress, retrospectively, from its first institution to this day, I think we may discover several marks of wisdom, fortitude, integrity and zeal: such as one would imagine, were sufficient to inspire the people with a good degree of confidence— Some things might, possibly, have been done, which they did not do, and some things, probably, might have been done better; but considering their situation, considering also, the state of the country, have we reason to believe, we could have selected a body of men, that would have acquitted themselves with more honour, and answered the expectations of the people better?—Perfection, and infallibility are not to be looked for in human nature; and therefore, that all the measures of Congress were not so, is no way remarkable; sufficient is it to say, we could not reasonably expect more from men in like circumstances.

Congress does not, nor can want more extensive powers, than our respective assemblies have;—and why we should give unlimited powers to them, in matters of national policy, wherein we can have no expectation of a unanimity; and withhold competent powers from that body, in whom alone we can hope for a union, and why we should unreservedly intrust our political interests in the hands of men who must act partially, and the generality of whom cannot be but superficially acquainted with the arts of government and policy, and distrust that body, who are the best qualified to superintend the common interests of the nation, are, what I believe, no sufficient reason can be assigned for.— Congress, in all their measures have been uniform, and consistent with the principles of their institution.—Can as much be said, with respect to the measures of the assemblies of the States? Their measures also, if they have not been the best adapted to promote the general interest, yet, they have aimed at an equal influence on the property of the citizens,—but has this been the case with the views and measures of the different assemblies? Have they not, rather set the different interests of the people, at open war with one another? Most evidently the variety of their measures tends to destroy that equality in the burdens and advantages of government, which ought to prevail throughout the continent, and be a governing principle of administration.—The situation, and connections of the inhabitants of the United States are such, that 'tis impossible to decide their political interests, without destroying them. Furthermore, are not the members of Congress, equally members of the same community?—Are they not equally interested in the welfare of the States? Or, are they men of worse views; more corrupt in their principles, and of less abilities and integrity, than those are, who compose the assemblies?—These are questions every man may determine for himself; for my own part, I can see no reason, why as great confidence cannot be placed in that body; as in any legislative body on the continent;—if so, I see no reason, why Congress (in our present situation) ought not to be invested with full and ample powers, in all the political interests of the nation: for such a measure only, will put us upon an equal footing, and render our public measures uniform and effectual.—But, if the States are determined to proceed as they begun, retain their absolute sovereignty, and grant Congress occasional, temporary and interfering powers, we have nothing to expect, but that train of ruinous consequences, which naturally, and unavoidably proceeds from imbecility and disorder.

APPENDIX C

The Duane Papers from the First Continental Congress of 1774

PROPOSITIONS OFFERED BY J. DUANE TO THE COMMITTEE
FOR STATING RIGHTS, GRIEVANCES, & THE
MEANS OF REDRESS

IN CONGRESS AT PHILADEL[PHIA]
BETWEEN 7 & 22D SEPT. 1774[1]

[ORIGINAL DRAFT]

A firm Union between the Parent State and her Colonies ought to be the great object of this Congress. It is
~~mutual happiness~~ & the permanent
this alone which can ensure ∧ ~~the~~ Stability of the british Empire & the mutual Happiness of it's respective Members. In the Resolves therefore to be adopted ~~by this~~ [illegible word stricken out] ~~Congress~~ the Prerogatives of the Crown, the Interest of Great Britain and the
proper
Rights of the Colonies ought each to have their ∧ Influence, & our proceedings to be tempered not only with a Regard to Justice but a Desire of Reconciliation.
I. The Supremacy of the Crown ~~is to be considered.~~ ~~This~~ will be secured upon the Principle that the King is entitled to the same Allegiance and to the like royal Prerogatives in the respective Colonies as are due from his Subjects and appertain to his Sovereignty within the Realm of England.
II. The Rights of the british Nation. These may be divided into two Branches,
(1) The Advantages of Commerce.
(2) Aids from the Colonists for the Defence of the Empire.
(1) The Advantages of Commerce. These arise
a. By furnishing the parent State in preference to
Country
every other ~~Nation~~ with so much of the Produce of the Colonies as they can spare and she may require.
b. By receiving from her exclusively every Com-

1. So endorsed by Duane. The originals of the Duane papers here reprinted are in the possession of the New York Historical Society, New York City, through whose courtesy their reproduction here has been made possible.

1210

raise or

modity ~~which~~ she may ∧ Manufacture or & of which we stand in need.

3.[2] By admitting only her Ships navigated with her Subjects to an commercial Intercourse with the respective Colonies.

4. By yielding up to her the Power of regulating the general Trade of the Empire to answer these purposes, and to preserve a uniform System in this respect among the several Colonies.

The difficulty is to establish a Principle upon which we can submit this Authority to Parliament without the Danger of ~~a hurtful Precedent.~~ their pleading a Right *to bind us in all Cases whatsoever.*

I think a solid Distinction may be taken.

It has hitherto been a received Maxim that we

of England

brought over as our Birth right the Common Law ∧ and such Statutes, applicable to our local Circumstances, as existed at the Time of our Colonization; and that these, with our Charter Rights, and provincial Codes, form our Colony Constitutions. This principle seems indisputable: because every Charter comprehends a prohibitory Clause against enacting any Laws repugnant to those of England; which necessarily implies that the

originally have

latter must ∧ extended[3] and been[4] the Basis of our Constitution.

Some of the Colonies have been planted since the navigation Act passed in the Reign of King Charles the

explicitly asserts claims and reserves

Second, which ∧ ~~reserves~~ for the people of England the

have enumerated.

Commercial Advantages we ∧ ~~have enumerated. With~~

In

~~respect to~~ ∧ such Colonies therefore this Statute is a part of the Law of the Land. *Others* have adopted or ex-

it

tended ∧ or ~~this Statute~~ by positive Law. *All* have sub-

and acquiesced in

mitted to ∧ its Authority for more than a Century.

By all

~~With respect~~ therefore ~~to all~~ the Regulation of Trade may be yielded to Parliament upon the Footing of a Compact, reasonable in itself, & essential to the wellbeing of the whole Empire as a Commercial People.

2. Duane inadvertently changed from letters to numbers at this point. His "3" and "4" should be "c" and "d."

3. The syllable "ed" added afterward.

4. The letters "en" added afterward.

exclusive
The Principle from which our ~~internal~~ Colony Legislation with respect to Taxation and internal Polity is derived, will not be crossed by such a Concession & this is the point to be guarded.

(2) Aids from the Colonists for the Defence of the Empire.

These are founded in Justice, due for Protection, and necessary for common Preservation.

The Difficulty of drawing together the Strength, and the Just Contributions, of so many separate Branches of the Empire, and the Danger of leaving it to the discretion of each, is the great Basis on which the Reasonableness of parliamentary Interposition is built. Nothing coud be more conciliatory than to obviate this objec-
that
tion. For ~~this~~ Purpose it is proper

1. That each Colony shoud engage to provide a competent and honourable Support for the Administration of Government & Justice within its ~~own~~ own Limits.

2. That considering the present perilous State of the National Funds, & the protection we constantly derive from it's Fleets, a present Supply be recommended in Lieu of the Mony extorted from Us under the fallacious Idea of regulating the Trade.

3. That a Plan be offered for ascertaining the Quotas
securing
and ~~raising~~ the Aids of every Colony in case of ~~any~~ future Emergency.

Justly   ~~Justly~~
1st. The first we ∧ consider as a priviledge instead of a Burthen.

2. To a *present Supply* is objected the Danger of it's being employed as a Means of Corruption: but this
prevented
might be ~~remedied~~ by a specific Application: to the Support, for Instance, of a certain Number of ~~his~~ the
American
royal Navy on an [illegible word stricken out] Estab-
the Fund
lishment, ~~and~~ ∧ to be raised by the Authority & on the Inhabitants of each Colony in such proportion as might
general
be agreed upon in ∧ Congress.

Aids
3. The Plan for raising the ~~Aidds~~ of the Colonies in ~~Case of~~ future Emergencies can only be established by the mutual Consent of the Crown & the respective Colony Assemblies. Woud it not be sufficient for this

purpose if Deputies from each ~~resp~~ respective House of
Assembly shoud be authorized by provincial Laws,

~~to meet~~ it's Commissioners
when called Upon by the Crown ∧ , to meet ∧ in a
and

_{∧° a general
Continental Council} ~~Congress~~ [∧°] and adjust the several Quotas ~~and~~ their de-
termination to be declared decisive and binding upon
each Colony.

Dutch
I do not know that the ∧ States ~~of Holland~~ have any

Province
other Bond of Union; or ~~th~~ at least that one ∧ has by

~~Constitution~~ the terms of the Confederacy ~~any~~
~~their Constitution any~~ ∧ coercive Authority over the
other. Common Interest, which is the only Cement of
such States, will prove a sufficient Obligation.

III. The Rights of the Colonies.

~~Our~~ These as has been already intimated are derived
1. From the Common Law of England and such
antient Statutes, applicable to our local ~~Cir~~ Circumstances, as existed at the time of our Colonization which
are fundamentals in our Constitution. 2. From our respective Charters confirming these Rights. 3. From our
several Codes of provincial Laws.

Nothing seems necessary ~~to preserve these Rights but~~
~~an exclusive for~~ for the preservation of those ~~N~~ Rights
but *an exclusive provincial Legislation in each Colony
respecting Taxation and internal Polity*, & comprehending the Dispensation of Justice both civil and criminal;
Subject only to the Negative of the Crown where that
negative has not been ceded by royal Charter.

If these Ideas are Just and properly arranged, then the
Resolves of the Congress may be to the following
Effect.

I. That his Majesty is entitled to the same Allegiance
and to the like royal Prerogatives in these his loyal
Colonies as are due from his Subjects and constitute his
Sovereignty within the Realm of England.

II. That the Acts of Navigation, & for the Encouragement of Trade, passed in the reign of King Charles the
_{∧° tho' in some
Respects extremely
burthensome to ~~his~~ the
do
Colonies ~~are~~ in ~~the~~
their general
Tendency establish} second ∧° ~~are~~ wise and salutary ~~Laws~~ Regulations, on
which the Wealth Strength and Safety of the whole
british Empire ~~do~~ greatly depend; and having taken
place before the Settlement of some of the Colonies;
and been adopted ~~and extended~~ in others in their In-
provincial
fancy, by positive ∧ Law; and in all having been submitted to and acquiesced in for more than a Century
ought to be considered in the Light of a Compact be-

provided that such Au-
thority is bona fide re-
strained to the Regula-
tion of our foreign
Trade for the purpose
of securing the Com-
mercial Advantages of
the whole Empire to
&
Great Britain in
with a due Regard to
the first place ∧ & the
equal commercial bene-
fit of its respective
and
Members ∧ excluding
any Idea of Taxation
internal & external for
raising a Revenue on the
Subjects of America
without their Consent.⁷
C
∧
And these Colonies
which has reserved
to the british
the supreme direction &
Parliament [∧] an
superintending power
exclusive Authority [∧]
over the general Trade
of all his Majesty's
Dominions And that
this Authority inter-
woven with our Estab-
lishments from their
first Righ Rise ought not
to be drawn into Ques-
tion provided that it be
exercised it is bona fide
restrained to the regu-
lation of our Trade.
This was [two illeg-

C these
tween the Parent Kingdom ∧ and her Colonies which
British
has reserved and secured to the P English Parliament
an
and exclusive Authority over the general Trade of all
his Majesty's Dominions:⁵ And that their Authority
thus
which is interwoven with our Establishments from their
first Rise cannot &⁶ ought not to be drawn into Question or disputed.

III. That it is the Duty of the Several Colonies *not
only* to provide a Competent and honourable Support
for the Administration of his Majesty's Government
and the Dispensation of Justice within their respective
Limits: but also to grant a present and annual Supply
towards defraying the Expence of the royal Navy from
which we draw the great Blessing of Protection in
Common with the rest of our Fellow Subjects throughout the Empire.

IV That it is the Duty of the several Colonies on
every Emergency that may threaten the Security of any
part of the Empire to contribute their Aids of Men and
money in the common Cause, according to their several
Abilities and that this Congress is firmly persuaded
that the respective Legislatures of the Colonies will

5. As indicated, the words from "which" through "Dominions" were stricken out
separately from the other words in the passage. Unless the resulting resolution was
made internally contradictory by the attachment of the marginal proviso in its initial
form, the words in question must have been stricken out when that proviso was
attached. All the rest of the words after "Parent Kingdom" to the end of the paragraph then went out when the second marginal recasting was made.

6. The words "cannot &" were probably stricken out before the other words in
the passage. The same may also have been true of the words "or disputed."

7. This entire proviso was stricken out after completion.

ible words] And this
Authority exercised
bona fide for the pur-
poses of securing the
Commercial Advan-
tages of the whole
Empire to Great Britain
with a Just Regard to
the ~~Commercial benefit~~
Interest of its respective
Members ought not to
Questioned But in this
Declaration we ∧ ex-
clude every⁸ Idea of
Taxation internal & ex-
ternal for raising a
Revenue on the Sub-
jects of America with-
out their Consent.

[Ch. 13th]

agree to any reasonable Plan which shall be recommended by his Majesty for drawing forth the united

Branches
Strength and Aids of these ~~parts~~ of his ~~roy~~ royal
Dominions whenever it shall be found necessary.

V. That the ~~respective~~ Colonies are ~~bound by and~~
entitled to the benefits of the common Law of England

[and from experience have been found]⁹
and such of the Statutes of that ˣRealm ∧ applicable to

[their respective]
~~our~~ ∧ local Circumstances, ˣas existed at the time of our
Colonization.¹⁰ We do not however admit but absolute-

26th
ly reject the Authority of the Statutes of ∧ King Henry
8th and King Edward 6 respecting [the trial for]
[or Concealmts.] [committed out of ye Realm]
Treasons and Misprisions ∧ of Treasons ∧ which
[as applied to us by a late Constructn. which would effectually destroy all Security of
the Lives Liberties & Properties of the Colonists]
cannot nor were intended to be of force where ~~Justice~~
[Tribunals are Established for the due Administration of Justice]
~~is duly administered~~ ∧ according to the Laws of England,
but only in remote and foreign parts where offenders for
such
want of ~~proper~~ ∧ Tribunals cannot be brought to legal
Trial. That these his Majesty's Colonies are [illegible
word] entitled to all the Immunities and Priviledges
granted to them by the royal Charter and confirmed
and secured by their several ~~provincial Codes~~ Codes of
provincial Laws; And that these ~~several~~ respective
Rights cannot be altered or abridged by any other
Authority than that of their respective Legislatures.

8. The words "we exclude every" are written over other words which are illegible.

9. Bracketed words are in another hand than Duane's. Some of them replace other
illegible words in a strange hand which were stricken out.

10. The "x's" mark a transposition. As transposed and amended this sentence read:
"That the Colonies are entitled to the benefits of the common Law of England and
such of the Statutes of that Realm as existed at the time of our Colonization, and from
experience have been found applicable to their respective local Circumstances."

x And that ~~to~~ the Representatives of the
people in General As-
sembly constitute a
                indispensable
fundamental ʌ Branch in
such Legislation.

several
within their ʌ ~~respective~~ Colonies
VI. That the Colonists[11] ʌ are respectively entitled to
a free and exclusive power of Legislation ~~in all Cases~~
in all Cases of
~~respecting~~ ʌ Taxation and internal Polity, Subject only
to the negative of the Crown where that Negative has
not been ceded by royal Charter.ˣ

[SECOND DRAFT OF DUANE'S RESOLVE II]

That the Acts of Navigation and for the Encouragement of Trade passed in the Reign of King Charles the
second tho' in some Respects extremely burthensome to
the Colonies, do in their general Tendency establish
wise & salutary Regulations on which the Wealth
Strength and Safety of the whole british Empire great-

x
ʌ That from the Spirit
of this Compact,
~~the Protection we stand~~
        ~~from G. B.~~
~~in need of, & derive~~ ʌ &
        Supreme
the Necessity of a ʌ
controuling Power in
this Respect, ~~we chear-~~
~~fully acknowledge~~ &
for the Protection which
we have enjoyed & still
draw from Great Britain
we ~~chear~~ chearfully
acknowledge that it be-
longs only to Parlia-
ment to direct &
superintend

become necessary by the policy of the Nations &
ly depend; And having ʌ taken place before the Settlement of some of the Colonies; and been adopted in
others in their Infancy by positive Law; and in all ~~hav-~~
~~ing been~~ submitted to and recognized for more than a
Century ought to be considered in the Light of a Compact between the parent ~~King~~ State and these Colonies
x
ʌ ~~which has reserved to the Parliament of Great Britain~~
~~the Supreme Direction and Superintendance over~~ the
~~general~~ Trade of all his Majesty's Dominions And that
this Authority exercised bona fide for the Purposes of
securing the Commercial Advantages of the whole
Empire to Great Britain with a Just Regard to the Interests of its respective Members ought not to be drawn
into Question. But in this Declaration we absolutely exclude every Idea of Taxation internal & external for
raising a Revenue on the Subjects of America without
their Consent.

[THIRD DRAFT OF DUANE'S RESOLVE II]

That the Acts of Navigation and for the Encouragement of Trade passed in the Reign of King Charles the
second tho' in some Respects extremely burthensome
upon the Colonists, do in their general Tendency establish wise & Salutary Regulations on which the Wealth
Strength and Safety of the whole british Empire greatly
            ~~Justified by~~
depend; and ~~from the Policy of the European Nations~~
                        ~~That~~
~~they become indispensable~~ highly ~~expedient and~~ having
taken place before the Settlement of some of the Colo-

11. This word was "Colonies" as the resolve was originally written. It was changed
to "Colonists" when the words "within their several Colonies" were added.

                                    been adopted   ~~been adopted~~
nies ~~and been adopted~~ in others ∧ in their Infancy ∧ by
positive Laws and in all ~~having been~~ submitted to and
                            ~~they~~ [illegible word stricken out]
recognized for more than a century ∧ ought to be con-
                            an ancient ~~& beneficial~~
sidered in the Light of a ~~reasonable~~ Compact between
                            ~~Upon these principles~~ ~~From~~
From the Spirit whereof   the parent state and the Colonies. ∧ ~~From the Spirit~~
~~of these ancient~~   ~~that~~
     Expediency
~~Acts~~ the ~~Act~~   ~~therefore of this Compact, the Necessity of a supreme~~
~~Utility~~ of ~~one~~ a   ~~controuling power in in this respect, as well as for the~~
~~Supreme controu~~   ~~Protection which we have enjoyed & still draw from~~
controuling Power   ~~Great Britain~~ we chearfully acknowledge that it be-
over ~~the general Com~~   the british
~~in the for regulating~~   longs only to ∧ Parliament to direct and superintend the
the general Commerce   Trade of all his Majesty's Dominions, and that this
of the Empire, as well   while it is
as on Account of the   Authority ∧ exercised bona fide ~~and~~ for the Purposes of
Protection we have   the Commerce of
derived from the   Securing the Advantages of ∧ the whole Empire to
~~naval Strength of~~   Great Britain with a Just Regard to the Interests of it's
~~the Parent Kingdom~~
parent Kingdom

x   ought not to be questioned^x
   In this Declaration we   respective Members ∧ ~~excluding~~ every Idea of Taxation
nevertheless   internal and external for raising a Revenue on the Sub-
~~however we~~   jects of America without their Consent, ~~ought not to be~~
absolutely exclude   ~~drawn into Questioned~~

APPENDIX D

The Articles of Confederation

To all to whom these Presents shall come, we the under signed Delegates of the States affixed to our Names, send greeting.

Whereas the Delegates of the United States of America, in Congress assembled, did, on the 15th day of November, in the Year of Our Lord One thousand Seven Hundred and Seventy seven, and in the Second Year of the Independence of America, agree to certain articles of Confederation and perpetual Union between the States of Newhampshire, Massachusetts-bay, Rhodeisland and Providence Plantations, Connecticut, New York, New Jersey, Pennsylvania, Delaware, Maryland, Virginia, North-Carolina, South-Carolina, and Georgia in the words following, viz. "Articles of Confederation and perpetual Union between the states of Newhampshire, Massachusetts-bay, Rhodeisland and Providence Plantations, Connecticut, New-York, New-Jersey, Pennsylvania, Delaware, Maryland, Virginia, North-Carolina, South-Carolina and Georgia.

ARTICLE I. The Stile of this confederacy shall be "The United States of America."

ARTICLE II. Each state retains its sovereignty, freedom, and independence, and every Power, Jurisdiction and right, which is not by this confederation expressly delegated to the United States, in Congress assembled.

ARTICLE III. The said states hereby severally enter into a firm league of friendship with each other, for their common defence, the security of their Liberties, and their mutual and general welfare, binding themselves to assist each other, against all force offered to, or attacks made upon them, or any of them, on account of religion, sovereignty, trade, or any other pretence whatever.

ARTICLE IV. The better to secure and perpetuate mutual friendship and intercourse among the people of the different states in this union, the free inhabitants of each of these states, paupers, vagabonds and fugitives from justice excepted, shall be entitled to all privileges and immunities of free citizens in the several states; and the people of each state shall have free ingress and regress to and from any other state, and shall enjoy therein all the privileges of trade and commerce, subject to the same duties, impositions and restrictions as the inhabitants thereof respectively, provided that such restriction shall not extend so far as to prevent the removal of property imported into any state, to any other state, of which the Owner is an inhabitant; provided also that no imposition, duties or restriction shall be laid by any state, on the property of the united states, or either of them.

If any Person guilty of, or charged with treason, felony, or other high misdemeanor in any state, shall flee from Justice, and be found in any of the united states, he shall, upon demand of the Governor or executive power, of the state from which he fled, be delivered up and removed to the state having jurisdiction of his offence.

Full faith and credit shall be given in each of these states to the records, acts and judicial proceedings of the courts and magistrates of every other state.

ARTICLE V. For the more convenient management of the general interests of the united states, delegates shall be annually appointed in such manner as the legislature of each state shall direct, to meet in Congress on the first Monday in November, in every year, with a power reserved to each state, to recal its delegates, or any of them, at any time within the year, and to send others in their stead, for the remainder of the Year.

No state shall be represented in Congress by less than two, nor by more than seven Members; and no person shall be capable of being a delegate for more than three years in any term of six years; nor shall any person, being a delegate, be capable of holding any office under the united states, for which he, or another for his benefit receives any salary, fees or emolument of any kind.

Each state shall maintain its own delegates in a meeting of the states, and while they act as members of the committee of the states.

In determining questions in the united states in Congress assembled, each state shall have one vote.

Freedom of speech and debate in Congress shall not be impeached or questioned in any Court, or place out of Congress, and the members of congress shall be protected in their persons from arrests and imprisonments, during the time of their going to and from, and attendance on congress, except for treason, felony, or breach of the peace.

ARTICLE VI. No state, without the Consent of the united states in congress assembled, shall send any embassy to, or receive any embassy from, or enter into any conference, agreement, alliance or treaty with any King prince or state; nor shall any person holding any office or profit or trust under the united states, or any of them, accept of any present, emolument, office or title of any kind whatever from any king, prince or foreign state; nor shall the united states in congress assembled, or any of them, grant any title of nobility.

No two or more states shall enter into any treaty, confederation or alliance whatever between them, without the consent of the united states in congress assembled, specifying accurately the purposes for which the same is to be entered into, and how long it shall continue.

No state shall lay any imposts or duties, which may interfere with any stipulations in treaties, entered into by the united states in congress assembled, with any king, prince or state, in pursuance of any treaties already proposed by congress, to the courts of France and Spain.

No vessels of war shall be kept up in time of peace by any state, except such number only, as shall be deemed necessary by the united states in congress assembled, for the defence of such state, or its trade; nor shall any body of forces be kept up by any state, in time of peace, except such number only, as in the judgment of the united states, in congress assembled, shall be deemed requisite to garrison the forts necessary for the defence of such state; but every state shall always keep up a well regulated and disciplined militia, sufficiently armed and accoutred, and shall provide and constantly have ready for use, in public stores, a due number of field pieces and tents, and a proper quantity of arms, ammunition and camp equipage.

No state shall engage in any war without the consent of the united states in congress assembled, unless such state be actually invaded by enemies, or shall have received certain advice of a resolution being formed by some nation of

Indians to invade such state, and the danger is so imminent as not to admit of a delay till the united states in congress assembled can be consulted: nor shall any state grant commissions to any ships or vessels of war, nor letters of marque or reprisal, except it be after a declaration of war by the united states in congress assembled, and then only against the kingdom or state and the subjects thereof, against which war has been so declared, and under such regulations as shall be established by the united states in congress assembled, unless such state be infested by pirates, in which case vessels of war may be fitted out for that occasion, and kept so long as the danger shall continue, or until the united states in congress assembled, shall determine otherwise.

ARTICLE VII. When land-forces are raised by any state for the common defence, all officers of or under the rank of colonel, shall be appointed by the legislature of each state respectively, by whom such forces shall be raised, or in such manner as such state shall direct, and all vacancies shall be filled up by the state which first made the appointment.

ARTICLE VIII. All charges of war, and all other expences that shall be incurred for the common defence or general welfare, and allowed by the united states in congress assembled, shall be defrayed out of a common treasury, which shall be supplied by the several states in proportion to the value of all land within each state, granted to or surveyed for any Person, as such land and the buildings and improvements thereon shall be estimated according to such mode as the united states in congress assembled, shall from time to time direct and appoint.

The taxes for paying that proportion shall be laid and levied by the authority and direction of the legislatures of the several states within the time agreed upon by the united states in congress assembled.

ARTICLE IX. The united states in congress assembled, shall have the sole and exclusive right and power of determining on peace and war, except in the cases mentioned in the sixth article—of sending and receiving ambassadors—entering into treaties and alliances, provided that no treaty of commerce shall be made whereby the legislative power of the respective states shall be restrained from imposing such imposts and duties on foreigners as their own people are subjected to, or from prohibiting the exportation or importation of any species of goods or commodities, whatsoever—of establishing rules for deciding in all cases, what captures on land or water shall be legal, and in what manner prizes taken by land or naval forces in the service of the united states shall be divided or appropriated—of granting letters of marque and reprisal in times of peace—appointing courts for the trial of piracies and felonies committed on the high seas and establishing courts for receiving and determining finally appeals in all cases of captures, provided that no member of congress shall be appointed a judge of any of the said courts.

The united states in congress assembled shall also be the last resort on appeal in all disputes and differences now subsisting or that hereafter may arise between two or more states concerning boundary, jurisdiction or any other cause whatever; which authority shall always be exercised in the manner following. Whenever the legislative or executive authority or lawful agent of any state in controversy with another shall present a petition to congress stating the matter in question and praying for a hearing, notice thereof shall be given by order of congress to the legislative or executive authority of the other state in controversy, and a day assigned for the appearance of the parties by their lawful agents, who shall then be directed to appoint by joint consent, commissioners or judges to constitute a court for hearing and determining the matter in question: but if they cannot agree, congress shall name three persons out of each of the united states, and from the list of such persons each party shall alternately strike out one, the petitioners beginning, until the number shall be reduced to thirteen; and from that number not less than seven, nor more than nine names as congress shall direct, shall in the presence of congress be drawn out by lot, and the persons whose names shall be so drawn or any five of them, shall be commissioners or judges, to hear and finally determine the controversy, so always as a major part of the judges who shall hear the cause shall agree in the determination: and if either party shall neglect to attend at the day appointed, without showing reasons, which congress shall judge sufficient, or being present shall refuse to strike, the congress shall proceed to nominate three persons out of each state, and the secretary of congress shall strike in behalf of such party absent or refusing; and the judgment and sentence of the court to be appointed, in the manner before prescribed, shall be final and conclusive; and if any of the parties shall refuse to submit to the authority of such court, or to appear or defend their claim or cause, the court shall nevertheless proceed to pronounce sentence, or judgment which shall in like manner be final and decisive, the judgment or sentence and other proceedings being in either case transmitted to congress, and lodged among the acts of congress for the security of the parties concerned: provided that every commissioner, before he sits in judgment, shall take an oath to be administered by one of the judges of the supreme or superior court of the state, where the cause shall be tried, "well and truly to hear and determine the matter in question, according to the best of his judgment, without favour, affection or hope of reward:" provided also, that no state shall be deprived of territory for the benefit of the united states.

All controversies concerning the private right of soil claimed under different grants of two or more states, whose jurisdictions as they may respect such lands, and the states which passed such grants are adjusted, the said grants or either of them being at the same time claimed to have originated antecedent to such settlement of jurisdiction, shall on the petition of either party to the congress of the united states, be finally determined as near as may be in the same manner as is before prescribed for deciding disputes respecting territorial jurisdiction between different states.

The united states in congress assembled shall also have the sole and exclusive right and power of regulating the alloy and value of coin struck by their own authority, or by that of the respective states—fixing the standard of weights and measures throughout the united states—regulating the trade and managing all affairs with the Indians, not members of any of the states, provided that the legislative right of any state within its own limits be not infringed or violated—establishing or regulating post-offices from one state to another, throughout all the united states, and exacting such postage on the papers passing thro' the same as may be requisite to defray the expences of the said office—appointing all officers of the land forces, in the service of the united states, excepting regimental officers—appointing all the officers of the naval forces, and commissioning all officers whatever in the service of the united states—making rules for the government and regulation of the said land and naval forces, and directing their operation.

The united states in congress assembled shall have authority to appoint a committee, to sit in the recess of congress, to be denominated "A Committee of the States," and to consist of one delegate from each state; and to appoint such other committees and civil officers as may be necessary for managing the general affairs of the united states under their direction—to appoint one of their number to preside, provided that no person be allowed to serve in the office of president more than one year in any term of three years; to ascertain the necessary sums of money to be raised for the service of the united states, and to appropriate and apply the same for defraying the public expences—to borrow money, or emit bills on the credit of the united states, transmitting every half year to the respective states an account of the sums of money so borrowed or emitted,—to build and equip a navy—to agree upon the number of land forces, and to make requisitions from each state for its quota, in proportion to the number of white inhabitants in such state; which requisition shall be binding, and thereupon the legislature of each state shall appoint the regimental officers, raise the men and cloath, arm and equip them in a soldier like manner, at the expence of the united states; and the officers and men so cloathed, armed and equipped shall march to the place appointed, and within the time agreed on by the united states in congress assembled: But if the united states in congress assembled shall, on consideration of circumstances judge proper that any state should not raise men, or should raise a smaller number than its quota, and that any other state should raise a greater number of men than the quota thereof, such extra number shall be raised, officered, cloathed, armed and equipped in the same manner as the quota of such state, unless the legislature of such state shall judge that such extra number cannot be safely spared out of the same, in which case they shall raise officer, cloath, arm and equip as many of such extra number as they judge can be safely spared. And the officers and men so cloathed, armed and equipped, shall march to the place appointed, and within the time agreed on by the united states in congress assembled.

The united states in congress assembled shall never engage in a war, nor grant letters of marque and reprisal in time of peace, nor enter into any treaties or alliances, nor coin money, nor regulate the value thereof, nor ascertain the sums and expences necessary for the defence and welfare of the united states, or any of them, nor emit bills, nor borrow money on the credit of the united states, nor appropriate money, nor agree upon the number of vessels of war, to be built or purchased, or the number of land or sea forces to be raised, nor appoint a commander in chief of the army or navy, unless nine states assent to the same: nor shall a question on any other point, except for adjourning from day to day be determined, unless by the votes of a majority of the united states in congress assembled.

The congress of the united states shall have power to adjourn to any time within the year, and to any place within the united states, so that no period of adjournment be for a longer duration than the space of six Months, and shall publish the Journal of their proceedings monthly, except such parts thereof relating to treaties, alliances or military operations, as in their judgment require secrecy; and the yeas and nays of the delegates of each state on any question shall be entered on the Journal, when it is desired by any delegate; and the delegates of a state, or any of them, at his or their request shall be furnished with a transcript of the said Journal, except such parts as are above excepted, to lay before the legislatures of the several states.

ARTICLE X. The committee of the states, or any nine of them, shall be authorized to execute, in the recess of congress, such of the powers of congress as the united states in congress assembled, by the consent of nine states, shall from time to time think expedient to vest them with; provided that no power be delegated to the said committee, for the exercise of which, by the articles of confederation, the voice of nine states in the congress of the united states assembled is requisite.

ARTICLE XI. Canada acceding to this confederation, and joining in the measures of the united states, shall be admitted into, and entitled to all the advantages of this union: but no other colony shall be admitted into the same, unless such admission be agreed to by nine states.

ARTICLE XII. All bills of credit emitted, monies borrowed and debts contracted by, or under the authority of congress, before the assembling of the united states, in pursuance of the present confederation, shall be deemed and considered as a charge against the united states, for payment and satisfaction whereof the said united states, and the public faith are hereby solemnly pledged.

ARTICLE XIII. Every state shall abide by the determinations of the united states in congress assembled, on all questions which by this confederation are submitted to them. And the Articles of this confederation shall be inviolably observed by every state, and the union shall be perpetual; nor shall any alteration at any time hereafter be made in any of them; unless such alteration be agreed to in a congress of the united states, and be afterwards confirmed by the legislatures of every state.

And Whereas it hath pleased the Great Governor of the World to incline the hearts of the legislatures we respectively represent in congress, to approve of, and to authorize us to ratify the said articles of confederation and perpetual union. Know Ye that we the undersigned delegates, by virtue of the power and authority to us given for that purpose, do by these presents, in the name and in behalf of our respective constituents, fully and entirely ratify and confirm each and every of the said articles of confederation and perpetual union, and all and singular the matters and things therein contained: And we do further solemnly plight and engage the faith of our respective constituents, that they shall abide by the determinations of the united states in congress assembled, on all questions, which by the said confederation are submitted to them. And that the articles thereof shall be inviolably observed by the states we respectively represent, and that the union shall be perpetual. In Witness whereof we have hereunto set our hands in Congress. Done at Philadelphia in the state of Pennsylvania the ninth day of July, in the Year of our Lord one Thousand seven Hundred and Seventy-eight, and in the third year of the independence of America.

JOSIAH BARTLETT,
JOHN WENTWORTH, JUNR
August 8th, 1778,
} On the part & behalf of the State of New Hampshire.

JOHN HANCOCK,
SAMUEL ADAMS,
ELBRIDGE GERRY,
FRANCIS DANA,
JAMES LOVELL,
SAMUEL HOLTEN,
} On the part and behalf of the State of Massachusetts Bay.

WILLIAM ELLERY,
HENRY MARCHANT,
JOHN COLLINS,
} On the part and behalf of the State of Rhode-Island and Providence Plantations.

ROGER SHERMAN,
SAMUEL HUNTINGTON,
OLIVER WOLCOTT,   } On the part and behalf of the State of Connecticut.
TITUS HOSMER,
ANDREW ADAMS,

JAS DUANE,
FRA: LEWIS,   } On the part and behalf of the State of New York.
WM DUER,
GOUVR MORRIS,

JNO WITHERSPOON,   } On the Part and in Behalf of the State of New
NATHL SCUDDER,   Jersey, November 26th, 1778.

ROBERT MORRIS,
DANIEL ROBERDEAU,
JON. BAYARD SMITH,   } On the part and behalf of the State of Pennsylvania.
WILLIAM CLINGAR,
JOSEPH REED,
  22d July, 1778,

THOS McKEAN,
  Febr 22d, 1779,
JOHN DICKINSON,   } On the part & behalf of the State of Delaware.
  May 5th, 1779,
NICHOLAS VAN DYKE,

JOHN HANSON,
  March 1, 1781,   } On the part and behalf of the State of Maryland.
DANIEL CARROLL, do

RICHARD HENRY LEE,
JOHN BANISTER,
THOMAS ADAMS,   } On the Part and Behalf of the State of Virginia.
JNO HARVIE,
FRANCIS LIGHTFOOT LEE,

JOHN PENN,
  July 21st, 1778,   } On the part and behalf of the State of North Caro-
CORNS HARNETT,   lina.
JNO WILLIAMS,

HENRY LAURENS,
WILLIAM HENRY DRAYTON,
JNO MATHEWS,   } On the part and on behalf of the State of South
RICHD HUTSON,   Carolina.
THOS HEYWARD, JUNR.

JNO WALTON,
  24th July, 1778,   } On the part and behalf of the State of Georgia.
EDWD TELFAIR,
EDWD LANGWORTHY,

APPENDIX E

The Constitution of the United States

We the People of the United States, in Order to form a more perfect Union, establish Justice, insure domestic Tranquility, provide for the common defence, promote the general Welfare, and secure the Blessings of Liberty to ourselves and our Posterity, do ordain and establish this Constitution for the United States of America.

ARTICLE. I.

SECTION. 1. All legislative Powers herein granted shall be vested in a Congress of the United States, which shall consist of a Senate and a House of Representatives.

SECTION. 2. The House of Representatives shall be composed of Members chosen every second Year by the People of the several States, and the Electors in each State shall have the Qualifications requisite for Electors of the most numerous Branch of the State Legislature.

No person shall be a Representative who shall not have attained to the Age of twenty five Years, and been seven Years a Citizen of the United States, and who shall not, when elected, be an Inhabitant of that State in which he shall be chosen.

Representatives and direct Taxes shall be apportioned among the several States which may be included within this Union, according to their respective Numbers, which shall be determined by adding to the whole Number of free Persons, including those bound to Service for a Term of Years, and excluding Indians not taxed, three fifths of all other Persons. The actual Enumeration shall be made within three Years after the first Meeting of the Congress of the United States, and within every subsequent Term of ten Years, in such Manner as they shall by Law direct. The Number of Representatives shall not exceed one for every thirty Thousand, but each State shall have at Least one Representative; and until such enumeration shall be made, the State of New Hampshire shall be entitled to chuse three, Massachusetts eight, Rhode-Island and Providence Plantations one, Connecticut five, New-York six, New Jersey four, Pennsylvania eight, Delaware one, Maryland six, Virginia ten, North Carolina five, South Carolina five, and Georgia three.

When vacancies happen in the Representation from any State, the Executive Authority thereof shall issue Writs of Election to fill such Vacancies.

The House of Representatives shall chuse their Speaker and other Officers; and shall have the sole Power of Impeachment.

SECTION. 3. The Senate of the United States shall be composed of two Senators from each State, chosen by the Legislature thereof, for six Years; and each Senator shall have one Vote.

1225

Immediately after they shall be assembled in Consequence of the first Election, they shall be divided as equally as may be into three Classes. The Seats of the Senators of the first Class shall be vacated at the Expiration of the second Year, of the second Class at the Expiration of the fourth Year, and of the third Class at the Expiration of the sixth Year, so that one third may be chosen every second Year; and if Vacancies happen by Resignation, or otherwise, during the Recess of the Legislature of any State, the Executive thereof may make temporary Appointments until the next Meeting of the Legislature, which shall then fill such Vacancies.

No Person shall be a Senator who shall not have attained to the Age of thirty Years, and been nine Years a Citizen of the United States, and who shall not, when elected, be an Inhabitant of that State for which he shall be chosen.

The Vice President of the United States shall be President of the Senate, but shall have no Vote, unless they be equally divided.

The Senate shall chuse their other Officers, and also a President pro tempore, in the Absence of the Vice President, or when he shall exercise the Office of President of the United States.

The Senate shall have the sole Power to try all Impeachments. When sitting for that Purpose, they shall be on Oath or Affirmation. When the President
is tried,
of the United States ∧ the Chief Justice shall preside: And no Person shall be convicted without the Concurrence of two thirds of the Members present.

Judgment in Cases of Impeachment shall not extend further than to removal from Office, and disqualification to hold and enjoy any Office of honor, Trust or Profit under the United States: but the Party convicted shall nevertheless be liable and subject to Indictment, Trial, Judgment and Punishment, according to Law.

Section. 4. The Times, Places and Manner of holding Elections for Senators and Representatives, shall be prescribed in each State by the Legislature thereof; but the Congress may at any time by Law make or alter such Regulations, except as to the Places of chusing Senators.

The Congress shall assemble at least once in every Year, and such Meeting shall be on the first Monday in December, unless they shall by Law appoint a different Day.

Section 5. Each House shall be the Judge of Elections, Returns and Qualifications of its own Members, and a Majority of each shall constitute a Quorum to do Business; but a smaller Number may adjourn from day to day, and may be authorized to compel the Attendance of Absent Members, in such Manner, and under such Penalties as each House may provide.

Each House may determine the Rules of its Proceedings, punish its Members for disorderly Behaviour, and, with the Concurrence of two thirds, expel a Member.

Each House shall keep a Journal of its Proceedings, and from time to time publish the same, excepting such Parts as may in their Judgment require Secrecy; and the Yeas and Nays of the Members of either House on any question shall, at the Desire of one fifth of those Present, be entered on the Journal.

Neither House, during the Session of Congress, shall, without the Consent of the other, adjourn for more than three days, nor to any other Place than that in which the two Houses shall be sitting.

Section. 6. The Senators and Representatives shall receive a Compensation for their Services, to be ascertained by Law, and paid out of the Treasury of the United States. They shall in all Cases, except Treason, Felony and Breach of the Peace, be privileged from Arrest during their Attendance at the Session of their respective Houses, and in going to and returning from the same; and for any Speech or Debate in either House, they shall not be questioned in any other Place.

No Senator or Representative shall, during the Time for which he was elected, be appointed to any civil Office under the Authority of the United States, which shall have been created, or the Emoluments whereof shall have been encreased during such time; and no Person holding any Office under the United States, shall be a Member of either House during his Continuance in Office.

Section. 7. All Bills for raising Revenue shall originate in the House of Representatives; but the Senate may propose or concur with Amendments as on other Bills.

Every Bill which shall have passed the House of Representatives and the Senate, shall, before it become a Law, be presented to the President of the United States; If he approve he shall sign it, but if not he shall return it, with his Objections to that House in which it shall have originated, who shall enter the Objections at large on their Journal, and proceed to reconsider it. If after such Reconsideration two thirds of that House shall agree to pass the Bill, it shall be sent, together with the Objections, to the other House, by which it shall likewise be reconsidered, and if approved by two thirds of that House, it shall become a Law. But in all such Cases the Votes of both Houses shall be determined by yeas and Nays, and the Names of the Persons voting for and against the Bill shall be entered on the Journal of each House respectively. If any Bill shall not be returned by the President within ten days (Sundays excepted) after it shall have been presented to him, the Same shall be a Law, in like Manner as if he had signed it, unless the Congress by their Adjournment prevent its Return in which Case it shall not be a Law.

Every Order, Resolution, or Vote to which the Concurrence of the Senate and House of Representatives may be necessary (except on a question of Adjournment) shall be presented to the President of the United States; and before the Same shall take Effect, shall be approved by him, or being disapproved by him, shall be repassed by two thirds of the Senate and House of Representatives, according to the Rules and Limitations prescribed in the Case of a Bill.

Section. 8. The Congress shall have Power To lay and collect Taxes, Duties, Imposts and Excises, to pay the Debts and provide for the common Defence and general Welfare of the United States; but all Duties, Imposts and Excises shall be uniform throughout the United States;

To borrow Money on the credit of the United States;

To regulate Commerce with foreign Nations, and among the several States, and with the Indian Tribes;

To establish an uniform Rule of Naturalization, and uniform Laws on the subject of Bankruptcies throughout the United States;

To coin Money, regulate the Value thereof, and of foreign Coin, and fix the Standard of Weights and Measures;

To provide for the Punishment of counterfeiting the Securities and current Coin of the United States;

To establish Post Offices and post Roads;

To promote the Progress of Science and useful Arts, by securing for limited

Times to Authors and Inventors the exclusive Right to their respective Writings and Discoveries;

To constitute Tribunals inferior to the supreme Court;

To define and punish Piracies and Felonies committed on the high Seas, and Offences against the Law of Nations;

To declare War, grant Letters of Marque and Reprisal, and make Rules concerning Captures on Land and Water;

To raise and support Armies, but no Appropriation of Money to that Use shall be for a longer Term than two Years;

To provide and maintain a Navy;

To make Rules for the Government and Regulation of the land and naval Forces;

To provide for calling forth the Militia to execute the Laws of the Union, suppress Insurrections and repel Invasions;

To provide for organizing, arming, and disciplining, the Militia, and for governing such Part of them as may be employed in the Service of the United States, reserving to the States respectively, the Appointment of the Officers, and the Authority of training the Militia according to the discipline prescribed by Congress;

To exercise exclusive Legislation in all Cases whatsoever, over such District (not exceeding ten Miles square) as may, by Cession of particular States, and the Acceptance of Congress, become the Seat of the Government of the United States, and to exercise like Authority over all Places purchased by the Consent of the Legislature of the State in which the Same shall be, for the Erection of Forts, Magazines, Arsenals, dock-Yards, and other needful Buildings;—And

To make all Laws which shall be necessary and proper for carrying into Execution the foregoing Powers, and all other Powers vested by this Constitution in the Government of the United States, or in any Department or Officer thereof.

SECTION. 9. The Migration or Importation of such Persons as any of the States now existing shall think proper to admit, shall not be prohibited by the Congress prior to the Year one thousand eight hundred and eight, but a Tax or duty may be imposed on such Importation, not exceeding ten dollars for each Person.

The Privilege of the Writ of Habeas Corpus shall not be suspended, unless when in Cases of Rebellion or Invasion the public Safety may require it.

No Bill of Attainder or ex post facto Law shall be passed.

No Capitation, or other direct, Tax shall be laid, unless in Proportion to the Census or Enumeration herein before directed to be taken.

No Tax or Duty shall be laid on Articles exported from any State.

No Preference shall be given by any Regulation of Commerce or Revenue to the Ports of one State over those of another: nor shall Vessels bound to, or from, one State, be obliged to enter, clear, or pay Duties in another.

No Money shall be drawn from the Treasury, but in Consequence of Appropriations made by Law; and a regular Statement and Account of the Receipts and Expenditures of all public Money shall be published from time to time.

No Title of Nobility shall be granted by the United States: And no Person holding any Office of Profit or Trust under them, shall, without the Consent of the Congress, accept of any present, Emolument, Office, or Title, of any kind whatever, from any King, Prince, or foreign State.

Section. 10. No State shall enter into any Treaty, Alliance, or Confederation; grant Letters of Marque and Reprisal; coin Money; emit Bills of Credit; make any Thing but gold and silver Coin a Tender in Payment of Debts; pass any Bill of Attainder, ex post facto Law, or Law impairing the Obligation of Contracts, or grant any Title of Nobility.

the
No State shall, without the Consent of ∧ Congress, lay any Imposts or Duties on Imports or Exports, except what may be absolutely necessary for executing it's inspection Laws: and the net Produce of all Duties and Imposts, laid by any State on Imports or Exports, shall be for the Use of the Treasury of the United States; and all such Laws shall be subject to the Revision and
the
Controul of ∧ Congress.

No State shall, without the Consent of Congress, lay any Duty of Tonnage, keep Troops, or Ships of War in time of Peace, enter into any Agreement or Compact with another State, or with a foreign Power, or engage in War, unless actually invaded, or in such imminent Danger as will not admit of delay.

Article. II.

Section. 1. The executive Power shall be vested in a President of the United States of America. He shall hold his Office during the Term of four Years, and, together with the Vice President, chosen for the same Term, be elected as follows

Each State shall appoint, in such Manner as the Legislature thereof may direct, a Number of Electors, equal to the whole Number of Senators and Representatives to which the State may be entitled in the Congress: but no Senator or Representative, or Person holding an Office of Trust or Profit under the United States, shall be appointed an Elector.

The Electors shall meet in their respective States, and vote by Ballot for two Persons, of whom one at least shall not be an Inhabitant of the same State with themselves. And they shall make a List of all the Persons voted for, and of the Number of Votes for each; which List they shall sign and certify, and transmit sealed to the Seat of the Government of the United States, directed to the President of the Senate. The President of the Senate shall, in the Presence of the Senate and House of Representatives, open all the Certificates, and the Votes shall then be counted. The Person having the greatest Number of Votes shall be the President, if such Number be a Majority of the whole Number of Electors appointed; and if there be more than one who have such Majority, and have an equal Number of Votes, then the House of Representatives shall immediately chuse by Ballot one of them for President; and if no Person have a Majority, then from the five highest on the List the said House shall in like Manner chuse the President. But in chusing the President, the Votes shall be taken by States, the Representation from each State having one Vote; A quorum for this Purpose shall consist of a Member or Members from two thirds of the States, and a Majority of all the States shall be necessary to a Choice. In every Case, after the Choice of the President, the Person having the greatest Number of Votes of the Electors shall be the Vice President. But if there should remain two or more who have equal Votes, the Senate shall chuse from them by Ballot the Vice President.

The Congress may determine the Time of chusing the Electors, and the Day on which they shall give their Votes; which Day shall be the same throughout the United States.

No Person except a natural born Citizen, or a Citizen of the United States, at the time of the Adoption of this Constitution, shall be eligible to the Office of President; neither shall any Person be eligible to that Office who shall not have attained to the Age of thirty five Years, and been fourteen Years a Resident within the United States.

In Case of the Removal of the President from Office, or of his Death, Resignation, or Inability to discharge the Powers and Duties of the said Office, the Same shall devolve on the Vice President, and the Congress may by Law provide for the Case of Removal, Death, Resignation or Inability, both of the President and Vice President, declaring what Officer shall then act as President, and such Officer shall then act accordingly, until the Disability be removed, or a President shall be elected.

The President shall, at stated Times, receive for his Services, a Compensation, which shall neither be encreased nor diminished during the Period for which he shall have been elected, and he shall not receive within that Period any other Emolument from the United States, or any of them.

Before he enter on the Execution of his Office, he shall take the following Oath or Affirmation:—"I do solemnly swear (or affirm) that I will faithfully execute the Office of President of the United States, and will to the best of my Ability, preserve, protect and defend the Constitution of the United States."

SECTION. 2. The President shall be Commander in Chief of the Army and Navy of the United States, and of the Militia of the several States, when called into the actual Service of the United States; he may require the Opinion, in writing, of the principal Officer in each of the executive Departments, upon any Subject relating to the Duties of their respective Offices, and he shall have Power to grant Reprieves and Pardons for Offences against the United States, except in Cases of Impeachment.

He shall have Power, by and with the Advice and Consent of the Senate, to make Treaties, provided two thirds of the Senators present concur; and he shall nominate, and by and with the Advice and Consent of the Senate, shall appoint Ambassadors, other public Ministers and Consuls, Judges of the supreme Court, and all other Officers of the United States, whose Appointments are not herein otherwise provided for, and which shall be established by Law: but the Congress may by Law vest the Appointment of such inferior Officers, as they think proper, in the President alone, in the Courts of Law, or in the Heads of Departments.

The President shall have Power to fill up all Vacancies that may happen during the Recess of the Senate, by granting Commissions which shall expire at the End of their next Session.

SECTION. 3. He shall from time to time give to the Congress Information of the State of the Union, and recommend to their Consideration such Measures as he shall judge necessary and expedient; he may, on extraordinary Occasions, convene both Houses, or either of them, and in Case of Disagreement between them, with Respect to the Time of Adjournment, he may adjourn them to such Time as he shall think proper; he shall receive Ambassadors and other public Ministers; he shall take Care that the Laws be faithfully executed, and shall Commission all the Officers of the United States.

SECTION. 4. The President, Vice President and all civil Officers of the United

States, shall be removed from Office on Impeachment for, and Conviction of, Treason, Bribery, or other high Crimes and Misdemeanors.

ARTICLE. III.

SECTION. 1. The judicial Power of the United States, shall be vested in one supreme Court, and in such inferior Courts as the Congress may from time to time ordain and establish. The Judges, both of the supreme and inferior Courts, shall hold their Offices during good Behaviour, and shall, at stated Times, receive for their Services, a Compensation, which shall not be diminished during their Continuance in Office.

SECTION. 2. The judicial Power shall extend to all Cases, in Law and Equity, arising under this Constitution, the Laws of the United States, and Treaties made, or which shall be made, under their Authority;—to all Cases affecting Ambassadors, other public Ministers and Consuls;—to all Cases of admiralty and maritime Jurisdiction;—to Controversies to which the United States shall be a Party;—to Controversies between two or more States;—between a State and Citizens of another State;—between Citizens of different States,—between Citizens of the same State claiming Lands under Grants of different States, and between a State, or the Citizens thereof, and foreign States, Citizens or Subjects.

In all cases affecting Ambassadors, other public Ministers and Consuls, and those in which a State shall be a Party, the supreme Court shall have original Jurisdiction. In all the other Cases before mentioned, the Supreme Court shall have appellate Jurisdiction, both as to Law and Fact, with such Exceptions, and under such Regulations as the Congress shall make.

The Trial of all Crimes, except in Cases of Impeachment, shall be by Jury; and such Trial shall be held in the State where the said Crimes shall have been committed; but when not committed within any State, the Trial shall be at such Place or Places as the Congress may by Law have directed.

SECTION. 3. Treason against the United States, shall consist only in levying War against them, or in adhering to their Enemies, giving them Aid and Comfort. No Person shall be convicted of Treason unless on the Testimony of two Witnesses to the same overt Act, or on Confession in open Court.

The Congress shall have Power to declare the Punishment of Treason, but no Attainder of Treason shall work Corruption of Blood, or Forfeiture except during the Life of the Person attainted.

ARTICLE. IV.

SECTION. 1. Full Faith and Credit shall be given in each State to the public Acts, Records, and judicial Proceedings of every other State. And the Congress may by general Laws prescribe the Manner in which such Acts, Records and Proceedings shall be proved, and the Effect thereof.

SECTION. 2. The Citizens of each State shall be entitled to all Privileges and Immunities of Citizens in the several States.

A Person charged in any State with Treason, Felony, or other Crime, who shall flee from Justice, and be found in another State, shall on Demand of the executive Authority of the State from which he fled, be delivered up, to be removed to the State having Jurisdiction of the Crime.

No Person held to Service or Labour in one State, under the Laws thereof, escaping into another, shall, in Consequence of any Law or Regulation therein, be discharged from such Service or Labour, but shall be delivered up on Claim of the Party to whom such Service or Labour may be due.

SECTION. 3. New States may be admitted by the Congress into this Union; but no new State shall be formed or erected within the Jurisdiction of any other State; nor any State be formed by the Junction of two or more States, or Parts of States, without the Consent of the Legislatures of the States concerned as well as of the Congress.

The Congress shall have Power to dispose of and make all needful Rules and Regulations respecting the Territory or other Property belonging to the United States; and nothing in this Constitution shall be so construed as to Prejudice any Claims of the United States, or of any particular State.

SECTION. 4. The United States shall guarantee to every State in this Union a Republican Form of Government, and shall protect each of them against Invasion; and on Application of the Legislature, or of the Executive (when the Legislature cannot be convened) against domestic Violence.

ARTICLE. V.

The Congress, whenever two thirds of both Houses shall deem it necessary, shall propose Amendments to this Constitution, or, on the Application of the Legislatures of two thirds of the several States, shall call a Convention for proposing Amendments, which, in either Case, shall be valid to all Intents and Purposes, as Part of this Constitution, when ratified by the Legislatures of three fourths of the several States, or by Conventions in three fourths thereof, as the one or the other Mode of Ratification may be proposed by the Congress; Provided that no Amendment which may be made prior to the Year One thousand eight hundred and eight shall in any Manner affect the first and fourth Clauses in the Ninth Section of the first Article; and that no State, without its Consent, shall be deprived of it's equal Suffrage in the Senate.

ARTICLE. VI.

All Debts contracted and Engagements entered into, before the Adoption of this Constitution, shall be as valid against the United States under this Constitution, as under the Confederation.

This Constitution, and the Laws of the United States which shall be made in Pursuance thereof; and all Treaties made, or which shall be made, under the Authority of the United States, shall be the supreme Law of the Land; and the Judges in every State shall be bound thereby, any Thing in the Constitution or Laws of any State to the Contrary notwithstanding.

The Senators and Representatives before mentioned, and the Members of the several State Legislatures, and all executive and judicial Officers, both of the United States and of the several States, shall be bound by Oath or Affirmation, to support this Constitution; but no religious Test shall ever be required as a Qualification to any Office or public Trust under the United States.

ARTICLE. VII.

The Ratification of the Conventions of nine States, shall be sufficient for the Establishment of this Constitution between the States so ratifying the Same.

The Word, "the," being interlined between the seventh and eighth Lines of the first Page, The Word "Thirty" being done in Convention by the Unanimous Consent of the States present the Seventeenth Day of September in the Year of partly written on an Erazure in the fifteenth Line of the first Page, The Words "is tried" being interlined between the thirty second and thirty third Lines of the First Page and the Word "the" being interlined between the forty third and forty fourth Lines of the second Page.

Attest WILLIAM JACKSON Secretary

our Lord one thousand seven hundred and Eighty seven and of the Independence of the United States of America the Twelfth In witness whereof We have hereunto subscribed our Names,

G⁰ WASHINGTON—Presid ͭ
and deputy from Virginia

New Hampshire	JOHN LANGDON NICHOLAS GILMAN
Massachusetts	NATHANIEL GORHAM RUFUS KING
Connecticut	Wᴹ Samᴸ JOHNSON ROGER SHERMAN
New York	ALEXANDER HAMILTON
New Jersey	WIL: LIVINGSTON DAVID BREARLEY Wᴹ PATERSON JONA: DAYTON
Pennsylvania	B FRANKLIN THOMAS MIFFLIN Robᵀ MORRIS GEO. CLYMER Thoˢ FITZSIMONS JARED INGERSOLL JAMES WILSON GOUV MORRIS
Delaware	GEO: READ GUNNING BEDFORD JUN JOHN DICKINSON RICHARD BASSETT JACO: BROOM
Maryland	JAMES MCHENRY DAN OF Sᴛ Thoˢ JENIFER Danᴸ CARROLL
Virginia	JOHN BLAIR— JAMES MADISON JR.
North Carolina	Wᴹ BLOUNT Richᴰ DOBBS SPAIGHT HU WILLIAMSON
South Carolina	J. RUTLEDGE CHARLES COTESWORTH PINCKNEY CHARLES PINCKNEY PIERCE BUTLER
Georgia	WILLIAM FEW ABR BALDWIN

LETTER OF THE PRESIDENT OF THE FEDERAL CONVENTION, DATED SEPTEMBER 17, 1787, TO THE PRESIDENT OF CONGRESS, TRANSMITTING THE CONSTITUTION

IN CONVENTION, September 17, 1787.

SIR,

We have now the honor to submit to the consideration of the United States in Congress assembled, that Constitution which has appeared to us the most adviseable.

The friends of our country have long seen and desired, that the power of making war, peace, and treaties, that of levying money and regulating commerce, and the correspondent executive and judicial authorities should be fully and effectually vested in the general government of the Union: But the impropriety of delegating such extensive trust to one body of men is evident—Hence results the necessity of a different organization.

It is obviously impracticable in the federal government of these states, to secure all rights of independent sovereignty to each, and yet provide for the interest and safety of all: Individuals entering into society, must give up a share of liberty to preserve the rest. The magnitude of the sacrifice must depend as well on situation and circumstance, as on the object to be obtained. It is at all times difficult to draw with precision the line between those rights which must be surrendered, and those which may be reserved; and on the present occasion this difficulty was encreased by a difference among the several states as to their situation, extent, habits, and particular interests.

In all our deliberations on this subject we kept steadily in our view, that which appears to us the greatest interest of every true American, the consolidation of our Union, in which is involved our prosperity, felicity, safety, perhaps our national existence. This important consideration, seriously and deeply impressed on our minds, led each state in the Convention to be less rigid on points of inferior magnitude, than might have been otherwise expected; and thus the Constitution, which we now present, is the result of a spirit of amity, and of that mutual deference and concession which the peculiarity of our political situation rendered indispensible.

That it will meet the full and entire approbation of every state is not perhaps to be expected; but each will doubtless consider, that had her interest been alone consulted, the consequences might have been particularly disagreeable or injurious to others; that it is liable to as few exceptions as could reasonably have been expected, we hope and believe; that it may promote the lasting welfare of that country so dear to us all, and secure her freedom and happiness, is our most ardent wish.

With great respect, We have the honor to be, Sir,

Your Excellency's

most obedient and humble servants,

GEORGE WASHINGTON, President.

By unanimous Order of the Convention.

His Excellency the PRESIDENT OF CONGRESS.

RESOLUTION OF THE FEDERAL CONVENTION SUBMITTING THE CONSTITUTION TO CONGRESS, SEPTEMBER 17, 1787.

In Convention Monday September 17th 1787.

Present

The States of

New Hampshire, Massachusetts, Connecticut, Mr Hamilton from New York, New Jersey, Pennsylvania, Delaware, Maryland, Virginia, North Carolina, South Carolina and Georgia.

Resolved,

That the preceeding Constitution be laid before the United States in Congress assembled, and that it is the Opinion of this Convention, that it should afterwards be submitted to a Convention of Delegates, chosen in each State by the People thereof, under the Recommendation of its Legislature, for their Assent and Ratification; and that each Convention assenting to, and ratifying the Same, should give Notice thereof to the United States in Congress assembled.

Resolved, That it is the Opinion of this Convention, that as soon as the Conventions of nine States shall have ratified this Constitution, the United States in Congress assembled should fix a Day on which Electors should be appointed by the States which shall have ratified the same, and a Day on which the Electors should assemble to vote for the President, and the Time and Place for commencing Proceedings under this Constitution. That after such Publication the Electors should be appointed, and the Senators and Representatives elected: That the Electors should meet on the Day fixed for the Election of the President, and should transmit their Votes certified, signed, sealed and directed, as the Constitution requires, to the Secretary of the United States in Congress assembled, and that the Senators and Representatives should convene at the Time and Place assigned; that the Senators should appoint a President of the Senate, for the sole Purpose of receiving, opening and counting the Votes for President; and, that after he shall be chosen, the Congress, together with the President, should, without Delay, proceed to execute this Constitution.

By the Unanimous Order of the Convention

Go Washington Presidt

W. Jackson Secretary

AMENDMENTS TO THE CONSTITUTION

Article I

Congress shall make no law respecting an establishment of religion, or prohibiting the free exercise thereof; or abridging the freedom of speech, or of the press; or of the right of the people peaceably to assemble, and to petition the Government for a redress of grievances.

Article II

A well regulated Militia, being necessary to the security of a free State, the right of the people to keep and bear Arms, shall not be infringed.

ARTICLE III

No Soldier shall, in time of peace be quartered in any house, without the consent of the Owner, nor in time of war, but in a manner prescribed by law.

ARTICLE IV

The right of the people to be secure in their persons, houses, papers, and effects, against unreasonable searches and seizures, shall not be violated, and no Warrants shall issue, but upon probable cause, supported by Oath or affirmation, and particularly describing the place to be searched, and the persons or things to be seized.

ARTICLE V

No person shall be held to answer for a capital, or otherwise infamous crime, unless on a presentment or indictment of a Grand Jury, except in cases arising in the land or naval forces, or in the Militia, when in actual service in time of War or public danger; nor shall any person be subject for the same offence to be twice put in jeopardy of life or limb; nor shall be compelled in any criminal case to be a witness against himself, nor be deprived of life, liberty, or property, without due process of law; nor shall private property be taken for public use, without just compensation.

ARTICLE VI

In all criminal prosecutions, the accused shall enjoy the right to a speedy and public trial, by an impartial jury of the State and district wherein the crime shall have been committed, which district shall have been previously ascertained by law, and to be informed of the nature and cause of the accusation; to be confronted with the witnesses against him; to have compulsory process for obtaining witnesses in his favor, and to have the Assistance of Counsel for his defence.

ARTICLE VII

In Suits at common law, where the value in controversy shall exceed twenty dollars, the right of trial by jury shall be preserved, and no fact tried by a jury, shall be otherwise re-examined in any Court of the United States, than according to the rules of the common law.

ARTICLE VIII

Excessive bail shall not be required, nor excessive fines imposed, nor cruel and unusual punishments inflicted.

ARTICLE IX

The enumeration in the Constitution, of certain rights, shall not be construed to deny or disparage others retained by the people.

ARTICLE X

The powers not delegated to the United States by the Constitution, nor prohibited by it to the States, are reserved to the States respectively, or to the people.

Article XI

The Judicial power of the United States shall not be construed to extend to any suit in law or equity, commenced or prosecuted against one of the United States by Citizens of another State, or by Citizens or Subjects of any Foreign State.

Article XII

The Electors shall meet in their respective states, and vote by ballot for President and Vice-President, one of whom, at least, shall not be an inhabitant of the same state with themselves; they shall name in their ballots the person voted for as President, and in distinct ballots the person voted for as Vice-President, and they shall make distinct lists of all persons voted for as President, and of all persons voted for as Vice-President, and of the number of votes for each, which lists they shall sign and certify, and transmit sealed to the seat of the government of the United States, directed to the President of the Senate;—The President of the Senate shall, in the presence of the Senate and House of Representatives, open all the certificates and the votes shall then be counted;—The person having the greatest number of votes for President, shall be the President, if such number be a majority of the whole number of Electors appointed; and if no person have such majority, then from the persons having the highest numbers not exceeding three on the list voted for as President, the House of Representatives shall choose immediately, by ballot, the President. But in choosing the President, the votes shall be taken by states, the representation from each state having one vote; a quorum for this purpose shall consist of a member or members from two-thirds of the states, and a majority of all the states shall be necessary to a choice. And if the House of Representatives shall not choose a President whenever the right of choice shall devolve upon them, before the fourth day of March next following, then the Vice-President shall act as President, as in the case of the death or other constitutional disability of the President.—The person having the greatest number of votes as Vice-President, shall be the Vice-President, if such number be a majority of the whole number of Electors appointed, and if no person have a majority, then from the two highest numbers on the list, the Senate shall choose the Vice-President; a quorum for the purpose shall consist of two-thirds of the whole number of Senators, and a majority of the whole number shall be necessary to a choice. But no person constitutionally ineligible to the office of President shall be eligible to that of Vice-President of the United States.

Article XIII

Section 1. Neither slavery nor involutary servitude, except as a punishment for crime whereof the party shall have been duly convicted, shall exist within the United States, or any place subject to their jurisdiction.

Section 2. Congress shall have power to enforce this article by appropriate legislation.

Article XIV

Section 1. All persons born or naturalized in the United States, and subject to the jurisdiction thereof, are citizens of the United States and of the State wherein they reside. No State shall make or enforce any law which shall abridge the privileges or immunities of citizens of the United States; nor shall any State deprive any person of life, liberty, or property, without due process of law; nor deny to any person within its jurisdiction the equal protection of the laws.

Section 2. Representatives shall be apportioned among the several States according to their respective numbers, counting the whole number of persons in each State, excluding Indians not taxed. But when the right to vote at any election for the choice of electors for President and Vice President of the United States, Representatives in Congress, the Executive and Judicial officers of a State, or the members of the Legislature thereof, is denied to any of the male inhabitants of such State, being twenty-one years of age, and citizens of the United States, or in any way abridged, except for participation in rebellion, or other crime, the basis of representation therein shall be reduced in the proportion which the number of such male citizens shall bear to the whole number of male citizens twenty-one years of age in such State.

Section 3. No person shall be a Senator or Representative in Congress, or elector of President and Vice President, or hold any office, civil or military under the United States, or under any State, who, having previously taken an oath, as a member of Congress, or as an officer of the United States, or as a member of any State legislature, or as an executive or judicial officer of any State, to support the Constitution of the United States, shall have engaged in insurrection or rebellion against the same, or given aid or comfort to the enemies thereof. But Congress may by a vote of two-thirds of each House, remove such disability.

Section 4. The validity of the public debt of the United States, authorized by law, including debts incurred for payment of pensions and bounties for services in suppressing insurrection or rebellion, shall not be questioned. But neither the United States nor any State shall assume or pay any debt or obligation incurred in aid of insurrection or rebellion against the United States, or any claim for the loss or emancipation of any slave; but all such debts, obligations and claims shall be held illegal and void.

Section 5. The Congress shall have power to enforce, by appropriate legislation, the provisions of this article.

Article XV

Section 1. The right of citizens of the United States to vote shall not be denied or abridged by the United States or by any State on account of race, color, or previous condition of servitude—

Section 2. The Congress shall have power to enforce this article by appropriate legislation.—

Article XVI

The Congress shall have power to lay and collect taxes on incomes, from whatever source derived, without apportionment among the several States, and without regard to any census or enumeration.

Article XVII

The Senate of the United States shall be composed of two Senators from each State, elected by the people thereof, for six years; and each Senator shall have one vote. The electors in each State shall have the qualifications requisite for electors of the most numerous branch of the State legislatures.

When vacancies happen in the representation of any State in the Senate, the executive authority of such State shall issue writs of election to fill such vacancies: *Provided*, that the legislature of any State may empower the executive thereof to make temporary appointments until the people fill the vacancies by election as the legislature may direct.

This amendment shall not be so construed as to affect the election or term of any Senator chosen before it becomes valid as part of the Constitution.

ARTICLE XVIII

SECTION 1. After one year from the ratification of this article the manufacture, sale, or transportation of intoxicating liquors within, the importation thereof into, or the exportation thereof from the United States and all territory subject to the jurisdiction thereof for beverage purposes is hereby prohibited.

SEC. 2. The Congress and the several States shall have concurrent power to enforce this article by appropriate legislation.

SEC. 3. This article shall be inoperative unless it shall have been ratified as an amendment to the Constitution by the legislatures of the several States, as provided in the Constitution, within seven years from the date of the submission hereof to the States by the Congress.

ARTICLE XIX

The right of citizens of the United States to vote shall not be denied or abridged by the United States or by any State on account of sex.

Congress shall have power to enforce this article by appropriate legislation.

ARTICLE XX

SECTION 1. The terms of the President and Vice President shall end at noon on the 20th day of January, and the terms of Senators and Representatives at noon on the 3d day of January, of the years in which such terms would have ended if this article had not been ratified; and the terms of their successors shall then begin.

SEC. 2. The Congress shall assemble at least once in every year, and such meeting shall begin at noon on the 3d day of January, unless they shall by law appoint a different day.

SEC. 3. If, at the time fixed for the beginning of the term of the President, the President elect shall have died, the Vice President elect shall become President. If a President shall not have been chosen before the time fixed for the beginning of his term, or if the President elect shall have failed to qualify, then the Vice President elect shall act as President until a President shall have qualified; and the Congress may by law provide for the case wherein neither a President elect nor a Vice President elect shall have qualified, declaring who shall then act as President, or the manner in which one who is to act shall be selected, and such person shall act accordingly until a President or Vice President shall have qualified.

SEC. 4. The Congress may by law provide for the case of the death of any of the persons from whom the House of Representatives may choose a President whenever the right of choice shall have devolved upon them, and for the case of the death of any of the persons from whom the Senate may choose a Vice President whenever the right of choice shall have devolved upon them.

SEC. 5. Sections 1 and 2 shall take effect on the 15th day of October following the ratification of this article.

SEC. 6. This article shall be inoperative unless it shall have been ratified as an amendment to the Constitution by the legislatures of three-fourths of the several States within seven years from the date of its submission.

ARTICLE XXI

SECTION 1. The eighteenth article of amendment to the Constitution of the United States is hereby repealed.

SEC. 2. The transportation or importation into any State, Territory, or possession of the United States for delivery or use therein of intoxicating liquors, in violation of the laws thereof, is hereby prohibited.

SEC. 3. This article shall be inoperative unless it shall have been ratified as an amendment to the Constitution by conventions in the several States, as provided in the Constitution, within seven years from the date of the submission hereof to the States by the Congress.

ARTICLE XXII

No person shall be elected to the office of the President more than twice, and no person who has held the office of President, or acted as President, for more than two years of a term to which some other person was elected President shall be elected to the office of the President more than once. But this Article shall not apply to any person holding the office of President when this Article was proposed by the Congress, and shall not prevent any person who may be holding the office of President, or acting as President, during the term within which this Article becomes operative from holding the office of President or acting as President during the remainder of such term.

APPENDIX F

Letter of Jasper Yeates to William Tilghman
Reproduced by Permission of the Historical
Society of Pennsylvania

LANCASTER July 20. 1806.

DEAR SIR

I have received your Favor of the 17th Instant.—The Appointment of the Court of nisi prius, to be held for two Weeks on the 24th November, is very agreeable to me. But it would seem, that the late Law cannot be well executed, unless by the Adoption of some general System. Besides the Advantage of the Times of the Sittings being generally known & the consequent Benefits of convenient Preparations for Trial, there is no other Mode of equalizing our own Labors.—Sittings of four Weeks twice in the Year, the one immediately after the December Term or before the March Term, and the other at a convenient Day after our Return from the Spring Circuit, would tend to cleanse the Augean Stable. These Periods I would have fixed so as to suit the Gentlemen of the Profession as much as possible, and we would be enabled to arrange our private Affairs so as to meet every probable Contingency, with the smallest Inconvenience to ourselves. I think we talked of some such Plan at our last Conference: Pray turn it over in [y]our Mind, or Suggest some other System.

Mr. Brackenridge called on me three Days ago, and said it would be proper that our several Tours on the ensuing Circuit should be ascertained, and that I had the Choice between the new Counties & the Westmoreland &c. Circuit. I informed him, that my present State of Health was so precarious, that it was highly uncertain, whether I should be able to go on to Pittsburgh; but if I could accomplish that Journey, I would go to the Counties North & West of the Allegheny. Motives of a public as well as private Nature, induced this Option.—

Should my Health admit of this distant Ride, I must confer with my Friends on the Bench, as to the Construction to be put on the Law of 3d April 1792. I have read with great Care, the Opinion of the Majority of the Judges of the Supreme Court of the United States, but I cannot reconcile it to my own Ideas of the Meaning of the Act. If such had been the Judgment of our Court of Errors & Appeals, the Path of Conduct would be easy & could not be mistaken. Tho' my Doubts might not be removed or my individual Sentiments changed, they would be over-ruled, & my Acquiescence would be the necessary Consequence, in Order to preserve an Uniformity of Decision. But will this apply to the relative Situation of our own Judiciary with that of the Union? Is it implied by the two Constitutions, that the Opinion of the Highest Court in the Union on a *State Law*, shall be the paramount Rule of Construction binding on the State Courts? Is not our Honor,—our Integrity & Independence contemplated by our Constitution as a Barrier for the Citizens in such a Case?

I can see a plain Difference between the Construction of a Treaty with foreign Powers, or a Law of the United States, and a Law of our own State which may be decided on by the Judiciary of the Union. Upon Principles of public Policy, Safety & Security, the Opinion in the first Cases thus expressed would seem to have a controlling Operation on ourselves. But will this Reasoning hold, when a State Law is the mere Object of Disquisition? On the other Hand, it appears to be a strange Solecism in Jurisprudence, that the same Subject should receive different Determinations, in the different Courts of one connected Government! Shall the Rights of Foreigners and Citizens of other States be judged of by other Rules, than are applied in the Cases of our own Citizens! Would not this be the Adoption of the Measure of the Chancellor's Foot in landed Titles, with a Vengeance!

I have conversed with some of my professional Friends on this Subject: Their Opinion *generally* has been that we are bound to follow the Precedent set to us by the Supreme Court of U.S. But I see great Difficulties in the Way; the more I reflect on the Matter, my Difficulties are increased.—I must request you & Judge Smith to take the Affair into Consideration, & inform me of the Result when I have the Pleasure of seeing you.

The Paroxysm of my Gout is passed, but my Feet remain very tender, & ill support my body. With my large Cloth Shoes on, I shuffled painfully over two Squares on Friday last; but it cost me a Night's Sleep. If I possess this cursed Disorder by Hereditary Right (as I clearly think, I do) and if my Ancestors have entailed it on their Descendents by their voluntary Acts, what must they not have to answer for?

My best Respects to Judge Smith. I am with Esteem

Dear Sir

Your very obedient Servt.

J: YEATES

HONORABLE WILLIAM TILGHMAN, ESQ.

APPENDIX G

The Supreme Court's First Paid Reporter

The resentment aroused, in certain quarters, by the sweeping doctrines of *Martin* v. *Hunter's Lessee*, 1 Wheat. 304 (1816), is well indicated by the history of a certain bill that friends of the Supreme Court, in Congress, were seeking to get enacted when the case was decided. The bill was one to provide the Court with a paid reporter of its decisions. The proposal was to pay the reporter an annual salary of one thousand dollars, conditioned upon his prompt publication of each year's cases, and to allow him to make whatever, in addition, he could, from the sale of the reports. Much time was spent over this simple bill by both the Senate and the House, in committee of the whole. Of what was said, there appears to be no record. The bill, however, had finally passed the Senate and was under consideration, in committee of the whole House, on March 20, 1816, when *Martin* v. *Hunter* was decided. (Annals, XXIX, 142, 146, 178, 181, 184, 1202, 1207, and 1222.)

In so important a case, the Washington newspapers, it might naturally be supposed, must have been given the Supreme Court's opinion for publication. Instead, however, they were given only Justice William Johnson's separate opinion concurring in the result in the case, but not in much of the reasoning of the Court. This odd action is the first of the evidence that opposition to the Supreme Court's appellate jurisdiction over the courts of the states was what lay behind the slow progress the bill for the paid reporter was making. For Justice Johnson's opinion was very different from the one Justice Story had delivered for the Court.

The Johnson opinion *began* with a declaration that, because the Court, in the Martin case, had "disavow[ed] all intention to decide on [its] right to issue compulsory process to the state courts," the case had left the Supreme Court "*where*"—"in [Justice Johnson's] opinion"—"*the constitution* and laws [of Congress had] place[d it]*—supreme over persons and cases as far as [its] judicial powers extend[ed], *but not asserting any compulsory control over the state tribunals.*"* The Justice then proceeded to argue, in a very strange way, that the provision, in section 25 of the Judiciary Act, empowering the Supreme Court, "at their discretion," to execute their own judgments upon appeals from state courts, in any case wherein the state courts should prove recalcitrant, was actually intended as a recognition of *the state courts' right* to disobey a Supreme Court mandate of reversal, as the Virginia Court of Appeals had done. It is true, before he finished, he had also managed to say, *in the middle of his long opinion*, that it was "a momentous question" whether the judiciary provisions of the Constitution "d[id] not *necessarily*

---

* Justice Story had said: "We have not thought it incumbent on us to give any opinion upon the question, whether this court have authority to issue a writ of mandamus to the court of appeals to enforce the former judgments, as we do not think it necessarily involved in the decision of this cause." 1 Wheat. 362. As to what was probably meant by this, see footnote at page 806 *supra*.

carry with [them] a right to exercise appellate power *over the state tribunals*"—
by which, he made clear, he meant "*compulsory control* over [them]." And
seemingly forgetful of his initial assertion, he added that this was a question
"on which [he] sh[ould] reserve [him]self uncommitted for each particular
case as it sh[ould] occur." "It [was] enough, at present, to have shown that
congress ha[d], not asserted, and th[e] court ha[d] not attempted, to exercise
that kind of authority *in personam* over the state courts which would place
them in the relation of an inferior responsible body *without their own acquiescence*." "God forbid," he said, "that the judicial power in these states should
ever, for a moment, even in its humblest departments, feel a doubt of its own
independence." And then he *wound up* his very odd opinion with the con-
fident-seeming, but self-contradictory assertion that "the full extent of the
constitutional revising power m[ight] be secured to the United States, and
the benefits of it to the individual, without ever resorting to compulsory or
restrictive process upon the state tribunals; a right which, I repeat again,"
he said, "congress has not asserted, nor does there appear any necessity for
asserting." (1 Wheat. 362, 365–67, 376–77, and 381–82.)

The foregoing opinion of Justice Johnson's was the only thing published,
at the time, about the Court's decision in the Martin case. It appeared in
the semi-official *Daily National Intelligencer*, on April 6th. The House of
Representatives nevertheless voted, a short while later, to discharge its
committee from further consideration of the bill to provide the Court with
its paid reporter; and the bill itself was indefinitely postponed. (Annals, XXIX,
1458.) In the Senate, a proposal for a very badly needed increase in the
salaries of the Justices was likewise indefinitely postponed. (*Ibid.*, 193, 231–33,
and 234.)

That the action the House took with reference to the bill for the paid
reporter was due to opposition the Court had aroused by its opinion in the
Martin case is not actually of record; but the difficulties this simple bill had
been having anyway, and the extraordinary action of withholding the Court's
opinion from the newspapers and giving them, instead, Justice Johnson's
strange and self-contradictory views, make such an explanation of the House's
action seem probable. And the correctness of this conjecture is confirmed
by what happened in Congress the next winter. For, when Congress met
again, in December, the Judiciary Committee of the House reported another
bill, similar to that which had been postponed in the spring; and three days
later, after what, apparently, was a rather extended debate, the House de-
feated the bill "by a vote of 76 to about 40." The debate on the bill was not
reported; but a brief summary of it appeared in the *National Intelligencer*
and was later reprinted in the *Annals of Congress*. It appears, from this, that
the friends of the bill "urged the great importance of having correct and
early reports of the decisions of a court, whose decrees," they said, "*if not
law in themselves, [were] evidence of the law*."* They also urged "the advantage of a reporter of proper abilities, made responsible for the proper
exercise of his duties." These things, they said, the bill would secure. And
without the "inducement" it provided, they were afraid no reports of the
Court's cases would be published. Some of the states, they added, had deemed
the reporting of the decisions of their local supreme courts, so important
that they were paying more to their reporters than the bill proposed to pay

---

* This meant that they were binding precedents. *Cf.*, *Swift v. Tyson*, 16 Pet. 1
(1842); also Blackstone, I, 69.

"to a reporter of the decisions of *a higher court*." The opposition replied by attacking the bill, though without the slightest warrant, as a proposal to create a monopoly, whereas the right to publish the Court's decisions ought, they said, to be free to all. They also argued that, inasmuch as "the effect" of the Supreme Court's decisions would "pervade the Union," the demand for reports of its cases would be so great that no salary need be paid to induce some man of ability to undertake their publication. And one of their number, probably more candid than the rest, declared that he was against the bill because he "was opposed to any act which would sanction the idea of [the Supreme Court's decisions] having a permanent effect over the law, or [which would] make [the Court's] constructions of laws binding on their successors *and on other authorities.*" (*Ibid.*, XXX, 357 and 366–67.) So, it is clear the Court's opinion in the Martin case was causing some, at least, of the trouble.

The friends of the Court, in Congress, in spite of their two defeats, apparently determined to make another attempt to obtain a paid reporter for the Court. This time, they began in the Senate; and Dudley Chase, of Vermont, one of the Senate's Judiciary Committee, wrote Chief Justice Marshall, asking " '[his] views relative to the object and utility of the proposed act.' " The Chief Justice replied on the 7th of February 1817. (*American State Papers*, Class X, Vol. II, pp. 419–20.) The letter he wrote was in the nature of an argument in support of the bill. Written, apparently, to meet the views of the opposition in Congress, as the *Intelligencer* had reported them, the letter suggests, without actually expressing them, views of the Supreme Court's appellate jurisdiction over the courts of the states, which it is utterly impossible to reconcile with John Marshall's earlier behavior, as lawyer and litigant, in 1795–96–and, for that matter, as a litigant, in 1813 and 1816–in seeking to settle the title to the Fairfax estate, through a Supreme Court decision in an ejectment action relating merely to a tiny part of that estate. (See chapter xxiv hereof.) In addition to this, the views hinted in this letter are of a kind impossible to reconcile with Marshall's action, as Chief Justice, in 1805, in deciding the case of *Huidekoper* v. *Douglass* as he did; for, unless the Court's decision in that case was going to settle the Holland Land Company's title to its West Allegheny lands, it was a frivolous thing to disregard the Pennsylvania state-court precedents. (See chapter xxiii hereof.) And the views the Chief Justice suggested in his letter were likewise inconsistent with the actual decision the Supreme Court had made in his own Fairfax case, in 1813; and with the views which five of his six brethren on the Court had expressed in his Martin case, in the year before; views, it may be added, with which, according to Justice Story, fifteen years later, the Chief Justice, though not, of course, participating in the case, had fully concurred. (See W. W. Story, *Life and Letters of Joseph Story* [Boston, 1851], II, 49.) The only thing in the past of the Court which the Chief Justice's vague hints in this letter of 1817 at all resembled was Justice Johnson's separate opinion in the Martin case, which had been given to the Washington newspapers, in somewhat similar circumstances, in the spring before. So, the reasonable conclusion would seem to be that the Chief Justice's letter was written merely to procure the passage of the bill pending in Congress. The vague hints it contained would in no way bind the Court; and the Court, at the time, had the services of an extraordinarily able reporter, Henry Wheaton, whom they were no doubt anxious to retain. And for the purpose for which the letter was written, it was successful. It was communicated to the Senate on the day Marshall wrote it, and was no doubt afterwards made known to the House; and on the

1st of March 1817, the bill for the Court's paid reporter became a law. (Annals, XXX, 90, 96–97, 108, 131, 132, 193, 996, 1019, 1043, and 1044.)

The letter ran as follows:

"WASHINGTON, February 7, 1817

"SIR:

"Your letter, enclosing a copy of the bill to provide for reports of the decisions of the Supreme Court, in which you do me the honor to request, for the committee, 'my views relative to the object and utility of the proposed act,' was yesterday received, and communicated to the judges. We all concur in the opinion that the object of the bill is in a high degree desirable.

"That the cases determined in the Supreme Court should be reported with accuracy and promptness, is essential to correctness and uniformity of decision in all the courts of the United States. It is also to be recollected that from the same tribunal the public receive that exposition of the constitution, laws, and treaties of the United States as applicable to the cases of individuals which must ultimately prevail. It is obviously important that a knowledge of this exposition should be attainable by all.

"It is a minor consideration, but not perhaps to be entirely overlooked, that, even in cases where the decisions of the Supreme Court are not to be considered as authority except in the courts of the United States, some advantage may be derived from their being known. It is certainly to be wished that independent tribunals having concurrent jurisdiction over the same subject should concur in the principles on which they determine the causes coming before them. This concurrence can be obtained only by communicating to each the judgments of the other, and by that mutual respect which will probably be inspired by a knowledge of the grounds on which their judgments respectively stand. On great commercial questions, especially, it is desirable that the judicial opinions of all parts of the Union should be the same.

"From experience, the judges think there is much reason to apprehend that the publication of the decisions of the Supreme Court will remain on a very precarious footing if the reporter is to depend solely on the sales of his work for a reimbursement of the expenses which must be incurred in preparing it, and for his own compensation. The patronage of the Government is believed to be necessary to the secure and certain attainment of the object.

"Law reports can have but a limited circulation. They rarely gain admission into the libraries of other than professional gentlemen. The circulation of the decisions of the Supreme Court will probably be still more limited than those of the courts of the States, because they are useful to a smaller number of the profession. Only a few of those who practice in the courts of the United States, or in great commercial cities, will often require them. There is, therefore, much reason to believe that no reporter will continue to employ his time and talents in preparing those decisions for the press after he shall be assured that the Government will not countenance his undertaking.

"With very great respect, I am, sir, your obedient servant,

"J. MARSHALL

"THE HON. DUDLEY CHASE"

APPENDIX H

Unusual Abbreviations Used in the Notes

Am. D. Adv.	*Dunlap's* [Philadelphia] *American Daily Advertiser*
Am. Her.	*The* [Boston] *American Herald*
Am. Merc.	*The* [Hartford] *American Mercury*
Am. Mus.	*The* [Philadelphia] *American Museum*
Annals	*Annals of the Congress of the United States* (Washington, 1834)
Ann. Gaz.	*The* [Annapolis] *Maryland Gazette*
Archives	PETER FORCE, *American Archives* (Washington, 1837–53)
ASP	*American State Papers* (Washington, 1834), Class X, Volume I
Balt. Gaz.	*The* [Baltimore] *Maryland Gazette*
B. Cont. Jour.	*The* [Boston] *Continental Journal*
Beveridge	A. J. BEVERIDGE, *Life of John Marshall* (Boston and New York, 1916–19)
B. Ind. Chr.	*The* [Boston] *Independent Chronicle*
Blackstone	SIR WILLIAM BLACKSTONE, *Commentaries on the Laws of England* (1st American ed.; Philadelphia, 1771–72)
Bost. Chr.	*The Boston Chronicle*
Bost. Ev. P.	*The Boston Evening Post*
Bost. Gaz.	*The Boston Gazette*
Ch. City Gaz.	*The* [Charleston] *City Gazette*
Ch. Ev. Gaz.	*The Charleston Evening Gazette*
Ch. G. A.	*The* [Charleston] *South-Carolina Gazette and General Advertiser*
Ch. Mng. P.	*The Charleston Morning Post*
Ch. P. A.	*The* [Charleston] *South-Carolina Gazette and Public Advertiser*
Ch. St. Gaz.	*The* [Charleston] *South-Carolina State Gazette and Daily Advertiser*
Ch. Wkly. Gaz.	*The* [Charleston] *South-Carolina Weekly Gazette*
Clarke & Hall	M. S. CLARKE and D. A. HALL, *Legislative and Documentary History of the Bank of the United States* (Washington, 1832)

Col. Her.	*The* [Charleston] *Columbian Herald*
Com. Int.	MALACHY POSTLETHWAYT, *Great-Britain's Commercial Interest Explained and Improved* (2d ed.; London, 1759)
Conn. Cour.	*The* [Hartford] *Connecticut Courant*
Conn. Jour.	*The* [New Haven] *Connecticut Journal*
Conn. Rec.	*The Public Records of the State of Connecticut* (Hartford, 1894 and later)
Coxe	TENCH COXE, *A View of the United States of America* (Philadelphia, 1794)
Cumb. Gaz.	*The Cumberland* [Maine] *Gazette*
DHC	*Documentary History of the Constitution of the United States of America* (Washington, 1894)
Dickinson	*The Political Writings of John Dickinson* (Wilmington, 1801)
Durfee	THOMAS DURFEE, *Gleanings from the Judicial History of Rhode Island* (Providence, 1883)
Elliot	JONATHAN ELLIOT, *The Debates in the Several State Conventions on the Adoption of the Federal Constitution* (2d [24 cm.] ed.; Washington, 1936)
Ess. Jour.	*The* [Newburyport, Mass.] *Essex Journal*
Fal. Gaz.	*The Falmouth* [Me.] *Gazette*
Ga. Gaz.	*The* [Augusta] *Georgia State Gazette*
Gaz. S.C.	*The* [Charleston] *Gazette of the State of South-Carolina*
Gaz. U.S.	New York *Gazette of the United States*
Hamilton	*The Works of Alexander Hamilton* (Federal ed.; New York, 1904)
HLR	*The Harvard Law Review*
Holdsworth	SIR WILLIAM HOLDSWORTH, *A History of English Law*
Jackson	JONATHAN JACKSON, *Thoughts upon the Political Situation of the United States* (Worcester, 1788)
Jefferson	*The Works of Thomas Jefferson* (Federal ed.; New York, 1904–5)
John Adams	*The Works of John Adams* (Boston, 1850–56)
Journals	W. C. FORD et al., *Journals of the Continental Congress* (Washington, 1904–37)
Kent	JAMES KENT, *Commentaries on American Law* (New York, 1827)
Knox	SAMUEL F. DRAKE, *Life and Correspondence of Henry Knox* (Boston, 1873)
Lee	*The Letters of Richard Henry Lee* (New York, 1911–14)
Letters	E. C. BURNETT, *Letters of Members of the Continental Congress* (Washington, 1921–36)

Madison	*The Writings of James Madison* (New York, 1900–1910)
Marsden	R. G. MARSDEN, *Law and Custom of the Sea* ([British] Navy Records Society, 1915)
Massachusettensis	*Massachusettensis* (4th ed.; Boston printed; London reprinted for J. Matthews, 1776)
Mass. Cent.	*The* [Boston] *Massachusetts Centinel*
Mass. Gaz.	*The* [Boston] *Massachusetts Gazette*
McCulloch I	J. R. MCCULLOCH, *A Select Collection of Early English Tracts on Commerce* (London, 1856)
McCulloch II	J. R. MCCULLOCH, *A Select Collection of Scarce and Valuable Tracts on Commerce* (London, 1857)
Md. Jour.	*The* [Baltimore] *Maryland Journal*
Mid. Gaz.	*The* [Middletown, Conn.] *Middlesex Gazette*
Monroe	*The Writings of James Monroe* (New York, 1898–1903)
N. & P. Jour.	*The Norfolk & Portsmouth* [Va.] *Journal*
Newp. Her.	*The Newport* [R.I.] *Herald*
Newp. Merc.	*The Newport* [R.I.] *Mercury*
N.H. Ct. Gaz.	*The New-Haven Gazette* (later *The New-Haven Gazette and Connecticut Magazine*)
N.H. Gaz.	*The* [Portsmouth] *New-Hampshire Gazette*
N.H. Merc.	*The* [Portsmouth] *New-Hampshire Mercury*
N.H. Spy	*The* [Portsmouth] *New-Hampshire Spy*
N.J. Gaz.	*The* [Trenton] *New-Jersey Gazette*
N.J. Pol. Int.	*The* [Elizabeth-Town, N.J.] *Political Intelligencer*
N. L. Gaz.	*The* [New London] *Connecticut Gazette*
Norw. Pack.	*The Norwich* [Conn.] *Packet*
N.Y. Adv.	*The* [New York] *Daily Advertiser*
N.Y. Ind. Jour.	*The* [New York] *Independent Journal*
N.Y. Jour.	*The New-York Journal* (This paper was published for a time, during the Revolution, at Poughkeepsie)
N.Y. Mng. P.	*The New-York Morning Post*
N.Y. Wkly. Merc.	*The New York Gazette and Weekly Mercury*
Otis	JAMES OTIS, *The Rights of the Colonies Asserted and Proved* (2d ed.; reprinted for J. Almon, London)
Oxford	*The Oxford English Dictionary* (Oxford, 1933)
Pa. Chr.	*The* [Philadelphia] *Pennsylvania Chronicle*
Pa. Gaz.	*The* [Philadelphia] *Pennsylvania Gazette*
Pa. Her.	*The* [Philadelphia] *Pennsylvania Evening Herald*
Pa. Jour.	*The* [Philadelphia] *Pennsylvania Journal*

Pa. Merc.	The [Philadelphia] *Pennsylvania Mercury*
Pa. Pack.	The [Philadelphia] *Pennsylvania Packet*
Ph. Fr. Jour.	The [Philadelphia] *Freeman's Journal*
Ph. Ind. Gaz.	The [Philadelphia] *Independent Gazetteer*
Po. Fr. Jour.	The [Portsmouth, N.H.] *Freeman's Journal*
Pownall	THOMAS POWNALL, *The Administration of the British Colonies* (5th ed.; London, 1774)
Prov. Gaz.	The *Providence* [R.I.] *Gazette*
P. Web.	PELATIAH WEBSTER, *Political Essays* (Philadelphia, 1791)
Rawle	WILLIAM RAWLE, *A View of the Constitution of the United States of America* (2d ed.; Philadelphia, 1829)
Records	MAX FARRAND, *The Records of the Federal Convention* (New Haven, 1937)
Reed	WILLIAM B. REED, *Life and Correspondence of Joseph Reed* (Philadelphia, 1847)
Rutherforth	THOMAS RUTHERFORTH, *Institutes of Natural Law* (Cambridge [Eng.], 1754–56)
Sal. Merc.	The *Salem* [Mass.] *Mercury*
Sav. Gaz.	The [Savannah] *Gazette of the State of Georgia*
SEAALH	*Select Essays in Anglo-American Legal History* (Boston, 1907)
Seabury	SAMUEL SEABURY, *Letters of a Westchester Farmer*, as reprinted in PUBLICATIONS OF THE WESTCHESTER COUNTY HISTORICAL SOCIETY, Vol. VIII (White Plains, N.Y., 1930)
Smith	ADAM SMITH, *An Enquiry into the Causes of the Wealth of Nations* (Modern Library ed.; New York, 1937)
Story	JOSEPH STORY, *Commentaries on the Constitution of the United States* (Boston, 1833)
Sullivan	JAMES SULLIVAN, *The History of Land Titles in Massachusetts* (Boston, .1801)
Swift	ZEPHANIAH SWIFT, *A System of the Laws of the State of Connecticut* (Windham, Conn., 1795)
True Sys.	MALACHY POSTLETHWAYT, *Great-Britain's True System* (London, 1757)
Tucker	ST. GEORGE TUCKER, *Blackstone's Commentaries* (Philadelphia, 1803)
U.S. Chr.	The [Providence, R.I.] *United States Chronicle*
Va. Am. Adv.	The [Richmond] *Virginia Gazette or the American Advertiser*
Va. Her.	The [Fredericksburg] *Virginia Herald*
Va. Ind. Chr.	The [Richmond] *Virginia Independent Chronicle*

Va. Jour.	*The* [Alexandria] *Virginia Journal*
VLR	*The Virginia Law Review*
Vt. Gaz.	*The* [Bennington] *Vermont Gazette*
Warren	CHARLES WARREN, *The Supreme Court in United States History* (Boston, 1924)
Warren-Adams	*The Warren-Adams Letters* (The Massachusetts Historical Society, 1917)
Wbg. Va. Gaz.	*The* [Williamsburg] *Virginia Gazette*
Webster	*Webster's International Dictionary of the English Language* (Springfield, Mass., 1933)
Wharton	FRANCIS WHARTON, *State Trials of the United States during the Administration of Washington and Adams* (Philadelphia, 1849)
Wilson	*The Works of the Honourable James Wilson* (Philadelphia, 1804)
Wm. Smith	WILLIAM SMITH, *The History of the Province of New York* (2d ed.; Philadelphia, 1792)

Notes

NOTES TO CHAPTER I

1. George Chalmers, *Political Annals of the Present United Colonies, from their Settlement to the Peace, of 1763* (London, 1780), 16.

2. Alexander Hamilton's son, John Church Hamilton, was one of the skeptics. After drawing attention to Madison's presentation of his notes as "an authentic exhibition of the objects, the opinions, and the reasonings" of the Federal Convention, young Hamilton declared his own belief that the notes had not that character. More specifically, he said that he could not credit his father's ever having seen and approved Madison's report of his speech of June 18th, as Madison affirmed had been the case. In support of his incredulity, he adduced some very cogent reasons. See J. C. Hamilton, *The Life of Alexander Hamilton* (New York, 1841), II, 466–67 and 490 (footnote). A reviewer of the *Life of Hamilton*, in THE NEW YORK REVIEW, VIII, 121, 155 (1841), confessed that he was not "backward to admit the possible thought which the recent perusal of the Madison Papers had . . . awakened from many internal marks, viz., that Madison's notes of the convention of 1787 [were] not, in a strict sense, an original document, but b[o]r[e] the color of subsequent thought." "And if so," he went on, "it is easy to divine what tinge would be given them, whether intentionally or unintentionally, touching a party [the Federalist party] he had abandoned, principles he had forsaken, and, above all, the man [Alexander Hamilton] whom, beyond all other men, he hated and feared." These views, of the Reverend Francis L. Hawkes, were published again, five years later, in THE LIVING AGE, VIII, 425, 437 (1846). So, the skepticism in regard to Madison's notes must, originally, have been fairly widespread.

3. Max Farrand, in Records, I, xv. Mr. Farrand spoke of Madison's notes in THE PENNSYLVANIA MAGAZINE OF HISTORY, LXII, 130, 133 (April 1938), as "comprehensive, accurate, impartial, and impersonal." He said that, "oddly enough, the latter virtues are now our chief cause of complaint"; that Madison's "notes are too impartial and impersonal." That this estimate of Madison's notes is, at many points, totally unawarranted will eventually appear from the evidence and discussion to be presented in this book. Even lawyers, whose training ought to fortify them against such things, have accepted Madison's notes with complete naïveté. Cf., Rodell, *Fifty-five Men* (New York and Harrisburg, 1936), 7 and 8.

4. See Worthington Chauncey Ford (theretofore in charge of the Madison papers as chief of the manuscript division of the Library of Congress), in Proc. Mass. Hist. Soc., 2d Ser., XV, 119 (1901): "Madison lived long enough to have some doubts on certain of his actions, and to destroy a part of his correspondence bearing upon those actions." Cf., the reference by Gaillard Hunt to "the suspicious investigator, who thinks that Madison may have made alterations in his original record so as to suppress or distort the truth or give a coloring to the facts." Hunt and Scott, *The Debates in the Federal Convention of 1787* (New York, 1920), xxi. Mr. Hunt was Mr. Ford's successor as chief of the manuscript division of the Congressional Library.

5. This view of the role of Taney has recently been denied. See Frankfurter, *The Commerce Clause under Marshall, Taney and Waite* (Chapel Hill, 1937), 47 *et seq.* But the facts fully justify the statement in the text.

NOTES TO CHAPTER II

1. The cases explaining the nature of interstate commerce are very numerous. Those mentioned by Justice Sutherland in *Carter* v. *Carter Coal Co.*, 298 U.S. 238, 297 *et seq.* (1936), are typical.

2. Typical recent cases are: *National Labor Relations Board* v. *Jones & Laughlin Steel Corp.*, 301 U.S. 1 (1937); *Santa Cruz Fruit Packing Co.* v. *National Labor Relations Board*, 303 U.S. 453 (1938); *Consolidated Edison Co.* v. *National Labor Relations Board*, 305 U.S. 197 (1938); *United States* v. *Darby*, 312 U.S. 100 (1941); *Kirschbaum* v. *Walling*, 316 U.S. 517 (1942); *McLeod* v. *Threlkeld*, 319 U.S. 491 (1943); *Borden Co.* v. *Borella*, 325 U.S. 679 (1945); *10 East 40th Street Building, Inc.* v. *Callus*, 325 U.S. 578 (1945); *Mulford* v. *Smith*, 307 U.S. 38 (1939); *United States* v. *Rock Royal Co-operative, Inc.*, 307 U.S. 533 (1939); *H. P. Hood & Sons, Inc.* v. *United States*, 307 U.S. 588 (1939); *Sunshine Anthracite Coal Co.* v. *Adkins*, 310 U.S. 381 (1940); *Wickard* v. *Filburn*, 317 U.S. 111 (1942); *United States* v. *Wrightwood Dairy Co.*, 315 U.S. 110 (1942).

3. See, for example, *Schechter Poultry Corp.* v. *United States*, 295 U.S. 495, 548, 554 (1935).

4. *Ibid.*, 550; *National Labor Relations Board* v. *Jones & Laughlin Steel Corp.*, 301 U.S. 1, 30 (1937). The position is implied in many earlier cases; and nothing in any of the cases subsequent to those cited has any tendency to indicate that the Court has changed its mind.

5. *Op. cit.* note 3 *supra*, 546–48.

6. The power of Congress to act upon non-interstate commerce has always been supposed to rest upon the fact that the non-interstate commerce acted upon has effects upon interstate commerce which make the action taken with respect to the non-interstate commerce necessary to the achieving of the regulation of interstate commerce. Where effects giving rise to the necessity for such action actually exist, it is not easy to see what bearing the directness or indirectness of the effects can have upon the existence of the necessity. Actually, it was never possible to say just what effects the Court would call "direct"; and what, "indirect." About all that could be said was that the Court seemed to mean "not too remote," rather than "proximate" or "immediate." In other words, the Court tolerated some indirectness, provided there was not too much. Besides this, it should be mentioned that, when the accomplishment of some effect upon interstate commerce appeared *as the end* for which intrastate acts were done, the power of Congress was held to extend to the intrastate acts, however indirect their relation to the interstate commercial end might be; and the end in such cases was described by the Court as a "direct" effect of the intrastate acts. See *Coronado Coal Co.* v. *United Mine Workers of America*, 259 U.S. 344 (1922), and 268 U.S. 295 (1925). There was also much inconsistency in the cases. A striking instance of this may be seen if *Local 167* v. *United States*, 291 U.S. 293 (1934), and *Schechter Poultry Corp.* v. *United States*, 295 U.S. 495 (1935), are compared with each other. It is especially evident when the record in the former case is examined.

7. *National Labor Relations Board* v. *Jones & Laughlin Steel Corp.*, 301 U.S. 1, 31 and 37 (1937).

8. *United States* v. *Darby*, 312 U.S. 100, 119 (1940).

9. *Burns Mortgage Co.* v. *Fried*, 292 U.S. 487 (1934); *Erie Railroad Co.* v. *Tompkins*, 304 U.S. 64 (1938).

10. An exception to this statement should be noted to cover the case of *Davis* v. *Department of Labor,* 317 U.S. 249 (1942).

11. *Santa Cruz Fruit Packing Co.* v. *National Labor Relations Board,* 303 U.S. 453, 466–67 (1938).

12. *Kirschbaum* v. *Walling,* 316 U.S. 517, 526 (1942).

13. *Polish National Alliance* v. *National Labor Relations Board,* 322 U.S. 643, 652 (1944).

14. *The Employers' Liability Cases,* 207 U.S. 463 (1908).

15. 35 U.S. Stat. 65, c. 149, sec. 1. This statute was upheld in *Second Employers' Liability Cases,* 223 U.S. 1 (1912). Somewhat later, the Court indicated a willingness to relax somewhat the position taken in *The* [first] *Employers' Liability Cases,* in 1908 (note 14 *supra*). *Illinois Central R. Co.* v. *Behrens,* 233 U.S. 473, 477 (1914). But Congress never took action on the Court's hint until August 1939. See 53 U.S. Stat. 1404, c. 685, sec. 1.

16. *Shanks* v. *Delaware, Lackawanna & Western R. Co.,* 239 U.S. 556, 558 (1916).

17. *Chicago & North Western R. Co.* v. *Bolle,* 284 U.S. 74, 79, 80 (1931); *Chicago & Eastern Illinois R. Co.* v. *Industrial Commission of Illinois,* 284 U.S. 296, 299 (1932). The words of the statute of 1908 (note 15 *supra*) were: "Every common carrier by railroad while engaging in commerce between any of the several States . . . shall be liable in damages to any person suffering injury while he is employed by such carrier in such commerce. . . ."

18. *New York Central R. Co.* v. *Winfield,* 244 U.S. 147 (1917); *Philadelphia, B. & W. R. Co.* v. *Smith,* 250 U.S. 101 (1919); *Southern Pacific R. Co.* v. *Industrial Accident Commission,* 251 U.S. 259 (1920); *Kinzell* v. *Chicago, M. & St. P. Ry. Co.,* 250 U.S. 130 (1919); *Erie R. Co.* v. *Szary,* 253 U.S. 86 (1920); *Erie R. Co.* v. *Collins,* 253 U.S. 77 (1920).

19. *Petersen* v. *Delaware, Lackawanna & Western R. Co.,* 229 U.S. 146 (1913); *Philadelphia & R. R. Co.* v. *Di Donato,* 256 U.S. 327 (1921); *New York Central R. Co.* v. *Porter,* 249 U.S. 168 (1919); *Chicago & North Western R. Co.* v. *Bolle,* 284 U.S. 74 (1931).

20. How considerable the evil may be, from this point of view, may be seen from the number of cases cited to U.S.C.A., Tit. 45, sec. 51, notes 121–266. See, also, Schoene and Watson, *Workmen's Compensation on Interstate Railways,* 47 HLR, 389, 397.

21. 284 U.S. 74 (1931).

22. 258 Ill. App. 545 (1930). The opinion rendered at this stage of the proceedings contains the fullest statement of the case. The date of the injury is, however, misstated as "December 4, 1925," instead of December 4, 1922. See Record on Appeal to United States Supreme Court, pp. 1, 15, 17, 18.

23. The following citations cover the various stages in the litigation as stated in the text: 235 Ill. App. 380 (1924); 324 Ill. 479 (1927); 251 Ill. App. 623 (1929); 258 Ill. App. 545 (1930); 284 U.S. 77.

24. The cases were *Erie R. Co.* v. *Collins,* 253 U.S. 77 (1920), and *Erie R. Co.* v. *Szary,* 253 U.S. 86 (1920). They were overruled in *Chicago & Eastern Illinois R. Co.* v. *Industrial Commission of Illinois,* 284 U.S. 296, decided on January 4, 1932. The case discussed in the text was decided November 23, 1931. However, the Court, in effect, overruled the Collins and Szary cases in the Bolle case, since it refused to follow them therein. 284 U.S. 79–80; *cf.,* 284 U.S. 299. Reference to the briefs in the Bolle case will show that the argument was largely directed to the point not decided *formally* until six weeks after the Bolle case was disposed of.

25. The author is indebted for this information, to the plaintiff's counsel, Mr. Joseph D. Ryan, of Chicago.

26. 284 U.S. 78–80.

27. The disregard of the statutory language was not accidental. The statute was quoted. *Ibid.*, 78.

28. *Ibid.*, 79–80.

29. 52 U.S. Stat. 1060, c. 676, secs. 3(b), 6, and 7.

30. *McLeod* v. *Threlkeld*, 319 U.S. 491 (1942). The Bolle case is cited at pp. 495 and 496. Justice Murphy, who, with Justices Black, Douglas, and Rutledge, dissented, had the following to say (pp. 500–501) of the situation that has developed under the act: "The necessary effect of rejecting the *Smith* case [250 U.S. 101] for the restrictive concept of 'in [interstate] commerce' which was used in the *Shanks, Bolle, Commission,* and *Bezue* cases [239 U.S. 556; 284 U.S. 74; 284 U.S. 296; and 284 U.S. 415] is to introduce into the administration of the Fair Labor Standards Act that concededly undesirable confusion which characterized the application of the Federal Employers' Liability Act and prompted the 1939 amendment (53 Stat. 1404) which in effect repudiated the narrow test of the Shanks line of cases. The reality of this confusion is readily demonstrable. We have held that a rate clerk employed by an interstate motor carrier [*Overnight Motor Co.* v. *Missel*, 316 U.S. 572] and a seller of tickets on a toll bridge over which interstate traffic moves [*Overstreet* v. *North Shore Corp.*, 318 U.S. 125] are both 'engaged in [interstate] commerce' within the meaning of the Fair Labor Standards Act. Yet, in the view of the majority of the Court, when the employee's activities are in the field of transportation, the Act apparently will not cover those who work in an interstate carrier's repair shop on facilities to supply power for machinery used in repairing instrumentalities of transportation, or who heat cars and depots used by interstate passengers, or who store fuel for the use of interstate vehicles, or who work on such vehicles when withdrawn for the moment from commerce for repairs. The anomaly of this is clear—there is no sound reason for extending the benefits of the act to a rate clerk employed in the office of an interstate motor carrier and denying them to the janitor who keeps the office clean and warm, or the employee who works in the carrier's shop on machinery used to repair interstate vehicles, or on the vehicles themselves.

31. 52 U.S. Stat. 1060, c. 676, sec. 3(b).

32. *10 East 40th Street Building, Inc.* v. *Callus*, 325 U.S. 578, 587–88 (1945). *Cf., Kirschbaum* v. *Walling*, 316 U.S. 517 (1942); and *Borden Co.* v. *Borella*, 325 U.S. 679 (1945).

33. *10 East 40th Street Building, Inc.* v. *Callus*, 325 U.S. 578, 579–80 (1945).

34. *Ibid.*, 583 and 584.

35. *Kirschbaum* v. *Walling*, 316 U.S. 517, 520, 521, and 525.

36. *Thornhill* v. *Alabama*, 310 U.S. 88 (1940); *Carlson* v. *California*, 310 U.S. 106 (1940); and *Bakery & Pastry Drivers & Helpers Local* v. *Wohl*, 315 U.S. 769 (1942). The writer has heard workingmen laugh aloud at these decisions when the ground of the decisions was made clear to them. A reaction more articulate than these laughs, but based upon the same very sensible notions, is Charles O. Gregory, *Peaceful Picketing and Freedom of Speech*, 26 AMERICAN BAR ASSOCIATION JOURNAL, 709 (1940).

37. Pownall, I, 116–18.

38. *Pillans* v. *Van Mierop*, 3 Burr. 1664, 1672 (1765).

39. Blackstone, I, 43: "As it is impossible for the whole race of mankind to be united in one great society, they must necessarily divide into many; and form separate states, commonwealths, and nations, entirely independent of each other and yet liable to a mutual intercourse. Hence arises a third kind of law to regulate this mutual intercourse, called 'the law of nations': which, as none of these states will acknowlege [sic] superiority in the other, cannot be dictated by either; but depends entirely upon the rules of natural law, or upon mutual compacts, treaties, leagues, and agreements between these several communities; in the construction also of which compacts, we have no other rule to resort to, but the law of nature; being the only one to which both communities are equally subject; and therefore the civil law very justly observes, that *quod naturalis ratio inter omnes homines constituit, vocatur jus gentium.*"

Ibid., I, 44: "Municipal or civil law [is] the rule by which particular districts, communities, or nations are governed; being thus defined by Justinian, *'jus civile est quod quisque sibi populus constituit.'* "

Ibid., I, 74–75: "The second branch of the unwritten laws of England are particular customs, or laws which affect only the inhabitants of particular districts.

. . . .

"To this head may most properly be referred a particular system of customs used only among one set of the king's subjects, called the custom of merchants or *lex mercatoria*: which, however different from the general rules of the common law, is yet ingrafted into it, and made a part of it; being allowed, for the benefit of trade, to be of the utmost validity in all commercial transactions: for it is a maxim of law, that *'cuilibet in sua arte credendum est.'* "

Ibid., I, 273: "Whereas no municipal laws can be sufficient to order and determine the very extensive and complicated affairs of [foreign] traffic and merchandize; neither can they have a proper authority for this purpose. For, as these are transactions carried on between subjects of independent states, the municipal laws of one will not be regarded by the other. For which reason the affairs of commerce are regulated by a law of their own, called the law merchant or *lex mercatoria*, which all nations agree in and take notice of. And in particular it is held to be part of the law of England, which decides the causes of merchants by the general rules which obtain in all commercial countries; and that often even in matters relating to domestic trade, as for instance with regard to the drawing, the acceptance, and the transfer, of inland bills of exchange."

Ibid., IV, 66–68: "The law of nations is a system of rules, deducible by natural reason, and established by universal consent among the civilized inhabitants of the world; in order to decide all disputes, to regulate all ceremonies and civilities, and to insure the observance of justice and good faith, in that intercourse which must frequently occur between two or more independent states, and the individuals belonging to each. This general law is founded upon this principle, that different nations ought in time of peace to do one another all the good they can; and, in time of war, as little harm as possible, without prejudice to their own real interests. And, as none of these states will allow a superiority in the other, therefore neither can dictate or prescribe the rules of this law to the rest; but such rules must necessarily result from those principles of natural justice, in which all the learned of every nation agree: or they depend upon mutual compacts or treaties between the respective communities; in the construction of which there is also no judge to resort to, but the law of nature and reason, being the only one in which all the contracting parties are equally conversant, and to which they are equally subject.

"In arbitrary states this law, wherever it contradicts or is not provided for by the municipal law of the country, is enforced by the royal power: but since in England no royal power can introduce a new law, or suspend the execution of the old, therefore the law of nations (whenever any question arises which is properly the object of it's jurisdiction) is here adopted in it's full extent by the common law, and is held to be a part of the law of the land. And those acts of parliament, which have from time to time been made to enforce this universal law, or to facilitate the execution of it's decisions, are not to be considered as introductive of any new rule, but merely as declaratory of the old fundamental constitutions of the kingdom; without which it must cease to be a part of the civilized world. Thus in mercantile questions, such as bills of exchange and the like; in all marine causes, relating to freight, average, demurrage, insurances, bottomry and others of a similar nature; the law-merchant, which is a branch of the law of nations, is regularly and constantly adhered to. So too in all disputes relating to prizes, to shipwrecks, to hostages, and ransom bills, there is no other rule of decision but this great universal law, collected from history and usage, and such writers of all nations and languages as are generally approved and allowed of.

"But, though in civil transactions and questions of property between the subjects of different states, the law of nations has much scope and extent, as adopted by the law of England; yet the present branch of our enquiries will fall within a narrow compass, as offences against the law of nations can rarely be the object of the criminal law of any particular state.

. . . .

"The principal offences against the law of nations, animadverted on as such by the municipal laws of England, are of three kinds; 1. Violation of safe-conducts; 2. Infringement of the rights of embassadors; and, 3. Piracy."

40. (London, 1783), 92: "The Law of Nations is another constituent part of British jurisprudence, and has always been most liberally adopted and attended to by our municipal tribunals, in matters where that rule of decision was proper to be resorted to, as questions respecting the privileges of ambassadors, and the property in maritime captures and prizes.

"But the branch of the law of nations, which there have been the most frequent occasions of regarding, especially since the great extension of commerce, and intercourse with foreign traders, is called the law of merchants. This system of generally received law has been admitted to decide controversies touching bills of exchange, policies of insurance, and other mercantile transactions, both where the subjects of any foreign power, and (for the sake of uniformity) where natives of this realm only, have been interested in the event. Its doctrines have of late years been wonderfully elucidated, and reduced to rational and firm principles, in a series of litigations before a judge, long celebrated for his great talents, and extensive learning in general jurisprudence, and still more venerable for his animated love of justice. Under his able conduct and direction, very many of these causes have been tried by a jury of merchants in London; and such questions of this kind as have come before the court of King's Bench in term time, are laid before the public by a copious and elaborate compiler.

"The law of merchants, so far as it depends on custom, constitutes a part of the voluntary, not of the necessary, law of nations. It may therefore, so far as it is merely positive, be altered by any municipal legislature, where its own subjects only are concerned. Innovations may also be made in the whole voluntary law of nations, so as to affect the inhabitants of different regions, by treaty between the respective powers. But no change can be wrought in the natural law of nations, or the rules of moral justice applied to men as the members of different states, either by the sovereigns thereof, or any confederated union of human authority."

41. Marshall, *A Treatise on the Law of Insurance* (1st American ed., Boston, 1805, from 1st English ed. of 1802), 18–20: "The law of insurance is considered as a branch of marine law, and was borrowed by us from the Lombards, who first introduced the use of this contract into England. It is also a branch of the law of merchants, being founded in the practice of merchants, which is nearly the same in all the countries where insurance is in use; and, indeed, merchants themselves were, for a long time, the only expounders of it. The law of merchants not being founded in the particular institutions, or local customs of any particular country, but consisting of certain principles which general convenience has established to regulate the dealings of merchants with each other in all countries, may be considered as a branch of public law. *Non erit alia lex Romae, alia nunc, alia post hac; sed et apud omnes gentes, et omni tempore, una eademque lex obtinebit.*

"Besides the general law of merchants, there are certain usages which prevail in particular countries, and sometimes in particular branches of commerce. These, like local customs in England, have the force of law where they prevail; and where they are in force, are always supposed to be in the contemplation of the parties; and the contract of insurance is construed as having been made with reference to them; But then they must appear to have been long established; that is, as I humbly apprehend, they must be immemorial, or at least coeval with the branch of commerce to which they belong. They must also be reasonable and legal; otherwise no notice can be taken of them in any court of justice.

"If it be asked where the law of insurance is to be found; the answer is, in the marine law, and in the custom of merchants, which may be collected, 1. From the ordinances of different commercial states; 2. From the treatises of learned authors on the subject of insurance; 3. From judicial decisions in this country, and others professing to follow the general marine law and the law of merchants.

"1. Particular ordinances have, as we have already seen, been made in many countries upon the subject of marine law; and many have been made to regulate marine insurances. But these have seldom gone farther than to define, and to sanction by legislative authority, those principles which were already received as law in all commercial countries. Some, indeed, have added regulations, dictated only by national or particular interest; but these are wholly disregarded elsewhere.

"The ordinances of other countries are not, it is true, in *force** in England; but they are of authority, at least as expressing the usage of other countries upon a contract which is governed by general rules, which are understood to form a branch of public law. *Non habent vim legis, sed rationis.*"

Weskett, *A Complete Digest of the Theory, Laws, and Practice of Insurance* (3d ed.; Dublin, 1794), 321: "It is not less, nay it is often more requisite

* Italics in the original.

for merchants and insurers, to be acquainted with the law of nations, than with the municipal law of their own country; since it is by the former that the greater part of all commercial and maritime affairs is regulated."
See, also, *Luke* v. *Lyde*, 2 Burr. 883, 887 (1759).

42. See Wilson, I, 374–75; and III, 355 and 375–76. These passages are quoted in chapter xviii hereof, pp. 571–72 *supra*.

43. Sullivan, 337–38: "There have been motions, in some of the Legislatures in the Union, to prohibit the reading of English reports in our courts of justice. These attempts have been considered, by prudent and wise men, to be sudden, rash, and improper. None will undertake to maintain the propriety of them; but yet, perhaps they are more reprehensible on account of the time and form, in which they were made, than for the intention and substance of them. The judges themselves, in several of the States, have, with great propriety, inclined to reject the reports of cases determined in England since the American Revolution. These motions, however crude and indigested they may have been, no doubt had their origin in a strong love to our national independence: And the motive is therefore a laudable, rather than a reprehensible one.

"It will be seen, even by the small treatise to which these observations are attached, that it is impossible, by acts of legislation, to govern, define and direct the various tenures and incidents of real estates. There is yet a greater difficulty in conducting all the rights to personal estates, and to define the nature of, and to give a remedy on, contracts. The soil of a country is, generally speaking, governed by the power of the Legislature, or by customs peculiar to the country where the soil is; but personal estate is not fixed to any place or country, and contracts depend on the *jus gentium* (the general law of nations) for their origin and their expositions, rather than on any municipal regulations of particular countries."

44. Tucker, Bk. I, Pt. 1, p. 75, note 6: "The *lex mercatoria*, or general law and custom among Merchants, stands I presume upon the same authority in Virginia [as in England]; what that law is, is to be ascertained and determined by judicial decisions and not by any local usages amongst merchants and Traders; for these form no part of the common law of England, as the general law of Merchants doth. See Lord Mansfield's report, in the case of Edie and another against the East India Company; and Justice Foster's opinion in the same case. . . . 2 Burrow, 1222, and 1226.

"But where the law is not settled, it would seem that evidence of local usages, which are so settled and established among merchants and traders, as to be clear and plain beyond a doubt is proper for the consideration of a Jury. Lord Mansfield. . . . Ibid. 1221, 1222."

Ibid., App. 407: "From that moment [July 4, 1776], there was no common law amongst them [the states] but the general law of nations, to which all civilized nations conform."

Ibid., App. 429–30: "We may fairly infer from all that has been said that the common law of England stands precisely upon the same footing in the federal government, and courts of the United States, *as such,** as the civil and ecclesiastical laws stand upon in England: That is to say, it's maxims and rules of proceeding are to be adhered to, whenever the written law is silent, in cases of a similar, or analogous nature, the cognizance whereof is by the constitution vested in the federal courts: it may govern and direct the course of proceeding, in such cases, but cannot give jurisdiction in *any case,** where juris-

---

* Italics in the original.

diction is not expressly given by the constitution. The same may be said of the *civil law;** the rules of proceeding in which whenever the written law is silent, are to be observed in cases of equity, and of admiralty, and maritime jurisdiction. In short, as the matters cognizable in the federal courts, belong, (as we have before shewn, in reviewing the powers of the judiciary department) partly to the law of nations, partly to the common law of England; partly to the civil law; partly to the maritime law, comprehending the laws of Oleron and Rhodes; and partly to the general law and custom of merchants; and partly to the municipal laws of any foreign nation, or of any state in the union, where the cause of action may happen to arise, or where the suit may be instituted; so, the law of nations, the common law of England, the civil law, the law maritime, the law merchant, or the *lex loci*, or law of the foreign nation, or state, in which the cause of action may arise, or shall be decided, must in their turn be resorted to as the rule of decision, according to the nature and circumstances of each case, respectively. So that each of these laws may be regarded, so far as they apply to such cases, respectively, as the law of the land."

See, also, *ibid.*, App. 421.

45. *A Digest of the Law of Evidence in Criminal Cases and a Treatise on Bills of Exchange and Promissory Notes* (Hartford, 1810), 245: "Bills of exchange were unknown to the ancients, and have been introduced in modern times for the purpose of facilitating and extending commerce by the means of credit. They constitute a branch of universal commercial law, to be governed by the customs and usages of nations, and not by municipal law."

46. Owing to the small amount of American law reporting in the eighteenth century, cases are few; but there are two early Pennsylvania cases which shed a good deal of light upon the notions of the time, relating to the subject in question. They are *Steinmetz* v. *Currie*, 1 Dall. 269 (1788); and *Hunter* v. *Blodget*, 2 Yeates 480 (1799). These cases are outlined and discussed in chapter xviii hereof, at pp. 572–73 *supra*.

47. The *De Conflictu Legum* was a very small part of a three-volume treatise, *Praelectiones Juris Civilis* (Franeker, 1689–1701). See Lorenzen, *Huber's De Conflictu Legum*, 13 ILLINOIS LAW REVIEW, 199 (1918).

48. 370 *et seq*.

49. See cases mentioned in note 46 *supra*.

50. The conflict of laws made its way into our law on the plea that our situation was different from that of England, in that our government was nonunitary. See Livermore, *Dissertations on the Questions Which Arise from the Contrariety of the Positive Laws of Different States and Nations* (New Orleans, 1828), 12 and 19; Story, *Commentaries on the Conflict of Laws* (Boston, 1834), 9. The pre-Civil War attitude toward the national power (see, for example, Redfield, *The Proper Limits between State and National Legislation and Jurisdiction*, 6 AMERICAN LAW REGISTER [N.S.], 193) and the gradual frittering away, both then and later, of the constitutional limitations on the states naturally favored the spread of these alien notions. When, after the Civil War, the great deterrent to national legislation was seemingly removed, lawyers were so habituated to the territorial notions of the conflict of laws, that the interterritorial theory of the national commerce power, which was by then pretty well established anyhow, seemed quite natural. The conflict-of-laws technique of artificially localizing contracts in the locus of the final consummatory act of acceptance also influenced the conceptions of the national power.

* Italics in the original.

This influence is plainly apparent in *Paul* v. *Virginia*, 8 Wall. 168 (1869). There were, of course, political pressures, also, to account for these developments; but the point is that the territorial conflicts theories made the developments in question easier. *Cf.*, Redfield, *op. cit. supra*, 197.

The conflict of laws was urged upon the English courts on a somewhat similar basis: that the empire included many colonies having diverse sorts of local law that ought to be given recognition. See Henry, *The Judgment of the Court of Demerara in the case of Odwin v. Forbes*, [*etc.*] (London, 1823), ix; Burge, *Commentaries on Colonial and Foreign Laws* (London, 1838), 77. The extent to which Burge depended on Story and American cases should be noted.

51. *Cf.*, Kent, *An American Law Student of a Hundred Years Ago*, 1 SEAALH, 837, 843.

52. For further evidence of the widespread character of the sentiment in favor of uniform commercial law and the slowness of the shift to the modern conflicts notions, see chapter xviii hereof. It is noteworthy that the early conflict of laws writers, both here and in England, seem to have been interested mainly in legal diversities in non-commercial fields. Livermore urged the need for knowledge of conflicts rules in reference to the rights of married persons, intestate successions, and wills, though he also observed that Louisiana law differed from that of the other states, in certain respects, in reference to sales. *Op. cit.* note 50 *supra*, 19. Story's treatise purported to deal "especially" with "marriages, divorces, wills, successions and judgments." See title page to original edition. And Henry (*op. cit.* note 50 *supra*, viii–ix) spoke of the need of recognizing foreign law "in those cases which are of an universal nature, as those of bankruptcy, idiocy, lunacy, majority, minority, marriages, and wills, . . . which necessarily affect the intercourse of different states with each other." He also had said, in the opinion in *Odwin* v. *Forbes* (*ibid.*, 94–95): "That there is a kind of law now existing in Europe which has no locality of principle, will be evident, from considering the universal effect given to marriages and wills, and that these, together with contracts, under some restrictions, have (if I may use the term) a legal ubiquity, which is highly useful and necessary. The law of merchants, who, by the gradual incorporation and adoption of their customs, seem to have rendered themselves *quasi* subjects of almost every state of Europe, may, in many of its parts, also serve to illustrate this principle." That commercial cases were then still dealt with in England by "the-general-commercial-law" technique explains the fact that, in 1825, an English judge—*i.e.*, a judge of the nation then having the most extensive foreign commerce of any nation in the world—could nevertheless say, in *Arnott* v. *Redfern*, 2 C. & P. 88 (1825), that conflicts cases were of rare occurrence.

53. Sullivan, 353–54.

54. See, for example, *Western Union Telegraph Co.* v. *Call Publishing Co.*, 181 U.S. 92 (1901), and *Western Union Telegraph Co.* v. *Brown*, 234 U.S. 542 (1913); but *cf.*, *Pennsylvania R. Co.* v. *Hughes*, 191 U.S. 477 (1903).

55. Except, of course, in the District of Columbia. *Cf.*, McCurdy, *Uniformity and a Proposed Federal Sales Act*, 26 VLR, 572, 584 (1940).

56. *Burns Mortgage Co.* v. *Fried*, 292 U.S. 587 (1934); *Erie R.R. Co.* v. *Tompkins*, 304 U.S. 64 (1938).

57. *Cf.*, Thomas, *The Federal Sales Bill as Viewed by the Merchant and Practitioner*, 26 VLR, 537, 539 (1940).

58. Llewellyn, *The Needed Federal Sales Act*, 26 VLR, 558, 561 (1940).

59. *Ibid.*, 559.

60. See *A Symposium: The Proposed Federal Sales Act*, 26 VLR, 537 *et seq.* (1940).

61. Section 1 of the proposed act, H.R. 8176, 76 Cong., 3d Sess. (1940); reprinted 26 VLR, 668.

62. McCurdy, *op. cit.* note 55 *supra, passim;* Williston, *A Statement*, 26 VLR, 637 (1940).

63. *Burns Mortgage Co.* v. *Fried*, 292 U.S. 487 (1934).

64. The case cited in the next preceding note involved an instance of divergent state judicial interpretation of the Uniform Negotiable Instruments Law.

65. *Cf.*, McCurdy, *op. cit.* note 55 *supra.*

66. Smith, 700.

67. Wickersham, *Federal Control of Interstate Commerce*, 23 HLR, 241, 258 (1910); Morawetz, *The Power of Congress to Enact Incorporation Laws and to Regulate Corporations*, 26 HLR, 667, 672 (1913).

68. The matter is discussed in Henderson, *The Position of Foreign Corporations in American Constitutional Law* (Cambridge, 1918), 24 *et seq.*

69. Wilson, III, 405 *et seq.* Pelatiah Webster, in a pamphlet published in 1786, made substantially the same argument as Wilson made. P. Web., 427, 450 *et seq.*

70. Clarke & Hall, 13.

71. Henderson, *op. cit.* note 68 *supra*, 25; Wilson, III, 400–402; P. Web., 433 and 452.

72. Some of the early ones are listed in 2 Davis, *Essays in the Earlier History of American Corporations* (Cambridge, 1917), 29–30; but others turn up from time to time in the United States Supreme Court Reports of the nineteenth century.

73. 96 U.S. 1, 21: "The position advanced, that if a corporation be in any way engaged in commerce [*i.e.*, interstate or foreign commerce] it can enter and do business in another State without the latter's consent is novel and startling." There was a federal statute involved in the Pensacola case; but it should not have altered the result, since Congress was not given its commercial power in order that it might return it to the states. Besides, the Pensacola case is generally regarded as establishing the doctrine stated in the text independently of Congressional enactment. There are of course many other cases; *e.g.*, *Crutcher* v. *Kentucky*, 141 U.S. 47, 56, 57 (1891); *International Text-Book Company* v. *Pigg*, 217 U.S. 91, 108–12 (1910).

74. *First National Bank* v. *Fellows*, 244 U.S. 416 (1917).

75. Some national railroad and telegraph charters were granted. See *California* v. *Central Pacific R. Co.*, 127 U.S. 1 (1887). There was also pressure for nation-wide insurance charters and, apparently, for such charters in some other lines of business, also. *Cf.*, Redfield, *op. cit.* note 50 *supra*, 197.

76. Prentice, *The Federal Power over Carriers and Corporations* (New York, 1907), was one of the replies.

77. *Ibid.*, 4; Wickersham and Morawetz, *op. cit.* note 67 *supra.*

78. See *United States* v. *Delaware & Hudson*, 213 U.S. 366 (1909). The doubts that troubled the Court in this case related largely to the extent of Congressional power over the mode of organizing business. See, also, the dissent of White, J. (afterwards C.J.), with the concurrence of Chief Justice Fuller and Justices Peckham and Holmes, in *Northern Securities Co.* v. *United States*, 193 U.S. 197 (1904). White treated as quite untenable (367) the proposition "that the ownership of stock in railroad corporations created by a State is

interstate commerce, wherever the railroads engage in interstate commerce"; he said (368) that "the ownership of stock in railroads [was] not commerce at all." It would be interesting to be able to quote John Marshall on this point, in view of the realistic way he treated corporations in the case of *The Bank of the United States* v. *Deveaux,* 5 Cranch 61 (1809); but, unfortunately, Marshall never had the chance to explain how utterly false White's position appears to any mind not misled by the corporate fiction.

79. The Securities Act of 1933; the Securities Exchange Act of 1934; the Public Utility Holding Company Act of 1935.

NOTES TO CHAPTER III

1. Oxford, on "among," A, II, 9; I, 835; on "between," A, II, 10. Webster, on "among," 4; on "between," 4.

2. Oxford, on "between," A, II, 9. It is added, in A, V, 19, that "in all senses, *between* has been, from its earliest appearance, extended to more than two." Webster, on "between," 2. Webster, like Oxford, recognizes the propriety of the use of "between" with more than two entities.

3. *Ibid.*

4. *Cf.,* Hamilton and Adair, *The Power to Govern* (New York, 1937), 141; 191–92; and 232, notes 94 and 95; Lawson, *The General Welfare Clause* (Washington, 1934), 26–27; Jerome, *The Problem of the Constitution* (New York, 1939), 130; Stern, *That Commerce Which Concerns More States than One,* 47 HLR, 1335, 1347, 1348 (1934). The title of the article last mentioned is of course based upon Chief Justice Marshall's formula for the internal commercial power of Congress, in *Gibbons* v. *Ogden,* 9 Wheat. (U.S.) 1 (1824). There has been a tendency of late years to try to support Marshall's formula as justified by the meaning of the word "among." See Stern, *op. cit.,* 1347–48; Hamilton and Adair, *op. cit.,* 141. But "among" does not mean, and has never meant, "to concern more than one of"; that is, "to be of importance to more than one of," which is what Marshall plainly meant. No dictionary records such a meaning, and Marshall made not the slightest pretense that "among" carried such a meaning. The Jerome book takes the novel position that "among the several States," in the Commerce Clause, is an adverbial phrase modifying the verb "to regulate," rather than an adjective phrase modifying "Commerce." This interpretation would be grammatically possible if the phrase "among the several States" stood alone in the Commerce Clause. But it appears therein in parallel with the phrases "with foreign Nations" and "with the Indian Tribes." Since neither of these two phrases can possibly be taken in any adverbial sense that will justify the parallelism of construction, an adverbial interpretation of "among the several States" would appear to be out of the question.

5. *Cf.,* Oxford, on "among," A, I, 1 and 2; Webster, on "among," 1.

6. *Cf.,* Webster, on "among": "Among denotes a mingling or intermixture with distinct or separable objects." There are some exceptions, and seeming exceptions, to the foregoing statement; but they do not affect the argument in the text. See note 106 *infra.*

7. Further examples are: Samuel Williams, *History of Vermont* (Walpole, N.H., 1794), 30: "All the streams and rivers of Vermont, have their origin *among* the green mountains." William Robertson, *The History of the Reign of the Emperor Charles V* (London, 1769), I, 202: "A few miserable people . . . had taken shelter *among the ruins of the churches.*" N.Y. Jour., May 25, 1786,

reprinted as proof of what was going on *"among the mountains* of Vermont," a London rumor "that the Vermonteers [had] made private overtures to come under the British government."

8. Hamilton, I, 149.

9. Newp. Merc., September 10, 1785, speaks of "the advantages *this country have* wantonly sacrificed." Conn. Cour., March 27, 1786: *"The adjacent country were* soon called in to his assistance." Warren-Adams, I, 148: Abigail Adams to Mercy Warren, October 19, 1775: *"The Country appear* much exasperated."

10. Oxford, on "state," IV, 30.

11. II, 760; (ed. of 1809), II, 83.

12. See note 6 *supra.*

13. Harrison's edition (London, 1786) is the edition that was consulted.

14. The minor dictionaries consulted were: Bailey, *A Universal Etymological English Dictionary* (Harwood's ed., 1790); Dyche, *A New General English Dictionary* (London, 1765); J. K[ersey], *A New English Dictionary* (1772); Martin, *Lingua Britannica Reformata* (1749); Sheridan, *A Complete Dictionary of the English Language* (Philadelphia, 1789).

15. See, for example, *No. XXXIX* (by Madison): "individuals composing . . . the distinct and independent States *to which they* respectively *belong";* and *No. LXXVI* (by Hamilton): "candidates . . . from the same State *to which he* particularly *belonged."*

16. Blackstone, IV, 66: "intercourse . . . between two or more independent states, and the individuals belonging to each."

17. Benjamin Huntington, of Connecticut, February 4, 1790: "In the state *to which I belong,* no person can be naturalized but by an act of the legislature." Annals, I, 1120.

18. Pa. Pack., August 27, 1785: "A number of invalids *belonging to this commonwealth."* Newp. Merc., May 8, 1784: "a young Man *belonging to Rhode-Island* . . . was knocked overboard by the Boom and drowned." Gaz. S.C., November 27, 1786: "I am an honest farmer's son, who do not belong to this state."

19. Amendment XIV, sec. 1.

20. Wilson, I, 304, 305, 315. See, also, *ibid.,* I, 86, 160, and 373; and II, 436.

21. See also: Pa. Pack., March 22, 1786: "A true American will feel for the reputation and interest of his country, as keenly as for the immediate emolument of *the state of which he is a member."* Conn. Cour., March 25, 1793: "The principal end and design of a free government is to preserve inviolate the life, liberty and property of each *individual member of a state."*

22. Lord Kames, *Sketches of the History of Man* (Edinburgh, 1788), I, 93: "A lasting division of the land among *the members of the state."* Josiah Tucker, *A Treatise Concerning Civil Government* (London, 1781), 306: "Villains of any Sort, were never considered as Citizens at Large, *or as Members of the State."*

23. Constitution of New York, of 1777, article 13: "No *member of this state* shall be disfranchised . . . unless by the law of the land, or the judgment of his peers."

24. Mass. Gaz., April 17, 1787.

25. Journals, XXVI, 119.

26. Article I, sec. 2.

27. (6th Connecticut ed.; Hartford, 1800), II, 34.

28. (New Haven), 144.

29. Adams, a graduate of Harvard, of 1755, ordinarily used the singular verb and pronoun; but the way in which men preferring the singular usage slipped sometimes into the plural is well exemplified in a letter he wrote to James Warren, on May 20, 1776. He said, in part: "The Delegates from Georgia made their Appearance this day in Congress with unlimited Powers and these Gentlemen themselves are very firm. _South Carolina, has_ erected _her_ Government and given her Delegates ample Powers, and they are firm enough. _North Carolina have_ given _theirs_ full Powers after repealing an Instruction given last August against Confederation and Independence." Letters, I, 460. See, also, John Adams to James Warren, March 6, 1777, Warren-Adams I, 297–98: "_This State_ of Pennsilvania _have_ at last compleated their Government." Cf., ibid., I, 230, 269, 293, 333.

30. See, for example, three letters of Bowdoin's to Meshech Weare, president of New Hampshire:—August 16, 1776: "_This state have_ erected eleven forts. . . ." October 17, 1776: "_Your state were_ informed. . . ." And December 6, 1776: "_The State_ of Connecticut . . . _have_ thought fit. . . ." Archives, 5th Ser., I, 990; II, 1107; and III, 1104. Bowdoin, however, like John Adams, seems usually to have followed the singular usage. He was a graduate of Harvard, of 1745. President Weare, of New Hampshire, another graduate of Harvard, used the plural forms, at least at times. See note 36 _infra_.

31. See letter to William Churchill Houston, of January 27, 1778: "_The State_ of Massachusetts _have_ besides large Taxes called in all their own Paper Money to be paid." Letters, III, 57.

32. Wolcott's letters were not searched; but that the plural usage was rationally acceptable to him seems apparent from his repeated use of the plural forms in the following passage from a letter he wrote to Jonathan Trumbull, on December 18, 1780: "In _North Carolina, who have_ not yet adopted the money system of Congress, [the old bills] are very low, but yet pass at twice the value of a late state emission which _they_ have issued. In _Virginia, who_, it is said, _are_ issuing a State emission, the depreciation is also very great. . . . _This State have_ put out a few of [the new Continental bills] and made them a tender at 75 for one. _Pennsylvania are_ about to pass an act relative to the new money system." Coll. Mass. Hist. Soc., 7th Ser., III, 167. It will be noted that, in the foregoing excerpt, the words "North Carolina" and "Virginia" each serve simultaneously in a sense apparently territorial in the "in" phrases, and in a societal sense as the subjects, by reference, in the "who" clauses. This type of construction was common. James Monroe, for example, in one of his letters to Thomas Jefferson, says: "_The county jn w[hic]h_ I reside _have_ plac'd me in the Legislature." Monroe, I, 174.

33. A search of the published letters of Jonathan Trumbull disclosed the following: August 16, 1777: "_The State_ of Rhode Island _rely_ on us for assistance." Coll. Mass. Hist. Soc., 7th Ser., II, 114. February 22, 1779: "_The State_ of Rhode Island _have_ received [sic] a grant of seven thousand bushels of grain. . . ." Ibid., 362. April 22, 1779: "_This State intend_ to complete _their_ quota. . . ." Ibid., 5th Ser., X, 135. August 31, 1780: "_This State have_ at New London four or five hundred barrels of best Irish mess beef." Ibid., 203. July 20, 1781: "_This state hold_ the Articles of Confederation inviolate." Ibid., 7th Ser., III, 251. November 25, 1776: "_This State have_ not a sufficiency [of blankets] for the supply of the men sent from _it_." Archives, 5th Ser., III, 845. November 25, 1776: "_This state beg_ leave for the present to decline." Ibid. December 4, 1776: "_This state have_ declined. . . . _This state have_ made the Continental bills and _its_ own bills of credit a legal tender in all payments."

Ibid., 1077. December 12, 1776: "We were . . . called upon for aid, as *were the Massachusetts, who have* sundry valuable towns lying on . . . that bay. But we learned that *the Massachusetts are* drafting every fourth man . . . to supply the deficiency of *their* proportion in the New Army." *Ibid.*, 1194–95. October 14, 1776: "*This state* readily *submit* to your Excellency's directions what is requisite. . . ." *Ibid.*, II, 1041. October 31, 1776: "*This state* . . . *have* thought proper to send a reinforcement. . . ." *Ibid.*, 1315. As may be seen from the foregoing, Trumbull occasionally lapsed from the plural usage. There are two or three other instances of this in his published letters; but it is plain to be seen that the plural usage was his usual mode of speech and, presumably, his deliberate preference.

34. See, also: Md. Jour., October 25, 1785: "*The Commonwealth* of Massachusetts *have* laid the following duties." Balt. Gaz., January 14, 1785: "*The state* of Vermont *have* chosen delegates." See, also, other notes *infra*.

Other instances of the plural usage noted in Pa. Pack. are as follows: March 6, 1786: "A Customer" says that "the *state* of Delaware, wishing to take advantage of our unhappy divisions, *are* endeavouring to turn them to *their* own benefit, and for this purpose *have* passed an act, making New-Castle and Wilmington free ports." March 21, 1786: "A Settler at Wyoming" says: "The *state* of Pennsylvania *are* aiming for the destruction of that settlement [at Wyoming]." May 16, 1786: "Our sister *state, New York*, has granted to Congress the impost—but *have* reserved to *themselves* the appointment of the officers to collect it." (Note, in this item, the quick lapse from the feminine personification.) May 18, 1786: "The *state* of New York *have* voted the continental impost." May 25, 1786: "The *state* of Connecticut *have* appointed . . . delegates." August 3, 1786: "The *state* of Rhode-Island . . . *have* lately imposed an arbitrary fine of 100 *l.* on every person refusing [its paper money]." See, also, Pa. Her., April 30, 1785: "The *commonwealth* of Massachusetts *have* passed an act. . . ." For other instances of the plural usage in Pennsylvania sources, see notes 43 and 48 *infra*.

35. Other similar items noted in New York papers are: N.Y. Jour., April 6, 1786: "The *state* of Virginia *have* passed an act. . . ." N.Y. Mng. P., August 14, 1788: "The *State* of North-Carolina *have* rejected the New Constitution by a majority of 100." N.Y. Adv., September 3, 1787: "The *State* of Georgia *have* agreed to confirm whatever cessions of land the Indians may make." In N.Y. Jour., of June 1, 1786, there appeared an item, entitled "A Cursory Perspective of the States of America," in which the following appeared: "*Connecticut:* Complaining of hard times, but *do* not yet express great uneasiness. *A branch of them*, however, *are* determined to hold their Wyoming settlements at the expence of blood and treasure, in opposition to the demand of Pennsylvania." This item also appeared in Ch. Mng. P., July 4, 1786; Gaz. S.C., July 3, 1786; Conn. Cour., June 5, 1786; N.H. Ct. Gaz., June 8, 1786; and Am. Her., June 12, 1786. For other New York items showing the plural usage, see notes 39, 43, 45, 47, and 48 *infra*.

For New Jersey instances of such usage, see note 31 *supra* and notes 45 and 48 *infra*.

36. Other similar items in N.H. Gaz. are:—March 25, 1785: "The *state* of Virginia *have* ever since chosen him as a delegate." November 28, 1787: "The *State* of Virginia *have* resolved to choose Delegates." January 2, 1788: "The *State* of Delaware *have* [adopted the Constitution]." N.H. Merc., March 21, 1787: "*The state* of Vermont *have* lately repealed [a certain law for the rendition of fugitives]." See also letter of President Meshech Weare, of New Hamp-

shire, of August 19, 1778, printed in Slade, *Vermont State Papers* (Middlebury, 1823), 90: "The pretended *state* of Vermont . . . *have* extended *their* pretended jurisdiction over the river [Connecticut], and taken into the union (as *they* phrase it) sixteen towns on the east side of [the] river." Additional New Hampshire items are listed in notes 39, 43, and 47 *infra*.

37. Other similar items noted in Conn. Cour. are: March 2, 1784: "The little *State* of Rhode-Island . . . *merit* the execrations which are so liberally uttered against *them*. . . ." July 31, 1786: "The *State* of Rhode-Island, at the election in May last, having changed the whole administration of *their* government, in the course of seven days issued a flood of paper money, from a pretended necessity, and made it a tender in all cases, and *have* lately imposed an arbitrary fine of 100 *l.* on every person refusing it." February 5, 1787: "The *state* of New-York *have* supported the credit of their money, and had similar measures been adopted by the *state* of Rhode-Island, in all probability *they* might have supported the credit of theirs." March 26, 1787: "The plan proposed is nearly similar to what the *state* of New-York *have* adopted. . . . That state, it is true, *have* adopted a paper currency." (This item also appeared in Mass. Cent., April 18, 1787.) June 9, 1788: "The *state* of Georgia *have* granted thirty millions of acres of land to the new confederacy." September 30, 1799: "The *state* of New York *have* long had a general act of bankruptcy." Am. Merc., October 25, 1784, says, "The *state* of New-York *boast*. . . ." Conn. Jour., May 9, 1787, says, "The *State* of Maryland *have* appointed deputies." N.H. Ct. Gaz., June 8, 1786, says, "The *state* of New-Jersey *have* passed an act for the emission of 100,000 *l.* in paper-money." See, also, *Remarks on* [Pelatiah Webster's] *Pamphlet, entituled a Dissertation on the Political Union and Constitution of the Thirteen United States of North America*, by "A Connecticut Farmer" (1784): "[Congress] have . . . determined, that *the state* of Connecticut *have* no just and legal claim . . . to hold any lands . . . west of the state of New-York" (p. 16). "This *state* . . . *have* already acceded to the alteration of the 8th article [of the Articles of Confederation]" (p. 35). "I have never heard that the *State* of Rhode-Island *have* ever refused to fund *their* quota of the national debt." Other Connecticut items showing the plural usage will be found in notes 40, 43, 45, and 48 *infra;* and note 35 *supra*.

38. Wbg. Va. Gaz., January 15, 1780, records that "the *State* of New-Hampshire *have* . . . repealed [a certain tender] law . . . and *have* empowered *their* judges not barely to sit in the seat of nominal justice, but really to dispense it between man and man." Va. Jour., May 19, 1785, says, "*The Commonwealth* of Massachusetts *have* passed an act imposing duties on licensed vellum, parchment, and paper." The same paper, on August 4, 1785, records that "the *Commonwealth* of Massachusetts *have* lately passed an act, laying very heavy duties on all Foreign Manufactures imported into that Commonwealth, by Land or Water." And, on November 3, 1785, that "the *Commonwealth* of Massachusetts *have* laid the following duties on the articles hereinafter enumerated." N. & P. Jour., March 12, 1788, says that "the *State* of New-Hampshire *have* adjourned *their* Convention *sine die*, without coming to any determination [on the Constitution]."

39. This item also appeared in Md. Jour., July 3, 1787; N.Y. Adv., July 9, 1787; Sal. Merc., July 17, 1787; Mass. Cent., July 14, 1787; N.H. Gaz., July 21, 1787; and Ga. Gaz., September 8, 1787.

40. Other similar items noted in the Charleston, S.C., papers are:—Ch. G. A., June 22, 1784: "The *State* of Virginia *have* wisely forbid any grain to be exported for a limited time, on account of the long drought prevailing in that

State." Ch. Wkly. Gaz., March 29, 1783: "The *State* in which [Continental troops] serve . . . *are* under no obligation to support them." Ch. G. A., January 11, 1786: "The *state* of New-Hampshire *have* passed an act to prevent the body of any debtor being taken by execution." Mid. Gaz., February 11, 1788, carried "a letter from a mercantile house in Charleston (S.C.) to one in [Philadelphia]," which said: "The *State of Georgia* have adopted the Federal Constitution." This letter may also be found in Mass. Gaz., February 12, 1788, and Mass. Cent., February 13, 1788. Another letter from Charleston, in Newp. Merc., April 14, 1788, says, "*This state feel their* interest deeply concerned in adopting the new Constitution." See, also, notes 45, 47, and 48 *infra;* and note 26 *supra.*

41. Other examples of the plural usage noted in Vt. Gaz. are:—March 14, 1785: "The *state* of Maryland *have* lately passed an act for the Naturalization of Major General the Marquis de la Fayette." July 7, 1788: "We are informed that the important *State* of Virginia *have* adopted the Federal Constitution." See also Slade, *op. cit.* note 36 *supra,* 156–58 (question propounded by committee of Congress to agents of Vermont, and their answer thereto): "Question 3d. What are the ideas of the *people of Vermont* relative to the claim of private property, under grants or patents from New-Hampshire, or New-York, previous to the present revolution? *Answer,* Although the *State* of Vermont *have* not, hitherto, authorized any Courts to take cognizance of such causes, as respect titles of lands, nevertheless *they* have had, and still have it in contemplation to adopt such modes, as the circumstances, arising out of each case, may justify, without adhering to the strict rules of law." See, also, note 46 *infra.*

42. Other examples of the plural usage noted in Massachusetts papers are as follows: B. Ind. Chr., April 8, 1784: "*The State of New-York have* possessed *themselves* of three hundred townships [of public lands deemed by the writer to belong to Massachusetts]." March 15, 1787 (letter of General Benjamin Lincoln to Governor Bowdoin): "*The State of New-York are* perfectly disposed to serve us." (This letter may also be found in Ga. Gaz., April 21, 1787.) May 17, 1787: "*The Commonwealth of Massachusetts have* never pursued measures to establish a credit." Mass. Gaz., September 19, 1788: "Governour Sevier [of the quondam state of Franklin] has lately put himself at the head of the federalists, and menaces the *state of Northcarolina,* for putting *themselves* out of the Union, by rejecting the new Constitution." Am. Her., November 12, 1787: "*The Commonwealth* of Massachusetts *have* pledged *their* sacred honor." Mass. Cent., August 11, 1787: "Whatever benefit may be derived to desperate debtors, spendthrifts, &c. from the Tender-Law, *the State at large,* by painful experience, *find* it, without a pun, a very Tough-Law." See, also, notes 29, 35, 37, 39, and 40 *supra;* and 43, 45, and 48 *infra.*

In Maine, then a part of Massachusetts, in Fal. Gaz., June 11, 1785, an advocate of separation from Massachusetts, says: "What *the State lose* by our leaving *them* will probably be made up to *them* in five or six years, by *their* natural increase." A Maine item in Pa. Pack., September 24, 1785, says: "*All that part of the state* twenty miles west of Boston, and upwards, *are* still anxious for the removal of the general court [to a more central spot]." See, also, Cumb. Gaz., April 6, 1787, and September 20, 1787; and next note *infra.*

43. Other examples in which the noun "state" in the singular number and a plural verb are used in immediate juxtaposition are: N.Y. Jour., May 25, 1786: "*This state have* an emission of [paper] money now in the press." (This item may also be found in Pa. Pack., May 30, 1786.) N.H. Spy, May 22, 1787,

prints a Rhode Island item which says: "*This state have* not [the contracting of new debts] to fear." Mass. Gaz., January 14, 1788: "We are informed . . . from Georgia, that *that state have* ratified the Federal Constitution." Conn. Cour., February 23, 1795: "*This state do,* indeed, claim a title to those lands." September 16, 1799: "*The state are* in no distress for money." Also: "*The state* not only *are* bound to warrant the title, *they are* bound to provide a government." The item last mentioned is a good example of consistent plural usage in an extended composition, by a man of obvious ability and education. It contains, however, one apparently accidental lapse into the singular. A Rhode Island letter, published in Conn. Cour., April 2, 1787, and Cumb. Gaz., April 6, 1787, says: "We have often heard of sinking funds—but we know of no *nation who have* provided one so productive as that with which *this state are* now furnished [under the paper-money law]."

44. Other examples of the plural usage noted in Rhode Island papers are: Newp. Merc., March 6, 1784: "*The State* of New-York *have* made choice of [persons] to represent that State in Congress." May 22, 1784: "*The State* of South-Carolina *have* passed an act. . . ." May 29, 1786: "We hear *the State* of Connecticut *have* appointed the following delegates." February 16, 1789: "*The State* of Vermont *have* appointed . . . Agents . . . to treat with [Congress]." August 26, 1789: "*The State* of South-Carolina *have* determined to call a Convention for the purpose of revising *their* State Constitution." Newp. Her., May 24, 1787: "*Every state* in the Union . . . *have* appointed Delegates to the Grand Convention, . . . Rhode-Island only excepted." U.S. Chr., September 22, 1785: "*The State* of Maryland (notwithstanding *their* tobacco) . . . *are* upon some plan [for a paper money emission]. . . . *The State* of New-Hampshire *have* impolitickly [handled their paper-money]." Prov. Gaz., January 8, 1785: "*The State* of Vermont *have* chosen delegates. For other Rhode Island examples of the plural usage, see notes 45 and 48 *infra;* and note 43 *supra.*

45. N.Y. Jour., March 15, 1787: "*Maryland* . . . *have* nominated three delegates." N.J. Pol. Int., April 21, 1784: "*South-Carolina* . . . *are* [now] inclining to . . . mild principles." This last item may also be found in Ch. G. A., June 29, 1784. N.J. Gaz., March 2, 1784: "*Virginia,* by a late act, *have* empowered her delegates in Congress, to convey by a deed to the United States, all lands on the north side of the Ohio." This item also appeared in U.S. Chr., April 1, 1784. It originated from Annapolis. N.Y. Adv., May 6, 1788, printed "from *The Nova-Scotia Packet,*" the following: "*Georgia,* in consequence of the refusal of Congress [to assist against the Indians] *have* withdrawn *their* delegates [from Congress] and formally renounced their authority." Am. Merc., December 17, 1787, printed, from "a letter from a gentleman in New-York," the following: "*Delaware have* set us a good example—*their* convention met on the 3d and unanimously ratified the proposed constitution on the 6th inst." Conn. Cour., March 9, 1784: "As soon as *New-York have* adopted the measure [*i.e.,* a state impost], we shall pay yearly the sum of about fifteen thousand pounds to *them* in duties." N.H. Ct. Gaz., June 8, 1786, says "*Vermont care* but little for the confederation." That, of June 7, 1787, reports "Col. Wadsworth" as having said in the Connecticut legislature that "*Massachusetts have* given no evidence of *their* having done wrong in separating *their* judges [from the council]." B. Ind. Chr., April 26, 1787: "Nor would the nation have been one whit better off, if all the States of the Union had granted the impost in the same manner that *Massachusetts have* granted it." Mass. Cent., April 24, 1784, reprints a New York item saying that "*New-Jersey,* taking advantage of our [New York'] political discussions, *are* determined to profit by them. . . ."

N.H. Spy, March 27, 1787: "*Maryland . . . have* nominated delegates to the grand convention."

46. Slade, *op. cit.* note 36 *supra*, 119. See, also, another letter of Governor Chittenden's of October 28, 1779. *Ibid.*, 114–15. Also, committee report in Vermont House of Representatives, February 12, 1781. *Ibid.*, 128, 130.

47. Elliot, I, 108. This item was published in identical form in at least the following papers: Ch. Ev. Gaz., June 1, 1786; N.H. Merc., March 15, 1786; and N.Y. Jour., May 4, 1786. A reprint of the report in its original form will be found in Journals, XXX, 93. Another report on the same subject was made, on October 23, 1786, by a committee made up of Charles Pinckney, of South Carolina; Melancton Smith, of New York; and John Henry, of Maryland. It was published in N.Y. Jour., December 21, 1786. It states that "*South Carolina . . . have* invested . . . Congress with [certain powers]"; that "*New Hampshire, by their* Act of the 23d of June, 1785, invested . . . Congress with [certain powers]"; and that "*North-Carolina by their* Act of the 2d of June, 1784, *have* authorised *their* delegates to agree to [certain stated changes in the Articles of Confederation]." However, in this report, there is a lapse into the singular usage with reference to the state of Delaware. For the original form of this report, see Journals, XXXI, 907. It, also, is reproduced by Elliot with the plural verbs changed to singulars. Elliot, I, 109.

48. Ph. Ind. Gaz., May 28, 1785; N.Y. Ind. Jour., June 1, 1785; N.J. Gaz., June 6, 1785; Bost. Gaz., June 6, 1785; Newp. Merc., June 11, 1785; Prov. Gaz., June 11, 1785; U.S. Chr., June 16, 1785; Norw. Pack., June 16, 1785; Ch. P. A., June 22, 1785.

49. See, also, *Civil Prudence* (Norwich, 1776), 20. The author of this pamphlet refers to the great amounts in Rhode Island and New Hampshire bills, which, according to Sherman's *Almanack*, were held by persons residing in Connecticut, in 1752. "Surely," he then concludes, "*Connecticut must have been an industrious and frugal people*, to purchase bills in such quantity."

50. May 1, 8, 22, and 29, and June 26, 1797.

51. May 29, 1797.

52. June 26, 1797.

53. 30. See, also, 8, 23, 27, and 30.

54. Article II, sec. 1.

55. Ford, *Letters of Joseph Jones to James Madison, 1788–1802* (Cambridge, 1901), 9, 10.

56. George Mason, according to Madison's notes on the Federal Convention, "argued very cogently [in that body] that punishment could not in the nature of things be executed *on the States collectively*, and therefore that such a Gov-[ernmen]t was necessary as could directly operate on *individuals*, and would punish those only whose guilt required it." Records, I, 34. In the Connecticut ratifying convention, William Samuel Johnson said, according to Conn. Cour., January 14, 1788: "The Convention saw this imperfection [under the Articles of Confederation] in attempting to legislate for states *in their political capacity. . . .* They have formed one new nation out of the individual states. . . .*" In the Vermont ratifying convention, of 1791, "Mr. Chipman, of Rutland," said, according to Pa. Pack., February 15, 1791, that "the national legislature . . . legislate, *not upon the states collectively, but upon the citizens of the union.*"

57. Records, I, 263. An anonymous pamphlet published in Richmond in 1798, *An Enquiry whether the Act of Congress . . . generally called the Sedition Bill is Unconstitutional or Not*, seems to refer to the same subject in the

same way. It says that the several inducements to the adoption of the Constitution were the raising of a national revenue, the regulation of our "intercourse with foreign powers, defending us from them—and prevent[ing] *disputes among the states.*" The subsequent discussion shows that the author had in mind both intrastate and interstate disputes, and it would seem that this was probably true in the passage quoted. It is not, however, quite so clear as the passage in the text.

58. All reports of Randolph's sentiments accord with the interpretation given in the text. *Cf.*, Records, I, 24, 25, and 256.

59. Hancock's speech was reported in the newspapers all over the country; among others, in the following: Pa. Merc., March 11, 1788; Pa. Jour., March 12, 1788; Va. Ind. Chr., March 26, 1788; Va. Her., March 27, 1788; N.Y. Jour., March 7, 1788; Col. Her., April 17, 1788.

60. Article I, sec. 8; Article II, secs. 2 and 3; Article IV, sec. 4.

61. Records, I, 586. *Cf.*, *ibid.*, II, 220.

62. Records, I, 349. The sense of Mason's remarks accords with the interpretation in the text, in all the reports of it. *Cf.*, Records, I, 339, 346, and 351.

63. *Op. cit.* note 22 *supra*, I, 191.

64. (6th ed.; London, 1793), 299.

65. *Op. cit.* note 7 *supra*, I, 142. See, also, *ibid.*, I, 197: "the enthusiastick passion for war, which prevailed *among the barbarous nations.*" I, 210: "*Among most of the* [Indian] *tribes*, the Sachem or chief is elective." I, 211: "*Among the Americans* [*i.e.*, the Indians], the magistrate has scarce any criminal jurisdiction." And I, 230: "*Among all the barbarous nations*, long hair was a mark of dignity and of freedom." It seems evident that in all the foregoing excerpts, and likewise in that in the text, Robertson's mode of thought was the same; and, further, that there was nothing territorial, or interstate, or intertribal, or international about it.

66. (London, 1829), IV, 14.

67. *Ibid.*, V, 383. "Aristus was sent as [Lacedaemonian] minister to Syracuse; [but] no title of harmost [governor] was assumed." The harmost ruled through oligarchical cliques in—*i.e.*, "among"—the various conquered states.

68. *Ibid.*, V, 125. The full text of the passage is as follows: "Nor was it now any longer the time when Spartan ladies could take and use arms like men. *Among the smaller Grecian states* the sight of an enemy, often recurring, became less terrible through familiarity. But at Lacedaemon, for centuries, it had almost ceased to be supposed that an enemy could ever be seen there. To the Spartan ladies now the sight even of the smoke, says the contemporary historian, from the buildings fired by the invaders was intolerable. Not only however the consternation of the fearful and inconsiderate, but the reasonable apprehension of the best informed and firmest, was very great." In other words, it was not the same "*among* the smaller Grecian *states*," as it was *among the Spartans*. Another passage, at V, 391, also brings out clearly the multitudinal sense of "state," as Mitford used it. After referring to "the unexampled prosperity which Syracuse [attained] under Dionysius," Mitford adds that this prosperity shows "that [Dionysius'] administration must have been not only able, but liberal, beneficent, and such as altogether clearly infused a general confidence, *both among those living under it, and among foreign states.*"

69. *Ibid.*, V, 374–75. *Cf.*, a reference by Henry Knox, Washington's Secretary of War (in Conn. Cour., February 13, 1792), to "certain turbulent and malignant characters, residing *among some of the northern and western tribes* [of Indians]."

70. Mitford, *op. cit.* note 66 *supra*, I, 359. He adds: "Everywhere this evil appears to have had its root in the institution of slavery; whence the operation of wealth has been remarkably similar *among all the ancient republics,* and remarkably different from anything known in modern Europe."

71. *Ibid.,* V, 481.

72. Ch. St. Gaz., March 22, 1785: *"The polite Athenians* taught [agriculture] to *the more rustic states* of Greece." Tucker, *op. cit.* note 22 *supra*, 220: "That which made the Conduct of *the Athenians* to appear different from that of most of *the other States,* was the Use of the Ostracism."

73. (6th ed.; London, 1809), I, "Preface to the First Edition," xi; "Introduction," iii, iv, and viii.

74. Thomas Lloyd, *The Congressional Register* (New York, 1789), I, 70.

75. Webster, 216: On "between": "AMONG always implies more than two objects."

76. Other similar items are: Richard Price, *Observations on the Importance of the American Revolution* (London, 1785), 49: "Would the *United States . . .* deny such men . . . all places of trust and power *among them?" Ibid.,* 68: "One of the circumstances . . . favorable to the *American States . . .* has been the equality which subsists *among them."* (Price did not mean "interstate equality," but that equality between man and man which "subsisted *among the people* of the American States.") Gaz. S.C., July 1, 1784: "The encouragement which the American *states* give to foreigners settling *among them."*

77. *An Addition to the Present Melancholy Circumstances of the Province Considered, &c.* (Boston, 1719), 8.

78. (Williamsburg, 1746), 5; reprinted in Boyd, *Some Eighteenth-Century Tracts Concerning North Carolina* (Raleigh, 1927), 55 at 72–73.

79. (Philadelphia, 1774), Letter II, 20; Letter VIII, 82.

80. *Political Essays* (1772), 376. See, also, Dickinson, I, 363, note.

81. Reprinted in Dickinson, I, 45, at 55 and 56.

82. Tucker, Bk. I, Pt. 1, App. 140, 158, and 191. *Cf., ibid.,* 103: "Those [counties] which have few or no slaves *among them."*

83. (Richmond, 1820), Editor's preface, iii.

84. 12 NORTH AMERICAN REVIEW, 290, 306.

85. 175

86. *Cf.,* the following miscellaneous materials: Mass. Cent., March 15, 1788: *"The bank are* a company consisting of gentlemen of the first fortunes." Charter of the Bank of North America, May 26, 1791, reprinted in Clarke and Hall, 13: *"The said corporation are* hereby declared [etc.] . . . That, for the well governing of the said *corporation* and the ordering of *their* affairs, *they* shall have such officers as *they* shall hereafter direct or appoint." Ch. P. A., December 7, 1785: *"The Episcopal English Church* in the United States, *have* lately expunged from *their* liturgy, the Nicene and Athanasian creeds." U.S. Chr., July 1, 1784: *"The University* of Pennsylvania *have* conferred the honorary degree of Doctor of Laws on Charles Thompson. . . .'" Mass. Gaz., May 9, 1788: *"The town* of Hingham, *have* made choice of the Hon. Benjamin Lincoln, Esq. and Col. Theophilus Cushing, to represent *them* the ensuing year." U.S. Chr., September 6, 1787: "The *city* of Philadelphia . . . *have* recently formed . . . 'The Pennsylvania Society, for Encouragement of Manufactures, and the Useful Arts.'" N.H. Ct. Gaz., November 8, 1787: *"This county* [of Somerset, N.J.] *do* highly approve of [the Constitution]." Oliver Ellsworth, in the Connecticut state convention, as reported in Mass.

Gaz., January 18, 1788: "*The province* of Holland *have* ever been opposed to the appointment of a stadtholder." N.Y. Jour., January 5, 1786: "The republic [of Venice] *have* actually prohibited all games [of chance]." Gaz. S.C., May 4, 1786: "There is not a *power* in Europe that *have* made such a rapid progress." Ch. P. A., July 28, 1784 (reprinted from THE BOSTON MAGAZINE): "Since the war began, these schools have been neglected, so that *few towns* have any such *among them*." Tench Francis, *Considerations on a Paper Currency*, reprinted in Pownall, II, 272, 287: "The convenience of [paper] will appear, if we suppose the debtor *a member of the society amongst whom* the paper passes." Dunbar, *Essays on the History of Mankind in Rude and Uncultivated Ages* (London, 1780), 6–7: "It is the arts of life which . . . have annihilated *personal* independence, and formed an immense chain of connexions *among collective bodies*." A "state," of course, was a "collective body"; indeed, the very sort of "collective body," of which Dunbar was speaking.

87. (Philadelphia), 22.

88. Further examples of the plural usage with "nation" are the following: N.Y. Jour., January 12, 1786: "No *nation* under heaven *have* greater advantages." Wilson, II, 85: "*Among untutored nations*, the want of letters is supplied, though imperfectly, by the use of visible and natural signs." There are many similar passages.

89. *Op. cit.* note 7 *supra*, 174. See, also, 151, 152, and 182.

90. Sullivan, 22. See, also, Sullivan, *History of the District of Maine* (Boston, 1795), 94: "That authority which nature gives to the parent, was not wholly disregarded *among the wild tribes* of our wilderness. . . . At what age the young Savage became his own guardian is very uncertain; nor is it probable that any general rule was observed *in the tribes*." The complete equivalence of "in" and "among" in this passage should be noted.

91. Pa. Pack., August 21, 1786.

92. Examples of the plural verb forms with "tribe" are: Fal. Gaz., March 26, 1785: "*The Chickamawga tribe have* abandoned and burnt their towns." Va. Am. Adv., August 21, 1784: "*The Oneida tribe have* made a donation of land to the Stockbridge Indians."

93. 269, 295, 306, and 348.

94. Examples of the type of usage last mentioned in the text are: Robertson, *op. cit.* note 7 *supra*, I, 225: "*In Italy*, the same revolutions happened in property, and succeeded each other in the same order. There is some ground, however, for conjecturing that allodial property continued longer in estimation *among the Italians*, than *among the French*." *Ibid.*, 226: "The progress of the feudal system *among the Germans* was perfectly similar to that which we have traced *in France*." Jackson, 88: "Agriculture is said to be encouraged *among the Chinese* to an high degree." Tucker, Bk. I, Pt. 2, App. 90, 92: "*Among the Muscovites*, emigration is not permitted." Examples of the types of usage first mentioned in the text at this point will be found in the notes that follow.

95. Wilson, II, 338: "He . . . attempted to palm upon the court, as a unanimous verdict, one contradictory to that which had been agreed on *among the jury*."

96. Dickinson, I, 74: "The people of Great-Britain who have come *among us*." Wilson, I, 315: "*Those states* which manage their affairs best, will offer the strongest inducements to *their* own citizens to remain, and to others to incorporate *among them*." Letter of Pierce Butler to ——, May 30, 1786.

in the South Carolina Historical Society's collections: "I wish to God, at the time You thought of sitting down *among Us,* that My friend Thos. Fitzsimons had consented to it."

97. Wm. Smith, 207–8: "Trinity church . . . is, within, ornamented beyond any other place of worship *among us.*" Dickinson, II, 254: "The best houses *among us.*"

98. Dickinson, I, 53: "All the money brought *among us* in the course of the late war." Cumb. Gaz., February 23, 1787: "If the immense sums of money which are sent over the Atlantic for [calico] were saved *among us,* it would be not a little help towards restoring a circulating medium." Am. Her., August 6, 1787: "[With low domestic prices] the difficulties and disadvantages of making remittances will gradually turn in our favor, and money will flow in *among us.*"

99. Dickinson, I, 54: "We are prohibited by new and stricter restraints being laid on our trade, from . . . instituting *among ourselves* bills of credit in the place of [specie] in our internal traffic."

100. In N.Y. Jour., May 4, 1786, a letter from New Jersey speaks of "the necessity of producing that valuable article [flax] *among ourselves.*" Pa. Pack., September 16, 1785: "Thirty-one of the principal gentlemen in New-Haven have formed themselves into a society, by the name of 'The Connecticut Silk Society,' for the purpose of raising and manufacturing that article *among them,* which will employ large numbers of both sexes, grown people and children, besides saving vast sums of money *among us* which are now constantly sent to other countries."

101. Dickinson, I, 77: "It is surprising to see the linen and cloth that have been lately made *among us.* . . . I believe in a few years we shall have very different kinds of cloth *among us* from these we now make."

102. Dickinson, I, 75: "We have our choice of these two things—to continue our present limited and disadvantageous commerce—or to promote manufactures *among ourselves.*" Col. Her., September 28, 1785: "Let us encourage manufacturies *among ourselves.*" Newp. Merc., June 16, 1788: "The people in the back part of [South Carolina], are very anxious to get the machines for ginning, carding, and spinning cotton *amongst them.*"

103. Pa. Pack., July 4, 1786: "However dull trade may be here, it has met with much less stagnation *among us,* than in any part of the continent, Charleston perhaps excepted." Mass. Cent., December 5, 1787: "We have not secured even our own coasting trade *among ourselves.*" Col. Her., May 8, 1786: "The paper medium . . . cannot be sent out of the state, but will answer all the purposes of intercourse *amongst ourselves.*"

104. *Wikoff* v. *Coxe,* 1 Yeates (Pa.) 353, 357 (1793): "We have no chancery jurisdiction *amongst us.*" *Warder* v. *Bell,* 1 Yeates (Pa.) 531, 532–33 (1795): "There is no fixed rule *amongst us* in such cases. . . . No decision that we know of *amongst us,* has fixed any general rule." *McCarty* v. *Emlen,* 2 Yeates (Pa.) 190, 193 (1797): "This objection does not occur *amongst us,* from a different arrangement of the judicial powers." *Dehuff* v. *Turbett,* 3 Yeates (Pa.) 157, 161 (1801): "What species of suit could Turbett or his executors, *amongst us,* have brought against Dehuff?" In all the foregoing cases, the "among" phrases mean "in" the state of Pennsylvania. Newp. Merc., September 10, 1785: "We might furnish *among ourselves* almost every article of consumption." Pa. Pack., February 1, 1786: A correspondent says that the action of "certain watchmen of the city" in "depriving [one Captain Procter] of his liberty" by "false imprisonment" should be "resented by

every inhabitant *among us* who values his citizenship." Am. Her., June 20, 1785: "With folded arms, we have permitted . . . their merchants to pursue a British *commerce among us.*" Jackson, 157: "Not a man, from this time forward born *among us*, should be suffered to pass on to the age of twenty-one years, . . . without having been instructed in the military art." Ch. City Gaz., January 24, 1788: General C. C. Pinckney to the South Carolina House of Representatives, January 17, 1788: "We obtained a representation for our property, and I confess I did not expect [to] be told on our return, that we had conceded too much to the Eastern *states* when they allowed us a representation for a species of property which they have not *among them.*"

105. Conn. Cour., July 22, 1793: "*Some among them* [fugitives from the massacres at Cape François] may have, by their guilt, drawn the misfortunes they feel, on their own heads." Dickinson, II, 170–71: "*Some among us* were . . . overheated." *Ibid.*, 197: "*Those among us* who have supposed [etc.]." Jackson, 63: "*Very few among them* have considered the subjects on which they are called upon to determine." *Ibid.*, 105: "*Some among them* are more capable than others." *Ibid.*, 128: "*Every one among us* [has] undoubtedly a right to think for himself." *Ibid.*, 130: "*None among us* are more than sufficient [in information] to project the best political institutions."

106. The greater frequency with which "among" was used may be further inferred from the following examples: Pa. Pack., July 4, 1786, records that one Sarah Vanpelt had recently killed her husband by giving him rat-poison "*among some clam soup.*" Newp. Merc., June 5, 1790: "Extract of a letter from Cooper's Town, on Lake Otsego: 'We are working away *among the* [maple] *sugar* here.' " N. L. Gaz., October 20, 1786: "A fluctuation of the medium [of commerce] in a state makes more fatal ravages *among the morals of people*, than a pestilence *among their lives.*" Mitford, *op. cit.* note 66 *supra*, I, 11: "In progress of ages, and *among revolutions*, arose circumstances tending to hold the [Grecian] people southward [of Macedonia and Epirus]."

107. In the great mass of materials examined, no evidence at all was found that the phrase "interstate commerce" was in use in 1787. It seems to have come into use along toward the middle of the nineteenth century.

108. See pp. 35–36 *supra*.

109. Blackstone, I, 43, 75, and 273; and IV, 66–68. These passages are set forth in full in note 39 to chapter ii of this book. See, also, Blackstone, III, 69.

110. (London), 92.

111. *Loc. cit.* notes 42–45 to chapter ii *supra*.

112. *The Elements of Commerce and Theory of Taxes*, reprinted in Schuyler, *Josiah Tucker* (New York, 1931), 51, 127. *The Elements of Commerce* was an unfinished, unpublished work; but the same mode of expression may be found in other eighteenth-century economic writings. See, for example, Com. Int., II, 371–75: "This definition [of 'the general operation of commerce'] naturally divides *trade* into two parts, *home and foreign.* . . . The *home trade* of a nation is that which the several members of a society carry on among themselves. It holds the first rank in *trade in general.* . . . *Foreign trade* is that which a political society carries on with others."

113. Mansfield resigned from the chief-justiceship of the King's Bench in June 1788.

114. *Pillans* v. *Van Mierop*, 3 Burr. 1664, 1672 (1765).

115. Sullivan, 337 *et seq.*, especially 352–54.

116. *Cf.*, note 4 to chapter ii *supra*.

NOTES TO CHAPTER IV

1. This most general sense of "commerce," now rare and rather stilted, was very common in the eighteenth century. A good example is the following from Conn. Cour., July 12, 1790: "Amiableness and politeness of manners are not only pleasing, but useful, in our *commerce* with the world." See, also, Thomas Jefferson's statement in his *Notes on Virginia* (Jefferson, IV, 82) that "the whole *commerce* between master and slave is a perpetual exercise of the most boisterous passions"; and Robert James's statement, in his *Treatise on Canine Madness*, of 1760 (p. 13), that "the distemper [therein treated of] is in man generally excited by the bite of some animal previously mad, and principally from domestic animals, which have the greatest *commerce* with mankind." The commonplace character of this sense of "commerce," in the eighteenth century, is indicated by its occurrence in idiomatic phrases; as in Fanny Burney's statement in her *Diary* for 1791 (edition of 1876, Vol. III, p. 371), that a certain bishop of Dromore was "of good commerce." Her meaning was that the bishop was "good company."

2. True Sys. 233: "The most active Principle of *useful Commerce* [is] Rivalship." In other words, "competition is the life of trade." Am. Mus., I, 210 (March 1787): "Study agriculture; carry it to the greatest perfection. It is the basis of our wealth; of manufactures; and of all *gainful commerce.*"

3. See either Oxford or Webster. Not all dictionaries give clearly this particular meaning of "general."

4. Book XXIV, line 230.

5. Act I, scene iv.

6. See Oxford. A good example of the use of the phrase "the general mass" may be found in Thomas Mortimer's translation of Jacques Necker's *De l'administration des finances de la France* (2d ed.; London, 1786), III, 77: "From the above probabilities, we ought not to infer that *the general mass* of the circulating specie in France bears an equal proportion to *the general mass* of the specie, circulating throughout the rest of Europe."

7. Reprinted in McCulloch I, 93, 94, 95, 98, 99, and 109.

8. Pownall, I, 20.

9. (London), 247–48.

10. *A Brief Essay on the Advantages and Disadvantages which respectively attend France and Great Britain, With regard to Trade*, reprinted in McCulloch II, 317–21, especially 321.

11. *Passim,* especially 4.

12. Reprinted in Coxe, 337 *et seq.*

13. A letter from Dr. Benjamin Rush to Richard Price, dated the 22d of April 1786, contains the following: "The States have *almost generally* appointed a Convention to sit next September at Annapolis, for the sole purpose of conferring upon Congress additional powers, especially for the purpose of regulating our trade." *Letters to and from Richard Price. D.D., F.R.S., 1767–1790* (Cambridge, 1903), 82. Rush's meaning was that the states had "almost all" made such appointments. Not nearly all of them had in fact done so; but Rush's letter was written at the peak of optimism about the Annapolis Convention, when the general belief was in accord with his statement. James Madison wrote to Thomas Jefferson, in Paris, three weeks later than the date of Rush's letter, that "most if not all the States except Maryl[an]d, ha[d] appointed deputies for the proposed Convention at Annapolis." Madison, II, 238.

14. Coxe, 331 *et seq.*

15. A writer in B. Ind. Chr. July 21, 1787, used the word "general" with the triad, "commerce, agriculture, and manufactures," in the sense of "entire" applying to all three members of the triad. He said: "To ascertain the quantity of currency requisite for any Government, we must first enquire the amount of their annual taxes, for the discharge of their foreign and domestic debt; also the sum necessary for their public exigencies; and *their general [i.e., their entire] commerce, agriculture, and manufactures.*" James Madison used the word "general" similarly, in reference to "trade" in the sense of "merchandize," in a letter he wrote to Robert Walsh, on March 2, 1819. He referred therein to "the British Factors chiefly from Scotland, who [before the American Revolution] carried on *the general [i.e., the entire] trade external and internal* of the Colony [of Virginia]." Madison, VIII, 428–29. So, also, John Dickinson said, in a pamphlet of his on Parliamentary power, in 1774: "Without [regulation], *our general [i.e., our entire] commerce with foreign nations* might have been injurious to [Great Britain]." Dickinson, I, 413. In the last item, the words *"foreign nations"* were italicized in the original. This, of course, tends to confirm that "general commerce" *ordinarily* meant all home trade, as well as all foreign trade. *Cf.,* discussion of Dickinson's pamphlet of 1774, in chapter v hereof. In a speech to the Massachusetts General Court, in 1785, Governor Bowdoin reported that he had sent to the other states a copy of Massachusetts' act for regulating commerce; that New Hampshire had also passed such a law; and that he hoped the remaining states would do the same. "Such correspondent acts," he said, "would be productive of happy effects, until Congress should ordain regulations for *the general [i.e., the entire] commerce* of the confederated body." Pa. Pack., November 5, 1785. In this case, "general" marked the distinction between "the commerce of the whole," and "the commerces of the parts."

16. *Cf.,* the use of the phrase "business of alienation" in the passage quoted in the text, at p. 95 hereof, from William Barton, *The True Interest of the United States* (Philadelphia, 1786).

17. See the discussion "Concerning the National *Industry*" in Coxe, 355. It begins: "An enquiry into the knowledge or skill, assiduity, economy, or frugality, and good management, with which the several descriptions of citizens in the United States pursue their employments, has never yet been made. The subject is copious, and would require much previous enquiry and detail. It is not intended, therefore, in this place to attempt a development of it; yet it may be serviceable to bestow upon it a few brief reflections. The learned professions will not be brought into view, as they are not strictly of the nature of the object contemplated. *The planters, the farmers, the merchants, the navigators, the fishermen, the shipbuilders, the manufacturers and the mechanics, with the persons immediately employed by them,* are all which are conceived to be comprehended in the subject." See, also, "The Retrospect" in Conn. Cour., September 29, 1800: "The beneficial effects of the Government under the Constitution [gave] . . . a universal spring . . . to the various branches of *industry both agricultural and mechanical as well as commercial.*" And Smith, 644: "The political oeconomy of the nations of modern Europe, has been more favorable to manufacturers and foreign trade, the *industry* of the towns, than to agriculture, the *industry* of the country."

18. The sense of "trade" and "commerce" which included manufactures,

but not agriculture, or "husbandry," is discussed in the fifth section of the present chapter.

19. 4.

20. 30 and 59.

21. 5 and 18.

22. *Cf.*, the definition of "article" as "a particular part of a whole" in Samuel Johnson, *A Dictionary of the English Language* (Harrison's ed.; London, 1786).

23. Com. Int., I, 130: "Nations, who have considered nothing farther in the culture of their lands, than the bare means of self-subsistance, have always lived in perpetual fear of dearths, and have often felt them. Those, on the contrary, who have considered agriculture as *an object of commerce*, have enjoyed such a series of plenty, as has enabled them, at all times, to supply the necessities of others." *Ibid.*, II, 404: "From what has been said in the preceding part, it is plain that agriculture cannot flourish, when not considered as *an object of trade*." "Object," in these passages, means "article," "part," or "branch."

24. *Cf.*, Hugh Henry Brackenridge, before the Pennsylvania legislature, as reported in Pa. Pack., January 4, 1787: "We talk of a *medium of commerce* amongst the citizens of the state: what is meant by this? Just so much money as in all dealings amongst the people will supercede the use of barter. . . . This sum will depend on the number of the people, the nature of their occupation, whether *agricultivators, manufacturers or merchants*."

25. Thus, the eighteenth century spoke of "raising and *manufacturing* wheat"—*i.e.*, raising it and threshing it and grinding it into flour. *Cf.*, Archibald Kennedy, *loc. cit.* note 21 *supra*. In the same way, "A Humble Enquirer," in N.H. Merc., January 3, 1786, asks how the state's impost can benefit those "who employ themselves in *manufacturing* fish."

26. Hamilton, III, 322, 334, 339, and 340.

27. Wilson, II, 114; and III, 193 and 194.

28. The pamphlet was published anonymously, but was ascribed to Barton by Matthew Carey, when reprinted, in part, in Am. Mus. for May 1788. The ascription was correct. See DHC, V, 66. The quoted passage will be found in Am. Mus., III, 442 and 443.

29. Reprinted in Am. Mus. (July 1787), II, 31.

30. An item advocating the cultivation of the sugar maple, in Mass. Gaz., July 4, 1765, says: "If we would be further stimulated to the proposed [cultivation], we need only to reflect . . . on the *Manufactures* in some of our Southern Provinces; whose Opulence arises from . . . the most diminutive Plants, and proceeds more from Art in the Improvement of these, than from Industry in laborious Employments." The "Manufactures in the Southern Provinces" in 1765 were rice, indigo, and tobacco, "from diminutive Plants"; and pitch and tar. In a "supplement" to the same paper for April 4, 1765, it is said: "They write from Bristol, that a ship just arrived from Charlestown, has brought over several Stalks of Hemp, the Growth of that Province, 17 feet high and two Inches Diameter at the Base. A sure Prognostic, that this *Manufacture* will soon arrive to great Perfection in the Southern Colonies." *Cf.*, Thomas Jefferson's reference to "making a bushel of wheat" in his opinion, rendered to President Washington, February 15, 1791, on the constitutionality of a national bank, reprinted in Clarke & Hall, 91, 92. Also, James Madison's statement, in a letter to Jefferson, of July 23, 1784, that "the slaveholders are Tob[acc]o *makers*." Madison, II, 62. See, also, Edwin

Cannan, *Lectures on Justice, Police, Revenue and Arms, Delivered in the University of Glasgow, by Adam Smith, Reported by a Student in 1763* (Oxford, 1896), 224: "The produce of agriculture is much greater than that of *any other manufacture.*"

31. The following Boston item was printed in Pa. Pack., June 5, 1786: "A plan for establishing a whale-fishing company, from the port of Halifax, has lately been proposed there, and meets with great encouragement, all the most opulent characters engaging in it with alacrity. . . . The spirit of enterprize diffused through all ranks is so great, as must, if not prevented by a like spirit here, eventually monopolize the greater part of *a commerce* which has heretofore proved so advantageous to the citizens of this state."

32. The following paragraph appeared in Pa. Pack., April 19, 1786: "The best writers upon *the internal trade* of nations agree, that the more equally manufacturers are distributed through a country, the greater improvements will be made in their different fabricks. . . . The arts of industry thrive in retirement where neither avocations nor expensive and idle pleasures can lure workmen from the pursuits of trade."

33. Also printed in Am. Merc., August 16, 1784.

34. The pamphlet has been variously ascribed to Robert Keale and John Roberts.

35. 31, 43, 51, 52, 55, and 56.

36. Reprinted in Josiah Child, *Brief Observations concerning Trade, and Interest of Money* (London, 1668), 25; also reprinted in the same year in London by Sir Thomas Culpeper, Jr., in *A Tract Against the high rate of Usury,* 3.

37. Reprinted by Sir Thomas Culpeper, Jr. in *op. cit.* note 36 *supra,* 21.

38. For an early use of the phrase "trade of merchants," see Henry Parker, *Of a Free Trade* (London, 1648), 21. For "trade of merchandize," see Thomas Mun, *A Discovrse of Trade from England vnto the East Indies* (London, 1621), reprinted in McCulloch I. Mun first says (p. 5) that "*the Trade of Merchandize,* is not onely that laudable practise whereby the entercourse of Nations is so worthily performed, but also . . . the very Touchstone of a Kingdomes prosperity." Later (p. 40), he speaks of his "observations in *the Trade of Merchandize,* which is my profession." A later, American example of the use of the phrase "trade of merchandize" may be found in a bill, introduced in the Pennsylvania legislature in 1785, "for the regulation of bankruptcy." The proposed act was to apply to "any merchant or other person using *the trade of merchandize.*" Pa. Pack., September 20, 1785. The language of the first national bankruptcy act, of 1800, was similar: "any merchant or other person . . . actually using *the trade of merchandise.*" 2 U.S. Stat., 19.

39. 1, 2, 4, 5, 72–74, 154, 172, 228, 245, and 246.

40. Smith, xxv, 282, 283, 426, and 690–716 (especially 699 and 713–15). Smith was a Scot; and Scottish usage differed on many points from that further south. It cannot, therefore, always be taken as evidence of general English usage; but upon the point now at issue, Smith's diction was in complete accord with south British and American usage.

41. The index in the Modern Library edition of *The Wealth of Nations,* which is the edition cited herein, is, except as to the bracketed items in it, a reprint of the original index of the third English edition, of 1784. See Smith, 907.

42. *Ibid.,* 341.

43. 339.
44. II, 528.
45. (London), iv. Note that "the mercantile commerce" is apparently not the whole of "commerce."
46. There is no pagination in the *Universal Dictionary*, except in the introduction referred to, in the next note *supra*.
47. (London), 12, 50, 65, and 66.
48. Blackstone, IV, 421.
49. (London, 1787), III, 172, 183, 289, and 315.
50. (2d ed.; London), 13 and 266.
51. (London, 1801), 145, 146, and 148.
52. *Op. cit.* note 41 to chapter ii *supra*, xxii. Referring to the great amount of litigation in connection with insurance contracts at the time he wrote, Weskett says: "What a Degradation is this of mercantile Character and Abilities, even in a single *Branch of Commerce!*"
53. (4th ed.; London, 1800), xx of the "Introduction." In the course of a discussion of the origin of insurance, Park observes that "the passage upon which those, who contend for the antiquity of this *branch of commerce,* have chiefly relied, is one to be found in Suetonius."
54. (Condy's American ed.; Philadelphia, 1810), I, xv. In the course of the preface to the original London edition, reprinted in the edition referred to, Marshall discusses the place of equity in the law of insurance. He says, in part: "It is said that good faith should preside in all the transactions of *commerce,* and equity in the decisions of the questions to which it gives rise.—That good faith should preside in all the transactions of *commerce,* is a truth which cannot be too frequently repeated, or too forcibly inculcated. —And that equity should on proper occasions, have its due weight in the decision of *commercial* questions, I am also ready to admit. But . . . under pretence of equity, the law is not to be forsaken."
55. The following remarks may be added from Malachy Postlethwayt's discussion of "Assurance" in his *Universal Dictionary of Trade and Commerce.* "The whole practice of insurance, in it's present state," says Postlethwayt, "is so perplexed with frauds, of such manifest tendency to the obstruction of *fair commerce,* that it absolutely requires some legal regulations." But it ought not, he thinks, because of these frauds, to be totally prohibited. "With regard to single acts of fraud, committed by particular men, it is not to be supposed," he says, "but that they have not been detected in this, as in all other *branches of traffic,* nor do I conceive that any argument can be drawn from them against the practice [of insurance]; for if every *part of commerce* is to be prohibited, which has furnished villains with opportunities of deceit, we shall contract *trade* in to pretty narrow compass." Note the apparent synonymy of "commerce," "traffic," and "trade" in their extensive sense, in the foregoing passage; and the apparent applicability therein of each to insurance.
56. Otis, 114.
57. Monroe, I, 84. See, also, *Four Dissertations on the Reciprocal Advantages of a Perpetual Union between Great-Britain and her American Colonies* (Philadelphia, 1776), 48 and 62.
58. The phrase "writer on trade" may be found in Archibald Kennedy, *op. cit.* note 21 *supra*, 31. Cf., *Four Dissertations*, etc., note 57 *supra*, 62.
59. The term "oeconomics" is met very infrequently. An American instance of its use may be found in an anonymous pamphlet entitled *Frag-*

ments on the Confederation of the American States, which was published in Philadelphia, in 1787, just after the convening of the Federal Convention. The pamphlet advocated, among other things, what was therein termed "an Equalizing Court." It was suggested that the judges thereof should be "skilled in *oeconomics* and jurisprudence." Precisely what the writer of this pamphlet intended by "oeconomics" is uncertain. Blackstone used the term as a synonym for "police" or "polity." Blackstone, I, 274. The meaning of "police" and "polity" is discussed herein in chapter vi. The "Equalizing Court" is considered in chapter xxviii.

60. Late in 1786, there was a long controversy in Pa. Pack., as to the nature of banks. "Great mistakes have arisen on this subject," said an item therein, on December 6, "from considering a bank *merely as a trading company.* Though it is in a degree of that nature, it is most an object of attention as a branch of political oeconomy." In reference to a proposal to "limit the bank [*i.e.,* the Bank of North America] as to the articles it [was] to deal in," another correspondent said, on December 20, that it would be time enough to do this when the bank should engage in other than money dealings "to the injury of *private commerce*"; that "the bank [had theretofore] facilitated, but never injured the *private commerce* of the country."

61. The following from the article on "commerce" in Malachy Postlethwayt's *Universal Dictionary of Trade and Commerce* points the distinction intended to be made in the text: "I have endeavoured to make *practical trade,* and it's natural circulation in a state, the foundation of what is suggested argumentatively; for I judge it as irrational and absurd to reason upon *trade,* without making the practices of traders the basis thereof; as to philosophize without experimental knowledge; the *theory* and *practice* (or rather the *political* and *practical* consideration of *trade*) should go hand in hand, as well as the theory and practice in other sciences; for *practical trade,* and facts arising consequentially from it's national circulation, must be the touchstone of all *political* researches: that is to say, in other words, *the theory of trade, considered in a national light,* must be founded in the practical ways and methods of carrying it on."

62. Blackstone, IV, 154 *et seq.*

63. See Com. Int., I, 99: "It is a known axiom in *practical commerce* that a commodity bears a low price where there are more sellers than buyers." *Cf.,* note 61 *supra.*

64. See, generally, Joseph Massie, *A Representation concerning the Knowledge of Commerce as a National Concern* (London, 1760).

65. II, 368.

66. 234–37.

67. *Cf.,* note 61 *supra.*

68. *Op. cit.* note 64 *supra.*

69. *Cf.,* note 61 *supra.*

70. Strangely enough, the term "national commerce" was also sometimes used to signify "domestic commerce only." Thus, Jeremy Belknap, in his *History of New Hampshire* (Boston, 1792), III, 205, says: "[New Hampshire's] foreign trade [before the Revolution], as distinguished from national, was very inconsiderable." By "foreign trade," Belknap meant "trade with non-British non-Americans." This appears from the preceding discussion. "National trade," then, was apparently all trade within the Empire. This was an unusual usage; foreign and domestic trade were both ordinarily included.

71. Clear examples of the use of "general trade" and "general commerce,"

in a doctrinal, as distinct from a phenomenal, sense, are not very plentiful. A probable example occurs in the translator's preface to an English version of a French work on commerce, by Jean François Melon, which was published in Dublin, in 1738. The work, entitled in translation *A Political Essay on Commerce*, covered colonies and exclusive companies, among many other topics. The translator, David Bindon, observed in his preface, that these were "attendant upon independent countries only." He expressed the hope, however, that his Irish readers would "not be displeased with the Translator's Endeavours to explain some of th[e]se Branches of *general Commerce*." Even in this instance, the reader will note, "general Commerce" may mean only "general economics"—that is, more general than applied to Ireland only.

72. *The Elements of Commerce, and the Theory of Taxes*. This work was never completed by Tucker. A copy from the private printing of what Tucker did complete is in the New York Public Library. It is reprinted in Schuyler, *Josiah Tucker* (New York, 1931). The passage referred to in the text is at p. 90 of the latter volume.

73. (London), 124.

74. Cf., Smith, 22: "When the division of labour has been once thoroughly established, it is but a very small part of a man's wants which the produce of his own labour can supply. He supplies the far greater part of them by exchanging that surplus part of the produce of his own labour, which is over and above his own consumption, for such parts of the produce of other men's labour as he has occasion for. Every man thus lives by exchanging, or becomes in some measure a merchant, and the society itself grows to be what is properly *a commercial society*."

75. Joseph Harris, *An Essay upon Money and Coins* (London, 1757), 22–25; reprinted in J. R. McCulloch, *A Select Collection of Scarce and Valuable Tracts on Money* (London, 1856), 360–63.

76. (Dublin), II, 18.

77. (London), II, 556.

78. *Op. cit.* note 51 *supra*, 68–69.

79. *The Virginia Gazette* states that the item was copied from N.Y. Ind. Jour. It also appeared in some other papers; but a record of these was not kept.

80. Smith, 397.

81. The term "commercial oeconomy" may be found in a letter from James Monroe to Thomas Jefferson, of June 16, 1785, in which Monroe observed that "the effect [of creating a national power over commerce, which project was then under discussion in Congress,] would be to put *the commercial economy* of every state *entirely* under the hands of the Union"; that, once the power was granted, "the measures necessary to obtain the carrying trade, to encourage domestic by a tax on foreign industry, or *any other* ends which in the changes of things bec[a]me necessary, [would] depend *entirely* on the Union." Monroe, I, 84. See, also, the speech of George III to Parliament, January 14, 1766, as reported in Mass. Gaz., March 27, 1766: "If any alterations should be wanting in the *commercial oeconomy* of the Plantations, which may tend to enlarge and secure the mutual and beneficial intercourse of my Kingdoms and Colonies, they will deserve your most serious consideration." A letter of Alexander Hamilton's to William Seton, of January 18, 1791, exhibits the tendency to distinguish between "commercial economy," and "political economy" in the sense of "fiscal arrangements." Hamilton refers to the forming of a third bank in New York as "a dangerous tumor in [the state's] *political and commercial economy*." Hamilton, IX, 476. The

statement in Pa. Pack., December 6, 1786 (see note 60 *supra*), that a bank is "not merely a trading company," but "a branch of political oeconomy," should be compared with Hamilton's statement. "Political oeconomy," in the Pa. Pack. statement, probably included the idea of "commercial regulation." See, also, Pa. Pack., December 21, 1786, wherein a correspondent insists that "the bank [is not] an important branch of political oeconomy in this country; however it may be considered in other countries, where it is more immediately connected with the governments." The sense of the phrase "commercial system," as comprehending a national system of division of labor, and of exchange of products and services, may be inferred from the contents of Tench Coxe's *An Enquiry into the Principles on which a Commercial System for the United States should be founded* (Philadelphia, 1787), reprinted in Coxe, 435 *et seq.* "Commercial system" and "commercial oeconomy" were, in many cases, merely synonyms for "commerce" and "trade" in their extensive gainful senses; but the synonymy, it must be remembered, worked both ways.

82. *Cf.*, for example, Jeremy Dummer, *A Defence of the New-England Charters* (Boston: [Re]printed, 1745): "A great Minister once said to me, That the Regulation of [colonial] Charters must be look'd on as Part of *the publick Oeconomy*, and not as the Affair of any particular Person or Province."

83. See note 72 *supra*.

84. Schuyler, *op. cit.* note 72 *supra*, 52.

85. See, for example, the passages set forth at the beginning of the second section of this chapter.

86. 41 and 43; also the preface.

87. The book containing this advertisement is in the University of Chicago Library.

88. II, 89.

89. Coxe, 436 and 513.

90. Records, I, 287 and 329.

91. 100 and 101.

92. The excerpts quoted in the text are from the article on the "Royal Society."

93. Coxe, 7, 36, and 240. B. Ind. Chr., July 21, 1787. Smith, 296; *cf.*, 282.

94. P. Web, 175, 435, and 440.

95. *Ibid.*, 430.

96. *Ibid.*, 154 and 235.

97. *Ibid.*, 102, 120, 241, 383, and 430. The following should be especially noted: "all business both of merchandize, husbandry, and mechanic arts" (*ibid.*, 120, 241, 235, and 430) and "any man of business, whether he be merchant, farmer, or tradesman" (*ibid.*, 240). *Cf.*, "agricultivators, manufacturers, or merchants," in note 24 *supra*.

98. See, for example, the article on "Treaties of Commerce and Navigation" in Malachy Postlethwayt's *Universal Dictionary of Trade and Commerce.* The phrase "treaty of trade and navigation" is used in the article as an equivalent. See, also, True Sys. 11, 13, 26, 29, 78, 116, 130, 131, 230, 240, 266. Also, a recommendation by Governor Moultrie, of South Carolina, that the Continental Congress be vested with "full power to regulate *commerce and navigation*." Pa. Pack., March 9, 1786, and Ch. Mng. P., February 2, 1786.

99. See, for example, Sir Francis Brewster, *Essays on Trade and Navigation* (London, 1695). "The Contents" shows that "trade" in the title must have

included every branch of gainful activity with the single exception of navigation. "The Contents" includes, among other topics: "Trade in general," "the Manufactory and Dispose of Sheeps-Wool," "Exports," "Fishing," "Building Ships," "Banks and Lumbers," "Agriculture and Rural Employments." Again, see a reference, in John Smith, *op. cit.* note 77 *supra*, I, 7, to Huet's *History of the Commerce and Navigation of the Ancients*. Smith remarks that "the Reader who expects from [Huet's book], *by reason of the Title,* any very particular Account of Trade *and Manufacture*, as exercised among the Ancients, will find himself disappointed."

100. This meaning of "trade" and "commerce" is familiar today and is listed in all dictionaries, both of today and of the eighteenth century. Probably, it is the central core of meaning of "trade" and "commerce" in the eighteenth-century triads "commerce, agriculture, and manufactures," "trade, husbandry, and manufactures," and the like, already referred to. Nevertheless, clear examples of this sense of "trade" and "commerce" are rather difficult to find. In most cases, the words can be taken as well in their extensive sense, as in this narrow sense. A statement, in *The Commercial Conduct of the United States of America Considered &c,* by "a Citizen of New-York" (New York, 1786), that "the profession of a merchant is trade," is typical. So, also, a statement, in the death notice of Thomas Hancock (Mass. Gaz., August 16, 1764) that he first "enter'd into the Stationery Business, but having a genius for a more extensive *commerce*," eventually became one of Boston's greatest merchants. In this instance, however, "a more extensive commerce" may simply have meant "a more extensive business."

101. See Coxe, 333: "The *balance of trade* has been aptly denominated *the metaphysics of commerce*." James Monroe to Thomas Jefferson, June 16, 1785: "An opinion seems to be entertained by the late commercial writers and particularly a Mr. Smith on the wealth of nations that the doctrine of the *balance of trade* is a chimera." Monroe, I, 84. The term "balance of trade" was the usual one with Adam Smith. See Smith, 357, 456, 461, 464, 911.

102. See Com. Int., II, 532: "It will next be necessary to observe the means of procuring a state an advantageous *balance of commerce*, by the increase of the number of workmen."

103. Pa. Jour., July 31, 1782: "America requires more from *commerce* than any country in the world. Agriculture is the proper business of her citizens. . . . It will for centuries to come be oeconomy in her to owe to *commerce* the principal manufactures that will be necessary for her." Am. Her., August 8, 1785, says, "*Commerce* with America [*i.e., for* America] is only a secondary object;—the primary, and from whence the principal resources and splendor of America must spring is AGRICULTURE. . . . America must desist in its *trade*, to become rich and flourishing. . . . An American ship comes freighted principally with SPECIE." *Commerce and Luxury* (Philadelphia, 1791), 11: "If the maxim, that money is the sinew of war, was ever verified, it is now. *Trade* which alone furnishes that sinew [*i.e.*, through a favorable international trade balance], is deemed the strength and security of nations." In this connection, it ought perhaps to be noted that Thomas Mortimer, at the beginning of his *Elements of Commerce, Politics, and Finances* (cited in note 51 *supra*), took the position that "commerce," when properly used, "serve[d] to distinguish the mercantile negotiations carried on by the inhabitants of different nations with each other, from the operations of inland traffick, commonly known under the name of trade, wholesale and retail, and limited to one particular country or town." No reasons

for this view were given by Mortimer. He admitted that the "propriety" to which he alluded was not generally observed; and added that he would not strictly observe it himself. The actual usage of the eighteenth century undoubtedly contains as many examples of the appropriation of "trade" to foreign trade as of the appropriation of "commerce" to that subject.

104. Material illustrative of the broad sense of "industry" has already been presented in note 17 *supra*.

The extensive sense of "traffic" may be seen in an item first published in Mass. Cent., April 30, 1785, and thence afterwards copied by N.J. Pol. Int., May 18, 1785, and Col. Her., July 13, 1785. In the item, "America" calls upon her "Friends and Guardians" to "defend my Merchandize, my Navigation, and Fishery, and every other branch of *Traffic*—more especially defend the mechanical part of my Family, on whom hangs the greatest dependence for my safety." The word is used as including agriculture in *Commerce and Luxury* (Philadelphia, 1791), 15: "The class of husbandmen, who exercise the surest *traffic*, and whose children are their riches, is, of all others, the fittest and most inclined to multiply." See, also, the excerpts from *The Trade's Increase*, cited at the beginning of the third section of the present chapter.

Examples of the comprehensive gainful sense of "business" are the following: Pelatiah Webster speaks, in his *Political Essays* (1791), of "*all business* both of merchandize, husbandry, and mechanic arts*" (P. Web., 120, 235, 241); and of "*any man of business*, whether he be merchant, farmer or tradesman" (*ibid.*, 240). He also says (p. 42) that "people are more settled in *business*, than they were three years ago." Tench Coxe, in his *View of the United States of America* (1794), says (Coxe, 71) that "shipbuilding is *a business* in which the port of Philadelphia exceeds most parts of the world," and, also (*ibid.*, 354) that "in the United States, [bank] directors [are] selected . . . on account of their property, integrity, talents, and attention to *business*." He likewise speaks of "the fishing business" (p. 91), of "the hatting business" (p. 157), and of "the progress of the state of Pennsylvania in the great business of agriculture" (p. 76). There are many other similar passages; but the phrase "to regulate business" was not, apparently, in use. "Commerce" and "trade" were the words used in that connection, with the phrase "to regulate traffic" once in a while occurring.

105. Oxford, V, 390: *Intercourse*, 1.

106. Wilson, I, 306.

NOTES TO CHAPTER V

1. Sav. Gaz., June 9, 1785.

2. Dickinson, I, 228: "The judges ought, in a well *regulated* state, to be equally independent of the executive and legislative powers." Pa. Pack., July 13, 1785: "It is my misfortune to live in a quarter of this well-*regulated* city, nightly serenaded with all the melody of canine music." July 14, 1785: "In well-*regulated* countries in Europe, there are positive laws against breaking horses in the streets, whether for draft or saddle."

3. Pages 442–43 of the partial reprint in Am. Mus., III (May, 1788).

4. *Op. cit.* note 49 to chapter iv *supra*, I, 537; and III, 302.

5. 242, 243, 250, 253, 267–69, 274–82, and 291.

6. Otis, 114 (appendix). Not all the opinions entertained of Postlethwayt were equally complimentary to him. The British writer, Arthur Young, referred to him, in his *Political Essays* (London, 1772), footnote p. 496, as "this

prince of Plagiarists, whose great work is a continual quotation without the acknowledgement of a line."

7. See, for example, an "Extract from the ingenious Mr. Postlethwayt" published in Pa. Gaz., January 1, 1766. The item also appeared in Bost. Gaz. See, also, the same paper, August 29, 1768, and Mass. Gaz., October 18, 1764.

8. See Pa. Gaz., November 19, 1767, and Pa. Chr., December 28, 1767.

9. See, for example, Alexander Hamilton, *The Farmer Refuted* (1775), reprinted in Hamilton, I, 53, notes at 144 and 148; Po. Fr. Jour., July 27, 1776; Pa. Pack., June 18, 1785, and February 16, 1791; Col. Her., November 7, 1785; Gaz. U.S., January 20, 1790.

10. *Bank of Augusta* v. *Earle*, 13 Pet. 519, 602.

11. See Dickinson, I, 50, 51, 52, 63, 73, 78, 80, 190, 191, and 192.

12. Dickinson, I, 151.

13. Dickinson, I, 151–52. At this point, Dickinson appends a footnote which may require some notice. The footnote consists of a series of "recitals from the former acts of parliament relating to these colonies." Not nearly all the former acts are represented, however; the series is far from complete. Yet, at the end of it, Dickinson says: "These are all *the most considerable* statutes relating to *the commerce* of the colonies; and it is thought to be utterly unnecessary to add any observations to these extracts, to prove that they were all intended *solely as regulations of trade*." As the acts represented in the series all related to the import and export trade of the colonies, it may be that Dickinson used "commerce" in this footnote to mean "external commerce only." We have seen, from other materials cited in the text, that it was not infrequent for eighteenth-century writers to pursue a shifting usage of "trade" and "commerce" (*cf.*, for example, the two passages cited at the beginning of the second section of chap. iv hereof); and if Dickinson did so use "commerce" in this footnote, it is another example of this shifting usage. On the other hand, it should be noted that the words, "the most considerable," make the sense of "commerce," in Dickinson's footnote, quite uncertain. His statement that "all" the statutes he cites were "intended solely as regulations of trade" means that they were *not intended* to raise a revenue. Most of them involved imposts of one kind or another on imports.

14. Dickinson, I, 152. As indicated by the citation, the passage quoted in the text is given as it appears in Dickinson's collected works. These appeared during Dickinson's lifetime and, it has been said, were gotten out under his supervision. P. L. Ford, *Writings of John Dickinson*, in Memoirs of the Historical Society of Pennsylvania, Vol. XIV. The text of the *Letters from a Farmer* in Dickinson's collected works was taken from the Virginia edition of 1769. Dickinson, I, 135. This Virginia edition, printed by William Rind, of Williamsburg, included a local Virginia production, called *The Monitor's Letters*, and was put out under the title, *The Farmer's and Monitor's Letters to the Inhabitants of the British Colonies*. The quoted passage appears therein as it is given in the text. The passage also appears as given in all the other American pamphlet editions of "the Farmer's Letters" that the writer has been able to find, with the single exception of the edition put out by Mein and Fleeming, of Boston, in 1768. Specifically, the passage so appears in the first Philadelphia pamphlet edition of the "letters," put out by David Hall and William Sellers, publishers of the Pa. Gaz., in 1768; in the New York edition put out by John Holt, in 1768; in the Boston edition put out by Edes & Gill, in 1768; and in the Philadelphia edition put out by Thomas Bradford, in 1769. The "letters" first appeared, however, in the Philadelphia newspapers. They probably were given

simultaneously to Pa. Chr. and Pa. Gaz., though, because of a difference in the publication dates of these two papers, "Letter I" appeared in Pa. Chr., on December 2, 1767, and in Pa. Gaz., on December 3. "Letter II," from which the passage under discussion is taken, appeared in Pa. Chr., on December 7. As printed in Pa. Chr., it read, however, as follows: "*All before*** are calculated to preserve or promote a mutually beneficial intercourse between the several constituent parts of the empire; and though many of these imposed duties on trade, yet those duties were always imposed *with design,*** to restrain the commerce of one part that was injurious to another, and thus to promote the general welfare. The raising a revenue was never intended." In short, the words, "regulate trade and," were somehow left out. "Letter II" appeared in Pa. Gaz. three days later, on December 10, in the form in which it afterwards appeared in the pamphlet editions of the "Letters," and in Dickinson's collected works. The third Philadelphia paper, Pa. Jour., printed the first and second letters together on the same day, December 10, following in the case of the second letter, the form in which that letter had appeared in Pa. Chr. The publishers of Pa. Jour. were William and Thomas Bradford. As already indicated, the Thomas Bradford pamphlet edition of the "Farmer's Letters," gotten out in 1769, followed the version of "Letter II" which appeared in Pa. Gaz. The version published by the newspapers outside Philadelphia varied in accordance with the particular Philadelphia paper from which the outside paper copied. Bost. Chr., published by Mein & Fleeming, apparently copied from Pa. Chr., and when Mein & Fleeming published their pamphlet edition in the spring of 1768, they still followed, at least in the case of "Letter II," the version which had originally appeared in Pa. Chr. Their pamphlet edition was first advertised for sale in Bost. Chr., of March 21, 1768. About a month later, on April 25, they added to their advertisement of the pamphlet, that it was "printed exactly from the Philadelphia papers, in which these Letters were first published." On May 30, 1768, Edes & Gill advertised in Bost. Ev. P., a "correct edition" of the "Farmer's Letters." See, also, Bost. Gaz., June 6, 1768. As already indicated, this Edes & Gill pamphlet edition followed the version of "Letter II" which is quoted in the text of this book. The foregoing is the only public notice of any confusion, or confusions, in the text of the "Farmer's Letters" that appears ever to have been taken; and if the reference was only to the inaccuracy in "Letter II," it does not seem that the printers of these two Boston editions of the "Farmer's Letters" had very much to quarrel about. It may be noted, however, that John Dickinson was disturbed at the time when the "Letters" were running serially in the newspapers, because many of the papers in New England were copying from Pa. Chr. "The only correct [version] publish'd here [in Philadelphia]," he wrote to James Otis, on January 25, 1768, "is printed in the *Pennsylvania Gazette* of Hall and Sellers. I find that the 'Letters' publish'd to the Eastward, are taken from our *Chronicle*, which being incorrect, I should be glad if you would be so kind as to mention to any of the Printers you may happen to see, that the *Gazette* is much the most exact." Warren-Adams, I, 5. It would appear from Dickinson's mode of speaking that there must have been other errors in the *Chronicle* and *Journal* versions, besides that which has been described above; but what those other errors were has not been determined.

15. 25 Geo. II, c. 6, § 10. Besides this act in reference to the Statute of Frauds, there were several acts related, in various ways, to the raising and governing of troops in the colonies which could be regarded as "relating to the colonies" in a certain sense, though probably not in the sense—*i.e.*, applying to the colo-

---

* Italics in the original.

nists—which Dickinson meant. See 29 Geo. II, c. 5; 29 Geo. II, c. 35; 30 Geo. II, c. 6, § 73.

16. *Hudson* v. *Flood*, 5 Boyce 450, 460–64; 94 Atl. 760, 764–66 (1915); *Anonymous*, 1 Dall. (4th ed., 1882) 1 (1754) and note thereto appended; 1 Bioren, *Laws of the Commonwealth of Pennsylvania (1700–1810)* (Philadelphia, 1810), chap. dclxix, p. 389, and note thereto appended at p. 390; *cf., The Report of the Judges of the Supreme Court of Pennsylvania* (1808), 3 Binn. 593; and see 1 Reed, *A Treatise on the Law of the Statute of Frauds, and Other Like Enactments in Force in the United States of America and in the British Empire* (Philadelphia, 1884), 4 and 5.

17. 23 Geo. II, c. 29.

18. Dickinson, I, 182.

19. Dickinson, I, 161–62.

20. *Cf.,* passage cited at p. 61 in chapter iii hereof. The Americans of the time seem to have been greatly concerned over the nail situation; but what the precise facts in regard to it were is unknown to the writer.

21. 5 Geo. II, c. 22.

22. Dickinson, I, 181 and 182.

23. 14 Geo. II, c. 37.

24. See legal opinion published in Pa. Gaz., May 7, 1767.

25. 5 Geo. II, c. 7.

26. (2d ed.; reprinted for J. Almon, London, 1766), 46, 47, and 52.

27. 9 Anne, c. 10.

28. 3 & 4 Anne, c. 10, §§ 6 & 7; 9 Anne, c. 17; 8 Geo. I, c. 12, §§ 5 & 6; and 2 Geo. II, c. 35.

29. 6 Anne, c. 30. As to the Queen's prerogative in this respect, see Blackstone, I, 273 and 278.

30. 24 Geo. II, c. 53.

31. "We are prohibited," said Dickinson, in the pamphlet of 1765, "*by new and stricter restraints being laid on our trade*, from procuring [specie] as we used to do; and *from instituting among ourselves bills of credit* in the place of such portions [thereof] as are required in our internal traffic." Dickinson, I, 54. See, also, a letter from Portsmouth, New Hampshire, in Pa. Pack., February 27, 1786: "It must be pleasing to hear that Congress is impowered *to regulate trade* [New Hampshire had acted sweepingly in the matter, in the preceding June; and the writer seems mistakenly to have assumed that similar action had been taken by the other states]; and they [*i.e.,* Congress] may, perhaps, find it expedient to establish a mint for the coinage of money, or issuing public notes on some fund—which will give a spring to *agriculture* and *commerce*."

32. Otis, 94.

33. See Mass. Gaz., January 12, 1764.

34. Smith, 682.

35. 4 Geo. I, c. 11, 65.

36. 13 Geo. II, c. 7; 2 Geo. II, c. 44.

37. II, 532.

38. See the partial reprints in Am. Mus., III, 442, 443.

39. Ct. Acts and Laws, 1784–90, pp. 268, 269.

40. Madison, II, 344, 345.

41. The statutes will be found listed in 24 Pickering, [*British*] *Statutes at Large* (Cambridge [Eng.], 1765), 437, under the head of "Plantations."

42. In some of these writers, there was an undercurrent of resentment over the way in which Parliament had recently been exercising its power; but a Parliamentary legislative power without statable limits was generally admitted.

The denial of power, at that time, when any was made, related to the power to tax. The following are typical:

James Otis, *The Rights of the British Colonies Asserted and Proved* (2d ed.; reprinted for J. Almon, London), 49: "I . . . lay it down as one of the first principles from whence I intend to deduce the civil rights of the British colonies, that all of them are subject to, and dependent on Great-Britain; and that therefore as over subordinate governments, the parliament of Great-Britain has an undoubted power and lawful authority, to make acts for the general good, that by naming them, shall and ought to be equally binding, as upon the subjects of Great-Britain within the realm. This principle, I presume, will be readily granted on the other side of the atlantic. It has been practiced upon for twenty years to my knowledge, in the province of the Massachusetts-Bay; and I have ever received it, that it has been so from the beginning, in this and the sister provinces, through the continent." Otis claimed only a *subordinate* legislative power for the colonial legislatures. "Under [God, the King, and Parliament]," he said, "it seems easy to conceive subordinate powers in gradation, till we descend to the legislative of a town council, or even a private social club. These have each 'a one whole legislative' subordinate, which, when it does not counteract the laws of any of its superiors, is to be indulged" (p. 73). The legislative power of Parliament was, however, "fiduciary" and to be exercised, in equity and good conscience, only "for the good of the whole" (p. 98). Otis further declared "that no parts of his Majesty's dominions c[ould] be taxed without their consent: that every part ha[d] a right to be represented in the supreme or some subordinate legislature [for this purpose]: that the refusal of this, would seem to be *a contradiction in practice to the theory of the constitution*" (p. 99). Yet, if the colonists were so taxed by Parliament, they "must and ought to yield obedience to [the] act . . . , though erroneous, till repealed." The foregoing ideas are not entirely free from seeming contradictions; but in another of his pamphlets, *A Vindication of the British Colonies against the Aspersions of the Halifax Gentleman* (Boston, 1765), Otis was specific in his admission of the naked power of Parliament to tax the colonies. He said (pp. 4–5): "I cannot think Mr. [Stephen] H[op]k[in]s, [of Rhode Island,] or any other of the writers, who have the misfortune to fall under the sore displeasure of the Halifax gentleman, ever really intended to encourage so groundless a claim as an independent, uncontroulable Provincial legislative. Most of them 'tis well known expressly disavow such a claim. It is certain that the Parliament of Great Britain hath a just, clear, equitable and constitutional right, power and authority, to bind the colonies, by all acts wherein they are named. Every lawyer, nay every Tyro knows this. No less certain is it that the Parliament of Great Britain has a just and equitable right, power and authority, *to impose taxes on the colonies, internal and external, on lands, as well as on trade.** This is involved in the idea of a supreme legislative or sovereign power of state. It will however by no means from thence follow, that 'tis always expedient, and in all circumstances equitable for the supreme and sovereign legislative to tax the colonies, much less that 'tis reasonable this right should be practised upon without allowing the colonies an actual representation. An equal representation of the whole state is, at least in theory, of the essence of a perfect parliament, or supreme legislative."

Stephen Hopkins, *The Rights of the Colonies Examined* (Providence, 1764), reprinted in *Records of the Colony of Rhode Island and Providence Plantations* (Providence, 1861), VI, 420: "In the first place, let it be considered, that although each of the colonies hath a legislature within itself, to take care of its interests,

---

* Italics in the original.

and provide for its peace and internal government; yet there are many things of a more general nature, quite out of the reach of these particular legislatures, which it is necessary should be regulated, ordered and governed. One of this kind is, the commerce of the whole British empire, taken collectively, and that of each kingdom and colony in it, as it makes a part of that whole. Indeed, every thing that concerns the proper interest and fit government of the whole commonwealth, of keeping the peace, and subordination of all the parts towards the whole, and one among another, must be considered in this light. Amongst these general concerns, perhaps, money and paper credit, those grand instruments of all commerce, will be found also to have a place. These, with all other matters of a general nature, it is absolutely necessary should have a general power to direct them; some supreme and over ruling authority, with power to make laws, and form regulations for the good of all, and to compel their execution and observation. It being necessary some such general power should exist somewhere, every man of the least knowledge of the British constitution, will be naturally led to look for, and find it in the Parliament of Great Britain; that grand and august legislative body, must, from the nature of their authority and the necessity of the thing, be justly vested with this power. Hence, it becomes the indispensable duty of every good and loyal subject, cheerfully to obey and patiently submit to all the acts, laws, orders and regulations that may be made and passed by Parliament, for directing and governing all these general matters." Hopkins apparently regarded the Parliamentary prohibitions upon the carrying-on of certain manufactures in the colonies as entirely constitutional. He says (p. 427) that the colonists have "cheerfully submitted to every constitutional law; have as little inclination as they have ability, to throw off their dependency; have carefully avoided every offensive measure, and *every interdicted manufacture.*" That he regarded such interdictions as "commercial regulations" does not specifically appear; but it is, of course, highly probable.

Thomas Fitch, *Reasons why the British Colonies, in America, should not be charged with Internal Taxes, By Authority of Parliament* (New Haven, 1764), 17–18: "As the Parliament of Great-Britain is most certainly vested with the supreme Authority of the Nation, and its Jurisdiction and Power most capacious and transcendent, the Colonies will be far, very far from urging or even attempting any Thing in Derogation of the Power or Authority of that august Assembly, or pretending to prescribe Bounds and Limits to the Exercise of their Dominion. Nothing in the foregoing Observations, be sure, is intended, by way of Objection, but that the Crown by its Prerogative, or the Parliament by its supreme and general Jurisdiction, may justly order and do some Things, which may affect the Property of the American Subjects, in a Way which, in some Sense, may be said to be independent upon or without the Will or Consent of the People, as by Regulations of Trade and Commerce and the like; and by general Orders relative to and Restrictions of their Conduct for the Good of the Whole: For as the Colonies are so many Governments independent on each other, or not Subjected the one to the other, they can only establish Regulations within and for themselves respectively; and as they are all subordinate to and dependent on the Mother Country, and Propriety, Conveniency and even Necessity require that they should be subject to some general Superintendency and Controul, in order that the general Course of Trade and Business should be so uniform as to center in some general national Interest, it becomes plainly expedient that there should be some supreme Director over all his Majesty's Dominions; and this Character and Authority, all Men must acknowledge and allow, properly belong to the British Parliament." Despite the foregoing elaborate statement, there are some other passages in Fitch's pamphlet which seem to indicate a desire to limit Parliament, probably on the basis of expediency, to "external" regulations. They are not entirely clear; but the general position of the pamphlet seems to be, as in the case of the others of its date, that a power in Parliament to tax the colonies is altogether different from its general regulatory power.

A preface to the Virginia edition of John Dickinson's *Letters from a Farmer* (*The Farmer's and Monitor's Letters to the Inhabitants of the British Colonies* [Williamsburg, 1769]), supposed to have been written by Richard Henry Lee (Dickinson, I, 135), says: "It is really wonderful that this unhappy dispute between Great-Britain and her colonies should ever have existed, when a moment's retrospection shews the Mother Country for near two centuries exercising legislative authority here without complaint, while she abstained from that single destructive claim of taking our money from us without consent of our representatives." There is, however, in this preface an undertone of resentment over Parliamentary restrictions on American manufactures and the British attempt to monopolize the buying of American products. "Agriculture, without arts, and a trade so confined, will probably never pay [what Americans owe to Britons]."

The petition of the Stamp Act Congress of 1765, said that the "general Subordination [of the colonies] to Parliament [was] universally acknowledged," but "submitted, whether there [was] not a material Distinction, in Reason and sound Policy, at least, between the necessary Exercise of Parliamentary Jurisdiction in general Acts for the Amendment of the Common Law and the Regulation of Trade and Commerce through the whole Empire, and the Exercise of that Jurisdiction by imposing Taxes on the Colonies." Mass. Gaz., April 17, 1766.

43. See Dickinson, I, 138–42; also N. L. Gaz., April 8, 1768; Pa. Gaz., April 7, 1768, and June 9, 1768; Pa. Jour., September 1, 1768; Bost. Gaz., April 15, 1768; Prov. Gaz., April 30, 1768, and June 25, 1768.

44. Some of the laudatory expressions cover the matter of trade regulation specifically. Thus, the Grand Jury of Cumberland County, Pennsylvania, "addressing" the author of the "Farmer's Letters," said, in Pa. Gaz., June 9, 1768: "You, Sir, have solidly proved, that tho' the P——t of G——t B——n, may adjust the Trade and Commerce of the various Branches of the extensive Empire, as will best promote the Happiness of the whole, yet every Provincial Assembly has, and must have, the Power of Taxation; or American Britons are no more Freemen, nothing but Slaves, and Vassals of Power." See, also, the same paper, for April 7, 1768.

45. See 7 & 8 Wm. III, c. 22, § 9, and 2 Firth and Rait, *Acts and Ordinances of the Interregnum 1642–1660* (London, 1911), 425. Cf., *ibid.* 405; and see Andrews, *The Colonial Background of the American Revolution* (rev. ed.; New Haven, 1931).

46. Jefferson Papers, Library of Congress, Vol. 24, fols. 4149–50. Jefferson's notes and comments on Soulés's history are printed in the various editions of Jefferson's works; but in none is the quoted passage given in complete form. The words, "in his Farmer's Letters that they could put down our looms, slitting mills, & other instruments of Manufacture," have generally been omitted altogether by Jefferson's editors. The late Paul Leicester Ford attempted to supply the omission in part and added, in his edition of Jefferson's works (New York, 1894) (IV, 302), after the work "acknoleged" the words "in his Farmer's to Manufacture [illegible]." The words "*of* manufacture" are perfectly clear in the original manuscript; so are the words "in his Farmer's"; and the

"illegible" material comes between these two groups of words, not after the word "manufacture," as Ford has it. The "illegible" material (*i.e.*, the words, "Letters that they could put down our looms, slitting mills & other instruments") constitutes the last line of one of the pages of the manuscript, which is a letter-press copy of Jefferson's original notes. Due to some accident in taking the copy, the last line of the page in question is very imperfect. Only the word "put" and the first part of the word "down" are at all clearly recorded. For the rest, the tops of the taller letters appear, and, in some instances, parts of the remaining portions of the missing words are faintly outlined. However, a reading of the entire passage, of which the missing line is a part, leaves no doubt as to what, in general, Jefferson was talking about; and if one is familiar with Dickinson's *Letters from a Farmer* and with the Parliamentary enactments discussed in those letters, there is not much difficulty in making out the missing line. See Dickinson, I, 151, 152, 161, 162, 181, 182; and the British statutes, 10 & 11 Wm. III, c. 10, § 19, and 23 Geo. II, c. 29, § 9. The only word of the missing line about which there could possibly be any question is the word "looms." Save that the loop of the "l" is faintly outlined, the manuscript is a complete blank at the point where the word "looms" should appear. It will be noted, however, that, a few lines farther on in his comments to Soulés, Jefferson mentions the "putting down" of American looms. As this latter mention of the subject seems plainly a reference back to something previously said, a pretty sure clue is provided that "looms" is the missing word; and since careful measurement shows that the word, as Jefferson elsewhere wrote it, would fit nicely into the blank space at this point in the manuscript, there can be little doubt that all the words of the missing line of this Jefferson manuscript are correctly given in the text of this book. The writer is indebted to Mr. Thomas P. Martin, of the Division of Manuscripts, in the Library of Congress, for courteous assistance in working this matter out.

47. See note 50 *infra*.

48. For an early dissenting view of this kind, see Pa. Gaz., January 30, 1766. This item says that Daniel Dulany's distinction between the taxing power and the legislative power is unwarranted; that it is inconsistent with "English liberty" for the colonies to be bound in legislative matters in the absence of their consent. The item adds that representation in Parliament is impracticable because of distance, and suggests, instead, a "junction of the colonies" in such "matters of general concern, as should be proposed to them by his Majesty for concurrence." See, also, the outline of the William Hicks pamphlet in note 50 *infra*.

49. See p. 95 *supra*; also material on the usage of the word "manufacture" in note 30 appended thereto; and *cf.*, next note *infra*.

50. *The Nature and Extent of Parliamentary Power Considered*, by "A Citizen" (Philadelphia, 1768), 28 and 29. This pamphlet, according to an ascription in old script, in the copy thereof in the possession of the Library of Congress, was the work of William Hicks, presumably William Hicks, of Bucks County, Pennsylvania. Afterwards a member of the governor's council in the province, Hicks, like Dickinson, was a lawyer who had received his legal education at the Inns of Court, in England. His discussion—assuming it was his discussion—first appeared in Pa. Jour. (January 21 and 28; February 4, 11, 18, and 25; and March 10, 1768), while Dickinson's *Letters from a Farmer* were still running in that paper. When the Hicks papers began to appear, the "Farmer's Letters" were relegated, in Pa. Jour., to second place. The Hicks essay was afterwards published in pamphlet form in Philadelphia and New

York, and parts of it were copied in a few newspapers in other parts of the country. See Mass. Gaz., February 15 and 22, 1768; Bost. Ev. P., February 15 and March 7, 1768; N.Y. Wkly. Merc., February 29, 1768.

Hicks did not purport to differ with Dickinson; instead, he affected to agree with him and to be dealing only with the "general principles" underlying the "important particulars" which Dickinson had dealt with. But a little reading in Hicks's essay is sufficient to show that he and Dickinson were far apart in their respective views. Dickinson had denied that Parliament had constitutional power to tax the colonies, but had conceded its regulatory power. Hicks, on the other hand, denied that Parliament, consistently with the principles of the British constitution, could exercise any power of any kind over the colonies. More specifically, Hicks said: "The commons of Britain might indeed with great propriety propose *regulations for the trade, and restrictions for the manufactures* of those by whom they were appointed; but how they can, with any face of equity [or 'consistently with the principles of their own government'] resolve to extend these regulations and restrictions to those from whom they have received no *delegated power,** is what I can not easily comprehend. Would they but admit to their general council a certain number of deputies properly authorized from every colony, to support the interests of their constituents, to explain the nature of their situation, and remonstrate against acts of oppresssion, then, indeed, whatever *commercial regulations* they might think proper to form, would be fixed upon a constitutional basis, and their authority remain forever undisputed; as I can never be supposed to mean that it should extend to any other than such matters which immediately relate to *commerce;* while the internal policy of each colony should still be regulated by its proper representatives, in conjunction with the deputy of the crown, and their liberty should only be restrained and their property fairly disposed of by those who are legally vested with that authority" (pp. xiii and xiv). The latter portion of the foregoing passage could, no doubt, by itself be taken as an intimation that Hicks was not disposed to give to "a power of regulating commerce" so broad a scope as some others—including, one might surmise, the author of the "Farmer's Letters"—had given it; and very likely it will at first seem to most modern readers that Hicks meant to exclude such "internal" subjects as agriculture and manufactures from the field of "commercial regulation." The remark about "the internal policy of each colony" will seem to indicate this. The term "internal policy"—even if it is not actually a misprint for "internal police" or "internal polity"—did not, however, always have, in the eighteenth century, the strict and exhaustive intraterritorial signification which it would be likely to have at present. The adjective "internal" was then usually understood in the sense of "domestic," "provincial," or "local," rather than "intraterritorial." So, even alone, Hick's statement about "internal policy" would not be conclusive; and since he elsewhere makes himself perfectly clear on the point at issue, the statement obviously must have meant something other than what seems most natural to a reader of today. Thus, he elsewhere says, in so many words, that he is "ready to acknowledge the *necessity** of lodging in some part of the [imperial] community a restraining power, for the regulating and limiting the trade *and manufactures* of each particular county or colony, in such manner as might most effectually promote the good of the whole" (p. xii); and he says that he would "not obstinately object to the vesting of this power in the parlia-

* Italics in the original.

ment of Great Britain [*i.e.*, the Parliament as then constituted], if the [recent] violent measures . . . did not afford too much reason to believe that every concession which might . . . be made from a *principle of necessity*,* and a regard to the public utility, would be immediately considered as an acknowledgment of such a *subordination*,* as is totally inconsistent with the nature of our constitution." (P. xii; *cf.*, pp. 28 and 29; and see, to the same effect, the letter of "A Citizen" [presumably Hicks] in Pa. Jour., December 17, 1767.) So, taking all of Hick's statements together, his intention seems clear: though inclined, *possibly*, to interpret "commercial regulation" somewhat more narrowly than Dickinson had done, he nevertheless proposed to vest in a re-constituted imperial Parliament "a power to regulate commerce" that would extend to colonial "manufactures," a term which, as we have seen, was in common use at the time to include agriculture and its products, as well as "manufactures" in the modern sense. And that "manufactures" did include "agriculture" in this particular connection seems virtually certain because there was no basis, in the conventional objects of "commercial regulation," for distinguishing between it and the non-agricultural "manufactures." Cf., 12 Car. II, c. 34; 15 Car. II, c. 7, §§18 and 19; and 22 and 23 Car. II, c. 26, interdicting the growing of tobacco in England for the benefit of the colonial tobacco trade and English manufactures. The foregoing intimations in this Hicks pamphlet are, it may be added, the only thing even conceivably construable as an objection to Dickinson's view of the scope of "commercial regulation" which could be found from the period when the "Farmer's Letters" were written. This, however, is not to say, of course, that there were not some writers who objected to Parliament's wielding power over American "manufactures," quite without regard to the "commercial" or non-"commercial" character of a power over them. See, for example, Pa. Jour., August 4, 1768, and N.Y. Jour., December 31, 1767. The foregoing statements are based upon an examination of all the American pamphlets of the time, of which the writer has any knowledge, and upon an examination of all the American newspapers of 1767 and 1768, except those published in Charleston, South Carolina. Because of the late war, these were not available at the time it was desired to examine them; and it has been impossible for the author to make a trip to that city since.

51. James Wilson, *Considerations on the Nature and Extent of the Legislative Authority of the British Parliament* (Philadelphia, 1774), reprinted in Wilson, III, 199 *et seq.*

52. Dickinson, I, 289 and 290.

53. It is probable that Dickinson himself had not changed his mind as to the desirability of conceding to Parliament full commercial power. In his *Diary* for September 12, 1774, John Adams recorded that "Mr. Dickinson [was] *full and clear* for allowing to Parliament *the regulation of trade*, upon principles of necessity, and the mutual interest of both countries." John Adams, II, 379; Letters, I, 29. *Cf.*, chapter vi hereof.

54. Reprinted in Dickinson, I, 329 *et seq.*

55. Dickinson, I, 360; *cf.* 356–57. The slitting of bar iron into rods was the first step in the making of nails.

56. Dickinson, I, 361–65.

57. Dickinson, I, 386.

58. Dickinson, I, 401.

* Italics in the original.

59. Dickinson, I, 398.

60. Joseph Reed, of Pennsylvania, definitely a sympathizer, though not with every position which Dickinson had taken, spoke, in a letter to Lord Dartmouth, written on July 18, 1774, of the "attempt [then] making [in Pennsylvania] to draw what [was], called the necessary and equitable line between the Mother Country and the Colonies." "It [was] the work," he said, "principally of the gentlemen [sic] who wrote the Farmer's Letters. But as it seems *to advance* the Colonial claims rather than diminish them, I fear, if it should be adopted by the Congress, it would meet with an unkind reception." Reed, I, xvi; *cf., ibid.,* 83. For an unsympathetic view, see an "Extract of a Letter from London, to a Gentleman in New York, dated December 10, 1774," in Archives, 4th Ser., I, 1036–37: "Your Patriots . . . have convinced the world, by their *new claims,** that the smallest part of the foundation of Parliamentary jurisdiction cannot be impaired, without demolishing the whole super-structure. . . . The *'Pennsylvania Farmer,'* by the late instructions, which hold up a claim to an exemption from Acts of Parliament, has ruined the cause, *and drawn on himself the just charge of contradicting his own principles.*"

NOTES TO CHAPTER VI

1. The historians' discussions are not specific or rigorous upon this point, as, indeed, they are not specific or rigorous upon many points. Reference may be made, however, to the discussion of Dickinson's "Farmer's Letters" in A. C. McLaughlin, *A Constitutional History of the United States* (New York, 1936), 55–63, especially 58, 59, and 61. Mr. McLaughlin apparently noted Dickinson's statement in his "Farmer's Letters" that all the colonial acts of Parliament before the Stamp Act administration were for the regulation of trade; but he seems to have concluded that Dickinson, in making this statement, had fallen into error. Back of this conclusion, there seems to lie an assumption, which appears to run through Mr. McLaughlin's whole discussion, that, at the time in question, "the regulation of trade, or commerce," meant "the regulation of external trade, or external commerce, only." This assumption comes to the surface when the commercial power which Dickinson and the country generally were ready to concede to Parliament, at the date of the "Farmer's Letters," is described as an "authority to regulate intercolonial and foreign trade." A first-hand examination of nearly all the extant American newspapers of 1767–68 and most, if not all, of the American pamphlets of that period has failed to disclose any basis for so describing the commercial power which was quite generally conceded to Parliament in 1768.

Other historical works which seem to take this same narrow view of the eighteenth-century American understanding of "commercial regulation" include Miller, *Origins of the American Revolution* (Boston, 1943), wherein it is stated, at p. 381, that the First Continental Congress "conceded that Parliament had the right to regulate colonial trade"; Jensen, *The Articles of Confederation* (Madison, 1940), wherein, at pp. 67 and 68, "the regulation of external commerce" and "the right to regulate trade" appear to be regarded as equivalents; and Alexander, *A Revolutionary Conservative: James Duane of New York* (New York, 1938), 100–101, and Burnett, *Letters of Members of the Continental Congress* (Washington, 1921), I, 38–44, especially

* Italics in the original.

note 36, p. 44, and the reprint "A" of Duane's resolution II, at pp. 40–41, wherein somewhat similar assumptions seem to be made, indicative of a belief by these two writers that the eighteenth century understood "the regulation of trade, or commerce," very narrowly. Cf., note 2 *infra*. See, also, p. 188 of Jensen, *op. cit.*, where New Jersey is said to have complained, in reference to the Articles of Confederation, that "the sole power of regulating trade should be given to Congress." New Jersey, at the time to which Mr. Jensen has reference, actually urged only that "the sole and exclusive power of regulating the trade of the United States *with foreign nations* ought to be clearly vested in the Congress." Journals, XI, 648. The remarks at p. 177 of Becker, *A History of Political Parties in the Province of New York,* BULLETIN OF THE UNIVERSITY OF WISCONSIN, History Series, Vol. II, are probably, in view of what actually happened in the New York Assembly in 1775 (see pp. 166–67 of text hereof), another instance of this erroneous general assumption among historians, as to what Americans understood by "the regulation of commerce, or trade." Cf., notes 74 and 75 *infra*. An exception, possibly, is Van Tyne, *Causes of the American Revolution* (Boston and New York, 1922), 441, wherein the resolution finally adopted by Congress, conceding to Parliament power over "external commerce" only, is seemingly recognized to have been a compromise in point of substance. There may be others.

2. The papers to be referred to constitute items 22, 58, 97, 98, and 123, in Vol. I of Burnett, *op. cit. supra*, note 1. As pointed out in the preceding note, Mr. Burnett seems to make the common error of assuming that eighteenth-century Americans understood the subject of "commercial regulation" in a narrow, territorially external sense. It is this, it is believed, which has led him to print version "A" of Duane's resolution II, in item 58 of his book, in a way that makes that resolution self-contradictory. Thus, he makes the resolution recognize a "supreme [parliamentary] direction and superintendance over the *general* Trade of all his Majesty's Dominions," subject to a proviso that "such Authority" be "bona fide restrained to the Regulation of [the colonies'] *foreign* Trade" only. Because of the unsatisfactory way in which Mr. Burnett has printed this item, it has been reprinted as Appendix C to the present volume of this book. See note 5 to Appendix C. The original of the item there reprinted and, as well, the originals of the other Duane papers mentioned above, except items 97 and 98, are in the library of the New York Historical Society, New York City. Items 97 and 98 exist only in the form of copies from the now unknown originals. The copies are among the Bancroft papers in the New York Public Library.

3. Richard Henry Lee was in favor of Congress' making a single, uniform constitution for the various states, in 1776. John Adams, IX, 374. He fought to the bitter end for a Congressional general-welfare power, in 1777. Letters, II, 345 and 346. He was against the continental impost, in 1785. Letters, VIII, 66. He was against a general national commerce power, in May 1787, and apparently also against any considerable increase of national power, at that time, of any kind. Lee, II, 419. Nevertheless, he seemed to grow reconciled to the prospect of a national government of "higher tone" (*i.e.*, "greater strength") as the summer wore along. Lee, 423, 427, 430, and 432. Then, in October, he deplored the general-welfare power in the Constitution, but only, it would seem, because the power was not accompanied by what he regarded as an adequate bill of civil rights. This is apparent from the letters which Lee then wrote; particularly, from one which he wrote for public

consumption, to Edmund Randolph, on October 16, 1787. For, in that letter, as also in his other letters at the time and in his accompanying proposals for amendment of the Constitution, Lee advocated only a more extended and more specific bill of *civil* rights in qualification of the general-welfare power. He did not propose an expungement of the general power, and he did not propose a qualification of it by the stipulation of any *states'* rights, at all, though he did propose certain rules of voting in Congress to protect Southern interests. Lee, II, 440–42, 444, 445, 448, 449, 452, and 453. The letter of October 16, 1787, to Edmund Randolph, was afterwards published in pamphlet form and in the newspapers, and made its way into all parts of the country. The most important single publication from the group opposed to unqualified ratification, the letter was, apparently, the only thing from Lee's pen actually published during the ratification campaign. The *Letters from a Federal Farmer*, usually attributed to Lee, were not written by him. (See discussion of this point in a later volume.) However, Lee began to lean towards *states'* rights again, just before the Virginia ratifying convention met. Lee, II, 465 and 469. And after the adoption of the Constitution, as one of the first senators from Virginia, Lee became identified with the anti-federalist faction.

The facts relating to Samuel Adams are less specific; but there is nothing to be found in any of his published letters to indicate that he held views very different, in 1776, from those then held by Richard Henry Lee. (See discussion herein in a later volume; also, the letters of Samuel Adams published in his collected works and in Warren-Adams.) He was at first identified with the opposition to the Constitution in 1787–88; but when he found that his usual backers, the laborers and artisans of Boston, were for the proposed new government, he changed his stand and helped in the end to get the Constitution adopted. See letters of Henry Knox and Rufus King printed in Knox, 97 and 98, and discussion herein in a later volume.

Considerations of a kind which we now call "political" were doubtless at the bottom of the vagaries of Samuel Adams and Richard Henry Lee; but the exact character of these considerations is difficult in some instances to determine.

4. 3 Geo. III, c. 44.

5. 4 Geo. III, c. 19.

6. Reed, I, 80, 81.

7. Archives, 4th Ser., I, 333–34, 366–67, 352–53, 384–86, 392–93, 409, 417–18, 425–26, 518, 550–51, 350–51, 686–90.

8. 4 Geo. III, c. 83.

9. 4 Geo. III, c. 54.

10. 4 Geo. III, c. 39.

11. 4 Geo. III, c. 45.

12. Archives, 4th Ser., I, 167–69.

13. *Ibid.*, 172–75.

14. Coffin, *The Province of Quebec and the Early American Revolution*, in Bulletin of the University of Wisconsin, Economics, Political Science and History Series, I, 274, 447.

15. In Coffin, *op. cit.* note 14 *supra*, the view of the Quebec Act here suggested is rejected, partly on the ground, apparently, that the administration of the act did not bear out the Americans' fears, and partly on the ground that the anti-American purpose of the act was not avowed with sufficient blatancy, at a time when, according to Coffin, there was no reason to fear a want either of Parliamentary or popular support for anti-American measures.

The reasoning is not persuasive. The English people, as well as Parliament, may, perhaps, have been "consistently and overwhelmingly" anti-American, as Coffin ventures to assert; but it is not of record that they were pro-Popish. Witness to the contrary the "Lord George Gordon Riots," of a few years later, in 1780. There was good ground to fear the popular reaction to an open avowal of an attempt to use the Roman Catholic Canadians against the American colonists. As for the actual administration of the Quebec Act, that was no doubt affected by the unexpected reactions in Canada. Coffin's study seems to indicate, moreover, that the British government did secure the support of the *noblesse* and the clergy, but not the *habitants*, of the province, during the later American invasion of Canada. *Op. cit.*, 497–98.

16. Archives, 4th Ser., I, 214, 1836–37.

17. Reed, I, 79.

18. Letters, I, 79.

19. John Adams, II, 373–75; Letters, I, 46.

20. Vattel, *The Law of Nations* (London, 1759), Bk. I, chap. xiii, sec. 174.

21. The discussion of the "objects of government" begins in chap. vi, which is entitled in the original French edition (see facsimile reprint, Washington, [1916], 73): "*Principaux objets d'un bon Gouvernement; 10. Pourvoir aux besoins de la Nation.*" This "first principal object" (*i.e.*, "providing for the Necessities of the Nation") was equivalent to the "political" aspects of the "regulation of commerce, or trade," as the latter phrase was used among English writers of the time. As comprehended within this "first principal object," Vattel discusses "the Cultivation of the Earth" in chap. vii, under the title of "*De la Culture des Terres*"; in chap. viii, he discusses "*Commerce,*" which includes both domestic and foreign "merchandize"; in chap. ix, under the title of "*Du soin des Chemins publics, & de Droits de Peage,*" he discusses "the Care of the Public Ways of Communication, and the Right of Toll"; and, in chap. x, under the title of "*De la Monnaie & du Change,*" he discusses "Money and Exchange." Manufactures are treated in chap. vi and to some extent in certain of the other chapters just mentioned. Chapter xiii, "On Justice and Polity," is a part of the discussion of "the second [principal] Object of a good Government: to procure the true Felicity of a Nation" ("*procurer la vraie felicite de la Nation*"), which is begun in chap. xi.

22. The variant version appears as follows in the London edition of 1811: "§174. The *internal police* consists in the attention of the prince and magistrates to preserve every thing in order. Wise regulations ought to prescribe whatever will best contribute to the public safety, utility, and convenience; and those who are invested with authority, cannot be too attentive to enforce them. By a wise *police* the sovereign accustoms the people to order and obedience, and preserves peace, tranquility, and concord among the citizens."

23. Blackstone, I, 274; and IV, 162. In the former reference, Blackstone says that "the [royal] limitation of ['markets and fairs'] to such time and place as may be most *convenient* for the neighbourhood, forms a part of *oeconomics, or domestic polity; which, considering the kingdom as a large family,* and the king as the master of it, he clearly has a right to dispose and order as he pleases."

24. Blackstone, IV, chap. 12 *passim.*

25. Blackstone, IV, chap. 10.

26. *Loc. cit. supra* note 23.

27. *Cf.*, note 23 to chapter iv.

28. Vattel, *op. cit. supra* note 20, p. 133.

29. See the excerpt from the series of letters on good roads for Connecticut, quoted in the text hereof at p. 65 *supra;* also, the provision in the Quebec Act of 1774 giving power to "the inhabitants of any town or district within said province" to "authorise" the provincial council "to assess, levy, and apply, within the said town or district, *for the purpose of making roads, erecting and repairing public buildings, or for any other purpose respecting the local convenience and economy of such town or district*" (4 Geo. III, c. 83, §13); and *cf.,* the construction put upon this provision by the Continental Congress (Journals, I, 109).

30. Appendix A hereof, pp. 1193–94 *supra.* Also, Johnson, J., in *Gibbons* v. *Ogden,* 9 Wheat 1, 234, 235, 238 (1824): "It remains, to consider the objections to this opinion as presented by the counsel for the appellee. . . . [One] principal objection . . . arise[s] . . . from the unavoidable action of some of the municipal powers of the States, upon commercial subjects. . . . It is no objection to the existence of distinct, substantive powers, that, in their application, *they bear upon the same subject.* The same bale of goods, the same cask of provisions, or the same ship, that may be the subject of commercial regulation, may also be the vehicle of disease. And the health laws that require them to be stopped and ventilated, are no more intended as regulations on commerce, than the laws which permit their importation, are intended to innoculate the community with disease. *Their different purposes mark the distinction between the powers brought into action.* . . . [And] wherever the powers of the respective governments are frankly exercised, with a distinct view to the ends of such powers, *they may act upon the same object, or use the same means,* and yet the powers be kept perfectly distinct. *A resort to the same means, therefore is no argument to prove the identity of their respective powers.*" It should be noted that "object" is used by Justice Johnson in the above passage in a sense different from any of those mentioned in the text.

31. Appendix A hereof, pp. 1181 and 1184 *supra.*

32. *Ibid.,* p. 1184 *supra;* also Hamilton, III, 481.

33. Appendix A hereof, p. 1181 *supra.*

34. *Ibid.,* pp. 1193–94 *supra;* also, Johnson, J., in *Gibbons* v. *Ogden,* 9 Wheat. 1, 235 (1824), and Barbour, J., in *New York* v. *Miln,* 11 Pet. 102, 138 (1837).

35. This is the dictionary definition. See Samuel Johnson's *Dictionary of the English Language* (Harrison's ed.; London, 1786): "Police [is] the regulation and government of a city or country, so far as regards the inhabitants." Also, Webster, *American Dictionary of the English Language* (Boston, 1828): "Police [is] the administration of laws and regulation of a city or incorporated town or borough; the internal regulation and government of a kingdom or state."

36. This also is the dictionary definition. See Johnson, *op. cit. supra* note 35: "Policy [is] the art of government, chiefly with respect to foreign powers." Chamber's *Cyclopaedia, or Universal Dictionary* (5th ed.; London, 1793) defines "policy" more generally, but says: "Some divide policy into two parts, agoranomy, that relating to the affairs of merchandize; and astynomy, that concerning the civil and judiciary government of the citizens." The terms "agoranomy" and "astynomy" do not appear to have been in common use; but except for the disregard of war and diplomacy, the division signified is much like that discussed in the text.

37. The writer in *The New Haven Gazette* said that "policy"—or, to quote his exact words, the "political interest" of a nation—related "chiefly to foreign

powers"; but indicated clearly at several points that the term included "commerce" in the sense of all gainful activity, whether internal or external in character. See Appendix A hereof, p. 1181, *supra; cf.*, pp. 1182 and 1184.

38. The writer in *The New Haven Gazette* said that, "under these denominations, of War; or that in which the peace and safety of a nation consists;—and of Commerce; or the correspondence and connections of a nation with other nations *and with one another,* the whole *political* interest of a nation [might] be included and considered." See p. 1184 of Appendix A hereof.

39. Appendix A hereof, p. 1181 *supra.*

40. The difference appears to have been that "internal polity" meant, primarily, *the setting-up* of government for *provincial purposes,* in the sense explained in the text, and, by consequence, the *carrying-on* of such government. "Internal police" meant, primarily, the *carrying-on* of such government and perhaps implied the setting-up. Some of the "internal-police" limitations in 1776 were phrased as "the right of regulating internal government and police." "Regulating internal government" meant "local constitution-making." The reasons for the specification are discussed in a later volume hereof.

41. Journals, I, 68.

42. To be treated in a later volume hereof.

43. The complaints were many and bitter in Pennsylvania and apparently came from Whigs as well as Tories. See, for example, Pa. Jour., March 19, May 21 and 28, and June 11, 1777. The same was true in Delaware. See the same paper for October 23, and November 13, 1776.

44. To be treated in a later volume hereof.

45. See, for example, the claim of James Smith, of Pennsylvania, in the Continental Congress, on February 14, 1777, that the regulation of commerce was included in "internal," or, as he put it, "domestic police" (Letters, II, 250); the claim of Thomas Burke, of North Carolina, on February 25, 1777, that the trying of persons for desertion from the army was included (Letters, II, 277); a reference by Edward Rutledge, in a letter to Robert R. Livingston, on October 19, 1776, to the notion, entertained by Philip Livingston, that the appointment of military officers by the Congress was "interfering in the internal polity of the States" (Letters, II, 126); and Alexander Hamilton's reference to the view, in his *Letters of Phocion,* in 1784, that the treaty of peace, of 1783, was regarded as invasive of the "internal police" of the states, in its stipulation that the states should carry out no further forfeitures or discriminations against loyalists after the treaty took effect (Hamilton, IV, 230, 234, 240–41). There are, of course, examples to be found of uses of "police" which are different from those cited in the text, and which, but for the considerations pointed out by Hamilton, might seem to warrant, to some extent, some of the foregoing contentions. Thus, Adam Smith, for example, used the term in a sense which was not found in any other writer. He said, according to the notes of one of his students, that "the four great objects of law [were] justice, *police,* revenue, and arms." "The object of justice," he continued, "is the security from injury, and it is the foundation of civil government. The objects of *police* are *the cheapness of commodities,* public security and cleanliness, if the two last were not too minute for a lecture of this kind. *Under this head we will consider the opulence of a state.*" Cannan, *op. cit.* note 17 to chapter iv *supra,* 3. Under this usage, "police," obviously, would include "commerce." Adam Smith, of course, was a Scotchman; and Scotch usage differed in many respects from English usage. No evidence was found that this sense of "police" was current either in America

or England; but there are occasional loose uses of "police" in which the word seems to be practically synonymous with "government." It should also be observed that the terms "police," "polity," and "policy"—presumably because of the similarity in their spelling—were sometimes confused. This was especially likely to occur when the words were copied or set up for printing. *Cf.*, Letters, I, 44 and 74. The situation was not unlike that with respect to the words "gaol" and "goal," which were constantly confused in eighteenth-century writing and printing. It would be a mistake, however, to suppose that the distinction between a "gaol" and "goal" was not understood. And so with "police," "polity," and "policy."

46. Hamilton, IV, 230, 240–41.

47. Records, II, 26. The limitation was only a qualified one and made the power of Congress to act for the "general welfare" paramount. Nevertheless, the Convention promptly voted the proposal down and then proceeded to adopt a provision giving Congress power "to legislate in all cases for the general interests of the Union" without even a qualified "internal-police" limitation. Records, II, 21, 25–27.

48. Besides the proposal referred to in the next preceding note, which was made by Roger Sherman, of Connecticut, a second substantially identical proposal was made by the Committee of Detail on August 22d. Records, II, 367. In this case, also, the reservation was a qualified one, and power was proposed to be given to Congress "to provide . . . for . . . the general interests and welfare of the United States." The General Welfare Clause eventually went in without the "internal-police" limitation. Records, II, 493, 495, 497, and 499. A final effort to obtain an "internal-police" limitation was made by Sherman, of Connecticut, according to the notes left by James Madison, on September 15th. It was promptly voted down. Records, II, 630. On the motion of Morris, the clause guarantying the equal vote of the states in the Senate was inserted, ostensibly as a structural substitute. Records, II, 631.

49. The Preamble was added by the Committee on Style in its draft of September 12. *Cf.*, Records, II, 565, 582, 585, and 590. Morris was a member of this committee, and to him was confided the drawing of the final draft of the Constitution (Records, III, 170, 420, and 499), although it appears that James Wilson, of Pennsylvania, had a hand in the final draft, as well (Records, III, 170; and Warren, *The Making of the Constitution* [Boston, 1928], 687–88). The inference stated in the text, that Morris was responsible for the Preamble, thus seems fairly justified; especially, as we have his word for it that he tried, so far as possible, to incorporate in the final draft, his own ideas of what was for the best interest of the country. Records, III, 404 and 420. His view as to the undesirability of the "internal-police" limitation seems sufficiently established by the statement by him which is referred to in the text. Records, II, 26.

50. 9 Wheat. (U.S.) 208, and 209–10. The opinion reads "upon their interfering with"; but this is obviously a mistake.

51. 9 Wheat. (U.S.) 204–5.

52. *Ibid.*

53. The coining of the phrase "police power" is usually attributed to Marshall in *Brown* v. *Maryland*, 12 Wheat. 419, 442–43 (1827): "The counsel for defendant in error have endeavoured to illustrate their proposition, that the constitutional prohibition [*i.e.*, the Imports and Exports Clause] ceases the instant the goods enter the country, by an array of the consequences

which they suppose must follow the denial of it. If the importer acquires the right to sell by the payment of duties, he may, they say, exert that right when, where, and as he pleases, and the State cannot regulate it. . . . He may introduce articles, as gunpowder, which endanger a city, into the midst of its population. . . . [But] the power to direct the removal of gunpowder is *a branch of the police power, which unquestionably remains, and ought to remain, with the States.*" The phrase "police power" is so natural a phrase, in view of the notions of the time, that it is difficult to believe that it was never used before Marshall used it in this particular case; but if Marshall did originate the phrase, it is clear that he employed the word "police" in it in the technical, eighteenth-century sense.

54. 16 Pet. 539, 632–33. The case came up under section 2 of Article IV of the Constitution, relating to the return by the states, of slaves escaping into them from labor or service in another state. The Court held that the states, as distinct from Congress, had no power to legislate under the section. Taney dissented from this view. He said, in part: "It seems to be supposed that laws nearly similar to those I have mentioned, might be passed by [a] state in the exercise of her powers over her *internal police,* and by virtue of her right to remove from her territory disorderly and evil-disposed persons, or those who, from the nature of her institutions, are dangerous to her peace and tranquillity. *But it would be difficult perhaps to bring all the laws I have mentioned within the legitimate scope of the internal powers of police.* The fugitive is not always arrested in order to prevent a dangerous or evil-disposed person from remaining in her territory. He is himself most commonly anxious to escape from it [out of the country]; and it often happens that he is seized near the borders of the state when he is endeavouring to leave it, and is brought back and detained until he can be delivered to his owner. He may sometimes be found travelling peaceably along the public highway on his road to another state, in company with and under the protection of a white man who is abetting his escape. *And it could hardly be maintained that the arrest and confinement of the fugitive in the public prison, under such circumstances, until he could be delivered to his owner, was necessary for the internal peace of the state; and therefore a justifiable exercise of its powers of police.*" Story, J., delivering the opinion of the Court, said (p. 625), that the "police power" was "designed for the protection, safety, and peace of the state." Daniel, J., said (pp. 657–58) that "the police power of a state . . . is confined to matters strictly belonging to her internal order and quiet." McLean, J., referred (p. 666) to the "laws which regulate the police of a state, maintain the peace of its citizens, and preserve its territory and jurisdiction from acts of violence"; and he said (p. 671) that he thought it "a most important police regulation" for a state to forbid the removal of "persons of colour" from her territory by violent means. The other justices said nothing to indicate that they held a view of "the police power of a state" different from that which all the foregoing justices seem plainly to have entertained.

55. 5 How. (U.S.) 504, 582, 583.

56. Journals, I, 26–29.

57. Journals, I, 40–42.

58. Journals, I, 63 *et seq.* The legality of the earlier Parliamentary acts was not specifically disputed; but the power conceded to Parliament was not sufficient to cover them, and the theories "of English liberty and of all free govern-

ment" which the resolutions set forth were inconsistent with their validity. Cf., note 73 *infra*.

59. Journals, I, 28 and footnote.

60. See *op. cit.* note 1 *supra*. The possibility is recognized, however, in a footnote in McLaughlin, *op. cit.*, that the sense of "internal polity" in the fourth of the Congressional resolutions of October 14, 1774, may perhaps have been other than that generally assumed among historians.

61. The classic statement of the Supreme Court's present-day position is that of Taney, C.J., in *The License Cases*, 5 How. (U.S.) 504, 582 (1847), which is quoted in the text at p. *155 supra*. Other pronouncements commonly quoted are the following: Field, J., in *Barbier* v. *Connolly*, 113 U.S. 27 (1885): "But neither the [fourteenth] amendment—broad and comprehensive as it is—nor any other amendment, was designed to interfere with the power of the state, sometimes termed its police power, to prescribe regulations to promote the health, peace, morals, education, and good order of the people, and to legislate so as to increase the industries of the state, develop its resources, and add to its wealth and prosperity." Harlan, J., in *Chicago, B. & O. Ry. Co.* v. *Illinois*, 200 U.S. 561, 592 (1906): "The police power of a state embraces regulations designed to promote the public convenience or the general prosperity, as well as regulations designed to promote the public health, the public morals, or the public safety." Holmes, J., in *Noble State Bank* v. *Haskell*, 219 U.S. 104, 111 (1911): "The police power extends to all the great public needs." The inflating of the state police powers was, of course, just one phase of the process by which, in the pre–Civil War period, the powers of Congress were gradually frittered down.

62. The Duane paper which contains Duane's explanatory statement and the original draft of his resolutions was endorsed by him: "Propositions offered by J. Duane to the Committee for Stating Rights, Grievances, & the Means of Redress In Congress at Philadel[phia] between 7 & 22d Sept. 1774." The endorsement is too vague to settle when the "propositions" were offered. There is no endorsement of any kind on Duane's second and third principal drafts.

63. It is sometimes overlooked that the first of the "navigation acts" in the reign of Charles II (12 Car. II, c. 18) was something more than a navigation act; it contained a provision (sec. 2) forbidding aliens to exercise the occupation of merchant or factor in the colonies. Another of these early statutes relating to the trade of the colonies (15 Car. II, c. 7; *cf.*, §§ 5, 6, 7, and 18) contained a provision forbidding tobacco-raising in England as a measure for the benefit of English manufactures and the colonial tobacco trade. See, also, the comprehensive provisions relating to the colonies, in "An Act for the Advancing & Regulating of the Trade of this Commonwealth," of August 1, 1650 (2 Firth and Rait, *op. cit.* note 45 to chapter v *supra*, 403, 405), especially secs. 11 and 12. And *cf.*, "An Act for prohibiting Trade with the Barbadoes, Virginia, Bermuda, and Antego," October 3, 1650 (*ibid.*, 425).

64. See note 75 *infra*. Cf., also, Duane's bitter complaint that the resolution finally adopted, which "restrained" the power of Parliament to the colonies' "external commerce," had "rejected" the power "to regulate trade" or "pared it away to nothing." Page 166 of the text hereof.

65. John Adams, II, 373–75; Journals, I, 63, notes 1 and 2; Letters, I, 45–47, No. 62, note 2. Cf., note 75 *infra*.

66. N.Y. Pub. Library, Bancroft Collection, American Papers, II, 207; Letters, I, 72–74. The manuscript in the New York Public Library is a copy of certain undated notes of Duane's. The paper does not say so; but it appears,

from the length and detail of it, that it is an outline of a speech of Duane's and not his notes of a speech by some one else. The sentiments expressed also indicate Duane's authorship. The statement in the speech that "none mean to dispute [the right to regulate trade]" shows that the speech was delivered after September 24th, when the Congress voted not to consider colonial grievances antedating 1763. Since the committee on rights had fully reported by that time, this means that the speech was delivered before the full Congress. Mr. Burnett (Letters, I, 72) assigns October 13th as the probable date of the speech. The 12th is at least as likely. In the Bancroft papers, there is a copy of some notes of Duane's of debates upon the resolution "on trade," in which Duane speaks of John Adams as favoring his—*i.e.*, Duane's—amendment. It was apparently later, according to these same notes, though how much later is not known, that another amendment limiting Parliament's power to the colonies' external commerce was introduced. The Bancroft copy of these Duane notes is dated October 12, 1774. See Letters, I, 71. If this date is correct, it is obviously probable that Duane's speech was made on October 12th, though the 13th can not be altogether ruled out. *Cf.,* note 70 *infra.*

67. Letters, I, 74.

68. Journals, I, 68.

69. Letters, I, 72–74.

70. This fact is stated in John Adams' *Diary* for October 13, 1774, reprinted in Letters, I, 74. Adams added: "Mr. Duane has had his heart set upon asserting in our bill of rights the authority of Parliament to regulate *the trade of the Colonies.*" Apart from the fact that Adams said "trade," not "external trade," the reference to Duane would seem to settle that it was over *Duane's* proposed *complete* power that the deadlock occurred. Some further corroboration for the view presented in the text, if any further corroboration be needed, may be seen in the following facts: The split in the Rhode Island vote was due to the fact that Stephen Hopkins was favorable, and Samuel Ward unfavorable, to the concession of commercial power to Parliament. See Ward's *Diary* for October 13, 1774, reprinted in Letters, I, 74. Hopkins, one of the earliest and most judicious of the pamphleteers in behalf of the colonies, had from the first consistently favored the concession of commercial and other general powers to Parliament. *Cf.,* note 42 to chapter v. In his *Rights of the Colonies Examined,* of 1764, he conceded to Parliament, as part of its power over "the general concerns" of the Empire, the power of legislating with respect to the whole commerce of the British Empire, and also with respect to "the commerce of each Kingdom and colony in it" to the extent that the general interest of the Empire was concerned in any separate regulation of the commerce of one of these parts. Hopkins' precise language was "the commerce of the whole British empire, taken collectively, and that of each Kingdom and colony in it, as it makes part of the whole." *Cf.,* note 42 to chapter v. That the power thus conceded was not an exclusively external power appears from the hope which Hopkins then expressed that "amongst the general concerns [over which Parliament exercised power] perhaps, money and paper credit, those grand instruments of all commerce would be found to have a place." Money troubles, it should be remembered, had been perennial in the colonies, and a sound money system for the entire continent, and, indeed, the entire Empire, was very naturally one of the hopes of intelligent men, like Stephen Hopkins. It has also been pointed out in note 42 to chapter v that Hopkins deemed the interdiction of certain colonial manufactures a "constitutional" exercise of the "general" powers of Parliament. He may, of course, have changed his mind in the

ten years that had elapsed since 1764; but in the light of all the other facts set forth in the text, it seems improbable. In other words, it seems likely that we have, in the opinions which Hopkins expressed in his pamphlet of 1764, a pretty sure clue to the kind of Parliamentary commercial power for which he was voting in the First Continental Congress, in 1774. It may be added that, in certain newspaper essays, written by him, in 1765, in answer to the Tory pamphlet, *A Letter from a Gentleman at Halifax to his Friend in Rhode Island* (Newport, 1765), Hopkins spoke of the power of Parliament as covering "general commerce." Prov. Gaz., March 9, 1765. It seems probable that "general commerce," in this instance, meant "public," or "political commerce." See pp. 103–4 *supra*. In any event, local commercial power was apparently not excluded for the separate colonies, as Hopkins viewed the subject in 1765; but the local powers were subject to the overriding power of Parliament.

71. *Loc. cit.* note 65 *supra; cf.*, note 75 *infra*.

72. Journals, I, 68. The bases were (1) "that the foundation of English liberty, and of all free government, is a right in the people to participate in their legislative council"; and (2) "[that] the English colonists are not represented, and from their local and other circumstances, cannot properly be represented in the British Parliament."

73. *Ibid.*

74. Alexander, *op. cit.* note 1 *supra*, 100–101. The author of this work observes (p. 100) that "Duane thought the mother country entitled to regulate commerce throughout the empire in return for defending the colonies." He then sets out briefly Duane's various proposals; observes that most of these were "totally ignored"; and then adds (p. 101): "But [Duane] won his fight to acknowledge the right of Parliament to regulate external commerce." He adds, in a footnote, that "Burnett's analysis of Duane's share in the final resolves [*i.e.*, the analysis contained in Burnett's *Letters of Members of the Continental Congress*] is masterful and convincing"; and that, "without doubt, [Duane] was entitled to as much credit as was John Adams for the fourth resolve [of October 14, 1774] conceding commercial regulation." These statements of Duane's biographer seem incomprehensible, unless "trade," "commerce," "general trade," "general commerce," "foreign trade," and "external commerce" are all regarded as having been equivalent terms in the eighteenth century. In other words, the statements seem comprehensible only if "commercial regulation" is assumed to have meant the regulation of external trade, or external commerce, only. This, as already indicated, is an assumption which American historians seem generally to make. *Cf.*, the following note.

75. See the materials cited in note 1 *supra*. The Burnett analysis, referred to by the biographer of Duane mentioned in the next preceding note, is to be found in the notes appended by Mr. Burnett to his reprints of the Duane papers herein referred to, which are included in the first volume of his *Letters of Members of the Continental Congress*. Mr. Burnett seems to reach the conclusion in these notes (though the conclusion is not very explicitly stated) that article 4 of the Resolutions of Congress on the Rights and Grievances of the Colonies was *not* "essentially the work of John Adams." *Cf.*, Letters, I, 44, note 36 to No. 58. Yet we have the explicit statement of John Adams, who, when not engaged in controversy, seems to have been a thoroughly honest man, that he drew the resolution in question, both originally and finally. *Loc. cit.* note 65 *supra*. Adams' account of the doings of the First Continental Congress, written largely from memory in 1804, is inaccurate in certain particulars; but there is no reason to suppose that he laid claim to credit for any part in the

proceedings of the Congress that he did not take. Mr. Burnett seems to doubt Adams' claim to the authorship of article 4, because "the latter half of the [fourth] article, excepting the introductory clauses, is drawn," he says, "from Duane's article II [*i.e.*, Duane's resolution on Parliament's power over trade *with the proviso attached in its initial form*], and [because] Duane's article VI [*i.e.*, Duane's resolution on colonial power over taxation and internal polity] is embodied in the first half [of the fourth article] with but small alteration." Letters, *loc. cit.* He also even grudges to Adams the introductory and concluding phrases of that part of the fourth resolution which relates to Parliament's power over trade. Letters, I, 45, note 2 to No. 62, at p. 47.

Mr. Burnett's conclusions in this matter appear to be based upon an unstated assumption that *everything* contained in the several versions of the trade resolution found in the Duane papers which is in Duane's handwriting is also of Duane's authorship; and, more particularly, that this is true of the initial form of the proviso which was added to Duane's original resolution on the power to be conceded to Parliament over trade. This proviso was added to Duane's resolution, only after an omission from that resolution which Mr. Burnett, presumably because of his views on "commerce," apparently did not perceive. *Cf.*, note 2 *supra*. Apart from the resulting self-contradictory character of the initial form of the proviso to the trade resolution, Mr. Burnett's general assumption as to Duane's authorship of everything contained in his papers which is in his handwriting is obviously unsafe; only the *complete* series of resolutions *in their original form* and the two re-drafts of the trade resolution on the separate sheets can, with any confidence, be ascribed to him. And the conclusion to which Mr. Burnett's assumption leads, in the case of the initial form of the proviso added to the Duane resolution on trade, seems, for the reasons stated in the text, to be completely untenable. See pp. 160–61 *supra*. The conclusions reached by Mr. Burnett are, moreover, possible only if "trade," "commerce," "general trade," "general commerce," "foreign trade," and "external commerce" were all equivalent terms; that is to say, his conclusions are possible only if "the regulation of trade" or "commerce" really meant to Duane and the other members of the First Continental Congress "the regulation of external trade, or external commerce, only." That being true, the inference seems to follow that Mr. Burnett, in common with most other writers on the period, must have assumed that "the regulation of trade" or "commerce" did have this narrow meaning at the time in question. But since this assumption certainly is unwarranted, Mr. Burnett's conclusion also is unwarranted, that John Adams' claim to the "essential" authorship of resolution 4 is without foundation. Instead, as indicated in the text, Duane's papers tend, on the whole, to strengthen Adams' claim.

In this connection, it is interesting further to note that Mr. Burnett is apparently somewhat puzzled by his own conclusions; for, in his more recently published book, *The Continental Congress* (New York, 1941), he observes that "it is little short of remarkable that the Declaration of Rights [was] so restrained in tone, in view of the fact that 'the violent party' was in the ascendancy in Congress [when the declaration was adopted]." When it is considered that Mr. Burnett believes that the Congress agreed to *everything* in reference to the central question of Parliamentary and colonial power which, he supposes, conservatives like Duane desired, it is easy to see why he should think the action of that body "remarkable" in view of the so-called "fact" he mentions. Actually, the Congress was deadlocked up to the very last on the important subject of commercial power. Nevertheless, it would be "remarkable," even in this situation, if conservatives like Duane had gotten everything they wanted, on what John Adams described as "indeed the essence of the whole controversy"; and this consideration is, of course, one more excellent reason for believing that Mr. Burnett's theory of what happened is not correct.

76. N.Y. Hist. Soc., Duane Papers, IV, 260 (copy); Letters, I, 87, No. 123.

77. The usual assumption is, apparently, that the whole controversy in Congress was something of "a tempest in a teapot"; that it had no substantive significance; and that Duane was complaining, in his letter to Chase, only of the failure of the Congress to ground the power conceded to Parliament on military and naval protection, long acquiescence, and *ancient* compact; not merely upon current necessity, expediency, and the colonies' consent *at the time*. Cf., excerpt reprinted from John Adams' *Diary*, in Letters, I, 74; and see Jensen, *op. cit.* note 1 *supra*, 68 and 73. Unquestionably, Duane did dislike this aspect of the Congress' action; but the failure of Congress to comply with Duane's wishes in this respect would not have been described very aptly as "rejecting [the power to regulate trade] or paring [it] away to nothing." These words, on the other hand, are just about what a man would say of the "restraining" of Parliament's power to "external commerce" if what he had wanted was a power extending to the whole of the gainful activities of the colonies.

78. Archives, 4th Ser., I, 1286–87, 1289, 1290.

79. *Ibid.*, 1297–1303, 1309–21.

80. *Ibid.*, 1319–20; cf., *ibid.*, 1309–10.

81. See the speech of Isaac Wilkins. *Ibid.*, 1293, 1296.

82. *Ibid.*, II, 1253; cf., 1244.

83. *Ibid.*, 1265, 1271, 1312, 1315–18, 1326, 1327, 1329. The text of the plan is set forth at 1326 and 1327.

84. Journals, I, 48 and 51, note 1; Letters, I, 51, No. 68, note 2; and 51–59; John Adams, II, 387–91.

85. Journals, I, 49–51.

86. N.Y. Public Library, Bancroft Collection, American Papers, II, 117–19; Letters, I, 71, No. 97.

87. There is other evidence which at least suggests that Adams may have vacillated on the degree of power over trade which should be conceded to Parliament. Thus, after the Congress was over, and he had returned to Boston, he wrote to Edward Biddle, of Pennsylvania, on December 12, 1774, inquiring how "the fourth resolution in our bill of rights" was "relished" in other parts of the continent. "*I had more anxiety about that,*" he said, "*than all the rest. But I find it is extremely popular here. Our provincial Congress have approved and adopted it in strong terms. They consider it a great point gained. They think it has placed our connection with Great Britain on its true principles, and there is no danger from it to us, and there is quite as much allowed to her as either justice or policy requires.*" John Adams, IX, 348; Letters, I, 87. And cf., his entry in his *Diary*, for September 12, 1774: "Mr. Dickinson . . . has an excellent heart, and the cause of his country lies near it. He is *full and clear* for allowing to Parliament *the regulation of trade*, upon principles of necessity, and the mutual interest of both countries." John Adams, II, 379; Letters, I, 29; Cf., note 52 to chapter v *supra*.

88. See pp. 125–26 *supra*.

89. The same view of the "slitting-mill statute" may be found in a speech that was published in Alexander Purdie's [Williamsburg] *Virginia Gazette*, on July 14th, 1775. The speech is described in the *Gazette*, as having been "de-

livered to the inhabitants of a certain [Virginia] county [when] assembled to choose deputies to the colony convention." In the course of the speech, the slitting-mill statute and the act of Parliament which sought to regulate the colonial manufacture of hats and felts are both referred to as "instances in which the colonies were oppressed under the notion of [Parliamentary] right *to regulate our trade.*" The acts in question were of course reprobated by the speaker; first, because they were deemed oppressive; and, second, because the speaker would not concede that Parliament had any legislative power over the colonies at all. But the speech is devoid of any intimation that the acts were not acts which actually "regulated our trade."

90. N.Y. Hist. Soc., Duane Papers, IV, 201; Letters, I, 23.

NOTES TO CHAPTER VII

1. Seabury, 118.
2. Seabury, 118–19, 126–27.
3. Hamilton, I, 126.
4. Hamilton, I, 128–29.
5. Hamilton, I, 130
6. Hamilton, I, 126.
7. Massachusettensis, 9.
8. See the provision in the so-called Dickinson draft of the Articles of Confederation that "the United States assembled"—*i.e.*, the Continental Congress—should "never impose or levy any Taxes or Duties, except in managing the Post-Office." Journals, V, 552 (Art. XVIII). And *cf.*, Blackstone, I, 321–23. There are many other examples, in the usage of the times, indicating that "postage" was regarded as a tax.
9. Massachusettensis, 9, 39, 45, 54–55, 89, 91, 107–8. As to what "Massachusettensis" understood by the "regulation of trade" or "regulation of commerce," see pp. 26–27 and 98–101. These passages contain no direct statement upon the point; but they will probably be accepted by most readers as sufficiently indicative that his understanding was the same as John Dickinson's, in his "Farmer's Letters." For a Whig corroboration of the view of "Massachusettensis" that the "principles" of the resolves of Congress were a novelty, see a letter from Joseph Reed, of Pennsylvania, to Lord Dartmouth, written after the Congress had adjourned. Reed, I, 83. Reed therein observed: "The universal claim is, to be restored to the state we were in 1763, though a line drawn at that period includes some of those laws *to whose principles and binding authority we are now opposed.*" Cf., *ibid.*, I, xvi.
10. John Adams, IV, 99.
11. Thus, at p. 33, of John Adams, IV: "But, at the same time, [the people of Massachusetts] know that, in their own opinions, and in the opinions of all the colonies, parliament has no authority over them, *excepting to regulate their trade,* and this not by any principle of common law, but merely by the consent of the colonies, founded on the obvious necessity of a case which was never in contemplation of that law, nor provided for by it." At p. 38: "But there is no need of any other power than that of *regulating trade,* and this the colonies ever have been, and will be, ready and willing to concede to her. But she will never obtain from America any further concession while she exists." At p. 47: "More than a century since, Massachusetts and Virginia both protested against even the act of navigation, and refused obedience, for this very reason, because they were not represented in parliament and were therefore not bound; and

afterwards confirmed it [the navigation act] by their own provincial authority. And from that time to this, the general sense of the colonies has been, that the authority of parliament was confined to *the regulation of trade,* and did not extend to taxation or *internal legislation."* At p. 49: "We had considered ourselves as connected with Great Britain, but we never thought parliament the supreme legislature over us. We never generally supposed it to have any authority over us, but from necessity, and that necessity we thought confined to *the regulation of trade,* and to such matters as concerned all the colonies together. We never allowed them any authority in our *internal concerns."* In the next sentence, Adams says: "This writer says, 'acts of parliament for regulating our *internal polity* were familiar' [with the material footnoted, which is mentioned in the text]. This I deny." And so on, as the text explains.

12. John Adams, IV, 49.

13. Adams repeated his refrain twice more before finishing his fourth letter, which was the letter in which the horseplay about "internal polity" appeared. See John Adams, IV, 52.

14. *Ibid.,* 112.

15. *Ibid.,* 99–100.

16. *Ibid.,* IX, 348; Letters, I, 87.

17. The proceedings of the convention are printed in an appendix to Connecticut Records, I, 585–99.

18. *The Acts and Resolves of the Province of Massachusetts-Bay* (Boston, 1886), V, 583 and 642. The Massachusetts act was printed *in extenso* in B. Cont. Jour., February 6, 1777.

19. Conn. Rec., I, 599–606.

20. Journals, IX, 956.

21. Conn. Rec., I, 607–20. See, also, Baldwin, *The New Haven Convention of 1778,* in Papers of the New Haven Colony Historical Society (New Haven, 1882), III, 33.

22. Journals, XI, 569–70.

23. N.Y. Jour., January 18, 1779. He also said that "the whole *trade* of the country did, and does still consist of monopoly and extortion." *Ibid.*

24. N.J. Gaz., April 23, 1778.

25. December 1, 1779. See, also, "A Farmer," in the issues of June 9, September 29, and November 17, of the same year.

26. May 26, 1779.

27. The "representation" made by the New Jersey Legislature to Congress is printed in N.J. Gaz., October 13, 1779. The substance of it will be found in a later volume of this book.

28. Conn. Rec., II, 562–71.

29. Journals, XV, 1289.

30. N.J. Gaz., April 11, 1781.

NOTES TO CHAPTER VIII

1. Letters, VIII, 247.

2. *Ibid.,* 458–60.

3. Mass. Gaz., December 3, 11, and 14, 1787.

4. Mass. Gaz., December 14, 1787.

5. Mass. Gaz., November 30, and December 14 and 18, 1787; and January 14 and 25, 1788.

6. Mass. Gaz., January 14 and 25, 1788.

7. Pa. Pack., June 3, 1785. The circular was printed in nearly every newspaper in the country.

8. Am. Mus., II, 542; McMaster and Stone, *Pennsylvania and the Federal Constitution, 1787–1788* (Philadelphia, 1888), 463.

9. Annals, II, 1182 and 1197.

10. *Ibid.*, 1466.

11. *Ibid.*, 1204.

12. Madison's speech was delivered on February 12, 1790. The outline of the speech, as it appeared in Gaz. U.S., was published in many other newspapers. It may be found conveniently in Elliot, IV, 408.

13. Annals, II, 2023.

14. *Ibid.*, 1723.

15. See Am. D. Adv., December 22 and 23, 1790; *The* [Philadelphia] *Federal Gazette*, December 22, 1790.

16. Annals, II, 1738, 1739, 1741, 1745, 1746, 1748.

17. *Works of Fisher Ames, with a Selection from his Speeches and Correspondence* (Boston, 1854), I, 95.

18. *Journal of William Maclay* (New York, 1890), 355, 364, 368–73.

19. Ames, *op. cit.* note 17 *supra*, I, 94–96.

20. Annals, II, 1748, 1875, 1886, 1891–94.

21. *Ibid.*, 1894–1960.

22. *Ibid.*, 1894–1902.

23. *Ibid.*, I, 514–15.

24. *Ibid.*, 455–571; especially 461–64.

25. *Ibid.*, 436 and 441.

26. See chapter xxii hereof.

27. Annals, II, 1904.

28. *Ibid.*, 1910.

29. *Ibid.*, 1945–54; especially 1950–51.

30. *Ibid.*, 1905–6, 1914–15, 1919, and 1921–22. *The* [Philadelphia] *Federal Gazette*, of February 15, 1791, said, in part, that Fisher Ames, in defending the constitutionality of the Bank, "adverted to the preamble of the constitution, which declares that it was established for the general welfare of the Union; [that] this vested Congress with the authority over all objects of national concern or of a general nature; [that] a national bank undoubtedly came within this idea."

31. *Ibid.*, 1910–12.

32. *Ibid.*, 1906.

33. *Ibid.*, 1904 and 1909; and see note 30 *supra*.

34. *Ibid.*, 1912 and 1940.

35. The only record is as follows: "The power to regulate trade is said to involve this [incorporating power] as a necessary means; but the powers consequent on this express power are specified, such as regulating light houses, ships, harbors, &c." Annals, II, 1917. There are, of course, no "specified" powers over "light houses, ships, [or] harbors" in the Constitution. What Jackson said, or meant, is thus obscure.

36. Annals, II, 1957.

37. The inference of great incompleteness arises, in part, from the disparity between the total volume of the recorded debates, and the time known to have been consumed in them. The recorded speeches and, also, the opinions rendered to President Washington by Edmund Randolph and Thomas Jefferson contain references to arguments not found in the recorded speeches. There are also

references to speeches not recorded. And there is a want of fullness and logical coherence, in developing various doctrines in the recorded speeches, which indicates fragmentary reporting.

38. The suspicious character of the sudden outbreak in the Philadelphia newspapers was the occasion for remark on the floor of Congress. Annals, II, 1904, 1914, 1929.

39. Am. D. Adv., February 16, 1791.

40. Am. D. Adv., February 5, 1791. The port-preference argument had also been urged in an item in Am. D. Adv., of February 3, 1791.

41. Am. D. Adv., February 3, 4, and 16, 1791.

42. Am. D. Adv., February 16, 1791. There are other items critical of the Bank in Am. D. Adv., of January 31 and February 22, 1791. The items in this and the three preceding notes, some of which appeared also in other papers, include all items that were published, critical of the Bank. For an item defending it, see Am. D. Adv., February 10, 1791; cf., items, unconnected with the Bank controversy, in which a "general-concerns" power was claimed for Congress, in Am. D. Adv., February 8 and 15, 1791.

43. Clarke & Hall, 86–91. As the Randolph opinions are short, no page references to the particular quotations from them in the text are given in these notes.

44. See chapter xxii hereof.

45. Jefferson, VI, 197–204.

46. *Ibid.*, V, 368, 371.

47. *Ibid.*, 338, 340–41. The development in Jefferson's ideas that culminated in his letter to Wythe may be seen in *ibid.*, 283, 318–19, 331–32, and DHC, IV, 225–26, 241–42, 252–53. For a letter from Edward Carrington which was probably influential in affecting his ideas, see DHC, IV, 189.

48. Jefferson, V, 199.

49. Journals, II, 195–99.

50. Edmund Randolph recognized this in his opinion on the Bank. Clarke & Hall, 86–87.

51. Jefferson, V, 400, 401. The same may be said of his attitude in his letter to Madison, in the preceding December. *Ibid.*, 368.

52. *Ibid.*, VI, 198–99.

53. 1 Stat. at L. 191.

54. See pp. 132–34 *supra.*

55. Jefferson, VI, 199.

56. *Ibid.*, IX, 398.

57. 2 Stat. at L. 150, 152.

58. *Cf.*, Hamilton, I, 261, 273, where, in his "Continentalist" papers, of 1781, Alexander Hamilton seemed to feel it necessary to specify that a power to pay bounties was to be understood as included in "THE POWER OF REGULATING TRADE" which he was then strenuously urging for Congress.

59. Clarke & Hall, 86–113.

60. Hamilton, III, 445–93.

61. *Ibid.*, 446.

62. *Ibid.*, 469–70.

63. *Ibid.*, 481.

64. *Ibid.*, 481–82.

65. *Ibid.*, 467.

66. *Ibid.*, 470.

67. *Buckner* v. *Finley & Van Lear*, 2 Pet. 586 (1829), is generally regarded

as having settled the point; but though there was some slight difference of opinion antecedently, the view of this case had long been the prevailing view.

68. Mass. Gaz., December 14, 25, and 28, 1787; and January 1 and 14, and February 5, 1788.

69. Mass. Gaz., February 5, 1788.

70. Sullivan, 352–54; *cf.*, 337–38.

NOTES TO CHAPTER IX

1. See p. 73 *supra.*
2. Tucker, Bk. I, Pt. 1, App., p. 250 and note.
3. 2 Stat. at L. 274.
4. *Ibid.*, 451, 453, 473, 499, and 506.
5. Clarke & Hall, 115 *et seq.*
6. *Ibid.*, 140.
7. 9 Johns. (N.Y.) 507.
8. *Ibid.*, 539, 542.
9. Van Vechten Papers, New York State Library, Folders 57, 67, and 68.
10. 9 Wheat. iii and 3.
11. 9 Johns. (N.Y.) 568.
12. *Ibid.*, 578.
13. *Ibid.*, 560–61.
14. *Hicks* v. *Hotchkiss*, 7 Johns. Ch. (N.Y.) 297, 310 (1823).
15. 16 Johns. 233, 254 (1819).
16. See p. 1029 hereof.
17. William A. Duer, *Letter to C. D. Colden* (Albany, 1817), 82.
18. *Ibid.* See, also, *The Opinion of the Supreme Court of the United States in the case of Gibbons v. Ogden . . . , with a Preface containing an historical sketch of the Steam-Boat Controversy* (Albany, 1824), 4.
19. Madison, VIII, 379.
20. *Ibid.*, 342.
21. Annals, XXX, 296 and 1052.
22. *Ibid.*, XXXII, 1371.
23. Madison, VIII, 386.
24. Annals, XXX, 855–57.
25. *Ibid.*, 859.
26. *Ibid.*, 876.
27. *Ibid.*, 897.
28. *Ibid.*, 878.
29. Letter of Marshall to Joseph Story, September 18, 1821, *Proc. Mass. Hist. Soc.*, 2d Ser., XIV, 330.
30. Monroe, VI, 41–42.
31. Annals, XXXI, 1119.
32. Annals, XXXII, 1385–86; Gales & Seaton, *Register of Debates in Congress* (Washington, 1831), VII, App. xxxvi.
33. Annals, XXXI, 1140.
34. *Ibid.*, 1165.
35. 4 N.J. L. (1 South.) 192, 198.
36. 6 Wheat. 264, 413–14.
37. 1 Brock. (U.S.C.Ct.) 423, 431–32.
38. 4 Wheat. 316, 407.
39. 4 Stat. at L. 22.
40. Annals, XLI, 1417–21.

41. *Ibid.,* 1054–55.

42. *Ibid.,* 1242.

43. *Ibid.,* 1288.

44. *Ibid.,* 1406–7.

45. *Ibid.* 1443.

46. *Ibid.,* 1221, 1289, 1419.

47. *Ibid.,* 1447.

48. *Ibid.,* 1253 and 1258.

49. *Ibid.,* 1315.

50. *Ibid.,* 1220, 1221–22, and 1224.

51. *Ibid.,* 1299, 1301, 1306–8, and 1310–11.

52. *Ogden* v. *Gibbons,* 4 Johns. Ch. (N.Y.) 150, 153–54, 159.

53. 17 Johns. (N.Y.) 488, 503, 506, and 509.

54. 9 Wheat. 9, 10, and 14.

55. *Ibid.,* 209–21.

56. 6 Wheat. 264, 413–14.

57. The policy of Chief Justice Marshall in this regard will be developed more fully in chapter xxx hereof.

58. 9 Wheat. 194.

59. *Ibid.*

60. *Ibid.,* 195.

61. *Ibid.,* 194.

62. *Ibid.*

63. *Ibid.*

64. The Supreme Court recognized this in *Hylton* v. *United States,* 3 Dall. (U.S.) 171 (1796). It has never been questioned.

65. 9 Wheat. 195.

66. *Ibid.,* 229–30.

67. *Ibid.,* 189–90.

68. 9 Wheat. 235–36.

69. *Ibid.,* 203.

70. See pp. 147–48 hereof.

71. See pp. 150–51 hereof.

72. 9 Wheat. 203–4.

73. See *Barron* v. *Baltimore,* 7 Pet. (U.S.) 243 (1833), in which the Court, speaking through Marshall, C.J., refused to apply to the states any of the literally general prohibitions of the first eight amendments, because, as Marshall put it, their application to the states was not "directly expressed." *Cf.,* discussion of this whole topic in chapter xxx hereof.

74. 9 Wheat. 204. *Cf.,* Marshall's statement in *The Brig Wilson, loc. cit.* note 37 *supra,* that "the word commerce, as used in [the Commerce Clause], is to be considered a *generic* term, *comprehending* navigation, or, that a control over navigation is *necessarily incidental to* the power to regulate commerce."

75. 9 Wheat. 209–10.

76. *Ibid.,* 197.

77. Joseph Story, though technically a Republican, saw eye-to-eye with Chief Justice Marshall on constitutional matters. William Johnson, also a Republican Justice, seems to have been orthodox enough in the Gibbons case. That leaves Justices Todd and Duvall, of the Republican appointees, and Justice Bushrod Washington, originally a Federalist. But if we may judge from Justice Washington's opinion in the closely related case of

Ogden v. *Saunders,* 12 Wheat. 213 (1827), his Federalism had gotten pretty well diluted by this period.

78. Beveridge, IV, 435.

79. 9 Wheat. 15 and 18–20.

80. 1 Hopk. (N.Y. Ch.) 149 (1824); s.c. 3 Cow. (N.Y.) 711 (1825).

81. 1 Hopk. 150–51 and 198 *et. seq.;* 3 Cow. 714–24.

82. *Cf.,* Justice Johnson in *Gibbons* v. *Ogden,* quoted herein at p. 260; and see the extracts from James Sullivan's *History of Land Titles in Massachusetts* (Boston, 1801), quoted in chapter xviii hereof. There were other suggestions to the same effect in the early years of the nineteenth century.

83. The arguments on appeal were not reported by Cowen, because, he says, they did not differ materially from those in the chancery court, as reported by Hopkins. See 3 Cow. 724. The excerpts from the plaintiffs' argument given in the text hereof will be found in 1 Hopk. 152–56.

84. *Ibid.,* 157–72; *cf.,* next note *supra.*

85. 3 Cow. 725–27 and 731–33.

86. *Ibid.,* 739, 749–53, and 756.

87. (Washington, 1882), 188–89.

88. Annals, XLI, 560–61.

89. *The Richmond* [Va.] *Enquirer,* January 27, 1829.

90. *Ibid.,* January 20, 1829. See, also, Davis, *Lecture on the Constitutionality of Protecting Duties* (Charlottesville, 1832), 10–11.

91. *The Richmond* [Va.] *Enquirer,* January 22, 1829.

92. Madison, IX, 316.

93. Records, III, 478; *Letters and Other Writings of James Madison* (Philadelphia, 1865), IV, 14–15.

94. *Address of the Friends of Domestic Industry, assembled in Convention at New-York, October 26, 1831, to the People of the United States* (Baltimore, 1831), 12 *et seq.*

95. X, 444, 454–55.

96. (2d ed.; Boston, 1856), 276–77.

97. *City of New York* v. *Miln,* 11 Pet. 102, 138 (1837).

98. THE NORTH AMERICAN REVIEW, XLVI, 126, 154 (1838).

99. 5 How. (U.S.) 504, 574, and 582.

100. *United States* v. *De Witt,* 9 Wall. 41.

101. The statements in the text are not in accord with the record of the proceedings of the Stamp Act Congress, which was printed in Niles's *Register* in 1812. The record as there printed, though now apparently accepted, is pretty certainly garbled in the part corresponding to that quoted in the text. See *Journal of the First Congress of the American Colonies* (New York, 1845), 40. The statements in the text are taken from Mass. Gaz., April 17, 1766.

NOTES TO CHAPTER X

1. See the excerpts printed in the text hereof at pp. 306–7 and 309; also, "The Freeholder," in Conn. Cour., September 28, 1789. Excerpts from the latter writer are quoted at pp. 308–9 hereof.

2. 3 Dall. (U.S.) 171, 174 (1796).

3. See the materials mentioned in note 1 *supra.* The excerpts first mentioned therein are from an article with the title, "On Excise, *or Duties on Inland Trade and Business,*" in Gaz. U.S., January 9, 1790.

4. Gaz. U.S., January 23, 1790 (p. 328): "Monies raised on lands, polls,

houses, cattle, &c, are usually called taxes. Monies raised on goods imported or exported are called duties and imposts. Monies raised on manufactures and the retailing of liquors are called excises. But in a more enlarged sense, taxes and imposts comprehend every method of levying money on real or personal estate. Duties is usually restricted to taxes on goods, wares, and merchandize; excise only being confined, to a particular mode of laying duties, and, for the most part, to duties on manufactures." Except, possibly, for what is said about the "enlarged sense" of "impost," the foregoing seems typical of the American notions of the time. *Cf.*, the usage in the following Connecticut laws: "An Act for collecting and paying Rates and Taxes," Ct. Acts and Laws, 1784–90, p. 197; "An Act to enable the United States in Congress assembled, to levy certain Duties and Imposts &c.," *ibid.*, 270; and "An Act for laying an Excise on sundry Articles of Consumption within this State," *ibid.*, 318. Or the usage in following South Carolina laws: 4 S.C. Stat. at L. 365, 413, 487, 512, 565, 570, 582, 603, and 655. In these South Carolina laws, what is said, in the above-quoted excerpt, about the "enlarged sense" of "imposts," is, to some extent, borne out. The efforts to obtain what was universally called "a Continental impost," in the 1780's—*i.e.*, a *customs* duty on imports, to raise money for Congress—had, apparently, a considerable effect in emphasizing, in American usage, the limitation of the term "impost" to duties of that character.

5. Typical advertisements of the kind mentioned in the text may be found in the following papers: Sav. Gaz., March 22, and October 11, 1787, and April 3, and June 5, 1788; Col. Her., June 29, 1785; Ch. Wkly. Gaz., September 13, 1783.

6. Col. Her., November 26, 1787.

7. Mass. Cent., September 5, 1787.

8. N.H. Ct. Gaz., October 6 and 20, 1785.

9. N.Y. Jour., July 20, 1786; Newp. Merc., July 31, 1786.

10. Col. Her., February 14, 1785.

11. N.Y. Adv., September 5, 1787.

12. R.I. Acts and Resolves, June 1783, p. 26.

13. 12 Hening, Va. Stat. at L., 304, 305.

14. Col. Rec. of Ga., XIX, Pt. II, 498, 501.

15. Md. Laws of 1784, chap. lxxxiv.

16. 12 Hening, Va. Stat. at L., 289.

17. *Ibid.*, X, 501, 511; XI, 66, 67, 70, 112, 121, 122, 196, 197; and XII, 289.

18. Journals, XIX, 112.

19. State Rec. of N.C., XXIV, 561.

20. Records, I, 243.

21. Conn. Cour., March 27, 1797.

22. See "A Bye-Law [of New Haven, Connecticut,] to regulate Trade & Commerce," in Conn. Jour., October 6, 1784; also N.Y. Laws, 1797–1800, pp. 128 and 547.

23. Md. Laws, November 1786, chap. xvii.

24. An important instance of this occurred in Boston in 1785. The "tradesmen and manufacturers" of Boston had requested the "merchants and traders" to support measures to encourage the manufactures of the state. The "merchants and traders" consented to support "restrictions and excises" for the purpose, but, by implication, objected to an "impost." See Mass. Cent., May 7, 1785, and Bost. Gaz., May 9, 1785. The matter will be dealt with more fully in a subsequent volume.

25. Ct. Acts and Laws, 1784–90, p. 279.

26. Prov. Gaz., February 13, 1790; Conn. Cour., January 7, 1790; Gaz. U.S., January 9, 1790. The item appeared in many other papers.

27. Conn. Cour., January 14, 1790.

28. *Ibid.*, September 28, and October 5, 1789.

29. Ct. Acts and Laws, 1784–90, p. 389.

30. 12 Wheat. (U.S.) 419.

31. 5 How. (U.S.) 504.

32. The clearest statement upon this point was made by Woodbury, J. He said: "It has been contended, that the sum to be paid for a license, and the penalty imposed for selling without one, are in the nature of a duty on imports, and thus come within the principle really settled by *Brown* v. *Maryland*, and thus conflict with the Constitution. . . . But neither of these statutes purports to tax imports from abroad of foreign spirits, or imports from another State, either coastwise or by land, of either foreign or domestic spirits. . . . Nor does either of those statutes purport to tax the introduction of an article by the merchant importing it, much less to impose any duty on the article itself for revenue, in addition to what Congress requires. Neither of them appears to be, in character or design, a fiscal measure." *Ibid.*, 622–23. Grier, J., said: "The true question presented by these cases . . . is whether the States have a right to prohibit the sale and consumption of an article of commerce which they believe to be pernicious in its effects, and the cause of disease, pauperism, and crime." *Ibid.*, 631. Catron, J., said, in his opinion in the New Hampshire License Case, that "the first proposition [decided in *Brown* v. *Maryland*]"—*i.e.*, as to the application of the Imports and Exports Clause—"ha[d]no application to [the New Hampshire] case, as [in it] no tax or duty was imposed." *Ibid.*, 602. His opinion relating to the Massachusetts and Rhode Island License Cases (wherein fees, or "duties," some of 20 cents, and some of one dollar, were involved) treated entirely of regulation, though the taxing power of the states is twice mentioned in the opinion, apparently incidentally. *Ibid.*, 608–10. Taney, C.J., despite the fact that he delivered himself at large on the taxing power of the states with respect to imports, treated the Massachusetts and Rhode Island cases as presenting a question under the Commerce Clause and certain acts of Congress thereunder. Of the New Hampshire case, which had to do with a sale of domestic spirits, and in which there was no relevant legislation by Congress, Taney said that it presented the question, "whether the grant of [commercial] power to Congress [was] of itself a prohibition to [a] state [of 'regulation confined to its own territory, and made for its own convenience or interest, and not in conflict with any law of Congress']." "This," he said, "is the question on which the case turns; and I do not see how it can be decided upon any other ground." *Ibid.*, 572–85; especially 573, 577, and 578. Nelson, J., concurred with Taney's and Catron's opinions. McLean, J., seems clearly to have meant to decide all the License Cases under the Imports and Exports Clause, as well as the Commerce Clause; and probably the same was true of Justice Daniel.

33. *Ibid.*, 574–76. Cf., next note *supra*.

34. Cf., *ibid.*, 587, 610, 617, 622–23.

35. *Ibid.*, 594–95, 612, 622–23.

36. Records, II, 359 *et seq.* The character of these passages will be considered when the proceedings of the Federal Convention are dealt with.

37. Records, III, 478.

38. Madison, IX, 1 *et seq.*

39. To some extent, Madison's theories of the Commerce Clause were somewhat vaguely adumbrated in his veto of the so-called "Bonus Bill," as his last official act as President, in 1817. Madison, VIII, 386.

40. 24 How. 169.

41. *State v. Pinckney*, 10 Rich. L. (S.C.) 474 (1857); *Harrison v. Vicksburg*, 3 Smedes and Marshall (Miss.) 581 (1844); *Beall v. State*, 4 Blackf. (Ind.) 107 (1835).

42. *Padelford, Fay & Company v. Savannah*, 14 Ga. 438 (1854).

43. Besides *Woodruff v. Parham*, see *Paul v. Virginia*, 8 Wall. 168 (1868) and *United States v. De Witt*, 9 Wall. 41 (1870). Also, *Slaughter-House Cases*, 16 Wall. 36 (1873); *Civil Rights Cases*, 109 U.S. 3 (1883); and other cases related to these.

44. 8 Wall. 123. The companion case was *Hinson v. Lott*, *ibid.*, 148.

45. *Ibid.*, 140.

46. *Freeman v. Hewit*, 329 U.S. 249 (1946).

47. The first step toward ushering in the present deplorable condition was undoubtedly taken in *Sonneborn Bros. v. Cureton*, 262 U.S. 506 (1923).

48. Some of the recent cases indicating how very far the Court has lately gone in sustaining state taxes which manifestly offend the Imports and Exports Clause are the following: *McGoldrick v. Berwind-White Co.*, 309 U.S. 33 (1940); *Nelson v. Sears, Roebuck & Co.*, 312 U.S. 359 (1941); *McLeod v. Dilworth Co.*, 322 U.S. 327 (1944); *General Trading Co. v. State Tax Commission*, 322 U.S. 335 (1944); *Western Live Stock v. Bureau of Revenue*, 303 U.S. 250 (1938); *Coverdale v. Arkansas-Louisiana Pipe Line Co.*, 303 U.S. 604 (1938); *Indiana v. Ingram-Richardson Mfg. Co.*, 313 U.S. 252 (1941).

49. *Gregg Dyeing Co. v. Query*, 286 U.S. 472 (1932); *Henneford v. Silas Mason Co.*, 300 U.S. 577 (1937).

50. Smith-Hurd, *Illinois Annotated Statutes*, c. 120, §§453.1(3), 453.13, and 453.17.

51. *The Chicago Sun*, February 19 (p. 1), 20 (p. 17), and 21 (p. 3), and March 6 (p. 3) and 16 (p. 27), 1947; also *The Chicago Daily News*, February 19, 1947, p. 13).

52. See, for example, *A. Magnano Co. v. Hamilton*, 292 U.S. 40 (1934).

53. An egregious case of this kind is *Heisler v. Thomas Colliery Co.*, 260 U.S. 245 (1922).

54. See, for example, *Helson v. Kentucky*, 279 U.S. 245 (1929); *Edelman v. Boeing Air Transport, Inc.*, 289 U.S. 249 (1933); *Morf v. Bingaman*, 298 U.S. 407 (1936); *Bingaman v. Golden Eagle Western Lines, Inc.*, 297 U.S. 626 (1936); *McLeod v. Dilworth Co.*, 322 U.S. 327 (1944); and *General Trading Co. v. State Tax Commission*, 322 U.S. 335 (1944).

55. 67 Sup. Ct. 274, 277–78 (1946).

56. *Graves v. O'Keefe*, 306 U.S. 466, 491–92 (1939).

57. *Kansas v. Colorado*, 206 U.S. 46 (1907). The Court held, in this case, that Congress had no power either.

58. See *Carpenter v. Providence-Washington Insurance Co.*, 16 Pet. 495 (1842), and *Watson v. Tarpley*, 18 How. 517 (1855). These cases are no longer "law." But see *The Lottawanna*, 21 Wall. 558, 574–75 (1874); *Southern Pacific Co. v. Jensen*, 244 U.S. 205 (1917); and *Knickerbocker Ice Co. v. Stewart*, 253 U.S. 149 (1920). Also, *Ogden v. Saunders*, 12 Wheat. 213, 358 *et seq.* (1827), and *Shaw v. Robbins*, 12 Wheat. 369 (1827).

59. The law on this subject has never developed greatly, except as to

court judgments; and even as to these, it has developed imperfectly. The matter will be dealt with at later points. See pp. 554–56 hereof.

60. See pp. 552–54 hereof.

NOTES TO CHAPTER XI

1. Records, II, 640; IV, 59.

2. Records, II, 375–76, 435, and 439–40, including note 19 on p. 440.

3. II, 169 (August 1787). A list of the subscribers to Am. Mus. will usually be found printed in the opening pages of the bound volumes. The item, "On ex post facto laws," was likewise published in Col. Her., November 26, 1785.

4. *Helm's Lessee* v. *Howard*, 2 H. & McH. (Md.) 57, 96 (1784). Robert Hanson Harrison, C.J., in this case, also applied the phrase "*ex post facto*" to a civil matter. He said: "If a grantor uses expressions in his grant which admit of a double location, or a location either in this or that way, it is in the power of the grantee to determine, he being the first agent after the patent granted, by an *ex post facto act, his entry and possession*, which of the two locations he will have." *Ibid.*, 85.

5. *Donaldson* v. *Harvey*, 3 H. & McH. (Md.) 12, 17 (1790). It should be noted that one of the other counsel in this case said that "there m[ight] be an *ex post facto* law in civil, but not in criminal cases." *Ibid.*, 18. It is not entirely clear what he was talking about. His mode of speech shows he understood the phrase "*ex post facto* law" as applying "in civil cases." And this suggests that he was referring to the Maryland constitution, whose prohibition of "*ex post facto*" laws" could have been taken as limited expressly as he suggested. *Cf.*, pp. 344–46 *supra*. He was the same counsel whose argument, in *Helm's Lessee* v. *Howard*, is cited in the text hereof. See next preceding note. For other Maryland applications of "*ex post facto*" to civil matters, see *McFadon's Executor* v. *Martin, ibid.*, 153, 166 (1793), and *Dunlop* v. *Funk, ibid.*, 318, 319 (1793).

6. Ch. G. A., February 1, 1786.

7. *Ibid.*, March 2, 1786.

8. *Ibid.*, March 2 and 8, 1786.

9. "A Friend to Justice," in Ch. Mng. P., March 15, 1787.

10. February 11, 1786.

11. May 31, 1787.

12. Col. Her., June 5, 1788; N.Y. Adv., July 17, 1788.

13. Records, III, 99, 100.

14. The examples given by Jacob are that "an Act done, or Estate granted, may be made good by Matter *ex post facto*, that was not so at first, by Election, &c.," and that "sometimes a Thing well done at first, may afterwards become ill [in the same way]."

15. *Wilkinson* v. *Meyer*, 2 Ld. Raym. 1350, 1352.

16. Sheppard, *Touchstone of Common Assurances* (7th ed.; London, 1820), I, 63, 67, and 68; and II, 234, 250, 267, and 372.

17. Fearne, *An Essay on Contingent Remainders* (8th ed.; London, 1824), 274 and 362.

18. Powell, *An Essay upon the Learning of Devises* (London, 1788), 113, 133, and 134.

19. Wooddeson, *A systematical View of the Laws of England* (London, 1792), II, 641.

20. Blackstone, I, 46.

21. Elliot, III, 461–73 *passim*.

22. That is, he could not be heard by the reporter. Elliot, III, 473.

23. Edmund Randolph repeated this part of what Madison had said, which the reporter did not hear. Elliot, III, 477.

24. Elliot, III, 473–81 *passim*.

25. Elliot, IV, 168–87; especially 184–85.

26. Annals, II, 1196, 1205, 1214, 1220, 1227, 1241, 1249, and 1266; also Gaz. U.S., February 20 and 27, and March 3, 1790 (especially pp. 358, 366, and 369).

27. Statements are frequent, in the cases early in the nineteenth century, that, when the Constitution took effect, the states voluntarily repealed all *past* laws deemed to conflict in principle with the *future* prohibitions of the Constitution. See, for example, the statement of Johnson, J., in *Ogden* v. *Saunders*, 12 Wheat. (U.S.) 213, 278 (1827): "Every where, too, the principle was practically acquiesced in, that taking away the power to pass a law on a particular subject was equivalent to a repeal of existing laws on that subject." The cases alluded to, in the text at this point, show that the foregoing and other statements to the same effect cannot be relied upon. They were generally used to introduce a spurious kind of "practical construction" by the states, *in favor* of "States' Rights." Cf., *Owings* v. *Speed*, 5 Wheat. (U.S.) 420, 422 (1820).

28. *Turner* v. *Turner's Executrix*, 4 Call (Va.) 234, 237 (1792).

29. *Elliot's Executor* v. *Lyell*, 3 Call (Va.) 268, 286 (1802).

30. 1 N.J.L. 315, 319 (1795).

31. 9 N.J.L. 427, 444. See Erdman, *The New Jersey Constitution of 1776* (Princeton, 1929), 92.

32. See, also, argument of William Rawle, of Philadelphia, in *Warder* v. *Bell*, 1 Yeates (Pa.) 531, 532 (1795), and that of William Lewis, of the same place, in *Ross's Executors* v. *Rittenhouse*, ibid., 443, 453 (1795). Rawle said: "But should it be deemed eligible to fix a new rule of decision as to what shall be deemed early and convenient notice, of a protest [upon a bill of exchange], it is submitted that the plaintiffs should not be made the sacrifice to this doctrine. As to them, it would be an *ex post facto* law." Lewis said: "Olmstead and his little party were aliens to our laws, and had no voice in the choice of our representatives: they did not come voluntarily into the port of Philadelphia to be subjected to the laws of Pennsylvania, but were tortiously compelled thither by the superior force of two armed vessels, who seized their prize: and it is now pressed against them, that an *ex post facto* law of Pennsylvania . . . shall operate against them [to deprive them of recovery], in all these circumstances of hardship." For another Pennsylvania application of "*ex post facto*" to a civil matter, see McKean, C.J., in *Lessee of Joy* v. *Cossart*, ibid., 50, 54 (1791).

33. 2 Dall. (U.S.) 304, 319 (1795).

34. 3 Dall. (U.S.) 385, (1798).

35. Chase was not a Federalist, as so often has been erroneously stated. See, for example, 37 HLR, 49, 73. He had, instead, been one of the ringleaders of the opposition to the Constitution, in Maryland, in 1787 and 1788. In spite of his record, he was put on the Supreme Court, by Washington, in 1796, in the hope, presumably, that his allegiance and real abilities might thereby be enlisted in the service of the new government. The move was not a success. Chase was no sooner in office than he began to set afloat, in his opinions, a great many of the Anti-Federalist sophistries; views which had never been heard from a Supreme Court Justice, before his addition

to the Court. Chase's opinion in *Calder* v. *Bull* is no exception in this respect, and not one of the other Justices in the case agreed with all of what he had to say. The notion that Chase was a Federalist has probably arisen from the personal animosity that existed between him and Thomas Jefferson. The bad feeling between these two led Chase, in effect, to "campaign" from the bench against Jefferson, in 1800; and this, after Jefferson finally obtained the Presidency, in the following year, eventually led to Chase's impeachment.

36. See Justice William Johnson's memorandum on the subject, printed in the rear of the first edition of the second volume of Peters' United States Reports. The memorandum is discussed in the text hereof at a later point.

37. 2 Pet. (U.S., 1st ed.) 681, 685 (1829).

38. *Osborne* v. *Huger*, 1 Bay (S.C.) 184 (1791).

39. Coxe, 344. For the arguments of Rawle and Lewis, before the Pennsylvania Supreme Court, see note 32 *supra*.

40. *Adm'rs of Byrne* v. *Adm'rs of Stewart*, 3 Desaussure (S.C. Eq.) 466 (1812); *Grim* v. *Weissenberg School District*, 57 Pa. 433 (1868).

41. *Loc. cit.* note 37 *supra*.

42. *Dickinson* v. *Dickinson*, 3 Murphey (N.C., L. & Eq.) 327 (1819); *Baugher* v. *Nelson*, 9 Gill (Md.), 299, 306 (1850).

43. McRee, *Life and Correspondence of James Iredell* (New York, 1858), II, 168, 169.

44. Dallas' second volume was published at some time in 1798.

45. This seems to be the meaning of a note, not altogether clear in its intent, which is appended to p. 33 of Wright, *The Contract Clause of the Constitution* (Cambridge, 1938).

46. Records, III, 73 and 589; and IV, 72 and 73.

47. Annals, I, 417 and 1105–6.

48. Annals, III, 166, 708, and 741; IV, 142, and 970; V, 149 and 240; and VI, 1739–40.

49. The debate in Annals, IX, 2649–77, though not in all respects completely candid, gives a good insight into the essential nature of the politics involved.

50. *Jefferson*, VII, 193, 194, 196, 197, 198.

51. Annals, VII, 643, 644, 692, 786, 788, 796, 797, and 970; and VIII, 2426, 2441, 2465, 2489, 2552, 2556, 2577, 2582, 2649, 2656, and 2677.

52. There seems to be no direct record of this in the Annals; but James A. Bayard, of Delaware, referred to the matter in a speech in Congress, in 1799. The statement in the text is based on his statement. See Annals, IX, 2579.

53. Annals, IX, 2577–79.

54. See *The Dictionary of American Biography* on Morris.

55. See *The Dictionary of American Biography* on Wilson.

56. Annals, IX, 2577–79.

57. 2 U.S. Stat. 19.

58. Annals, XII, 551.

59. 5 Binn. (Pa.) 355, 370 (1812).

60. *The Writings of Thomas Jefferson* (Washington's ed.; New York, 1861), VI, 175–76.

61. 12 Wheat. (U.S.) 213, 286 (1827).

62. 2 Pet. (U.S.) 380, 416 (1829).

63. 2 Pet (U S., 1st ed.) 681 (1829).

NOTES TO CHAPTER XII

1. *Ogden* v. *Saunders,* 12 Wheat. 213 (1827), is still "the law."

2. It was a main reliance of the plaintiff in *Ogden* v. *Saunders.* See Marshall's re-statement of this branch of the plaintiff's argument at 12 Wheat. 336–37.

3. *Sinking Fund Cases,* 99 U.S. 700, 718 (1878); *Nichols* v. *Coolidge,* 274 U.S. 531 (1927); *Untermeyer* v. *Anderson,* 276 U.S. 440 (1928). *Cf., Coolidge* v. *Long,* 282 U.S. 582 (1931). See, also, the cases cited in Hale, *The Supreme Court and the Contract Clause,* 57 HLR, 512, 515–16 (1944).

4. Records, II, 547 and 597; IV, 59.

5. 12 Wheat. 213 (1827).

6. 4 Wheat. 209 (1819).

7. A national bankruptcy act had again failed of passage in Congress, just thirteen days before *Ogden* v. *Saunders* was decided. Gales and Seaton, *Register of Debates in Congress,* III, 289.

8. See *Journal of the Senate of Pennsylvania for 1834–35,* II, 164–65, for comment on the impossible situation which resulted from the decision in *Ogden* v. *Saunders.*

NOTES TO CHAPTER XIII

1. See, also, Bacon, *A New Abridgement of the Law* (3d ed.; London, 1768), IV, 645, 647–49.

2. See, also, St. Germain, *Doctor and Student* (17th ed.; London, 1787), a book first published in 1523, wherein it is said (pp. 49–50) that "equity" in interpretation of statutes is available "in the same court, and by the common law"; and that, in contrast with the "equity" of chancery, "mention is made [of it] many times, and often in the law of England." Other early books frequently cited as dealing with the subject, to which, however, the writer has not had access, are: T[homas] A[she], Επιεικεια; *et Table generall a les Annales del Ley* (London, 1609), and Sir Christopher Hatton, *Treatise concerning Statutes or Acts of Parliament* (London, 1677).

3. *Eyston* v. *Studd* (16 Eliz.), 2 Plowden 459, 465–68.

4. *Stowel* v. *Lord Zouch* (11 Eliz.), 1 Plowden 353, 366; *Wimbish* v. *Tailbois* (4 Edw. VI), 1 Plowden 38, 53, 57.

5. 2 Plowden 467.

6. *Stradling* v. *Morgan* (2 Eliz.), 1 Plowden 198, 205.

7. 1 Plowden 369.

8. Cowp. 540, 543. *Cf., Barker* v. *Reading,* W. Jones 163; Palmer 485 (1628).

9. *Wilson* v. *Knubley,* 7 East 128 (1806).

10. Viner, *A General Abridgement of Law and Equity,* XIX, 514–19.

11. Blackstone, I, 59–62; III, 430–31.

12. Rutherforth, II, chap. vii, *passim.*

13. Annals, I, 514.

14. (London, 1793), I, 62, note 10.

15. Tucker, Bk. I, Pt. 1, p. 61, note 12.

16. Story, I, 386, note 1.

17. Story, I, vi.

18. Story, I, 443–45; *cf.,* 387 and 404.

19. See pp. 146–55 *supra.*

20. Article III.

21. Article II.

22. See pp. 152–53 *supra.*

23. Rutherforth, II, 331–32. *Cf.*, Blackstone, I, 60.

24. Article VI, second paragraph.

25. The idea of legislative supremacy is emphasized and re-emphasized by John Locke, in his *Treatises on Civil Government* (1690), which had such great influence among the American colonists. Relying on Locke, James Otis, of Massachusetts, said, in his *Rights of the Colonies Asserted and Proved*, of 1764, that, "in a constituted common wealth, standing upon its own basis, and acting according to its own nature, that is, acting for the preservation of the community, there can be *but one supreme power which is the legislative, to which all the rest are and must be subordinate.*" Otis, 33. Locke was careful to indicate that he did not mean, by a "supreme" legislative, an "arbitrary" and "unlimited" legislative; and Otis, again relying on Locke, took the further position that "the legislative [was] only a fiduciary power, *to act for certain ends*"—that is, of course, for "the common good"—"[so that] there remain[ed] still, 'in the people, a supreme power to remove, or alter, the legislative when they find the legislative act contrary to the trust reposed in them.'" *Ibid.* The idea of legislative supremacy occurs over and over again in the American writings of the period. *Cf.*, for example, the argument of "J. R." in *The* [Hartford] *Connecticut Courant*, of June 10, 1776, in support of the view that delegates to the Continental Congress ought to be popularly elected: "The difference between legislative and executive powers"—the latter apparently used (as Otis and many other Americans also used it) to include the judicial—"are too obvious to need a moment's reflection. *To constitute legislators with power to make other legislators, is erecting a supreme authority upon a supreme authority;* the former elective only by the latter, and totally out of the reach of the people." Archives, 4th Ser., VI, 798, 799. The Lockian ideas of legislative supremacy were given further currency among the colonies, through their adoption by Blackstone and their repetition by him in his *Commentaries*. "By the sovereign power," says Blackstone, "is meant the making of laws . . . : and *all other powers of the state must obey the legislative power in the discharge of their several functions*, or else the constitution is at an end." In that case, he pointed out, "according to Mr. Locke (who," he said, "perhaps carried his theory too far [in not providing for any non-revolutionary mode of change in the constitution])," there resulted from "such a change, however effected," "an entire dissolution of the bonds of government; and the people [were] thereby reduced to a state of anarchy, with liberty to constitute to themselves a new legislative power." Blackstone, I, 49 and 52. See, also, St. George Tucker's reference to Congress as "the *supreme* national council," in his edition Blackstone, of 1803. Tucker, Bk. I, Pt. 2, p. 280, note 67; and Kent, *Commentaries on American Law* (New York, 1826), I, 207: "The power of making laws is the *supreme* power in a state."

NOTES TO CHAPTER XIV

1. 272 U.S. 52, 118, 135, 163–64 (1926).

2. Annals, I, 463–64 and 496 (1789).

3. 206 U.S. 46 (1906).

4. *Ibid.*, 82–84.

5. *Cf.*, *National Mutual Insurance Co.* v. *Tidewater Transfer Co., Inc.*, 337 U.S. 582 (1949).

6. See chapter xxvi hereof.

7. 206 U.S. 81 and 83–84.

8. See note 25 to chapter xiii *supra*.

9. *The Head Money Cases*, 112 U.S. 580 (1884); *Whitney* v. *Robertson*, 124 U.S. 190, 195 (1888); *Chae Chan Ping* v. *United States*, 130 U.S. 581, 600 (1889); *Hijo* v. *United States*, 194 U.S. 315, 324 (1904).

10. Rutherforth, II, 347–51.

11. Records, II, 590, 594–96.

12. The report of the Committee on Style, of September 12th, was not correctly printed in the official *Journal, Acts, and Proceedings of the Convention* (Boston, 1819), 351, 356 (*cf.*, *Memoirs of John Quincy Adams* [Philadelphia, 1875], VI, 124–27); nor in *The Madison Papers* (Washington, 1840), III, 1543, 1549. The earliest correct printing appears to have been in DHC, III, 720, 724, in 1900.

13. *Cf.*, Records, II, 590, 594–96, with *ibid.*, 651, 655–56.

14. Records, III, 379. Gallatin's remarks could have referred only to Gouverneur Morris, who was in Europe and could not answer, and Roger Sherman, who was dead. Gallatin's story is, moreover, inherently incredible, because incompatible with Sherman's known sentiments and actions in the Federal Convention and afterwards. *Cf.*, what is said of him in chapter xxii hereof. The whole subject will be more fully treated when the Federal Convention is taken up.

15. *Cf.*, for example, the groupings of the specifically enumerated Presidential powers in Article II.

16. Hamilton, IV, 70, 150–52.

17. *United States* v. *Butler*, 297 U.S. 1, 65–66 (1936); *Helvering* v. *Davis*, 301 U.S. 619, 640 (1937). The actual decision in the Butler case is, of course, impossible to justify under the Hamiltonian theory.

18. Elliot, IV, 552.

19. Madison, VIII, 386, 387: "A restriction of the power 'to provide for the common defense and general welfare' to cases which are to be provided for by the expenditure of money would still leave within the legislative power of Congress all the great and most important measures of Government, money being the ordinary and necessary means of carrying them into execution."

20. Madison, IX, 424–25 footnote.

21. Annals, I, 463–64 and 496 (1789); *cf.*, *ibid.*, II, 1945, 1946, 1950, 1951.

22. Records, II, 473, 481, 493, 496–97, 547, 553, 565, 590.

23. Madison, IX, 411 *et seq.*; Records, III, 483 *et seq.*

24. Madison, IX, 251, 255.

NOTES TO CHAPTER XV

1. Madison, VIII, 386, 387.

2. Madison, IX, 411, 420.

3. It must be remembered that the *Commentaries* were written primarily for laymen; and that they circulated widely among laymen in America may be seen from an inspection of the subscription list which Robert Bell, of Philadelphia, published in the first American edition of the *Commentaries*, of 1772. Blackstone, IV. Bell's list includes eight future members of the Federal Convention and many other names prominent in our history in and around 1787. Edmund Burke told Parliament, in 1775, that he had "been told by an eminent bookseller, that in no branch of his business, after tracts of popular devotion, [had] so many books as those on law [been] exported to the [American]

Plantations." He added that "the Colonists ha[d] now fallen into the way of printing them for their own use," and that he had "hear[d] that they ha[d] sold nearly as many copies of Blackstone's *Commentaries* in America as in England." Archives, 4th Ser., I, 1754.

4. See materials cited in note 8 to chapter vii *supra*.

5. *Cf.*, Holdsworth, IV, 321–22, 335–38; VI, 325–28, 334–37; X, 400–411. In reading Holdsworth, it should be remembered that he wrote with nearly a century and a half of hindsight which the men of the Federal Convention did not have.

6. 7 [British] *State Trials* (2d ed.; London, 1766), 493, 555 *et seq.*

7. See authorities cited in Holdsworth, VI, 334.

8. Forsyth, *Cases and Opinions on Constitutional Law* (London, 1869), 423.

9. The Blackstone passages are pointed out later in the text hereof.

10. Wilson, III, 199, 244–46.

11. Tucker, Bk. I, Pt. 2, notes pp. 249–80, especially notes 11, 13, and 67.

12. Blackstone, I, 250–78.

13. *Cf.*, Holdsworth, X, 340–41.

14. Blackstone, I, 250, 252–53, 257–61.

15. *Cf.*, Pownall, I, 104–29.

16. This matter is dealt with fully in chapter xix hereof.

17. Blackstone, I, 261.

18. Blackstone, I, 271–73.

19. Constitution, Article I, secs. 9 and 10; and Article VI of the Confederation.

20. Blackstone, I, 273–79; II, 407; and IV, 159.

21. Blackstone, I, 263–64.

22. Holdsworth, X, 386.

23. Blackstone, I, 262–63 and 264–66.

24. *Houston* v. *Moore*, 5 Wheat. 1, 17, 53–54 (1820).

25. Blackstone, I, 265.

26. An earlier act relevant to the situation on saltpeter when the act of George II mentioned in the text was passed is 21 Car. I, c. 21. It was passed to promote the production of gunpowder in England; and, to that end, it was provided that any British subject might "make and sell any quantities of gunpowder at . . . pleasure" and, likewise, "bring into th[e] kingdom any quantities of salt-petre, brimstone or any other materials necessary or requisite for the making of gun-powder." Nothing was said about any right of exporting saltpeter; and, considering the object of the act, none was to be inferred. And as stated in the text, no right to export saltpeter was given by the act of 12 Car. II, c. 4, though a heavy "rate outward" upon it was provided.

27. Blackstone, I, 266–71 and 334. Also, IV, 261.

28. *Ibid.*

29. In other words, *Marbury* v. *Madison*, 1 Cranch 137 (1803), seems plainly to have been inconsistent with the Constitution. For to add to the Supreme Court's original jurisdiction cases put by the Constitution tentatively within its appellate jurisdiction is obviously one way of making "Exceptions" from the Court's appellate jurisdiction as provided in the Constitution. And it is a way, moreover, which fully complies with that implied condition upon Congress' "excepting" power which grows out of the requirement in Article III, that "the [national] judicial Power" (which "shall be vested in" the courts therein referred to) "shall extend to" the several categories of "Cases" therein mentioned.

30. Journals, I, 68.
31. To be treated fully in a later volume of this book.
32. *Cf.*, Records, II, 565 and 574, with II, 590 and 600.
33. *Cf.*, Holdsworth, VI, 218 *et seq.*
34. *Cf.*, St. Germain, *Doctor and Student* (17th ed.; London, 1787), 45 and 49–50.
35. Pownall, I, 113–14.
36. Holdsworth says that a "pardon" differs from a "dispensation"; that a "dispensation" makes the act done "legal"; but that a "pardon" does not. Holdsworth, VI, 217–18. This is true; but a "pardon" "dispenses" with punishment, thereby making non-punishment "legal." The Bill of Rights, of 1689, spoke of "dispensing with laws, *or the execution of laws,* by regal authority." And that "pardons" were understood to be covered is shown by the inclusion of "pardons" granted before October 23, 1689, in the saving clause thereof. 1 W. & M. sess. 2, c. 2, §§ 1 and 13. It is in this broader sense that the term is used in the text hereof.
37. 1 W. & M. sess. 2, c. 2, §§ 2, 12, and 13.
38. 12 & 13 Wm. III, c. 2, § 3.
39. Constitution, Article II, sec. 1.
40. *The Case of Sutton's Hospital,* 10 Coke's Reports 1a (1615), at 29b.
41. See Davis, *op. cit.* note 72 to chapter ii *supra,* I, 75–107; and II, 8 *et seq.*
42. N.J. Hist. Soc. Proc., 3d Ser., III, 117 (1906).
43. See, for example, Elliot, II, 177 and 407; and IV, 246.
44. Annals, II, 1891–1960.
45. Hamilton, III, 445 *et seq.*
46. *McCulloch* v. *Maryland,* 4 Wheat. 316 (1819).
47. Iredell, J., in *Trial of the Northampton Insurgents,* Wharton, 458, 471 (1799). *Cf.*, Cockburn, *Nationality* (London, 1869), 27–28; also, Blackstone, I, 374, and Holdsworth, IX, 77.
48. Blackstone, I, 374.
49. 12 & 13 Wm. III, c. 2, § 3.
50. *Loc. cit.* note 47 *supra.*
51. Blackstone, II, 249.
52. Blackstone, II, 76–77.
53. Blackstone, I, chap. 8.
54. See Start, *Naturalization in the English Colonies in America,* ANNUAL REPORT OF THE AMERICAN HISTORICAL ASSOCIATION (1893), 319.
55. Annals, I, 1109–25. *Cf.*, the view of Iredell, J., in 1799, quoted in the next note *infra.*
56. Tucker, Bk. I, Pt. 1, App., pp. 256–57; Bk. I, Pt. 2, p. 272, footnote 55; *McClenaghan* v. *McClenaghan,* 1 Strob. Eq. (S.C.) 295, 317–18 (1847); 5 S.C. Stat. at L. 355. *Cf.*, Iredell, J., in *Trial of the Northampton Insurgents* (1799), Wharton, 458, 471, who, after defining denization as "a kind of *partial naturalization,*" observed: "Upon the dissolution of the royal government, *the whole authority* of naturalization, either whole or *partial,* belonged to the several States, and *this power* the people of the States have since devolved on the Congress of the United States."
57. Blackstone, I, 274.
58. Holdsworth, I, 535–44.
59. Blackstone, I, 267.
60. Holdsworth, X, 402–3.
61. Blackstone, I, 263–64; Coke's *Institutes,* IV, 148; Hale, *De Portibus Maris,*

in Hargrave's *Law Tracts* (London, 1787), 45–113, especially 50–51; Holdsworth, X, 386–89.

62. Chapters mxv and mccclxxxvii of Carey & Bioren, *Laws of Pennsylvania* (Philadelphia, 1803), are typical eighteenth-century provisions for an American town market.

63. *Cf.*, the port-preference prohibition in Article I, sec. 9, of the Constitution.

64. 21 Jac. I, c. 3.

65. Records, II, 181–82.

66. Records, II, 312, 315–16, 569–70, 594–95, 655.

67. Records, II, 312, 315–16.

68. Records, II, 312, 316, 595, 614–15.

69. Marsden, I, 99 (footnote).

70. Marsden, I, 84–89.

71. Coke's *Institutes*, III, 111–12.

72. *Rolls of Parliament*, 8 H. VI, No. 42; and 9 H. VI, No. 29.

73. 27 H. VIII, c. 4.

74. 28 H. VIII, c. 15.

75. *Cf.*, Benedict, *The American Admiralty* (New York, 1850), 2–3. The complete independence of American admiralty courts under the Constitution tends, of course, to obscure for Americans the very different character of "the court of the Admiral," in England, in the earlier days.

76. 11 & 12 Wm. III, c. 7.

77. There was some local colonial legislation in the seventeenth century. See Down and Edmonds, *The Pirates of the New England Coast* (Salem, 1923), 365; Jameson, *Privateering and Piracy in the Colonial Period* (New York, 1923), xiii and 217, including note 9; Hughson, *The Carolina Pirates and Colonial Commerce*, in Johns Hopkins University Studies, 12th Ser., 237, 254–58, 276–77.

78. See Jameson, *op. cit.* note 77 *supra*, 133, note 1; 143, including note 2; and 286, note 1. The law officers of the Crown, in 1684, had at first agreed with the view stated in the text hereof and then, later, had held that, though the act of 28 Hen. VIII did not extend to the colonies, so as to authorize commissions under it for trial of pirates *there*, the colonial vice-admirals' authorities did not extend to the trial of piracies and other capital crimes. See Crump, *Colonial Admiralty Jurisdiction in the Seventeenth Century* (London, 1931), 112–13. The result, eventually, was the statute of 11 & 12 Wm. III.

79. Section 14 of the act of 11 & 12 Wm. III provided that the commissioners under that act, and those under the act of Henry VIII, should, between them, have "the sole power and authority" to try persons for the crimes which the two acts covered, in the colonies or in England, respectively, "any letters patents, grants or charters of government, in and about the said plantations, or other usages heretofore had or made to the contrary notwithstanding."

80. Marsden, II, 252.

81. *Ibid.*, 255.

82. Acts of the Privy Council, Colonial Series, IV, 485–87. Earlier specimen commissions under the act of 11 & 12 Wm. III may be found in Benedict, *op. cit.* note 75 *supra*, 76–82 (dated 1701); and in N.J. Archives, 1st Ser., V, 196 (dated 1728). The act of William III did not apparently put a complete end to local proceedings for the trial of piracies in some of the colonies. See Charles Johnson, *A General History of the Robberies and Murders of the Most No-*

torious Pirates (Hayward ed.; London, 1926), 576, 578 (Bahamas, 1718); and Jameson, *op. cit.* note 77 *supra*, 286 (South Carolina, 1716).

83. John Adams, II, 224; and IX, 627–29.

84. *Blankard* v. *Galdy*, 2 Salkeld 411 (1693); *cf., Commonwealth* v. *Chapman*, 13 Metc. 68, 71–74 (Mass. 1848).

85. John Adams had appeared as counsel in such trials (*op. cit.* note 83 *supra*); and no doubt this was true of some of the older members of the Federal Convention, also.

86. Blackstone, IV, 71.

87. Blackstone, IV, 94 *et seq.*

88. Chalmers, *Opinions of Eminent Lawyers on Various Points of English Jurisprudence* (Burlington, 1858), 210, 525–27. Trials for murder, under the act of William III, seem nevertheless to have occurred. *Op. cit.* note 83 *supra*.

89. Rutherforth, II, 331; Dwarris, *A General Treatise on Statutes* (London, 1830), 766.

90. *Barber* v. *Wharton*, 2 Ld. Raym. 1452, 1453 (1726); *The King* v. *Coombes*, 1 Leach's Crown Cases (3d ed.), 432 (1785); 2 East, *Pleas of the Crown* (London, 1803), 803; *cf., The Queen* v. *Carr*, L. R., 10 Q. B. D. 76, 86 (1882). In the early part of his *Commentaries*, Blackstone speaks of "the high seas" as synonymous with "the main seas," which, he says, "begin at low-water-mark." But when he comes to speak of piracies and marine felonies, it is evident, if the words of the acts of Parliament are borne in mind, that he uses the phrase, "the high seas," in the sense which appears in the foregoing citations. Blackstone, I, 110; IV, 71, 72, and 265.

91. Coke's *Institutes*, III, 112.

92. *Cf., op. cit.* notes 79 and 88 *supra*.

93. Wooddeson, *loc. cit.* note 40 to chapter ii *supra;* and Wilson, III, 375–76.

94. Blackstone, IV, 68, 72.

95. Records, II, 595.

96. Records, III, 170, 419–20, and 499.

97. Records, II, 614–15.

98. Blackstone, IV, 68, 72.

99. *Triquet* v. *Bath*, 3 Burr. 1478 (1764); *Heathfield* v. *Chilton*, 4 Burr. 2016 (1767).

100. Blackstone, I, 253–57; IV, 67, 70–71.

101. See, besides Blackstone *loc cit.* note 100 *supra*, Boyer, *Annals of Queen Anne* (London, 1709), VII, 233–36, to which Blackstone referred.

102. *Rex* v. *Blake*, 3 Burr. 1731 (1765); *Rex* v. *Thomas*, Cas. temp. Hard. 278 (1735); Hawkins, *Pleas of the Crown* (6th ed.; Dublin, 1788), II, 301; Chitty, *Criminal Law* (London, 1816) I, 710; Russell, *Crimes* (2d ed.; London, 1826), I, 43. *Cf.,* the argument in Henfield's Case (1793), Wharton, 49, 78 *et seq.*

103. *Ibid.*

104. The facts in regard to the English practice before Mattueof's case are set forth in Adair, *The Law of Nations and the Common Law of England*, in THE CAMBRIDGE HISTORICAL JOURNAL, II, 290 (1928). See, also, chap. xii of the same writer's *Exterritoriality of Ambassadors in the Sixteenth and Seventeenth Centuries* (1929). Mr. Adair's strictures against the views of Lord Mansfield on Mattueof's case, as distinct from his statement of facts as to the prior English practice, do not seem to the present writer to be warranted. As indications of what the English courts would have done, had the need arisen, either in the first or the seventh decade of the eighteenth

century, Mansfield's statements are undoubtedly reliable. It was for that purpose that they were intended.

105. Boyer, *op. cit.* note 101 *supra*, VII, 234–42. Blackstone's statement is in accord with the Czar's letter, except that the Czar did add, after demanding that "a Capital Punishment, according to the Rigour of the Law, be inflicted on them all," that "at least such an one [be inflicted] as [was] adequate to the Nature of the Affront, which every particular Person [had] put upon the Ambassador." *Ibid.*, 242. So, the Czar did recognize that something less than "a Capital Punishment" might perhaps be "adequate" in the case of some of the sixteen persons who had been found implicated in the affair.

106. 3 Burr. 1480.

107. 7 Anne, c. 12.

108. 3 Burr. 1480–81.

109. Boyer, *op. cit.* note 101 *supra*, VIII, 141–58.

110. Adair, *loc. cit.* note 104 *supra*.

111. Blackstone, IV, 67.

112. Wilson III, 375–76; Records, II, 615.

NOTES TO CHAPTER XVI

1. Elliot, IV, 540. The argument was repeated seriously, by St. George Tucker, in one of the appendices to his edition of Blackstone's *Commentaries*, of 1803. Though his discussion shows that he must have been aware of the real reason for the enumeration of Congress' counterfeiting power, Tucker argued that "the special power [t]hereby granted, shew[ed] that it was not intended to vest congress with the power of punishing offences of this nature, generally"—such, he said, as forgery—"but such only as [were] enumerated: all others not enumerated being reserved to the jurisdiction of the states, respectively." In reference to the power over piracies, etc., his comment was that "the power of defining and punishing all felonies and offences committed upon land, in all cases not enumerated, [was] reserved to the states, respectively." Tucker, Bk. 1, Pt. 1, App. 414–15. It will be remembered that Tucker was fully aware that many of the enumerations in section 8 of Article I had been made to transfer "executive" powers to Congress.

2. Blackstone, IV, 92–93 and 370. See, also, *Rex* v. *Cameron*, 10 *State Trials* (London, 1766), 202, 204 (1753).

3. Blackstone, IV, 373–82.

4. Blackstone, IV, 75–84.

5. Blackstone, I, 76–81 and 84.

6. Blackstone, IV, 83–84, 88–90.

7. Blackstone, I, 88.

8. Wharton, *A Treatise on the Criminal Law of the United States* (Philadelphia, 1846), 6.

9. Blackstone, IV, 89.

10. *Ibid.*

11. For more detailed discussions of the background facts on copyrights under English law, which are summarized in section 2 of this chapter, see A. S. Collins, *Some Aspects of Copyright from 1700 to 1780*, The Library, 4th Ser., VII, 67 (1926); Birrell, *Copyright in Books* (London, 1899); Holdsworth, VI, 360–79. The views of these authorities are not entirely in accord with each other, or with everything stated in the text hereof.

12. The charter of the company is printed in Arber, *Transcript of the Stationers' Register*, I, xxxi *et seq.*

13. 8 Anne, c. 19.

14. *Cf.*, argument of Thurlow in *Tonson* v. *Collins*, 1 W. Bl. 301, 309. The booksellers apparently insisted on sales of "copy" in perpetuity, with obligation upon the author to assign the "return" term in the future, should the author survive the initial term. That they paid anything in addition for this contingency is, of course, extremely unlikely. See Birrell, *op. cit.* note 11 *supra*, 131 and note.

15. Collins, *op. cit.* note 11 *supra*, 69–73; Cobbett, *Parliamentary History of England* (London, 1813), XVII, 991 and 995.

16. Collins, *op. cit.*

17. 4 Burr. 2303 (K.B. 1769).

18. See especially 4 Burr. 2405 *et seq.*

19. 4 Burr. 2408 (H.L. 1774); also in 2 Bro. P.C. 129 and Cobbett, *op. cit.* note 15 *supra*, 953 *et seq.*

20. See discussion of this matter, in chapter xix hereof.

21. See Charles Evans, *American Bibliography* (Chicago, 1903), for the years in question.

22. *Ibid.*

23. The items recorded in Evans, *op. cit.*, show that only a handful of persons were engaged in the business.

24. See Noah Webster, *Origin of the Copyright Laws of the United States*, in the same author's *Collection of Papers on Political, Literary and Moral Subjects* (New York, 1843), 173.

25. Ct. Acts and Laws, 1784–90, p. 133.

26. Mass. Acts and Resolves, 1782–83, p. 143.

27. Journals, XXIV, 180, 211 note, and 326–27.

28. N.J. Acts, 1776–83, p. 325.

29. 4 N.H. Laws 521.

30. R.I. Acts and Resolves, December 1783, p. 6.

31. 11 Pa. Stat. at L. 271.

32. 4 S.C. Stat. at L. 618.

33. 24 N.C. State Records, 747.

34. 12 Hening, Va. Stat. at L., 30.

35. Marbury and Crawford, Digest of Laws of Georgia, 1755–1800, p. 342; N.Y. Laws, 1785–88, p. 298.

36. 8 Pet. (U.S.) 591, 660–62.

37. N.J. Acts, 1776–83, p. 270; N.Y. Laws, 1778–84, pp. 460, 556, 703; N.Y. Laws, 1785–88, pp. 146, 182, 290, 556, 592, 813; R.I. Acts and Resolves, June 1784, pp. 16–17; May 1786, p. 11; June 1787, p. 12; December 1788, p. 4; 5 N.H. Laws 44, 307; Mass. Acts and Resolves, 1782–84, pp. 9 and 660; 1784–85, pp. 27, 124, 485, 488, 507, 508, 522; 1786–87, pp. 5, 53, 571, 579.

38. 13 N.C. State Records 538, 553–54, 630–32, 637–38, 641, 647–48, 650–52, 654, 656, 711, 718–19, 761, 767–68, 819, 821, 848, 860–61, 935, 937, 941, 952–54.

39. 10 Hening, Va. Stat. at L., 129; 11 *ibid.*, 322; 12 *ibid.*, 261; 1 Kilty, Laws of Md., c. 6 of 1779; Marbury and Crawford, Digest of Laws of Ga., 1755–1800, p. 38; 4 S.C. Stat. at L. 600; 9 Pa. Stat. at L. 601.

40. 11 Hening, Va. Stat. at L., 154 and 316; Marbury and Crawford, Digest of Laws of Ga., 1755–1800, pp. 58 and 59; 1 Kilty, Laws of Md., c. 31 of 1783, and c. 32 of 1784; 5 S.C. Stat. at L. 15 and 92.

41. Ct. Acts and Laws, 1784–90, p. 102.

42. *Ibid.*, 83, 102, 268–69.

43. *Ibid.*, 88.

44. 4 Pa. Stat. at L. 171.
45. *Ibid.*, 211.
46. 6 *ibid.*, 392 and 459.
47. 7 *ibid.*, 347; 9 *ibid.*, 1; 11 *ibid.*, 396 and 528.
48. 11 *ibid.*, 1, 51, 157, 180, 186, 195, 330, 334. The practice of relieving individual debtors by private acts went back in Pennsylvania to the colonial period. See 7 *ibid.*, 69, 140, 265, 317.
49. 9 *ibid.*, 598.
50. 12 *ibid.*, 70.
51. *Ibid.*, 347; 13 *ibid.*, 66 and 175.
52. 1 Kilty, Laws of Md., c. 28 of 1774.
53. Chapter 42 of the Laws of Maryland of 1785, for the relief of five named individuals, is the only one of these private acts printed *in extenso* in Kilty's Laws. In other instances, the titles only are given. See c. 26 of 1783, c. 57 of 1784, and c. 16 of 1786.
54. N.Y. Colonial Laws, 1774–75, pp. 77, 80, 169, and 174.
55. N.Y. Laws, 1778–84, p. 649.
56. N.Y. Laws, 1785–88, 167; see, also, 570.
57. *Ibid.*, 242.
58. *Ibid.*, 639.
59. *Ibid.*, 835.
60. Conn. Rec., VI, 71, 82, 216, 256, 263, 276, 310, 373, 381, 445, 453, 458, 484, 514.
61. *Ibid.*, 66–67, 128, 187, 315, 325, 341, 428.
62. *Ibid.*, 53, 88, 119, 121, 389, 441, 458.
63. *Ibid.*, 181, 309, 320, 343, 371, 386, 387, 429, 463, 513, 527, 531.
64. *Cf.*, pp. 347–48 *supra.*
65. See the material cited in chapter xi hereof.
66. See chapter v hereof.
67. Journals, I, 68.
68. Journals, II, 195, 196; V, 546, 548, 552, 678, 682, 685.
69. Journals, II, 195; V, 456 and 674.
70. These background facts will be developed fully in Volume II hereof.
71. Records, III, 615–16.
72. *Cf.*, pp. 486–87 *supra.*
73. Journals, XXVI, 113; *cf.*, Treat, *The National Land System, 1785–1820* (New York, 1910), 8 and 9.
74. See especially Records, II, 446, 454–59, and 461–66. The whole history of the subject in the Federal Convention indicates that the whole of section 3 of Article IV grew bit by bit, as suggested in the text, from the original desire of the Convention to provide for power in Congress to admit new states.
75. A power merely "to dispose of the [nation's] Territory" might have had this effect. *Cf.*, pp. 486–87 *supra.*
76. See Story, III, 181–83.
77. See Swift, I, 73–79; Durfee, 21–23 and 34 *et seq.*
78. Blackstone, I, 250.

NOTES TO CHAPTER XVII

1. Madison, IX, 411, 420–21; Records, 483, 488.
2. *Northern Pacific R. Co.* v. *North Dakota*, 250 U.S. 135 (1919); *Dakota Central Telephone Co.* v. *South Dakota*, 250 U.S. 163 (1919); *Hamilton* v.

Kentucky Distilleries & Warehouse Co., 251 U.S. 146 (1919); *Jacob Ruppert, Inc.* v. *Caffey*, 251 U.S. 264 (1920).

3. *Ex parte Milligan*, 4 Wall. 2, 139 (1866). This passage is usually cited in the later cases.

4. 283 U.S. 605, 622–23 (1931).

5. Charles Evans Hughes, *Addresses and Papers* (New York, 1908), 139.

6. Oliver Wendell Holmes, Jr., *The Common Law* (Boston, 1881), 1; *idem*, *Collected Legal Papers* (New York, 1921), 173.

7. Felix Frankfurter and Henry M. Hart, Jr., *The Business of the Supreme Court at October Term, 1934*, 49 HLR, 68, 91–94 (1935); cited with apparent approval by the senior author in *Flournoy* v. *Wiener*, 321 U.S. 253, 264 (1944).

8. *United States* v. *Curtiss-Wright Export Corp.*, 299 U.S. 304 (1936).

9. *United States* v. *Butler*, 297 U.S. 1 (1936); *Helvering* v. *Davis*, 301 U.S. 619 (1937).

10. See chapter ii hereof.

11. Records, III, 478.

12. *Cf.*, pp. 405–407 *supra*.

13. See chapters xi and xii hereof.

14. See pp. 443–65 and 469–77 *supra*.

15. That such is the nature of this power of Congress as to statutes and judgments is the thesis of Cook, *The Powers of Congress under the Full Faith and Credit Clause*, 28 YALE LAW JOURNAL 421 (1919); reprinted as chap. iv of Cook, *The Logical and Legal Bases of the Conflict of Laws* (Cambridge, 1942).

16. Records, II, 151.

17. Section 13 of South Carolina Constitution of 1778.

18. N.J. Acts, 1776–83, p. 113; 11 Pa. Stat. at L. 557 (1785); and 11 Hening, Va. Stat., at L., 365 (1784) are typical enactments.

19. R.I. Acts and Resolves, March 1777, p. 18; Ct. Acts and Laws, 1784–90, p. 39.

20. Records, I, 314.

21. Article II, sec. 1.

22. See Stanwood, *A History of the Presidency, 1788–1897*, *passim*. As this author intimates, the exigencies of getting the new government organized and going, in 1789, undoubtedly were a factor in the origin of this practice.

23. See pp. 67–68 and 537–39 *supra*.

24. Records, III, 172, 195.

25. *The address, and reasons of dissent, of the minority of the convention of the state of Pennsylvania, to their constituents*, Am. Mus., II, 536, 544–45 (December 1787).

26. Elliot, II, 49–51 and 181.

27. *Ibid.*, IV, 50, 52, 55, 65; *cf.* 71.

28. Kent, I, 211–12.

29. Elliot, III, 367.

30. Records, II, 240–41.

31. Records, II, 139, and IV, 40. The inference of committee approval is drawn from the fact that, although there are emendations in the hand of John Rutledge, the chairman of the Committee of Detail, all through the Randolph scheme, the provision on voters' qualifications, as Randolph finally drew it, shows no such emendation. The pervasive Rutledge alterations undoubtedly mean that, when Randolph had finished his scheme to his own

satisfaction, it was taken up, provision by provision, by the committee as a whole; that, in this process, Rutledge as chairman, held the document and read off its provisions to the committee's members; and that he noted upon it the changes which the committee, or a majority of its members, decided to make.

32. Records, II, 150, 151, 152, 153, 155, 163–64, 165. As indicated earlier in the text hereof, the most primitive of the Wilson working papers which survive today contains the provision first quoted in the text hereof, at p. 525 *supra*. In this initial effort, Wilson carried the formal drafting only through the provisions relating to the House of Representatives and then began making mere scattered notes. In his next effort, he apparently began over and got part way through the provisions relating to the Senate, before trailing off. In his second effort, he included the following:

> The Members of the House of Representatives shall be chosen every second Year by the People of the several States comprehended within this Union *the Time and Place and the Manner of holding the Elections* and the Rules shall be appointed by the Legislatures of the several States; but the provisions which they shall make concerning them shall be *subject to the Control of the Legislature of the United States.*

In view of the meaning of "Manner" which appears in the more primitive Wilsonian provision on House elections, quoted in the text, it seems certain that the provision last quoted was intended to confer on the state legislatures tentative power, and on the Congress of the United States ultimate power, to prescribe "the Qualifications of Electors" in House elections.

Wilson apparently remained satisfied with the provision last quoted, until he got well along with the provisions relating to the Senate. He then apparently saw that, though the "Manner" of elections to that body was to be stipulated as "by the Legislatures of the States," "every sixth year," a "Time," a "Place," and a "Manner" provision, in reference to such elections, was nevertheless necessary for regulating various details of these elections which could not well be specified. So, he canceled his "time-place-and-manner" provision relating only to elections to the House and drew the following for insertion among the provisions, which he was beginning to draw, to apply to both houses of Congress:

> The Times and Places and the Manner of holding the Elections for the Members of each House shall be prescribed by the Legislature of each State; but their Provisions concerning them may, at any Time, be altered and superseded by the Legislature of the United States.

At the same time that he drew this provision, Wilson apparently perceived the different incidence which the "Manner" branch of his tentative and ultimate powers would have upon the elections of the House and Senate; and, so, he inserted, presumably as a precautionary measure, among the provisions relating solely to the House, a stipulation which read as follows:

> The Qualifications of Electors [in House Elections] shall be prescribed by the Legislatures of the several States; but their provisions concerning them may at any Time be altered and superseded by the Legislature of the United States.

If only this phase of the Wilson drafting were known, the argument could be made that control over "the Manner of holding Elections" was not understood to include control over "the Qualifications"—or, what is the same thing, over the identity—of the voters participating in them. But the survival of Wilson's more primitive effort, quoted in the text hereof, precludes such a view. Wilson undoubtedly knew that his "Manner" provision covered this point; but the complexity of its incidence produced his "Qualifications" provision relating to the House, for what, he seems temporarily to have thought, was a needed emphasis.

The scheme of draftsmanship just delineated was carried by Wilson into the final draft constitution which, the systematic emendations in it by John Rutledge show, must have been put before the whole committee. Apparently before this occurred, Wilson determined, however, ๖ change the particular provisions in which we are interested, and to change them to a tenor more in line with what the committee, in the Randolph draft, had previously approved. As a result of these changes, the final Wilson draft, as considered by the committee, provided, with respect to "the Qualifications of Electors" in House elections, that these "sh[ould] be the same from time to time as those of the Electors, in the several States, of the most numerous Branch of their own Legislatures." The "time-place-and-manner" provision was continued in the form last noted. There was also, in this Wilson draft, a Republican Government Clause identical with that now in the Constitution. The draft passed the committee, in all three of the foregoing respects, without any change; and the provisions above noted, which are, of course, very similar to those now in the Constitution on the points in question, were all included in the draft Constitution which the committee reported to the Convention, on August 6th.

33. The rule, that is, that any doubt as to the meaning of any part of a document is to be resolved by comparison of the different parts thereof and by interpretation of the document as a whole. Blackstone, I, 60; Rutherforth, II, 332–33.

34. Erdman, *The New Jersey Constitution of 1776* (Princeton, 1929), chap. iv.

35. Records, II, 201–8, 215–16.

36. *Loc. cit.* note 30 *supra.*

37. Cf., Holmes, *The Theory of Legal Interpretation*, 12 HLR, 417 (1899).

38. See pp. 67–68 *supra.*

39. Elliot, III, 494.

40. *Ibid.*, 493 and 495.

41. *Ibid.*, IV, 74 and 105.

42. See p. 68 *supra.*

43. *Fitzgerald* v. *Green*, 134 U.S. 377, 379 (1890); *Burroughs* v. *United States*, 290 U.S. 534 (1934).

44. *Minor* v. *Happersett*, 21 Wall. 162, 171 (1875).

45. See Flack, *The Adoption of the Fourteenth Amendment* (Baltimore, 1908), 97 *et seq.*

46. *Bradford Electric Light Co., Inc.* v. *Clapper*, 286 U.S. 145, 154–55 (1932); *John Hancock Mutual Life Insurance Co.* v. *Yates*, 299 U.S. 178, 183 (1936).

47. The Bradford case cited next note *supra* speaks of "a statute" as being "a 'public act' *within the meaning* of [the Full Faith and Credit] Clause." 286 U.S. 155. And Justice Jackson, of the present Supreme Court, says: "The Constitution by use of the term 'public acts' clearly *includes* statutes." Jackson, *Full Faith and Credit: The Lawyer's Clause of the Constitution* (New York, 1945), 19. The implication in both cases seems to be that "public Acts" may include something more.

48. Records, II, 188.

49. Records, II, 447–48.

50. Records, II, 445.

51. 1 Stat. (Boston, 1827) 93.

52. The Act of Congress of 1804 (2 Stat. [Boston, 1856] 298) has probably contributed to produce this view, though what the theory of the Congress was, that passed this act, is not known. *Cf.*, footnote at 547 hereof.

53. *Cf.*, the reference to "magistrates," in the petition to the New Jersey legislature from Monmouth county, in that state, after the decision of *Holmes* v. *Walton*, in 1780, referred to herein in chapter xxvii. See p. 950 *supra*. These "magistrates" were "justices of the peace." *Cf.*, N.J. Acts, 1776–83, App., p. 10.

54. Kirby's Connecticut Reports, the earliest published, came out in 1789.

55. Blackstone, I, 68–69 and 71.

56. See Blackstone, I, 63 and 73.

57. *Cf.*, Sullivan, 340–41: "And who is to decide on the question, whether a principle, urged as law, has heretofore been in practice? The judges are to decide; but yet not in an arbitrary manner. The *records* of the courts of law will generally witness whether a principle has been in practice in the country. . . ." Sullivan also said that "it would be well for us to have our own comments, and to reject those of other governments [*i.e.*, England], which have been issued since we became an independent nation. . . . We ought now to have our own reporters, compilers and compositors. Every one, who will attempt something in this way, ought to be encouraged by the public."

58. Some of the early cases (*e.g.*, *Peck* v. *Williamson*, Carolina Law Repository, 53 [1812]) appear to have been confused by the cases having to do with judgments which had arisen under the Articles of Confederation. These held that the judgments of courts of other states were required to be received *as evidence* by the "full faith and credit" provision of the Articles. See *James* v. *Allen*, 1 Dall. 188 (1786). This was proper; for such was the effect which such judgments *ought to* be given, by mere comity, under the law of nations. *Cf.*, *Hilton* v. *Guyot*, 159 U.S. 113 (1895). But these holdings were manifestly not to be taken as expositions of the *general* meaning of the phrase "to give full faith to"; they were merely expositions of what "giving full faith *to*" *judgments* meant under an *obligatory* observance of the law of nations.

59. 2 Dall. 302 (1794).

60. *Cf.*, *Chicago & Alton R.R.* v. *Wiggins Ferry Co.*, 119 U.S. 615, 622 (1887).

61. See *James* v. *Allen*, 1 Dall. 188 (1786); *Miller* v. *Hall*, 1 Dall. 229 (1788).

62. See chapters xviii–xxi.

63. *Pink* v. *A.A.A. Highway Express, Inc.*, 314 U.S. 201, 210 (1941).

64. Records, II, 448.

65. Records, II, 483–86 and 488–89.

66. Records, II, 489.

67. Story, III, 181–83.

68. There is an act of 1804 relating to non-judicial records. *Cf.*, note 52 *supra*.

69. *Cf.*, Jackson, *op. cit.* note 47 *supra*, 11–17.

70. *Ibid.*, 19.

71. *Kryger* v. *Wilson*, 242 U.S. 171, 176 (1916); *Klaxon Co.* v. *Stentor Electric Mfg. Co.*, 313 U.S. 487, 496–97 (1941).

72. *Western Union Telegraph Co.* v. *Brown*, 234 U.S. 542 (1914), is the chief of these.

73. With respect to the situation existing in this department of the subject, a member of the present Supreme Court has recently confessed that he "cannot say with any assurance where the line is drawn today between what the Supreme Court will decide as constitutional law and what it will leave to the states as common law." He also says he "can not discern any consistent pattern or design into which the cases [in the field] fit." Jackson, *op. cit.* note 47 *supra*, 21 and 28.

74. *Home Insurance Co.* v. *Dick*, 281 U.S. 397 (1930); *Hartford Accident & Indemnity Co.* v. *Delta & Pine Land Co.*, 292 U.S. 143 (1934).

75. *Cf.*, pp. 34 *et seq.* of chapter ii hereof *supra*. The statements herein made as to the chaos and confusion existing should be compared with those made by Justice Jackson of the present Court, in the work cited in note 47 *supra*. He says, in particular (p. 46), that the Court seems to him to have "adopt[ed] no rule, permit[ted] a good deal of overlapping and confusion, but interfere[d] now and then without imparting to the bar any reason by which the one or the other course is to be guided or predicted." He has also pointed out (pp. 21 and 47) the utter impossibility of reconciling the statements the Court has made about what it does in the field, in certain of its cases; notably, in *Klaxon Co.* v. *Stentor Electric Mfg. Co.*, 313 U.S. 487, 496–97 (1941), and *Griffen* v. *McCoach*, 313 U.S. 498, 507 (1941), on the one hand; and in *Pacific Employers Insurance Co.* v. *Industrial Accident Commission*, 306 U.S. 493, 502 (1939), on the other.

76. See materials cited in note 52 to chapter ii *supra*.

77. *Mills* v. *Duryee*, 7 Cranch (U.S.) 481 (1813).

78. *Hampton* v. *McConnell*, 3 Wheat. (U.S.) 234 (1818), and *Mayhew* v. *Thatcher*, 6 Wheat. (U.S.) 129 (1821). There were some other cases on the sufficiency of the proof offered.

79. See cases cited in Story, III, 181–83; also *Bartlet* v. *Knight*, and note attached thereto, in 1 Mass. (3d ed.; Exeter, N.H., 1821) 399, 410.

80. The result in the recent case of *Griffen* v. *McCoach*, 313 U.S. 498 (1941), is certainly impossible to justify under any rational system of jurisprudence. *Cf.*, same case, 116 F. (2d) 261; 123 F. (2d) 550; and 316 U.S. 683, 713. And see Cook, *The Logical and Legal Bases of the Conflict of Laws* (Cambridge, 1942), 126 *et seq.*

81. See *The Charming Betsy*, 2 Cranch 64, 118 (1804); *The Nereide*, 9 Cranch 388, 422–23 (1815).

82. *Kansas* v. *Colorado*, 206 U.S. 46 (1906). This law was described as "federal common law" by Brandeis, J., just after deciding *Erie Railroad Co.* v. *Tompkins*, 304 U.S. 64 (1938). See *Hinderlider* v. *La Plata River & Cherry Creek Ditch Co.*, 304 U.S. 92, 110 (1938).

83. *Southern Pacific Co.* v. *Jensen*, 244 U.S. 205, 215 (1917).

84. *Loc. cit.* note 28 to chapter vi, *supra*.

85. Blackstone, I, 86–87.

86. Blackstone, I, 49.

87. *Cf.*, Marshall, *loc. cit.* note 41 to chapter ii *supra*; *Steinmetz* v. *Currie*, 1 Dall. 269 (1788); and *Watson* v. *Tarpley*, 18 How. 517 (1855).

88. *Ibid.*

89. See Lord Mansfield in *Holman* v. *Johnson*, 1 Cowp. 341, 343 (1775): "Every action tried here [in England] must be tried by the law of England; but the law of England says that in a variety of circumstances, with regard

to contracts legally made abroad, the laws of the country where the cause of action arose shall govern." And *cf.,* Story J., in *Van Reimsdyk* v. *Kane,* 1 Gallison 371 (1812): "The rule is well settled, that the law of the place, where a contract is made, is to govern . . . ; and that being valid in such [place], it is to be considered as equally valid, and to be enforced everywhere. . . . This doctrine is explicitly avowed by *Huberus de conflictu legum* and has become incorporated into the code of national law"—*i.e.,* of "the law of nations"—"in all civilized countries. . . . If, in such a case, the Legislature [of another country] nullify such contracts [as to others than its own citizens], it is certain that they cannot be enforced within its own tribunals, but elsewhere they remain with the original validity, which they had by the *lex loci contractus.*"

90. *Loc. cit.* note 81 *supra.*

91. *Ibid.* See, also, Bishop, *Criminal Law* (7th ed.), 60.

92. Tucker, Bk. I, Pt. 1, App., p. 380.

93. *United States* v. *Coolidge,* 1 Wheat. (U.S.) 415 (1816); *cf., United States* v. *Hudson,* 7 Cranch (U.S.) 32 (1812). See, also, "the [anti-]Federalist judge, Chase," in *United States* v. *Worrall,* 2 Dall. (U.S.) 384 (1798).

94. Jefferson, IX, 86, 87.

95. Elliot, IV, 566.

96. *Erie Railroad Co.* v. *Tompkins,* 304 U.S. 64, 72, 77–78 (1937).

NOTES TO CHAPTER XVIII

1. Montesquieu, *The Spirit of the Laws* (Worcester, 1802), II, 161.

2. See Blackstone, I, 106–9.

3. Wilson, I, 374–75.

4. *Reports and Dissertations* (2d ed..; Rutland, 1871), 68–69.

5. Note to *Mandeville* v. *Riddle,* 1 Cranch 367, 374–75 (1804); reprinted in SEAALH, III, 72, 75.

6. Swift, I, 44.

7. *Livingston* v. *Jefferson,* 1 Brock. 203, 209 (1811).

8. Cf. the action of James Duane, of New York, referred to in a footnote to p. 463 *supra.*

9. Dall. (U.S., 3d ed.; Philadelphia, 1830) iv.

10. *Cf.,* Blackstone, I, 44.

11. The American mode of thought comes to the surface clearly in *Baker* v. *Wheaton,* 5 Mass. 509 (1809), and *Ogden* v. *Saunders,* 12 Wheat. 213, 358, 363 (1827).

12. *Cf.,* the Blackstone passages quoted in note 39 to chapter ii *supra.*

13. *Penn* v. *Lord Baltimore,* 1 Vesey, Sr., 444 (1750), was, of course, an exception to this general rule.

14. *Cf.,* Blackstone's usage in the first volume of his *Commentaries.* "The Rights of Persons," however, as Blackstone used it, included corporations, agency, master and servant, and much British constitutional law.

15. Conflict-of-laws cases are generally listed under this head in eighteenth-century lawbooks.

16. This view is expounded in Kames, *Principles of Equity* (Edinburgh, 1760), 266: "The common law of Britain regulates not foreign matters; and the law of a foreign country hath no authority here. Whence it follows, that foreign matters must be governed by the rules of common justice to which all men are subjected, or *jure gentium* as generally expressed." "Common law" is, of course, used by Kames in a sense different from that in which Blackstone

and other English writers used it when they declared that "the Common Law" included "the *jus gentium*." Kames wrote very early in Mansfield's Chief-Justiceship. He complains that the English courts, taking jurisdiction in conflicts cases by a fiction, apply to them "common law" in the sense in which he used the term. *Cf.*, Mansfield in *Holman* v. *Johnson*, Cowp. 341, 344 (1775). Lord Kames was a very frequently cited writer, among Americans, on conflict-of-laws points, in the early years. *Cf.*, Sack, *Conflict of Laws in the History of English Law*, 3 Law: A Century of Progress, 342 (1937).

17. *Op. cit.* note 52 to chapter ii *supra.*

18. *Cf.*, the statement in the English case, *Arnott* v. *Redfern*, 2 C. & P. 88 (1825), that conflicts cases were even then of rare occurrence in England.

19. *Cf.*, the statement of Jabez Henry in *Odwin* v. *Forbes*, quoted in note 52 to chapter ii *supra.* Henry plainly recognizes the law merchant as something distinct from the conflicts of laws, although the relation between the two is not made clear.

20. Reprisals as a sanction for the general law had, apparently, as a practical matter, ceased by 1787. *Cf.*, Holdsworth, X, 374–75. Nevertheless, Blackstone still talked about them in that connection. Blackstone, I, 258.

21. *Cf.*, Blackstone, I, 273, and Wooddeson, *loc. cit.* note 40 to chapter ii *supra.*

22. *Pillans* v. *Van Mierop*, 3 Burr. 1663, 1672 (1765).

23. Some cases, like *Hunter* v. *Blodget* (referred to later in the text), which recognize the interest exception refer to Fonblanque's edition of [Ballow], *A Treatise of Equity* (London, 1794); but the reason for the exception is not there discussed.

24. *Cf.*, passages quoted in note 39 to chapter ii *supra.*

25. *Cf.*, passage quoted in note 40 to chapter ii *supra.*

26. Wilson was not on the Committee on Style; but with the knowledge, apparently, of the Convention, the final draft of the Constitution was submitted to Wilson after it was prepared. Records, III, 170 and 419–20; *cf.*, Warren, *The Making of the Constitution* (Boston, 1929), 688 and note 1.

27. Wilson, it is clear, from the papers of the Committee of Detail, was the chief draftsman for that committee. Edmund Randolph's rambling sketch, which is sometimes called the first draft of the Constitution, was hardly more than a set of informal notes as to what should be done. Records, II, 129–89.

28. Wilson, I, 374–75.

29. Wilson, III, 375–76.

30. 1 Dall. (U.S.) 269 (1788).

31. 1 T.R. 167 (1786).

32. 2 Yeates (Pa.) 480 (1799).

33. *Minet* v. *Gibson*, 3 T.R. 481 (1789).

34. *Gibson* v. *Minet*, 1 H. Bla. 569 (1791).

35. 337–38 and 352–54.

36. 1 Southard (N.J.) 223, 229–30, and 231 (1818).

37. Griffith's *Annual Law Register of the United States*, III, 243–44 (1822). The statute is Pa. Laws of 1809, p. 136, c. 98.

38. *Loc. cit.* note 45 to chapter ii *supra.*

39. *Cf.*, Tucker's statement (Tucker, Bk. I, Pt. 1, App., p. 430) that it "may be said of the civil law [that its] rules of proceeding . . . , whenever the written law is silent, are to be observed in cases of equity, and of admiralty, and maritime jurisdiction."

40. Tucker, Bk. I, Pt. 1, App., pp. 407 and 429–30.

41. ASP, 479–80.

42. *Cf.*, note 19 *supra.*

NOTES TO CHAPTER XIX

1. Blackstone, I, 63, 67, 68, 74–75, 79, and 83.

2. The same notions as to the structure of the Common Law are found in chap. ii of Sir Matthew Hale's *History of the Common Law*, of 1713. They were, therefore, not new.

3. 1 Story, *Commentaries on Equity Jurisprudence* (Boston, 1836), §§ 24 and 25.

4. Blackstone, III, 441.

5. This view of Blackstone's was cited and relied upon, in the debate in the United States Senate, during the drafting of the Judiciary Act of 1789. *Journal of William Maclay* (New York, 1890), 92.

6. Blackstone, III, chap. xxvii.

7. Cf., Holdsworth, *Blackstone's Treatment of Equity*, 43 HLR, 1 (1929), in which, however, little sympathy is expressed with the Blackstonian and Mansfieldian views.

8. Cowp. 473–74 (1776). See, also, *Eaton v. Jaques*, 2 Doug. 455, 460 (1780); *Clark v. Shee*, 1 Cowp. 197, 199–200 (1774); and *Moses v. Macferlan*, 2 Burr. 1012 (1760); and cf., the similar views of Mansfield's associate judges in *Master v. Miller*, 4 T.R. 320, 344 (1791); *Winch v. Keeley*, 1 T.R. 619, 622–23 (1787); and *Corbett v. Poelnitz*, 1 T.R. 5 (1785).

9. See pp. 572–75 *supra*.

10. *Op. cit.* note 12 to chapter xvii *supra*, VII, 155–56; XII, 427, 430; XIII, 165–66; XVI, 155, 156.

11. *Livingston v. Jefferson*, 1 Brock. 203, 209 (1811).

12. Jefferson, XII, 246, 247–50, and footnote 250–59. For a portion of Johnson's letter in reply, see 57 HLR, 333 (1944).

13. The first legislative reform of this nature was the New York Code of Civil Procedure of 1848.

14. *Wheaton v. Peters*, 8 Pet. (U.S.) 591, 657 (1834).

15. Otis, 49 and 108.

16. The nine colonies were Massachusetts, Rhode Island, Connecticut, New York, New Jersey, Pennsylvania, Delaware, Maryland, and South Carolina.

17. Mass. Gaz., April 17, 1766.

18. The charters may be found in Poore, *The Federal and State Constitutions, Colonial Charters, and other Organic Laws of the United States* (Washington, 1877).

19. *An Essay upon the Government of the English Plantations on the Continent of America*, "by an American" (London, 1701), 17–18.

20. *Ibid.*, 51–52; cf., 18–19.

21. See Andrews, *op. cit.* note 45 to chapter v *supra*, 45–63; and cf., Reinsch, *The English Common Law in the Early American Colonies*, reprinted in SEAALH, I, 367.

22. In reference to the Common Law practice of following precedents, Zephaniah Swift said, in 1795: "This practice is founded in the highest wisdom, and produces the best effects. It establishes one permanent uniform, universal directory, for the conduct of the whole community, and opens the door for a constant progressive improvement in the laws, in proportion to the civilization of their manners, and the encrease of their wealth. [W]hile the legislature were passing acts for general regulations, the courts were polishing, improving, and perfecting a system of conduct, for the minuter subordinate transactions of life, which by the collective wisdom and experience of successive ages, have advanced to the highest pitch of clearness, certainty, and precision. Courts how-

ever are not absolutely bound by the authority of precedents. If a determination has been founded upon mistaken principles, or the rule adopted by it be inconvenient, or repugnant to the general tenor of the law, a subsequent court assumes the power to vary from or contradict it. In such cases they do not determine the prior decisions to be bad law; but that they are not law. Thus in the very nature of the institution, is a principle established which corrects all errors and rectifies all mistakes. . . . The validity of [the Common Law in Connecticut] in all cases depended upon its being approved of, and adopted by the courts, and the authority of the courts to admit it, originated in the general consent of the people, as no statute was ever made on that subject. In such cases our courts exercised the same discretionary power and jurisdiction, as have been exercised by all the English judges, from the earliest period of their government, to the present time. There are a vast many improvements which were introduced by the courts without any legislative act." Swift, I, 40–41 and 43–44. See, also, Wilson, II, 50 and 53; and Chipman, *op. cit.* note 7 to chapter xviii *supra*, 61–69.

23. Schlesinger, *Colonial Appeals to the Privy Council*, 28 POLITICAL SCIENCE QUARTERLY, 279 and 433, 446–49 (1913).

24. Wm. Smith, 371–72. For a Virginia complaint, of the middle 1730's, see *ibid.*, footnote to 379 at 382.

25. *Documents Relative to the Colonial History of the State of New York* (Albany, 1856), VII, 483, 485.

26. *Ibid.*, 500–501; and Pownall, I, 111 and 114–15.

27. Laussat, *An Essay on Equity in Pennsylvania* (Philadelphia, 1825), reprinted in 1 REPORTS OF THE MEETINGS OF THE PENNSYLVANIA BAR ASSOCIATION, 221 (1895); Rawle, *Equity in Pennsylvania* (Philadelphia, 1868); Fisher, *The Administration of Equity through Common Law Forms in Pennsylvania*, 1 LAW QUARTERLY REVIEW, 455 (1895); Rawle, Wharton, and Jones, *Report on the Administration of Justice*, JOURNAL OF THE SENATE OF PENNSYLVANIA (1834), II, 116 *et seq.*

28. *Op. cit.* note 24 *supra*, 385–89.

29. Pownall, I, 129–30.

30. *Ibid.*, 104–5.

31. *Ibid.*, 113–14.

32. *Ibid.*, 116–18.

33. *Cf.*, Col. Rec. of N.C., II, 161.

34. For a discussion of these aspects of the Resolutions on Rights and Grievances, see chapter vi hereof.

35. Journals, I, 69.

36. *Blankard* v. *Galdy*, 2 Salkeld 411 (1693).

37. For example, no legislative or constitutional direction was given to the courts in Massachusetts until four years after the Revolution occurred. See *Commonwealth* v. *Chapman*, 13 Metc. 68, 71–72 (1848). None was ever given in Connecticut. Zephaniah Swift, writing on that state in 1795, said: "At the late revolution, when we were separated from the British empire, the general consent and approbation of the people, establishd the common law of England, as far as it is warranted by reason, and conformable to our circumstances, to be the law of the land. . . . [N]o statute was ever made on that subject." Swift, I, 42 and 44.

38. *The Constitutions of the Several Independent States of America* (2d ed.; Boston, 1785), 74.

39. *Ibid.*, 100 and 103.

40. *Ibid.*, 65–66.

41. Story, I, 29–30.
42. 2 Hening, Va. Stat. at L., 43.
43. Sabin's Reprint (New York, 1865), 47.
44. Tucker, Bk. I, Pt. 1, App., p. 395.
45. *Ibid.*, 396.
46. 9 Hening, Va. Stat. at L., 127.
47. Tucker, Bk. I, Pt. 1, App., p. 405.
48. See Andrews, *op. cit.* note 45 to chapter v *supra*, 49.
49. Kirby's Connecticut Reports, the earliest of our American state law reports, was not published until 1789.
50. Ct. Act and Laws, 1784–90, p. 268.
51. *Cf.*, the mode of expression in the provision, in the original draft of section 34 of the Judiciary Act of 1789, that the national courts should follow as "rules of decision" the states' "unwritten or *common law* [then] in use, whether *by adoption from* the common law of England, *the ancient statutes of the same* or otherwise." A fascimile reproduction of this draft may be found in 37 HLR, 87. This usage followed Hale and Blackstone. *Cf.*, notes 1 and 2 *supra.*
52. Swift, I, 1–3, 42–45.
53. Swift, I, 3 and 74–78.
54. Sullivan, iii–iv and 18–19.
55. Kent, *An American Law Student of a Hundred Years Ago*, in SEAALH, I, 837, 842–43, and 844.
56. Elliot, IV, 566.
57. Wythe's and Washington's.
58. Tucker, Bk. I, Pt. 1, iv and v.
59. A summary of the state of equity in the New England states in 1825 may be found in an appendix to Laussat, *op. cit.* note 27 *supra*. It had not changed greatly, in those states in the years that had intervened since 1787. *Cf.*, Swift, I, 74–78, and Durfee, 23–25 and 119–23.
60. *Op. cit.* note 27 *supra.*
61. Swift, I, 74–78; Durfee, 21–22 and 34 *et seq.;* especially 61–62.
62. The states, besides Connecticut and Rhode Island, whose judges were without tenure during good behavior were Pennsylvania, New Jersey, Georgia, and South Carolina as to its chancery judges. Some of the other states limited such tenure to the higher courts. New Hampshire, Massachusetts, Delaware, and Virginia had provisions for "fixed" or "permanent" salaries. *Op. cit.* note 38 *supra, passim.* In *No. LXXIX* of *The Federalist*, Hamilton said: "The enlightened friends to good government *in every State*, have seen cause to lament the want of precise and explicit precautions in the State Constitutions on this head [of judicial salaries]. Some of these indeed have declared that *permanent* [these italics Hamilton's] salaries should be established for the judges; but the experiment has in some instances shown that such expressions are not sufficiently definite to preclude legislative evasions." The precise facts as to the legislative evasions to which Hamilton here alluded are not known to the present writer.
63. Chipman, *op. cit.* note 7 to chapter xviii *supra*, 62.
64. Blackstone, I, 63–64, 69, and 71.

NOTES TO CHAPTER XX

1. 1 U.S. Stat. 73 (1789).
2. See chapter xxiii hereof.
3. 2 U.S. Stat. 89 (1801).

4. 2 U.S. Stat. 132 (1802).

5. The lower federal courts first permanently obtained general jurisdiction, concurrent with the state courts, over cases arising under the Constitution, laws, and treaties of the United States, in 1875. 18 U.S. Stat. 470.

6. Records, I, 119 and 124.

7. Records, II, 45–46.

8. This apparently, was the view taken in the First Congress; and, accordingly, in the first Judiciary Act there were certain cases within the "Controversy" categories to which "the [national] judicial Power" was in no way "extended." *Cf.*, Story, J., in *Martin* v. *Hunter's Lessee*, 1 Wheat. 304, 333–37 (1816). The Justice indicated that the Court was not much impressed with this view, and the main body of the opinion is inconsistent with it.

9. This, also, was apparently the view in the First Congress; and the proviso in section 25 of the first Judiciary Act was drawn accordingly. In *Smith* v. *Maryland*, 6 Cranch 286, in 1810; and in *Fairfax's Devisee* v. *Hunter's Lessee*, 7 Cranch 603, and *Martin* v. *Hunter's Lessee*, 1 Wheat. 304, in 1813 and 1816, respectively, the Court refused to be bound by the strict letter of the proviso. *Cf.*, the discussion of these cases in chapter xxiv hereof.

10. The First Congress apparently recognized the Court's "judicial supremacy" in drawing the original "process" acts, the "rules-of-decision" section (§ 34) of the first Judiciary Act, and the provisions in the twenty-fifth section of that act empowering the Court to enforce its precedents on the courts of the states. *Cf.*, chapters xxiii–xxvi hereof.

11. The views presented in the text of the present chapter and that next following are a mere amplification of the views of the Court, in *Martin* v. *Hunter's Lessee*, 1 Wheat. 304 (1816); and of Alexander Hamilton, in *The Federalist, Nos. XXII* and *LXXXII*.

12. Records, I, 97 and 138; II, 73 and 74–75. See, also, pp. 1002–35 hereof.

13. The ideas expressed for the Supreme Court by Story, J., in *Martin* v. *Hunter's Lessee*, 1 Wheat. (U.S.) 304 (1816), were never acted upon by that body. These ideas must certainly have been understood by the Supreme Court in the earlier years. *Cf.*, the somewhat gloating views of the *Anti*-Federalist judge, Chase in *Turner* v. *Bank of North America*, 4 Dall. (U.S.) 8, 10 (1799): "The notion has frequently been entertained, that the federal courts derive their judicial power immediately from the constitution; but the *political* truth is, that the disposal of the judicial power (except in a few specified instances [*i.e.*, apparently, the instances in which the Supreme Court has original jurisdiction]) belongs to congress. If congress has given the power to this Court, we possess it, not otherwise: and if congress has not given the power to us, or to any other Court, it still remains at the Legislative disposal. Besides, congress is not bound, and it would, perhaps be inexpedient, to enlarge the jurisdiction of the federal Courts to every subject, in every form, which the constitution might warrant."

14. Records, I, 119 and 124; II, 431.

15. *Cf.*, Records, II, 183, 389, 417, 430–31, and 572.

16. See pp. 433–36 *supra*.

17. For a more detailed discussion of the Federal Convention's attitude toward this branch of the English law of the royal prerogative, see chapter xv hereof.

18. *Cf.*, Story, J., in *United States* v. *Coolidge*, 1 Gall. 488, 492 (1813).

19. For a more detailed discussion of the Federal Convention's attitude toward the English law of treason, see the opening pages of chapter xvi hereof.

20. See chapter xvi hereof.

21. Records, II, 564.

22. He wrote to Richard Henry Lee, in Congress, on the day the Convention arose. This appears from Lee's reply to him, under date of October 16, 1787. The character of the letter which Randolph had written is also inferable from the general tenor of Lee's reply. Lee, II, 450.

23. See Elliott, III *passim;* especially 207.

24. Randolph patronized, in the fall of 1788, the New York proposal of another convention to make changes in the Constitution. See Edmund Randolph to James Madison, August 13, 1788, and Francis Corbin to James Madison, October 21, 1788, in Library of Congress, Madison Papers, IX, 77, and X, 24. Corbin's opinion of Randolph was that "he [was] too Machiavellian and not Machiavellian enough."

25. ASP, 21–36.

26. 1 Stat. at L. 92; 28 U.S.C. § 725.

27. ASP, 25 and 33.

28. Wharton, 49, 78 *et seq.;* Conway, *Omitted Chapters of History Disclosed in the Life and Papers of Edmund Randolph* (New York, 1888), 182–83.

29. Wharton, 49 footnote.

30. So far as the writer is aware Madison's letter is not in existence. The statement in the text is an inference from Randolph's reply. See Conway, *op. cit.* note 28 *supra,* 184–86.

31. *Ibid.* The contemporary estimate of Randolph, among his fellow Virginians, was that he was a good deal of a trimmer. See DHC, IV, 321, 323, 579, and 787. Cf., note 24 *supra.* The surviving evidence undoubtedly bears this estimate out.

32. References to Virginia's preparations—building an armory in Richmond, distributing public arms to the citizenry to resist the national government, arming cavalry and infantry—may be found in *The Winchester* [Va.] *Gazette,* for May 29, 1799, and February 19, 1800. In the former issue, there is also a reference to similar measures in Tennessee. Winchester was a staunchly Federalist community, and the *Gazette* was a Federalist paper. Other Federalist references to the subject are: Hamilton, X, 330; and King, III, 147–48. Years later, John Randolph confessed, on the floor of Congress, that Virginia's measures had, in fact, been in preparation to resist the national government if the Federalists won the election of 1800, as the Federalists at the time believed. Annals, XXX, 795, 802, and 805.

33. See pp. 594–98 *supra.*

34. A late example of this is a letter, of August 1824, from James Madison, to Peter S. Du Ponceau, of Philadelphia, who had sent Madison a copy of a book he had just published, in which he had taken the position that the Common Law was a law of the United States for the purpose of deciding cases in the United States courts, but not for that of giving them jurisdiction. Madison declined to agree that the Common Law was a national law for any purpose. Madison, IX, 198. It must be confessed that, if the matter be looked at from Madison's point of view, he showed good sense. Du Ponceau made a strong case for the affirmative branch of his thesis; but his only "reasons" for excluding the Common Law from among "the Laws of the United States" in Article III were these: "That [section 2 of Article III] is altogether restrictive, and was intended to confine the powers of the federal judiciary within certain fixed bounds, and therefore its language is to be taken in its natural restrictive sense, and not as extending authority beyond the bounds prescribed by the

instrument. [And] that by the words 'the laws of the United States,' the framers of the Constitution only meant the statutes which should be enacted by the national Legislature; otherwise, if they had intended to include the common law, they would have expressed themselves otherwise, and no doubt have also specifically described those powers under the common law which they meant to confide to the judiciary, for the general expression *all cases arising under the common law* would have given them such a wide and undefined extent of jurisdiction as cannot be supposed to have been in contemplation." Du Ponceau, *A Dissertation on the Nature and Extent of the Jurisdiction of the Courts of the United States* (Philadelphia, 1824), 98–99. In short, Du Ponceau did not think the expression, "the Laws of the United States," in Article III, covered the Common Law, because he did not think it did; but Du Ponceau's unsupported opinion was not enough for Madison.

35. Elliot, IV, 561 *et seq.*

36. Tucker, Bk. I, Pt. 1, App., p. 378 *et seq.*, especially 406–7.

37. Elliot, IV, 565–66. In addition, Madison intimated, inconsistently, that there would be doubt that the Common Law could be changed even by Congress. *Ibid.*

38. Tucker, Bk. I, Pt. 1, App., pp. 424–26.

39. The quoted words are from the trial of Aaron Burr. At one point, Marshall refers to the Common Law as "that generally recognized and long established law, which forms the substratum of the laws of every state"—that is, every state in the Union. 2 *Burr's Trial* (Philadelphia, 1808), 482. At another point, he refers to the statute of treasons of 25 Edward III as "a very old statute of that country whose language is our language, and whose laws form the substratum of our laws"—that is, in this instance, national laws. *Ibid.*, 402.

40. 2 Salkeld 411 (1693); *cf., Commonwealth* v. *Chapman*, 13 Metc. 68, 71–74 (Mass., 1848).

41. Grotius, *De Jure Belli et Pacis*, 1. 2, c. 9, secs. 8 and 9.

42. For a lucid expression of this point of view, see *Lynch* v. *Clarke*, 1 Sandf. Ch. (N.Y.) 583, 646 *et seq.* (1844).

43. According to James Wilson, as reported by Madison in the Federal Convention, the Continental Court of Appeals in Cases of Captures (*cf.,* Article IX of the Confederation) decided for itself "facts as well as law & Common as well as Civil law"; that is, "Common law" in the sense of those questions which the Common Law decided in its own peculiar way, "as well as Civil law" in the sense of those questions, of maritime law and the law of nations generally, in which the Common Law adopted the Civil Law as being the common law of the world. Records, II, 431.

44. *Cf.,* James A. Bayard, of Delaware, in Congress in 1802, in the debate on the repeal of the Judiciary Act of 1801: "I have never contended that the whole of the common law attached to the constitution, but only such parts as were consonant to the nature and spirit of our government. We have nothing to do with the law of the Ecclesiastical establishment, nor with any principle of monarchial tendency. *What belongs to us, and what is unsuitable, is a question for the sound discretion of the judges.*" *Debates on the Judiciary* (Albany, 1802), 373.

45. Elliot, IV, 566; Tucker, Bk. I, Pt. 1, App., pp. 424–26.

46. Cases between foreigners on *foreign* causes of action would have come in as cases arising under that branch of the law of nations which we now know as the conflict of laws; for the law of nations, in all its departments, was

deemed part of the Common Law. See Wilson, II, 45. The omission from the mandatory categories, of the type of case between foreigners stated in the text, seems somewhat anomalous. Of rare occurrence, it was probably overlooked.

NOTES TO CHAPTER XXI

1. Blackstone, I, 253.

2. Records, II, 133; *cf.*, I, 22 and II, 147.

3. Charles Warren, *New Light on the History of the Federal Judiciary Act of 1789*, 37 HLR, 49, 81–83 (1923); Henry Friendly, *The Historic Basis of the Diversity Jurisdiction*, 41 HLR, 483 (1928). The ideas of these writers are repeated with approval in Felix Frankfurter, *Distribution of Judicial Power between United States and State Courts*, 13 CORNELL LAW QUARTERLY, 499, 520 (1928).

4. Friendly, *op. cit.* note 3 *supra*, 487.

5. Elliot, III, 533.

6. Madison, II, 344–52.

7. As already indicated, there is a suggestion to this effect in Blackstone, I, 258–59, with respect particularly to letters of marque and reprisal, "the prerogative of granting which," says Blackstone, "is nearly related, and plainly derived from, that . . . of making war; this being indeed only an incomplete state of hostilities, and generally ending in a formal denunciation of war." "These letters," he goes on, "are grantable by the laws of nations, whenever the subjects of one state are oppressed and injured by those of another; and justice is denied by that state to which the oppressor belongs. In this case letters of marque and reprisal (words used as synonimous; and signifying the latter a taking in return, the former the passing the frontiers in order to such taking) may be obtained, in order to seise the bodies or goods of the subjects of the offending state, until satisfaction be made wherever they happen to be found." Blackstone relied on Grotius, *De Jure Belli et Pacis*, 1. 3, c. 2, secs. 4 and 5 (*q.v.*), where Grotius discusses the use of reprisals in cases, among others, of failure, on the part of a national of one state, to obtain judgment, in the courts of another state, for a debt due from a national of such latter state; and of judgment entered, in such a case, contrary to law.

8. See Blackstone excerpts in note 39 to chapter ii hereof.

9. See pp. 578–79 *supra*.

10. See p. 572 *supra*.

11. See pp. 572–73 *supra*.

12. See *Talbot* v. *Seeman*, 1 Cranch (U.S.) 1, 43 (1801); *The Charming Betsy*, 2 Cranch (U.S.) 64, 118 (1804), and *The Nereide*, 9 Cranch (U.S.) 388, 422–23 (1815).

13. 1 Dall. (Pa.) 269, 270 (1788).

14. Tucker, Bk. I, Pt. 1, App., pp. 181–84, 407, and 421.

15. Records, II, 157. The paper referred to is apparently an excerpt from the so-called New Jersey Plan. Comparison with other versions of that plan indicates that Wilson added to the contents of it, certain items which he underlined, apparently as a mnemonic device. The item quoted in the text is one of these. The inference is that he intended to add these underlined items to his own draft. The "diversity" cases are the only categories of judicial jurisdiction in his own draft that answer to the description. See Records, II, 163, 173.

16. Wilson, I, 374–76 and 378–80.

17. See pp. 321–22 *supra*.

18. See *Cohens* v. *Virginia*, 6 Wheat. (U.S.) 264 (1821).
19. *No. LXXXII.*
20. ASP, 23.
21. Tucker, Bk. I, Pt. 1, App., pp. 183–84.
22. 1 Wheat. (U.S.) 304, 315 (1816).
23. Tucker, Bk. I, Pt. 1, App., p. 407.
24. See p. 601 *supra.*
25. Tucker, Bk. I, Pt. 1, App., pp. 404–5.
26. See pp. 606–7 *supra.*
27. *Blankard* v. *Galdy*, 2 Salkeld 411 (1693); cf., *Commonwealth* v. *Chapman*, 13 Metc. 68, 71–74 (Mass., 1848).
28. This is the view held by the Supreme Court, in the cases falling within the statutory "federal-question" jurisdiction of the lower national courts. *Siler* v. *Louisville & Nashville Railroad Company*, 213 U.S. 175 (1909).
29. 10 Pa. Stat. at L., 55; cf., 14 *ibid.*, 117.
30. SEAALH, I, 842–43.
31. The notion that judicial jurisdiction over questions of state law, and even of common law, is abnormal, accidental, and exceptional, has become common, in recent decades. See Holmes, J., in *Kuhn* v. *Fairmont Coal Co.*, 215 U.S. 349 (1910). Cf., Thayer, *The Case of Gelpcke* v. *Dubuque*, 4 HLR, 311, 316 (1891); Friendly, *The Historic Basis of Diversity Jurisdiction*, 41 HLR, 483 (1928).
32. See chapters xxv and xxvi hereof.
33. Jefferson, IX, 86, 87.
34. Elliot, IV, 566.
35. Tucker, Bk. I, Pt. 1, App., p. 380.
36. ASP, 36; cf., 25.
37. Records, II, 564.
38. Cf., James Madison's statement, in the early days of the Federal Convention, before the provision in the Supremacy Clause was decided upon, that "the judges of the state"—*i.e.*, the state whose law is concerned—"must give the state laws their operation, although the law abridges the rights of the national government." Records, I, 169.

NOTES TO CHAPTER XXII

1. Before the decision of *Barron* v. *Baltimore*, 7 Pet. (U.S.) 243 (1833), lawyers, with good reason, considered most of the first nine amendments, because of the generality of their terms, as applying both to the states and the nation. See p. 1076 of the text hereof.
2. N.H. Ct. Gaz., July 5, 1787.
3. There were many expressions of this point of view during the ratification campaign. The following, from the letters of "Giles Hickory"—probably, Noah Webster—in *The American Magazine* for December 1787, is typical: "A Bill of Rights against the encroachments of Kings and Barons, or against any power independent of the people, is perfectly intelligible; but a Bill of Rights against the encroachments of an elective Legislature, that is, against our *own* encroachments on *ourselves*, is a curiosity in government." In the issue of this periodical for January 1788, the same writer declared it incontrovertible that "a Legislature should be competent to pass any law that the public safety and interest may require." The right of free election was the true protection of all civil rights.

4. The state constitutions containing formal bills of rights were those of New Hampshire, Massachusetts, Pennsylvania, Delaware, Maryland, and North Carolina. Virginia had a long and formal bill of rights, in separate form, which apparently was not very religiously observed, and the exact status of which was considered dubious. See chapter xxvii hereof. Certain of the other states—South Carolina, New Jersey, and New York—had made provision, in the body of their constitutions, much as the original Constitution of the United States did, for a few rights. South Carolina went furthest in this respect. In Connecticut and Rhode Island, they had no written constitution, unless the old colonial charters be considered as such. See *The Constitutions of the Several Independent States of America* (2d ed.; *Boston*, 1785). The foregoing facts were pointed out, during the ratification campaign, in a rather widely copied item which appeared in *The* [Baltimore] *Maryland Journal*, on December 25, 1787, with a correction following, on December 28. But the dark insinuations continued.

5. The reference, of course, is chiefly to what has been done under the Fifth Amendment, in the name of what is somewhat strangely called *"substantive due process."* There are also the recent picketing decisions, which, though relating to the states, apply, "in principle," as well to the nation. They hold that picketing "struck" employers is a right of free speech. *Thornhill v. Alabama*, 310 U.S. 88 (1940); *Carlson v. California*, 310 U.S. 106 (1940); and *Bakery & Pastry Drivers & Helpers v. Wohl*, 315 U.S. 769 (1942). And employers, logically, have urged that all their actions involving speech in labor relations are rights of free speech, too. But the Court thinks there is a difference. *National Labor Relations Board v. Virginia Electric & Power Co.*, 314 U.S. 468, 477 (1941).

6. Records, II, 340–42, 587–88.

7. Records, II, 21, 25–27, 366–67, 493, 495, 497, 499.

8. Annals, I, 761; Gaz. U.S., August 22, 1789.

9. *Journal of the House of Representatives of the United States* (New York, 1789), 108.

10. *Journal of the First Session of the Senate of the United States* (New York, 1789), 122.

11. Gaz. U.S., August 22, 1789; Annals, I, 761.

12. Records, II, 21 and 25–27; III, 615–16.

13. James Madison wrote Edmund Randolph, on April 12, 1789, that "Conneticut [was] least inclined [toward] amendments"; that "a paper under the signature of a Citizen of New Haven unfold[ed] Mr. Sherman's opinions." "The Letters of a Citizen of New Haven" may be found in N.H. Ct. Gaz., for December 4 and 24, 1788, and in Ford, *Essays on the Constitution*.

14. *Loc. cit.* note 11 *supra*.

15. Annals, I, 761.

16. Sherman was apparently arguing by analogy with the doctrine of *The Case of Sutton's Hospital*, 10 Coke's Reports, 1a (1615), at 30b, that the mere creation of a corporation, without more, vests it with all customary powers for the attainment of the ends for which it was created.

17. *Cf.*, Oxford, on "expressly," 1a and 1b. See, also, Webster on "expressly."

18. *Cf.*, Oxford, on "express," noting what is said of the combined sense in legal usage.

19. Elliot, II, 547, 550; Am. Mus., III, 419, 421 (May 1788); Ann. Gaz., May 1, 1788.

20. Ph. Ind. Gaz., August 29, 1789.

21. *Ibid.*, September 9, 1789.

22. *Ibid.*

23. *Ibid.*, August 29, 1789.

24. Lee, II, 486.

25. See Letters, VIII, 678–79; Lee, II, 423, 424, 427, 432, 433. The views of these men will be considered fully at later points.

26. Lee, II, 440, 442 (including footnote), 445, 450–55, 457.

27. Lee, II, 463–74, especially 471.

28. The amendment covering state powers actually recommended by the Virginia Convention was in favor of "retained" powers, not "reserved" powers; but the pro-Constitutionalists succeeded in defeating, undoubtedly by a narrow margin, the proposal of the opposition, to include the word "expressly." See Elliot, III, 587–63; especially 601, 622–23, and 659. The amendment finally recommended read as follows: "That each state in the Union shall respectively retain every power, jurisdiction, and right, which is not by this Constitution delegated to the Congress of the United States, or to the departments of the federal government." If the actual provisions of the Constitution are considered, the amendment presents great difficulties of interpretation, whatever sense be given to the word "delegate," as will be seen from a reading of the further discussion in the text. Madison's substitution, in it, of the word "reserved" made it easy to interpret as a declaration in favor of concurrent state powers. This, of course, was by no means what the radical "States' Rights" Virginians, like Lee and Grayson, in 1789, wanted.

29. The Virginia Senators' letter may be conveniently found in Lee, II, 507, or DHC, V, 217. It was given to the newspapers at the time and widely copied from paper to paper. Lee wrote a personal letter to Patrick Henry, on September 14th, of much the same tenor as the joint letter which he and Grayson wrote to the Virginia legislature. In it, he said, in part: "The most essential danger from the present system arises, in my opinion, from its tendency to a consolidated government, instead of a union of Confederated States." Lee, II, 502.

30. *Loc. cit.* note 10 *supra.*

31. Peters wrote to Madison on August 24, 1789, as follows: "I have to acknowledge your favour of the 19th. I am obliged by your information & acknowledge that some of your Reasons [for amendments] are the best that can be given. They are such therefore as I knew you could give. But many of them are founded on Apprehensions which forgive me for saying I think too highly wrought. I believe that a firmness in adhering to our Constitution 'till at least it had a longer Trial would have silenced Anti federalists sooner than by magnifying their Importance by Acknowledgments on our Part & of ourselves holding up a Banner for them to rally to. All you offer comes not up to their Desires & as long as they have one unreasonable Wish ungratified the Clamour will be the same. I know there are among them good Characters but many of those who lead do it not from other Motives than to make or keep themselves Heads of a Party. Our Character abroad will never acquire Consistency while Foreigners see us wavering even in our Government about the very Instrument under which that Government acts. In short I fear worse Consequences from the good Disposition of the Conciliators (especially now when some Things done by Congress have startled even many Federalists) than I apprehend from an Adherence to the System. But I have agreed with myself not to enter far into a Subject which you have so long considered. . . ." DHC, V, 192–93.

32. Peters Papers, IX, 96, Hist. Soc. of Pa.

33. *Ibid.*, 102.

34. Annals, I, 433 and 441.

35. As stated in a footnote to the text at page 702 hereof (*q.v.*), the *Annals of Congress* for 1789 are copied from the contemporaneously published *Congressional Register*, of Thomas Lloyd. The length and particularity of the report of Madison's speech upon introducing his proposed amendments can leave no doubt, when compared with Lloyd's reporting generally, that it was the product of co-operation between Madison and Lloyd.

36. DHC, V, 334, 337–38.

37. Annals, I, 463–64 and 496.

38. 9 Johns. (N.Y.) 507.

39. 9 Wheat. (U.S.) 1.

40. 9 Johns. (N.Y.) 573–75.

41. *Ibid.*, 565–66.

42. 1 Paine (U.S. Circ. Ct.) 79, 83.

43. 5 Wheat. (U.S.) 1, 48–50; *cf., ibid.*, 8.

44. Story, I, 395 *et seq.*, and III, 752 *et seq.*

45. 9 Johns. (N.Y.) 575.

46. 9 Wheat. (U.S.) 209–10.

47. 11 Pet. (U.S.) 102, 139.

48. 16 Pet. (U.S.) 539. *Cf.*, note 54 to chapter vi *supra*.

49. 5 How. (U.S.) 504, 582, 583. *Cf.*, pp. 154–55 and 287–88 hereof *supra*.

50. *United States* v. *DeWitt*, 9 Wall. (U.S.) 41 (1870); *Kidd* v. *Pearson*, 128 U.S. 1 (1888); and *United States* v. *Knight Co.*, 156 U.S. 1 (1895), are typical cases; but the cases that might be cited are, of course, legion.

51. 117 U.S. 697, 705 (1864).

52. See, for example, the view of "the [Anti-]Federalist Judge, Samuel Chase," in *United States* v. *Worrall*, 2 Dall. (U.S.) 384, 393–94 (1798): "The departments of the [national] government can never assume any power, that is not *expressly* granted by [the Constitution]." Also, the language of the Jeffersonian judge, William Johnson, of South Carolina, in the judicial travesty called *United States* v. *Hudson and Goodwin*, 7 Cranch (U.S.) 32, 33 (1812): "The powers of the general government are made up of concessions from the several states—whatever is not *expressly* given to the former, the latter expressly reserve." This was one of those cases in which Chief Justice Marshall, "hav[ing] the misfortune to differ from th[e] Court, acquiesce[d] silently in its opinion." *Cf.*, *Bank of the United States* v. *Dandridge*, 12 Wheat. (U.S.) 64, 90 (1827); and see pp. 767, 782, and 1356–58 hereof. By 1819, he had succeeded, however, in getting his Court part way back on the reservation; for, in *McCulloch* v. *Maryland*, 4 Wheat. (U.S.) 316, 406 (1819), he was able to declare, without exciting any dissent, that there was nothing, either in the Constitution or the Tenth Amendment, "which required that everything granted sh[ould] be *expressly and minutely described*." The case, nevertheless, has its inconsistencies. *Cf.*, 406–7 of Marshall's opinion with 381–82 of argument of counsel; and, then, with the statement, at 405, that the government is one "of enumerated powers."

53. 7 Wall. (U.S.) 71, 76 (1868).

54. Examples are *Hammer* v. *Dagenhart*, 247 U.S. 251, 275 (1918), and *United States* v. *Butler*, 297 U.S. 1, 63 (1936).

55. Oxford, on "delegate," *v.*, 3.

56. Articles II and IX.

57. Blackstone, I, 252.

58. *Ibid.*, 266–67.

59. *Ibid.*, 268.

60. *Ibid.*, 60; Rutherforth, II, 325, and 330–32.

61. Rutherforth, II, 331–32.

62. Oxford, on "retain," *v.*, I, 3. See, also, Webster.

63. The essence of a technical "exception" is that "the thing excepted is exempted and doth not pass by the grant, neither is it parcel of the thing granted." 1 Sheppard's *Touchstone* (7th ed.; London, 1820), 77. *Cf.*, next note *infra*.

64. "A reservation is a clause of a deed whereby the . . . grantor . . . doth reserve some new thing to himself out of that which he granted before [in the deed. A reservation] doth differ from an exception, which is ever a part of the thing granted, and of a thing in *esse* at the time, but [a reservation] is of a thing newly created or reserved out of a thing [granted] that was not in *esse* before, so that [a reservation] doth always reserve that which was not before. . . ." *Ibid.*, 80.

65. *Op. cit.* note 9 *supra*, 108, 109; *op. cit.* note 10 *supra*, 102, 103, 106, 122, 123. See, also, the reprint of the proposed amendments, as passed by the House, on August 24th, in Gaz. U.S., August 29, 1789.

66. According to Annals, I, 761, 767, 768, Carroll, of Maryland, moved the addition of the words "or to the people" in committee of the whole House, on August 18th, and the addition was agreed to. Yet it would appear, from the record therein for August 21st, that it had not been agreed to. For Gerry, of Massachusetts, is represented as trying unsuccessfully, on that date, in the House, to have both "expressly" and "or to the people" added to the amendment. Immediately afterward, Sherman, of Connecticut, is represented as moving the addition of "or to the people" alone; and the House, as agreeing to Sherman's motion. But this is not in accord with the official *Journal. Loc. cit.* next note *supra*.

67. There are a few exceptions where the fact that the legislatures are meant is plain from the context; as, for example, the provision in sec. 10 of Article I, that "no State shall pass any Bill of Attainder, ex post facto Law, or Law impairing the Obligation of Contracts."

68. *Op. cit.* note 63 *supra*, 80.

69. See *Lane County* v. *Oregon*, 7 Wall. (U.S.) 71, 76 (1868); also, arguments of counsel for appellees in *United States* v. *Sprague*, 282 U.S. 716 (1931). The Virginia Senate, in 1789, also took this view. "It [was] not declared to be the people of the respective States," it complained, "but the expression applie[d] to the people generally as citizens of the United States, and le[ft] it doubtful what powers [were] reserved to the State Legislatures." *Journal of the Senate of the Commonwealth of Virginia for 1789* (Richmond, 1828), 64.

70. See Article XIII.

71. Blackstone, I, 44, 46.

NOTES TO CHAPTER XXIII

1. N.Y. Jour., January 31, and February 7 and 14, 1788.

2. See p. 633 *supra*.

3. Annals, I, 815; Gaz. U.S., September 5, 1789.

4. Jackson's exact words on this point, as reported, were: "But should there be some exceptions for the present, yet, sir, the precedent is so forcible, for it

goes so far as even to admit of constructions on some of the articles"—that is, some of the parts of the section—"that by some means or other those articles will in time be totally lost." "Those articles" ought probably to read "those exceptions," and it seems not unlikely that Jackson's words were, in certain other respects, somewhat garbled in the reporting; but the general drift of what he had to say seems sufficiently clear.

5. *Journal of William Maclay* (New York, 1890), 117.

6. 3 Cranch (U.S.) 1.

7. 14 Pa. Stat. at L. 232. The entire statute is given in the report of *Huidekoper's Lessee v. Douglass,* in 3 Cranch.

8. *Commonwealth v. Coxe,* 4 Dall. (Pa.) 170, 198.

9. *Ewalt's Lessee v. Highlands,* 4 Dall. (Pa.) 161; *Balfour's Lessee v. Meade, ibid.* (U.S. Circ. Ct.) 361.

10. 15 Pa. Stat. at L. 153; *cf., Campbell v. Galbreath,* 1 Watts (Pa.) 70, 84.

11. Robert Morris was one of these. *Cf., Morris's Lessee v. Neighman,* 2 Yeates (Pa.) 450.

12. James Wilson was a large purchaser. Alexander Dallas and Jared Ingersoll were the owners of warrants, at a later date; but whether they were original purchasers or not, is not known. See Evans, *The Holland Land Company* (1924), Buffalo Historical Society Publications, XXVIII, 125.

13. For facts about the Holland Land Company, see Evans, *op. cit.* next note *supra;* and Tiffany, *Harm Jan Huidekoper* (Cambridge, 1904), chap. iii and Appendix I, the latter being a brief sketch of the Holland Land Company's West Allegheny enterprise, written by Harm Jan Huidekoper's son, Alfred, in 1876. The account in the text is based, to some extent, upon these three accounts. As they are all short, systematic page references to them have not been attempted.

14. For the Population Company's prospectus, see *Dunlap's* [Philadelphia] *American Daily Advertiser,* May 11, 1792.

15. Evans, *op. cit.* note 12 *supra,* 109–10. Evans' account is an interesting and apparently reliable one, except where points of law are involved. *Cf., ibid.,* 154.

16. 4 Dall. (Pa.) 175.

17. *The* [Meadville, Pa.] *Crawford Weekly Messenger,* August 28, 1805; *The* [Erie (Presque Isle)] *Mirror,* September 15, 1810.

18. 4 Dall. (Pa.) 170. The date given by Dallas for this case is 1800; but the case was decided on the date stated in the text. See *The* [Philadelphia] *Aurora,* October 5, 1801.

19. See Evans, *op. cit.* note 12 *supra,* 125 and 126.

20. *Cf., Campbell v. Galbreath,* 1 Watts (Pa.) 70, and Justice Huston's dissenting opinion in *Barnes v. Irvine,* 5 Watts (Pa.) 557.

21. This case is reported in 4 Dall. (Pa.) 209, as tried in May 1800, and in 2 Yeates (Pa.) 450, it is reported as tried in May 1799. Which date is correct, is not known.

22. 4 Dall. (Pa.) 237.

23. 17 Pa. Stat. at L. 133.

24. 4 Dall. (Pa.) 238 n. *Cf.,* Evans, *op. cit.* note 12 *supra,* 136.

25. 14 Pa. Stat. at L. 117.

26. 18 Pa. Stat. at L. 61, 64.

27. *Cf., West v. American Telephone & Telegraph Co.,* 311 U.S. 223 (1940); *Fidelity Trust Co. v. Field, ibid.,* 169 (1940); and *Erie R.R. Co. v. Tompkins,* 304 U.S. 64 (1938).

28. 4 Dall. (Pa.) 240.

29. 5 Watts (Pa.) 557, 558.

30. Justice Washington said, on circuit, in reference to the Supreme Court's Huidekoper decision, that it was to be "consider[ed] as the law of the land"; that is, of course, "the law of the land [of Pennsylvania]." *Lessee of Huidekoper* v. *Douglass*, 1 Wash. C.C. 258, 259 (1805).

31. A copy of the unsuccessful Findley resolve is among the Huidekoper papers in the Crawford County Historical Society, at Meadville, Pennsylvania.

32. See *The* [Meadville, Pa.] *Crawford Weekly Messenger*, July 10, and September 25, 1806.

33. Pa. Arch., 4th Ser., IV, 550.

34. *The* [Meadville, Pa.] *Crawford Weekly Messenger*, May 8, August 28, September 11, 18, and 25, 1806.

35. There were other papers, besides *The Crawford Weekly Messenger*, which participated in this; but complete files of these other papers have not survived.

36. Hist. Soc. Pa., Sup. Ct. of Pa., Case 2, Box 13. The letter is reproduced as Appendix F to these volumes.

37. *Cf.*, pp. 84–89 hereof.

38. 1 Watts (Pa.) 101.

39. 1 Binn. (Pa.) 166.

40. *Cf.*, the statements by Shaler, J., to this effect, quoted in *Leasure* v. *Wilson*, 3 Watts (Pa.) 168, 169 (1834).

41. *Ross* v. *Barker*, 5 Watts (Pa.) 391, 397 (1836). See, also, *Leasure* v. *Wilson*, 3 Watts (Pa.) 168, 174–75 (1834).

42. 1 Watts (Pa.) 101.

43. *The Trial of Alexander Addison* (Lancaster, 1803), 138.

44. *Cf.*, Evans, *op. cit.* note 12 *supra*, 132 and note.

45. *Report of the trial and acquittal of Edward Shippen, . . . Jasper Yeates and Thomas Smith* (Lancaster, 1805).

46. *The Lancaster* [Pa.] *Intelligencer & Weekly Advertiser*, April 7, 1807; Pa. Arch., 4th Ser., IV, 604.

47. Two of these petitions are printed in ASP, 479–81. *Cf.*, pp. 575–76 *supra*. See, also, *The Lancaster* [Pa.] *Journal*, February 20, 1807, and December 1, 1810; and *The* [Meadville, Pa.] *Crawford Weekly Messenger*, January 22, 1807.

48. *Cf.*, "An Observer" in *The* [Erie (Presque Isle)] *Mirror*, August 20, 1808.

49. *Ibid.*, April 7, 1810; and *The* [Philadelphia] *Aurora*, January 12, 13, and 29, and February 14, 1810.

50. See PA. MAG. OF HIST. AND BIOG., XVI, 385, and Warren, *The Supreme Court in United States History* (Boston, 1922), I, 384.

51. Laws of Pa., 1810–11, chap. lxvii.

52. Laws of Pa., 1813–14, chap. xxvii; 1817–18, chap. clxvii.

53. Laws of Pa., 1813–14, chap. lxxii.

54. 7 S. & R. (Pa.) 303.

55. *Loc. cit.* note 40 *supra*.

56. See Evans, *op. cit.* note 12 *supra*, 120; Tiffany, *op. cit.* note 13 *supra*, 113, 115, and 163; and Gibson, C.J., in *Leasure* v. *Wilson*, 3 Watts (Pa.) 168 (1934).

57. Tiffany, *op. cit.* note 13 *supra*, 117–18.

58. *Ibid.*, 111, 123, 166, and 350; Evans, *op. cit.* note 12 *supra*, 154.

59. *Ibid.*, 159–60.

60. These are among the Huidekoper papers in the Crawford County Historical Society, at Meadville, Pennsylvania.

61. Hist. Soc. of Pa., Wallace Papers, VII, 22.

62. Evans, *op. cit.* note 12 *supra*, 161.

63. See, generally, Sedgwick and Wait, *The History of the Action of Ejectment in England and the United States*, SEAALH, III, 611.

64. *Loc. cit.* note 40 *supra*.

65. *Cf.*, discussion in chapter xxviii hereof.

66. Tiffany, *op. cit.* note 13 *supra*, 352.

67. 5 Watts (Pa.) 560.

68. 6 Pet. (U.S.) 291.

69. *Cf.*, his remarks on the Huidekoper case, in 1830, in the circuit-court case of *Thompson* v. *Phillips*, Baldwin (U.S. Circ. Ct.) 246, 285.

70. 1 Watts (Pa.) 70.

71. *Ibid.*, 121.

72. Tiffany, *op. cit.* note 13 *supra*, 131 and footnote.

73. 5 Watts (Pa.) 504–5.

74. *Ibid.*, and see Tiffany, *op. cit.* note 13 *supra*, 352. The act was No. 71 of the Laws of Pa., 1832–33.

75. 5 Watts (Pa.) 497.

76. *Ibid.*, 557.

77. *Ibid.*, 504–5.

78. *Loc. cit.* note 41 *supra*.

79. 3 Watts (Pa.) 175.

80. The sixth volume of Peters' United States Reports was registered for copyright on October 1, 1832. See Copyright Records of the Clerk's Office, U.S. District Court for the Eastern District of Pa., now in the Rare Book Division of the Library of Congress. It is, of course, possible that *Green* v. *Neal's Lessee* was published earlier, in some Pennsylvania newspaper; but in a rather extended examination of such papers, it was not encountered.

81. For an account of the Cherokee controversy, see Warren, *op. cit.* note 50 *supra*, Vol. I, chap. 19, and Beveridge, Vol. IV, chap. 10.

82. 3 Watts (Pa.) 174.

83. The act of the 3d of April 1833 sufficiently proves this.

NOTES TO CHAPTER XXIV

1. 1 Stat. at L. 73.

2. See pp. 592–93 *supra*.

3. *No. LXXXII.*

4. See p. 587 *supra*.

5. See excerpts from *The* [Philadelphia] *National Gazette,* January 5, and May 11, 1793, reprinted in Warren, I, 87 note.

6. ASP, 21.

7. A long and elaborate amendment of the Judiciary Article, evincing apparent confusion as to its meaning in certain respects, was proposed in Congress, by Egbert Benson, of New York, on March 3, 1791. Annals, II, 1976. Nothing more was ever heard of it.

8. ASP, 52.

9. 1 Stat. at L. 333.

10. ASP, 77.

11. *The Correspondence and Public Papers of John Jay* (New York, 1893), IV, 9.

12. *Ibid.*, 284, 285.

13. *The Life and Correspondence of Rufus King* (New York, 1894), I, 509.

14. Adams, IX, 137 and 144.

15. Annals, X, 643–47, 649, 665–66.

16. 2 Stat. at L. 89.

17. 2 Stat. at L. 132.

18. Jefferson, IX, 321, 340.

19. *Ibid.*, 86, 87.

20. *Ibid.*, 138, 139.

21. *Ibid.*, 73.

22. See pp. 560–61 *supra.*

23. 2 Stat. at L. 132.

24. *Ibid.*, 420, 421.

25. Warren, I, 400 and note.

26. Jefferson, XI, 153 note.

27. *Ibid.*, 152 note.

28. *Livingston* v. *Jefferson*, 1 Brock. (U.S. Circ. Ct.), 203; *cf.*, Beveridge, 100.

29. For an account of the delays that were encountered in filling Justice Cushing's place, see Warren, I, 400 *et seq.*

30. 7 Cranch (U.S.) 32.

31. *Commonwealth* v. *Clap*, 4 Mass. 163 (1809); *Commonwealth* v. *Morris*, 1 Va. Cas. 175 (1811).

32. 1 Stat. at L. 596.

33. Elliot, IV, 533, 536.

34. Jefferson, IX, 357.

35. The letter has also been published from Jefferson's draft copy in almost identical form in Jefferson, IX, 449.

36. William Dickinson, publisher of *The Lancaster* [Pa.] *Intelligencer & Weekly Advertiser*, was prosecuted and punished by McKean. See the issue of that paper for May 27, 1806, quoting from *The* [Philadelphia] *Aurora*, of May 17, 1806.

37. See *The People* v. *Croswell*, 3 Johns. Cases (N.Y., 1804) 337, a state prosecution for a libel of Thomas Jefferson.

38. An account, though not a very connected one, of these activities may be found in Purcell, *Connecticut in Transition* (Washington, 1918), chap. vi.

39. The Public Statute Laws of the State of Connecticut (Hartford, 1808), 355.

40. Conn. Cour., August 27, 1806.

41. Conn. Cour., May 21, 1806.

42. Jefferson, XI, 108, 111.

43. 2 Stat. at L. 156, 158.

44. *The* [Litchfield, Conn.] *Witness*, April 30, 1806.

45. W. W. Story, *Life and Letters of Joseph Story* (Boston, 1851), I, 299. There is, in the Library of Congress, a letter of John Marshall's, dated November 27, 1800, to some unknown correspondent, which indicates, though not with complete clarity, Marshall's views at that date. He began by denying that the Common Law of England had been "adopted by the Constitution." The affirmative of this proposition, which, he pointed out, the opposition were affecting to combat, was one, he declared, that he had never heard any one maintain. As indicated in chapter xx, this issue was, in fact, a mere fraudulent

pretense of the Jeffersonian party. "My own opinion," Marshall went on, "is that our ancestors brought with them the laws of England both statute and common law as existing at the settlement of each colony, so far as they were applicable to our situation. That on our revolution the preexisting law of each state remained so far as it was not chang[e]d either expressly or necessarily by the nature of the governments which we adopted. That on adopting the existing constitution of the United States the common and statute law of each state remained as before and that the principles of the common law of the state wou[l]d apply themselves to magistrates of the general as well as to magistrates of the particular government." It will be noted that Marshall does not say that "the principles of the [statute] law of the state wou[l]d apply themselves to magistrates of the general government." The only reason why the states' common law, as distinct from their statute law, could have been deemed so applicable was that their common law, unlike their statute law, was the *general* law of the country, applicable to everything of a state or national nature within it, when not displaced by a state or a national statute, as the case might be. "It was contended [by the Federalists]," Marshall concluded, "not that the common law gave the [national] courts jurisdiction in cases of sedition, but that the constitution gave it." What particular provision of "the constitution gave it," he did not say. In Aaron Burr's trial, in 1807, he spoke of the Common Law as "form[ing] the substratum of the laws of every state," and, at another point, as "forming the substratum of our [national] laws," as well. Cf., 2 *Burr's Trial* (Philadelphia, 1808), 402 and 481–82, and note 39 to chapter xx hereof.

46. Conn. Cour., April 23, and September 31 [October 1], 1806.

47. Annals, XX, 83.

48. *Ibid.*, XVI, 247–51; cf., *ibid.*, XIX, 1327–28, and XX, 75–89.

49. *Thomas Jefferson Correspondence Printed from the Originals in the Collections of William K. Bixby* (Boston, 1916), 137.

50. Jefferson, X, 366.

51. "Hampden," *A Letter to the President of the United States, touching the Prosecutions under his Patronage, before the Circuit Court in the District of Connecticut* (New Haven, 1808), iii.

52. *United States v. Reid*, 12 How. 361 (1851); *Funk v. United States,* 290 U.S. 371 (1933).

53. 2 *Burr's Trial* (Philadelphia, 1808), 481–82.

54. *Ex parte Kearney*, 7 Wheat. 38, 42 (1822).

55. 2 Stat. at L. 156, 159.

56. This was possible in the Connecticut prosecutions because the point involved was jurisdictional. *Cf., Ex parte Kearney*, 7 Wheat. 38 (1822).

57. 2 Stat. at L. 156, 157, 244, 471; cf., Conn. Cour.. May 13, 1807, and "Hampden," *op. cit.* note 51 *supra.*

58. Conn. Cour., September 31 [October 1], 1806.

59. Conn. Cour., May 13, 1807.

60. Conn. Cour., September 30, 1807.

61. The quotations in the paragraph of the text to which this note is appended are from a purported statement by Walker, in the handwriting of Henry Lee, now in the Library of Congress. The statement may be found conveniently, printed in full, in Malone, *Jefferson the Virginian* (Boston, 1948), 449–50.

62. *Op. cit.* note 49 *supra*, 114 and frontispiece.

63. Ford, *Thomas Jefferson and James Thompson Callender* (Brooklyn, 1897).

64. For the correspondence on this subject between Jefferson and Mrs. Adams, see Ford, *op. cit.* next note *supra*, 41–45; Jefferson, X, 84–90; *Letters of Mrs. Adams, the Wife of John Adams* (3d ed.; Boston, 1841), II, 247–60.

65. See, especially, the issue of October 27, 1802.

66. *Loc. cit.* note 62 *supra*.

67. "Hampden," *op. cit.* note 51 *supra*, iv.

68. Jefferson, XI, 108, 109–10.

69. 2 Stat. at L. 471.

70. "Hampden," *op. cit.* note 51 *supra*, 23; *cf.*, Annals, XIX, 1327–28.

71. Annals, XX, 79.

72. 7 Cranch (U.S.) 32.

73. *United States* v. *Coolidge*, 1 Gall. 488, 495 (1813).

74. Story, *op. cit.* note 45 *supra*, I, 299.

75. Pickering Papers, Mass. Hist. Soc., letters of March 20, and April 14, 1816, more fully quoted in Warren, I, 441.

76. Story, *op. cit.* note 45 *supra*, I, 247; *cf.*, also, letters reproduced at pp. 243–45.

77. *United States* v. *Coolidge*, 1 Gall. 488 (1813).

78. *United States* v. *Coolidge*, I Wheat. 415 (1816).

79. Story, *op. cit.* note 45 *supra*, I, 293–301.

80. 4 Stat. at L. 115.

81. 7 Cranch 603.

82. This appears to be the view in Warren, I, 444. Warren, it may be added, is mistaken as to certain of his facts.

83. 2 Shepherd, Va. Stat. at L., 22.

84. *Ibid.*, 140.

85. See Beveridge, II, 202–11, and IV, 144–67. In Groome, *Fauquier during the Proprietorship* (Richmond, 1927), 227–40, it is concluded that it was the Fairfax devisee, not the Marshall group, who was claiming contrary to the compromise. Groome's is, on the whole, the best account of the transactions leading up to the cases of *Fairfax's Devisee* v. *Hunter's Lessee* and *Martin* v. *Hunter;* yet it is very far, indeed, from being free from errors and inconsistencies. Beveridge brought out many new facts, but failed lamentably in putting these together. The accounts in Lerner, *John Marshall and the Campaign of History*, 39 COLUMBIA LAW REVIEW, 396, 415–16 (1939), and Myers, *History of the Supreme Court of the United States* (Chicago, 1925), are the sheerest fantasy.

86. See *Marshall* v. *Conrad*, 5 Call (Va.) 364, 385 (1805); and *Martin* v. *Hunter's Lessee*, 1 Wheat. 304, 356, 368 (1816).

87. 1 Munf. (Va.) 221; 5 Call (Va.) 402.

88. Harrison, *The Proprietors of the Northern Neck*, 34 VIRGINIA MAGAZINE OF HISTORY, 19, 27, 45, 48–49 (1926); *idem, Virginia Land Grants* (Richmond, 1925), 108; Groome, *op. cit.* note 85 *supra*, 68–69 and 242, note 35.

89. 11 Hening, Va. Stat. at L., 128–29.

90. *Marshall* v. *Conrad*, 5 Call (Va.) 364 (1805).

91. *Ibid.*, 366.

92. *Ibid.*, 365–66.

93. *Ibid.*, and 1 Munf. (Va.) 218, 219–20.

94. Groome, *op. cit.* note 85 *supra*, 232; and 5 Call (Va.), 370.

95. *Hunter* v. *Fairfax's Devisee*, 1 Munf. (Va.) 218, 222 (1810); Beveridge, IV, 148.

96. Record in the United States Supreme Court, in *Hunter* v. *Fairfax's*

Devisee, 3 Dall. 305 (1796); letter of David Hunter to Alexander Hamilton, July 7, 1796, Hamilton Papers, Library of Congress.

97. Beveridge, II, 202–11. It must be remembered that, at the date of the Fairfax-Marshall contract, Denny Fairfax, then sixty-eight years old, had been trying for ten years to get his estate.

98. 6 Cranch 286.

99. See sec. 22 of the Judiciary Act.

100. Record in the Supreme Court of the United States in *Hunter v. Fairfax's Devisee*, 3 Dall. 305 (1796); letter of Robert Morris to James M. Marshall, March 4, 1796, in Morris' Private Letter Book, in Library of Congress; Beveridge, II, 207.

101. *Hunter v. Fairfax's Devisee*, 3 Dall. 305 (1796), and record therein, in the Supreme Court of the United States; letter of David Hunter to Alexander Hamilton, July 7, 1796, in Hamilton Papers, Library of Congress.

102. Record in the Supreme Court of the United States, in *Hunter v. Fairfax's Devisee*, 3 Dall. 305 (1796).

103. These questions all appear in *Fairfax's Devisee v. Hunter's Lessee*, 7 Cranch 603 (1813).

104. 1 Munf. (Va.) 218, headnote and 223.

105. *Marshall v. Conrad*, 5 Call (Va.) 364, 397 (1805).

106. *Hunter v. Fairfax's Devisee*, 1 Munf. (Va.) 218, 232 et seq.

107. The four Virginia judges were St. George Tucker and William Nelson, Jr., in the trial court at Winchester, in 1794; and William Fleming and Spencer Roane, in the Court of Appeals, in 1810. The six national judges were James Iredell and Cyrus Griffin, in the Circuit Court at Richmond, in 1795; and Joseph Story, Brockholst Livingston, Gabriel Duvall, and William Johnson, in the Supreme Court in 1813. The point under the treaty of 1783, omitted in *Fairfax's Devisee v. Hunter's Lessee*, in 1813, was afterwards decided unanimously by the Supreme Court (Marshall, C.J., not sitting), in the manner the Fairfax title required, in *Orr v. Hodgson*, 4 Wheat. 453 (1819).

108. 1 Munf. (Va.) 218, and letter of John Marshall to James M. Marshall, April 1, 1804, Marshall Papers, Library of Congress.

109. The petition is in the possession of the Virginia State Library.

110. Madison, II, 214, 217, 218, 220, and 223–24. The legislatures of 1783 and 1784 had apparently intended loyally to observe the treaty. *Cf.*, 11 Hening, Va. Stat. at L., 289, 325, and 446; and Fleming, J., in *Hunter v. Fairfax's Devisee*, 1 Munf. (Va.) 235–37 (1810).

111. It was the period of reaction to the Jay treaty with Great Britain, of 1794. The Federalists were outnumbered in the legislature, about two to one. See Beveridge, II, 137.

112. 2 Shepherd, Va. Stat. at L., 22.

113. *Ibid.*

114. *Ibid.*

115. 2 Shepherd, Va. Stat. at L., 140; Beveridge, *loc. cit.* note 85 *supra*. Beveridge made the mistake of thinking that the conveyance of 1797 was unconnected with the purchase of 1793. Apparently, he was ignorant of the legislative resolution of December 23, 1797. *Cf.*, Groome, *loc. cit.* note 85 *supra*.

116. 1 Munf. (Va.) 218.

117. Patteson, *The Supreme Court of Appeals of Virginia*, 5 GREEN BAG. 310, 322 (1893).

118. 1 Munf. (Va.) 224.

119. *Marshall v. Conrad*, 5 Call (Va.) 364, 385 (1805).

120. 7 Cranch 603.

121. 1 Wheat. 304.

122. Marshall Papers, Library of Congress.

123. 5 Call (Va.) 364.

124. This was the date of publication of the fifth volume of Daniel Call's Virginia Reports, in which the report of *Marshall* v. *Conrad* appears.

125. 1 Munf. (Va.) 226. He also cites *Marshall* v. *Conrad* as then in manuscript. *Ibid.*

126. See articles on Peter Lyons and Paul Carrington, in *Dictionary of American Biography.*

127. Ambler, *Thomas Ritchie* (Richmond, 1913), 11.

128. 3 Shepherd, Va. Stat. at L., 299.

129. Acts of Va., 1810–11, p. 5. See, also, letter of St. George Tucker to James Monroe, April 2, 1811, in Virginia State Library, Richmond, Va.

130. Letters of St. George Tucker to William Fleming, May 10 and 11, 1809, in possession of the Virginia Historical Society, Richmond, Va. See, also, unpublished thesis on Spencer Roane, by Rex Beach, in the library of the University of Virginia, and other sources there cited. In his letter of resignation to Governor James Monroe (cited note 129 *supra*), Tucker gave other reasons.

131. Ambler, *op. cit.* note 127 *supra*, 27; Dodd, *Chief Justice Marshall and Virginia, 1813–1821*, 12 American Historical Review, 776 (1907); Wright, *Judge Spencer Roane*, 2 Virginia Law Register, 473, 480 (1896).

132. 5 Call 385, 392, 393.

133. 5 Call 385.

134. April 1, 1804, Marshall Papers, Library of Congress.

135. 5 Call 393, 394, 397 *et seq.*

136. 1 Munf. (Va.) 218, 232.

137. John Marshall to James M. Marshall, February 13, 1806, Marshall Papers, Library of Congress.

138. Record in the Supreme Court of the United States, in *Fairfax's Devisee* v. *Hunter's Lessee*, 7 Cranch 603 (1813).

139. *Fairfax's Devisee* v. *Hunter's Lessee*, 7 Cranch 603 (1813); cf., *Martin* v. *Hunter's Lessee*, 1 Wheat. 304, 360 (1816).

140. 6 Cranch 286.

141. 7 Cranch 632.

142. 1 Wheat. 304.

143. *Hunter* v. *Martin*, 4 Munf. (Va.) 1 (1815).

144. Cf., 4 Munf. (Va.) 55. His intimation that the court had erred could have related to nothing else, since *the court* had decided nothing else.

145. *Marbury* v. *Madison*, 1 Cranch 137 (1803). Cf., the discussion of the case in chapter xxix hereof.

146. 1 Wheat. 340–42.

147. 1 Wheat. 339.

148. 6 Wheat. 264 (1821).

149. 6 Wheat. 320.

150. 6 Wheat. 318.

151. 6 Wheat. 422.

152. 6 Pet. 291 (1832).

NOTES TO CHAPTER XXV

1. Stat. at L. 92.

2. *Wayman* v. *Southard*, 10 Wheat. 1, 24 (1825). See, also, *Golden* v. *Prince*, 3 Wash. C.C. 313, 316 (1814).

3. 1 Stat. at L. 93.

4. *Ibid.*, 123, 191, and 275.

5. 4 Stat. at L. 278; 17 *ibid.*, 196. Undoubtedly, the so-called "static conformity" of the "process" acts prior to that last cited was a result of doubts—well-founded on any rational view—of the constitutionality of an act such as that finally passed.

6. 3 Dall. 344 (1797).

7. Warren, *New Light on the History of the Federal Judiciary Act of 1789*, 37 HLR 49, 88, footnote 85 (1923).

8. This was necessarily true under the "process" act of 1792. *Cf.*, cases cited note 2 *supra.*

9. It was faintly and unsuccessfully contended by the appellant that section 12 of the Judiciary Act required the damages to be assessed by a jury. 3 Dall. 350.

10. Cases cited note 2 *supra.*

11. *Cf.*, pp. 570 and 573 *supra.*

12. 3 Dall. 425 (1799).

13. Warren, *op. cit.* note 7 *supra*, 85 *et seq.*

14. The case is cited in the argument (3 Dall. 455) by volume and page only: "2 Dall. 98."

15. 3 Wheat. 212 (1818).

16. *Kirk* v. *Smith*, 9 Wheat. 241, 297 (1824).

17. *Strother* v. *Lucas*, 12 Pet. 410, 452 (1838).

18. *Cf.*, note 5, and cases cited in note 2, *supra.*

19. 1 Cranch 45, 94–95 (1801).

20. 5 Cranch 22, 32 (1809). In this case, the state judicial usage antedated 1789.

21. 9 Cranch 87, 98 (1815).

22. 1 Wheat. 130, 132 (1816).

23. 2 Wheat. 316, 325 (1817).

24. 5 Wheat. 293, 302, 306, 307 (1820).

25. *Golden* v. *Prince*, 3 Wash. C.C. 313, 316–18 (1814), has sometimes been cited as establishing the contrary. See Jackson, *The Rise and Fall of Swift* v. *Tyson*, 24 AMERICAN BAR ASSOCIATION JOURNAL, 609, 610 (1938). The views of Justice Bushrod Washington in *Golden* v. *Prince* relate, however, only to statutes. They have to be read with the Huidekoper, Fairfax, and Martin decisions of the Supreme Court in mind.

26. 1 Gall. 371 (1812).

27. *Clark's Executors* v. *Van Reimsdyk*, 9 Cranch 153, 156–57 (1815).

28. 2 Gall. 105, 118, 137–38 (1814).

29. 8 Wheat. 495, 501, 515–16, 526, 534–35 (1823).

30. 1 Binn. (Pa.) 546 (1809).

31. 12 Wheat. 153 (1827).

32. See p. 605 *supra.*

33. *Anderson* v. *Jackson* ex dem. *Eden*, 16 Johns. (N.Y.) 382, 398 (1819).

34. See the opinions of Chancellor Kent and Senator Hammond, in the case cited in the note next above.

35. 1 Johns. 440 (1806).

36. *Jackson* v. *Blanshaw*, 3 Johns. 289 (1808); *Executors of Moffat* v. *Strong*, 10 Johns. 12 (1813); *Jackson* v. *Staats*, 11 Johns. 337 (1814).

37. 16 Johns. 382.

38. *Wilkes* v. *Lion*, 2 Cow. (N.Y.) 333, 342 (1823).

39. *Blight's Lessee* v. *Rochester*, 7 Wheat. 550 (1822).

40. 2 Pet. 170, 179 (1829).

41. *Cf.*, 2 Pet. 172.

42. 2 Pet. 586 (1829).

43. 2 Pet. 179.

44. See *Wells* v. *Whitehead*, 15 Wend. (N.Y.) 527, 530–31 (1836); *Halliday* v. *McDougall*, 20 Wend. 81, 84 (1838); s.c., 22 Wend. 264, 272 (1839); *Allen v. Merchants Bank of New York*, 22 Wend. 215, 226 (1839); *Commercial Bank of Kentucky* v. *Varnum*, 49 N.Y. 269, 275 (1872).

45. 2 Wheat. 66 (1817).

46. 2 Wheat. 75–76.

47. 10 Wheat. 152 (1825).

48. 10 Wheat. 159–60.

49. 11 Wheat. 361, 366–69 (1826).

50. 3 Wheat. 541 (1818).

51. See Warren, II, chap. 17.

52. Marshall Papers, Library of Congress.

53. 1 Brock. C.C. 539, 543 (1822).

54. *Cf.*, pp. 575–76 and 732–33 *supra*.

55. *Loc. cit.* note 52 *supra*.

56. See, for example, his letter of July 13, 1821, to Justice Story, Proc. Mass. Hist. Soc., 2d Ser., XIV, 328–31, reprinted, in its most essential part, in Beveridge, IV, 365–66.

57. 6 Pet. iii.

58. 6 Pet. 291 (1832).

59. 1 Wheat. 476 (1816).

60. 2 Pet. 240 (1829).

61. 6 Pet. 300–301.

62. 6 Pet. 298.

63. *Cf.*, Justice Henry Baldwin in *Thompson* v. *Phillips*, Baldwin C.C. 246, 285 (1830).

64. 8 Pet. 591, 658 (1834).

65. 8 Pet. 687.

66. 2 Sumner C.C. 366, 377–78 (1836).

67. 3 Sumner C.C. 220, 225 (1838).

68. 3 Sumner C.C. 270, 276–77 (1838).

69. 1 McLean C.C. 275, 277–78, 281 (1836).

70. *Waters* v. *The Merchants Louisville Insurance Co.*, 11 Pet. 213 (1837).

71. 1 McLean C.C. 540, 547 (1839).

72. 2 McLean C.C. 44, 52 *et seq.* (1839).

73. 2 McLean C.C. 589, 591–92 (1841); *cf.*, *Austen* v. *Miller*, 5 McLean C.C. 153, 157 (1850).

74. 2 Wheat. 66 (1817).

75. 2 Pet. 170 (1829).

76. *Carlisle* v. *Wishart*, 11 Ohio, 172, 190–92 (1842).

77. 16 Pet. 495.

78. 16 Pet. 1.

79. *Loc. cit.* notes 74 and 75 *supra*.

80. See record in the case, National Archives, District Court Records, Southern District of New York, Law 1790–1859, T. 2422.

81. 16 Pet. 18–19.

82. 16 Pet. 511–12.

83. 18 How. 517, 520–21 (1855).

84. 5 How. 144 (1847).
85. 15 Pet. 449 (1841).
86. 1 Wall. 175 (1863).
87. Cf., *Stalker* v. *McDonald*, 6 Hill 93 (N.Y., 1843).
88. 14 Wall. 661, 665–66 (1871).
89. For a clear statement of this strange theory of the Constitutional relationship between the state and national judiciaries, see *Burgess* v. *Seligman*, 107 U.S. 20, 33 (1883).

NOTES TO CHAPTER XXVI

1. Blackstone, III, 441.
2. *Erie R.R. Co.* v. *Tompkins*, 304 U.S. 64 (1938).
3. *Six Companies* v. *Highway District*, 311 U.S. 180 (1940); *West* v. *American T. & T. Co.*, 311 U.S. 223 (1940); *Stoner* v. *New York Life Insurance Co.*, 311 U.S. 464 (1940).
4. *Fidelity Union Trust Co.* v. *Field*, 311 U.S. 169 (1940); *King* v. *Order of United Commercial Travelers*, 333 U.S. 153, 158, 162 (1948).
5. 1 Stat. at L. 92.
6. Warren, *New Light on the History of the Federal Judiciary Act of 1789*, 37 HLR, 49 (1923).
7. A facsimile reproduction of this paper may be found in 37 HLR, 87.
8. Warren, II, 362–63.
9. 37 HLR, 85–88.
10. Cf., pp. 818–20 *supra*.
11. Cf., *Wayman* v. *Southard*, 10 Wheat. 1, 27, 32 (1825).
12. Cf., p. 633 *supra*.
13. See chapter xxi *supra*.
14. On this point see pp. 649–50 *supra*, and pp. 985–87 *infra*.
15. 1 Stat. at L. 93.
16. 1 Stat. at L. 275, 276.
17. Cf., p. 368 *supra*.
18. 1 Gall. 488 (1813).
19. *Ibid.*, 491.
20. *Ibid.*, 493.
21. See Holmes, Pitney, Brandeis, and Clarke, JJ., dissenting in *Southern Pacific Co.* v. *Jensen*, 244 U.S. 205, 218, 223, and 255 (1917), and in *Knickerbocker Ice Co.* v. *Stewart*, 253 U.S. 149, 166 (1920).
22. See, for example, *The General Smith*, 4 Wheat. 435 (1819), and *The Lottawanna*, 21 Wall. 558 (1874).
23. *Knickerbocker Ice Co.* v. *Stewart*, 253 U.S. 149, 160 (1920). See, also, *Southern Pacific Co.* v. *Jensen*, 244 U.S. 205 (1917). This view goes back, though in vaguer form, to *The Lottawanna*, 21 Wall. 558, 574–75 (1874).
24. *Southern Pacific Co.* v. *Jensen*, 244 U.S. 205, 214–15 (1917).
25. See cases cited note 23 *supra*.
26. 1 Stat. at L. 76–77, 83–84.
27. 326 U.S. 99 (1945).
28. 1 Stat. at L. 82.
29. 3 Wheat. 212, 221–23 (1818).
30. 3 Dall. 425 (1799), Cf., pp. 824–26 *supra*.
31. 3 Wheat. 223.
32. *York* v. *Guaranty Trust Co.*, 143 F. 2d, 503, 521 (1944).

33. 1 Gall. 491.
34. 3 Dall. 455.
35. 4 Wheat. 108, 115 (1819).
36. Cf., *Wayman* v. *Southard,* 10 Wheat. 1, 24 (1825).
37. 6 Pet. 648, 658 (1832).
38. 13 How. 268, 272 (1851).
39. *Jackson* v. *Chew* is not cited by name in *Neves* v. *Scott,* but only by volume and page—"12 Wheat., 153, 167"—at 13 How. 269.
40. 326 U.S. 101–2.
41. See especially chapter xix hereof.
42. N.H. Laws, November 1832, c. 89, sec. 9.
43. R.I. Public Laws, 1844, pp. 88–89.
44. Durfee, 23–25.
45. Mass. Laws, 1798, c. 77; 1817, c. 87; 1818, c. 98; 1821, c. 85; 1823, cc. 140 and 146; 1826, c. 109; 1855, c. 194; 1856, c. 38; 1857, c. 214; 1877, c. 178.
46. Maine Laws, 1821, c. 50; 1830, c. 462; 1874, c. 175.
47. 2 Cranch 419 (1805).
48. 7 Cranch 69 (1812).
49. 9 Cranch 153 (1815).
50. See 1 Gall. 642–43; *cf.,* 2 Bates, *The Law of Partnership* (Chicago, 1888), sec. 750.
51. Justice Story, on circuit, had allowed recovery of the principal amount of the bill, $8,595.20 (1 Gall. 632), plus 10 per cent damages for non-payment, and interest on these two sums from the time of non-payment to the time of the decree, or $11,526.14 in all. 1 Gall. 643. The Supreme Court disallowed the damages and interest thereon (9 Cranch 162–63), which would reduce the total recovered to $10,478.31.
52. 1 Mason, 191, 219–20 (1817).
53. *Brown* v. *Gilman,* 4 Wheat. 255, 290–91 (1819).
54. 2 Story C.C. 555, 567 (1843).
55. 2 Mason 244 and 342 (1821).
56. 8 Wheat. 174, 216 (1823).
57. 3 Mason 294 (1823).
58. 1 Pet. 1 (1828).
59. 12 Wheat. 498 (1827). The circuit-court stage of the case is reported in 3 Mason 178, under the name of *Gardner* v. *Gardner and Potter* (1823). There was a second appeal to the Supreme Court, in 1831, reported in 5 Pet. 718.
60. 3 Mason 308 (1824).
61. 15 Mass. 505 (1819).
62. 16 Mass. 9 (1819).
63. Maine Laws of 1821, I, 45, and II, 775.
64. *Ibid.,* I, 189.
65. Durfee, 24–25, and 121.
66. III, 243, note 2.
67. Cf., pp. 626–29 *supra.*
68. *Loc. cit.* note 59 *supra.*
69. 2 Gall. 105, 118, 137–38 (1814).
70. *Journal of William Maclay* (New York, 1890), 95–96.
71. Cf., the complaint in the letter printed in Griffith's *Annual Law Register,* quoted in the text hereof at pp. 896–97 *supra.*
72. 13 Pet. 195, 203 (1839).

73. *Cf.*, Miller, J., in *Brine* v. *Insurance Co.*, 96 U.S. 627, 639 (1877). The Court, in *Mason* v. *United States*, 260 U.S. 545, 557 (1922), relied largely upon Miller; and in *Guaranty Trust Co.* v. *York*, 326 U.S. 99 (1945), the Mason case is one of those on which the opinion is built.

74. *Holland* v. *Challen*, 110 U.S. 15 (1884); *Pusey & Jones Co.* v. *Hanssen*, 261 U.S. 491 (1923).

75. *Ruhlin* v. *New York Life Insurance Co.*, 304 U.S. 202 (1938).

76. U.S. Judicial Code, sec. 1652.

77. *Cf.*, Bradley, J., in *Burgess* v. *Seligman*, 107 U.S. 20, 33 (1883): "The Federal courts have an independent jurisdiction in the administration of State laws, co-ordinate with, and not subordinate to, that of the State courts, and are bound to exercise their own judgment as to the meaning and effect of those laws."

78. Schofield, *Swift* v. *Tyson: Uniformity of Judge-Made State Law in State and Federal Courts*, 4 ILLINOIS LAW REVIEW, 533 (1910).

79. There were those who defended the rule of *Swift* v. *Tyson*, whilst not perceiving that the Supreme Court was at fault in not going further, by enforcing its precedents on the courts of the states. *Cf.*, the articles cited (other than Schofield's) in note 22 to the opinion in *Erie Railroad Co.* v. *Tompkins*, 304 U.S. 77.

80. (New York, 1909), secs. 528–50.

81. Carter, *Law: Its Origin, Growth, and Function* (New York, 1907).

82. See his letter to James Kent, of June 26, 1837, published in W. W. Story, *Life and Letters of Joseph Story* (Boston, 1851), II, 270; and more accessibly, in 51 HLR, 412.

83. *Op.* cit. note 80 *supra*, sec. 534.

84. See pp. 594–98 *supra*.

85. *Graves* v. *O'Keefe*, 306 U.S. 466, 491–92 (1939).

86. 215 U.S. 349, 370 (1910).

87. Holmes, *Collected Legal Papers* (New York, 1921), 311.

88. 244 U.S. 205, 221–22 (1917).

89. 276 U.S. 518, 532 (1928).

90. Holmes, *op. cit.* note 87 *supra*, 204.

91. 304 U.S. 64 (1938).

92. 1 Wheat. 337–51.

93. *Ibid.*, 345.

94. There were two dissenters; Justice Cardozo lay mortally ill at the time; Justice Brandeis was eighty-two; and Chief Justice Hughes, seventy-six. Had the case been set for argument, it would, in view of the ground counsel would have had to cover, certainly have had to be postponed to the following year. By that time, the Court majority of April 25, 1938, which decided the case, might not have been *in esse;* and there was no way of telling what the views of new appointees might be upon the point to be decided. The precipitate behavior of the precariously constituted Court majority thus seems not too hard to understand.

95. 304 U.S. 88.

96. See pp. 837–842 *supra*.

97. 304 U.S. 74 note.

98. See, also, recent entries in Federal Digest, sec. 359 *et seq.*

99. The discrimination resulted from the inequality between defendants' rights of removal into the national courts, and plaintiffs' rights of suing in them, as provided in the act of Congress regulating the subject.

100. 16 Pet. 18.

101. *Wichita Royalty Co.* v. *City National Bank*, 306 U.S. 103, 107 (1939); *West* v. *American T. & T. Co.*, 311 U.S. 223, 237 (1940).

102. *Ibid.* See, also, *Fidelity Union Trust Co.* v. *Field*, 311 U.S. 169, 180 (1940).

103. *Six Companies of California* v. *Joint Highway District No. 13 of California*, 311 U.S. 180 (1940); *West* v. *American T. & T. Co.*, 311 U.S. 223 (1940); *Stoner* v. *New York Life Insurance Co.*, 311 U.S. 464 (1940).

104. 311 U.S. 237.

105. 311 U.S. 169 (1940). The facts in the text not stated in the Court's opinion are taken from the record in the case, in the Supreme Court.

106. *Thatcher* v. *Trenton Trust Co.*, 119 N.J. Eq. 408 (1936); *Travers* v. *Reid*, 119 N.J. Eq. 416 (1936).

107. *Field* v. *Fidelity Union Trust Co.*, 108 F. 2d, 521 (C.C.A. 3d, 1939).

108. 129 N.J. Eq. 233 (1941).

109. 311 U.S. 730; 313 U.S. 550; 314 U.S. 709.

110. *Lester* v. *Guenther*, 132 N.J. Eq. 496 (1942); *Franklin Washington Trust Co.* v. *Beltram*, 133 N.J. Eq. 11 (1943).

111. *Lester* v. *Guenther*, 134 N.J. Eq. 53, 56 (1943); *Wolf* v. *Wolf*, 136 N.J. Eq. 403, 405 (1945); *In re Weinstein's Estate* 176 N.Y. Misc. 592 (1941).

112. 333 U.S. 153 (1948).

113. *Ibid.*, 160.

114. The case was argued on December 10–11, 1947, and decided on March 8, 1948. *Ibid.*, 153.

115. Clark, *State Law in the Federal Courts: The Brooding Omnipresence of Erie* v. *Tompkins*, 55 YALE LAW JOURNAL, 267 (1946); Keeffe, Gilhooley, Bailey, and Day, *Weary Erie*, 34 CORNELL LAW QUARTERLY, 494 (1949); Harnett and Thornton, *Precedent in the Eerie Tompkins Manner*, 24 NEW YORK UNIVERSITY LAW QUARTERLY REVIEW, 770 (1949).

116. 313 U.S. 487 (1941).

117. *Ibid.*, 498 (1941).

118. Section 1391.

119. *Cf.*, discussion and citations at pp. 554–55 *supra*.

120. *Cf.*, Jackson, *Full Faith and Credit: The Lawyer's Clause of the Constitution* (New York, 1945), 19: "The Constitution by use of the term 'public acts' clearly includes statutes. But it makes no mention of decisional law." There has, nevertheless, been a vague intimation, in at least one case, that the Court may perhaps be prepared to give the clause some application to decisional law anyway. *Ibid.*, 20; *Magnolia Petroleum Co.* v. *Hunt*, 320 U.S. 430, 436, 445 (1943).

121. 313 U.S. 496.

122. *Ibid.*, 498 (1941). The facts stated in the text not found in the Court's opinion are taken from the record in the case, in the Supreme Court.

123. For the phases of the case subsequent to the Supreme Court's 1941 decision, see 123 F. 2d, 550 (C.C.A. 5th, 1941); certiorari denied 316 U.S. 683, 713 (1942).

124. *New England Mutual Life Insurance Co.* v. *Spence*, 104 F. 2d, 665, 668 (C.C.A. 2d, 1939). It is also followed in Quebec.

125. 241 U.S. 518 (1916). *Cf.*, *Sanders* v. *Armour Fertilizer Works*, 292 U.S. 190 (1934).

126. *Estin* v. *Estin*, 334 U.S. 541, 548 (1948).

127. Apparently, *Wayman* v. *Southard*, 10 Wheat. 1 (1825), is no longer "good law."

128. Some of the friends of the new rules had to whistle very loudly to keep their courage up, after the York decision. See Clark, *op. cit.* note 115 *supra,* 288; and *cf.,* cases cited in notes 131 and 132 *infra.*

129. 330 U.S. 183 (1947).

130. See *Sheldon* v. *Sill,* 8 How. 441 (1850), and cases therein cited.

131. *Ragan* v. *Merchants Transfer and Warehouse Co.,* 337 U.S. 530 (1949).

132. *Cohen* v. *Beneficial Industrial Loan Corp.,* 337 U.S. 541 (1949).

133. *Woods* v. *Interstate Realty Co.,* 337 U.S. 535 (1949).

NOTES TO CHAPTER XXVII

1. Frankfurter, *Distribution of Judicial Power between United States and State Courts,* 13 CORNELL LAW QUARTERLY, 499, 503 (1928).

2. *10 East 40th Street Building, Inc.* v. *Callus,* 325 U.S. 578, 587–88 (1945); *Borden Co.* v. *Borella,* 325 U.S. 679 (1945).

3. *Santa Cruz Fruit Packing Co.* v. *National Labor Relations Board,* 303 U.S. 453, 466–67 (1938).

4. See, for example, *New York* v. *United States,* 326 U.S. 572, 575 (1946), and *Helvering* v. *Hallock,* 309 U.S. 106, 119 (1940). Just how "empiric" this Justice himself can be, may be seen by comparing his positions in the two cases cited in note 2 *supra;* or in *McLeod* v. *Dilworth Co.,* 322 U.S. 327 (1944), and *General Trading Co.* v. *State Tax Commission,* 322 U.S. 335 (1944).

5. *Loc. cit.* note 7 to chapter xvii *supra.*

6. The Justice mentioned in the text has apparently been much troubled by these qualities in the Supreme Court's decisions. He insists that "problems" of the kind with which the Court must deal are "incapable of precise and arithmetical solution" (*Nashville, Chattanooga, & St. Louis R.R.* v. *Browning,* 310 U.S. 362, 365 [1940]); that, when what he calls "lines" have to be drawn, "they are bound to appear arbitrary when judged solely by bordering cases" (*10 East 40th Street Building, Inc.* v. *Callus,* 325 U.S. 578, 584 [1945]); that "to attempt to harmonize all that has been said in the past [by the Court] would neither clarify what has gone before nor guide the future," because the Court's decisions are "the product of preoccupation with their special facts" (*Freeman* v. *Hewitt,* 329 U.S. 249, 252 [1946]); that this, in fact, is "one of the greatest sources of strength of our law" (*New York* v. *United States,* 326 U.S. 572, 575 [1946]).

7. *Santa Cruz Fruit Packing Co.* v. *National Labor Relations Board,* 303 U.S. 453, 466–67 (1938); *Kirschbaum* v. *Walling,* 316 U.S. 517, 526 (1942).

8. 8 Co. Rep. 114a; 2 Brownl. 255.

9. 2 Shower, *475; see, also, Bacon's *Abridgment,* tit. Prerogative, D7.

10. See, generally, Plucknett, *Bonham's Case and Judicial Review,* 40 HLR, 30 (1926).

11. Blackstone, I, 91. The explanation referred to, in the text, first appeared in the ninth edition.

12. See Thayer, *Legal Essays* (Cambridge, 1927), 2, and references therein contained.

13. See Plucknett, *op. cit.* note 10 *supra;* Haines, *The American Doctrine of Judicial Supremacy* (2d ed.; Berkeley, 1932), chap. iii; Corwin, *The Establishment of Judicial Review,* 9 MICHIGAN LAW REVIEW, 102, 105 *et seq.* (1910). It is not meant to approve all that these writers have to say about this colonial evidence. There is a general tendency to exaggerate its impor-

tance. It should be remembered that evidence remote in time, or place, from the Federal Convention is of little relevancy.

14. See Jefferson, II, 330; and XI, 400, 407, 410 and footnote.

15. See Turner, *A Phantom Precedent*, 48 AMERICAN LAW REVIEW, 21 (1914). There has been a seemingly great reluctance in certain quarters to give up this case as a precedent for judicial review, and various speculations have been indulged to lend it some vitality for the purpose. See Haines, *op. cit.* note 13 *supra*, 89 *et seq*. Entirely apart from the specific evidence given, or referred to, in the Turner article, the imputing of judicial review to the Virginia of 1778 is highly anachronistic. *Cf.,* Jefferson's contemporary *Notes on Virginia.* Jefferson, IV, 20–37.

16. Hening, Va. Stat. at L., IX, 463.

17. *Ibid.,* 110.

18. See, generally, Turner, *op. cit.* note 15 *supra* and sources therein cited.

19. Elliot, III, 66–67, 137–40, 193, 222–23, 236, 298–99, 324, 450, and *passim*.

20. Tucker, Bk. I, Pt. 1, App., p. 293.

21. *Cf.,* p. 601 *supra*.

22. See Boudin, *Precedents for the Judicial Power: Holmes v. Walton and Brattle v. Hinckley,* 3 ST. JOHN's LAW REVIEW, 173 (1929); and *Government by Judiciary* (New York, 1932), I, 531 *et seq*. This author, like some of the writers on the other side of the question, is inclined to argue much beyond his evidence. Some of the things he has to say about the cases of *State v. Parkhurst* and *Taylor v. Reading* fall plainly in this category; especially, in the light of the contemporary newspaper notices of these cases. *Cf.,* Erdman, *The New Jersey Constitution of 1776* (Princeton, 1929), chap. v. But there can be no doubt he demonstrated the improbability with respect to *Holmes v. Walton,* alluded to in the text. His demonstration was variously received. One reviewer thought it unimpressive in view of "the evidence for what," he said, *"did* occur" in the case, which "evidence," he intimated, was to be found in Erdman, *op. cit.,* pp. 91–92. 26 AMERICAN POLITICAL SCIENCE REVIEW, 1107 (1932). But there is no evidence in reference to *Holmes v. Walton,* in Erdman, which was not also set forth in Scott, *Holmes vs. Walton: The New Jersey Precedent,* 4 AMERICAN HISTORICAL REVIEW, 456, in 1899; and that evidence, this same reviewer thought, in 1910, created only a probability that the case was one of judicial review. See Corwin, *op. cit.* note 13 *supra,* at 111. The factors in the case, pointed out in Boudin, *op. cit. supra,* certainly lessened this probability and, in fact, make it very improbable that the case was a case of that kind. *Cf.,* discussion in the text.

23. N.J. Acts, 1776–83, App. No. V.

24. *Ibid.,* ix.

25. See *Falkenburgh v. Cramer,* 1 N.J. L. 31 (1790); *Parker v. Munday,* 1 N.J. L. 70 (1791); *Ashcroft v. Clark,* 5 N.J. L. 577 (1819); *Jones v. Oliver,* 7 N.J. L. 123 (1823).

26. See Boudin, *op. cit.* note 22 *supra*.

27. Votes of N.J. Assembly, December 8, 1780.

28. Sparks, *The Life of Gouverneur Morris, with Selections from his Correspondence and Miscellaneous Papers* (Boston, 1832), III, 438.

29. *State v. Parkhurst,* 9 N.J. L. 427, 444 (1802). This is not a report of the case, but merely a printing of Chief Justice Andrew Kirkpatrick's dissenting opinion therein, twenty-six years after the case was decided. The reporter, William Halsted, noted that he was indebted to the late Chief Justice for the opinion, which Kirkpatrick had apparently handed him on January 28, 1828; that is, shortly before his death. 9 N.J. L. 427 note and

434 note. Whether the opinion is the actual opinion Kirkpatrick delivered in 1802, or a reconstruction thereof from notes, there is no way of telling. In either case, his treatment of *Holmes* v. *Walton*, therein, as an instance of judicial review, by no means settles the true character of that case. For Kirkpatrick had not been a member of the New Jersey Supreme Court when the case was decided; so far as is known he had no first-hand knowledge of the case; and his statement, twenty-two years after it was decided, is not very persuasive, in view of the evidence in the text, relating to the Josiah Philips case, as to what could happen to precedents, even in the minds of successor judges of the courts that decided them, when judicial decisions were not reported.

30. 4 Call (Va.) 5.

31. The famous dissent of Justice (later Chief Justice) John Bannister Gibson, of Pennsylvania, in *Eakin* v. *Raub*, 12 Serg. L.R. 330, 345, was delivered in 1825 and attracted considerable attention. The whole of the 1820's, as pointed out herein in chapter xxv, was a period of attack on the reviewing power of the Supreme Court with respect to the states; and Jacksonian Democracy, which came into power in 1829, was essentially anti-judicial.

32. Jefferson, IV, 20–37.

33. Jefferson, III, 318–20.

34. Jefferson, III, 321.

35. Records, II, 89 and 587–88.

36. "The history of the violations of the [Virginia] constitution," Edmund Randolph said, "extends from the year 1776 to this time—violations made by formal act of the legislature: everything has been drawn within the legislative vortex." Elliot, III, 66. This was plain enough; but since it was in support of this statement that Randolph made his extraordinary misrepresentation of the Josiah Philips case (dealt with in the text), that fact, along with many others, discredits Randolph as a reliable witness. It is, however, not very likely that he would have made this sweeping statement before the Virginia convention, unless its *general* truth was pretty notorious among his hearers; and that this was the case, is confirmed by what others in the convention had to say. Thus, George Nicholas averred that, besides the bill of attainder enacted in the Philips case, "the [Virginia] declaration of rights . . . ha[d] been violated in many other instances." Edmund Pendleton —President of the state's Court of Appeals, which decided the Caton case— though "hop[ing]" to give no offence," felt obliged to admit that "there ha[d] been some [violations]." And Patrick Henry confessed the truth of the general charge of violations; but "the failures and errors" which had occurred, he said, "might have happened in any government," and he "hope[d]" the state's "deviations from justice" would "be attributed to the errors of the head, and not those of the heart." *Ibid.*, 298, 325, 450.

37. Madison, V, 269, 272.

38. 4 Call (Va.) 135.

39. Va. Ind. Chr., May 21, 1788; Pa. Pack., May 24, 1788.

40. 4 Call (Va.) 148–50.

41. Force Transcripts, 8695–8719.

42. That is, the words, "the decision of which might involve consequences to which gentlemen may not have extended their ideas." 4 Call 17.

43. 4 Munf. (Va.) 1, 57.

44. Elliot, IV, 548.

45. Records, II, 90 and 92.

46. 4 Call 7.

47. Kirby (Conn.), 444–53.

48. Cf., *Calder* v. *Bull*, 3 Dall. (U.S.) 386 (1798).

49. Printed in Bancroft, *History of the Formation of the Constitution of the United States* (New York, 1882), II, 472–73.

50. Goodell, *An Early Constitutional Case in Massachusetts*, 7 HLR, 415 (1894).

51. *Arguments and Judgments of the Mayor's Court of the City of New York in a cause between Elizabeth Rutgers and Joshua Waddington* (New York, 1784); Dawson, *The Case of Elizabeth Rutgers versus Joshua Waddington, with an historical introduction* (Morrisania, 1866); Thayer, *Cases on Constitutional Law* (Cambridge, 1895), I, 63.

52. Blackstone, I, 91.

53. Dawson, *op. cit.* note 51 *supra*, xii and 25–40; Thayer, *op. cit.* note 51 *supra*, 72 footnote.

54. Hamilton, V, 227.

55. Cf., Meigs, *The Relation of the Judiciary to the Constitution* (New York, 1919), 73; and see Dawson, *op. cit.* note 51 *supra*.

56. Varnum, *The Case, Trevett against Weeden, &c.* (Providence, 1787). The material and statements in the text, when not otherwise indicated, are taken from this Varnum pamphlet.

57. Pa. Pack., April 25, May 2, 9, 16, and 23, 1787.

58. See, among others, Newp. Merc., October 2, 1786; Prov. Gaz., October 7, 1786; Ch. Mng. P., October 31, 1786; Bost. Gaz., October 2, 1786; U.S. Chr., October 5, 1786; New-York Gazetteer, October 6, 1786.

59. Records, II, 28.

60. R.I. Acts and Resolves, October (1st Session) 1786, p. 3.

61. *Ibid.*, p. 7.

62. *Ibid.*, October (2d Session) 1786, pp. 4–6; May, 1787, p. 7.

63. Cf., Corwin, *The Doctrine of Judicial Review* (Princeton, 1914), 73.

64. Laws of N.H., V, 101.

65. See N.H. Spy, June 30, 1787.

66. N.H. Constitution of 1783, Part I, Article 20.

67. N.H. State Papers, XX, 450; Plumer, *Life of William Plumer* (Boston, 1857), 59.

68. N.H. State Papers, XX, 592, 634, 639, 652, 676, 698, 704, 759; XXI, 30, 31, 72, 78, 79, 83.

69. Ph. Ind. Gaz., July 18, 1787; Pa. Pack., July 19, 1787.

70. N.H. State Papers, XXI, 23, 28, 29, 51, 53, 66, 72, 76.

71. Records, II, 84.

72. 1 Martin (N.C.) 42 (1787). See, generally, Biggs, *The Power of the Judiciary over Legislation*, 17 REPORTS OF THE NORTH CAROLINA BAR ASSOCIATION, 5 (1915).

73. N.C. State Records, XVIII, 42, 215–17, 428–29.

74. *Ibid.*, 361.

75. McRee, *Life and Correspondence of James Iredell* (New York, 1858), II, 168, 169.

76. Pa. Pack., June 27, 1787.

NOTES TO CHAPTER XXVIII

1. Pa. Pack., May 23, 1787. A copy of this pamphlet may be found in the Ridgeway Library, in Philadelphia.

2. The extract was copied into the following papers, among others: N.H. Merc., June 14, 1787; Balt. Gaz., June 22, 1787; Prov. Gaz., June 16, 1787; Sal. Merc., June 12, 1787; Ch. Mng. P., July 7, 1787; Va. Ind. Chr., June 20, 1787.

3. "Oeconomics," here, probably means "police"; or, perhaps, more generally, "the science of regulation." Cf., pp. 107 and 148–49 *supra*.

4. *Marbury* v. *Madison*, 1 Cranch (U.S.) 137 (1803).

5. *Dred Scott* v. *Sandford*, 19 How. (U.S.) 393 (1857).

6. *Myers* v. *United States*, 272 U.S. 52 (1926).

7. Records, I, 21, 93–95, 97–105, 107–10, 131, 138–41, 144–45; II, 73–80.

8. Records, I, 63, 65, 66, 70, 71, 74, 93, 96, 97, 105, 109, 254, 261, and 266.

9. This fact was pointed out by Nathaniel Gorham, of Massachusetts, on July 21st. Records, II, 79.

10. Records, II, 294–95, 298.

11. There are, also, certain types of question which the Court declines to decide, on the theory that they are addressed to the discretion either of Congress or of the President. See, generally, Post, *The Supreme Court and Political Questions* (Baltimore, 1936); Dodd, *Judicially Nonenforceable Provisions of Constitutions*, 80 UNIVERSITY OF PENNSYLVANIA LAW REVIEW, 54 (1931); Finkelstein, *Judicial Self-Limitation*, 37 HLR, 338 (1923); Weston, *Political Questions*, 38 HLR, 296 (1925).

12. Cf., Hamilton's treatment of "Cases, in Equity, arising under the Constitution," in *No. LXXX* of *The Federalist*. The now common equity suit to enjoin the enforcement of an unconstitutional legislative act seems not to have crossed his mind.

13. Cases, or excerpts from cases, illustrative of most of these devices may be found collected in Frankfurter and Shulman, *Cases on Federal Jurisdiction and Procedure* (Chicago, 1937).

14. See, for example, *State of Georgia* v. *Stanton*, 6 Wall. (U.S.) 50 (1867).

15. *Carter* v. *Carter Coal Co.*, 298 U.S. 238 (1936), a case involving "States' Rights" as against Congress, to which neither the nation nor any state was a party, illustrates this possibility.

16. 50 Stat. at L. 751.

17. *National Labor Relations Board* v. *Jones & Laughlin Steel Corp.*, 301 U.S. 1 (1937), marked the Court's definite capitulation. Cf., *Schechter Poultry Corp.* v. *United States*, 295 U.S. 495 (1935).

18. These are the clauses which were cited by Chief Justice Marshall as justifying the Court's claim of power in *Marbury* v. *Madison*, 1 Cranch (U.S.) 137 (1803). And they have been cited ever since.

19. Cf., Hamilton, in *No. LXXX* of *The Federalist;* Madison, in the Virginia ratifying convention (Elliot, III, 532); and W. R. Davie, in the North Carolina convention of 1788 (Elliot, IV, 156–57).

20. Records, II, 27–29.

21. Records, II, 27.

22. Records, I, 169.

23. Records, I, 228, 231, 232.

24. Records, I, 47, 54, 61. The Convention had declined, however, on June 8th, to broaden the power to one "to negative all [state] laws which to [Congress] sh[ould] appear improper." Records, I, 162–68.

25. Records, II, 27–28 and 390–91.

26. Records, II, 22 and 28–29.

27. Records, II, 183.

28. Records, II, 381–82 and 389.

29. Elliot, IV, 187.
30. "Letter of a Countryman," N.Y. Jour., December 15, 1787.
31. Cf., p. 972 *supra*.
32. Records, II, 90 and 92.
33. Records, II, 73. This is particularly dealt with, in chapter xxix hereof.
34. Journals, V, 575, 768, 813; VI, 1039, 1054.
35. Records, II, 22 and 28–29.
36. Records, II, 183.
37. Article VI of the Constitution.
38. Records, II, 22.
39. Records, II, 183.
40. Article IX of the Confederation.
41. Records, II, 131.
42. Records, II, 22, 183, 381, 409, 603, and 663.
43. Records, II, 22.
44. Records, II, 183.
45. Records, II, 181 and 182.
46. Records, II, 381 and 389.
47. Cf., pp. 503–5 *supra*.
48. Records, II, 381 and 389.
49. Records, II, 409 and 417.
50. Records, II, 603.
51. Cf., pp. 621–22 and 634–35 *supra*.
52. Records, II, 182, 571, and 601.
53. Article II, sec. 1.

NOTES TO CHAPTER XXIX

1. Records, III, 81; cf., *ibid.*, I, 2 note; II, 322, 328 and note, 368, 375, 399, 406; III, 69, 71, 73, 75, 98.
2. Madison, V, 294.
3. Annals, I, 461, 495, 500.
4. Elliot, IV, 548, 549.
5. Madison, IX, 142.
6. It was said of Madison that his inconsistency had extended to "almost every question which ha[d] divided the public into parties." Records, III, 516.
7. Elliot, IV, 566.
8. Records, I, 97.
9. *Ibid.*
10. The difficulty is that the "opinions of the justices" under the Massachusetts practice had to be requested by the executive or one of the branches of the legislature; and it is difficult to see how this practice in itself could, in view of this fact, constitute a very efficient protection to the judiciary prerogatives against the legislature. Probably, what Gerry said is imperfectly recorded.
11. Records, I, 109.
12. Records, I, 104 and 140.
13. Records, II, 73.
14. Records, I, 228.
15. Records, II, 73.
16. Records, II, 74–75.
17. Records, II, 75.

18. Records, II, 76–78.
19. Records, II, 80.
20. Records, II, 298.
21. *Ibid.*
22. Records, II, 299.
23. Records, II, 182.
24. Records, II, 308–10.
25. Records, II, 375–76.
26. Records, II, 301.
27. Records, II, 28.
28. Records, I, 228.
29. See Corwin, *The Doctrine of Judicial Review* (Princeton, 1914), 11 and note.
30. Records, II, 93.
31. See Corwin, *op. cit.* note 29 *supra*, 10 and 11 note, and, especially, 43 and 47; and Warren, *The Making of the Constitution* (Boston, 1929), 333–34.
32. *Cf.*, pp. 985 *et seq. supra.*
33. Records, II, 248.
34. Records, II, 428.
35. See Corwin, *op. cit.* note 29 *supra*, 10 and 11 note.
36. *Ibid.*, and Beard, *The Supreme Court and the Constitution* (New York, 1938), 42.
37. Records, II, 376.
38. It has been thought "obvious" by writers without adequate legal background that "the Judges could take hold of" the Ex-post-facto Clause "only" by declaring acts of Congress void. *Cf.*, Beard, *loc. cit.* note 36 *supra*.
39. *Cf.*, the statement about "tender laws," in Spaight's letter to Iredell, quoted herein at p. 972 *supra*. *Bayard* v. *Singleton*, which, it will be remembered, involved another point, was the earliest case of judicial review in North Carolina. See pp. 971–74 *supra*.
40. See Beard, *op. cit.* note 36 *supra*, 18, 49, and 51 note.
41. Records, I, 291.
42. Corwin, *op. cit.* note 29 *supra*, 49. See, also, Beard, *op. cit.* note 36 *supra*, 19, 44, 45, 54.
43. The underlying assumptions appear quite clearly in Beard, *op. cit.* note 36 *supra*, 44–45.
44. Blackstone, I, 250 and 257; *cf.*, discussion pp. 416–17 *supra*.
45. *Cf.*, Butler, *The Treaty-making Power of the United States* (New York, 1902), *passim*.
46. See Tucker, *Limitations on the Treaty-making Power* (Boston, 1915).
47. *Missouri* v. *Holland*, 252 U.S. 416, 433 (1920).
48. Annals, I, 455–585.
49. *Ibid.*, 459, 467, 473, 509, 536–37, 550, 573.
50. *Ibid.*, 461, 495, 546.
51. *Cf.*, *Myers* v. *United States*, 272 U.S. 52, 111–14 (1926).
52. Elliot, IV, 532–39.
53. 1 Cranch 137 (1803).
54. Annals, I, 459, 509, 579.
55. Annals, II, 1459.
56. Annals, II, 1927.
57. *Cf.*, p. 200 *supra*.
58. Elliot, IV, 528, 540; *cf.*, *ibid.*, 548–49.

59. *Ibid.*, 534.
60. *McCulloch* v. *Maryland*, 4 Wheat. 316 (1819).
61. *Cf.*, chapter xi hereof.
62. *Cf.*, Warren, I, 269 *et seq.*
63. McRee, *op. cit.* note 75 to chapter xxvii *supra*, II, 293–96.
64. 1 Cranch 299 (1803).
65. The device used in the case of *Meyers* v. *United States*, 272 U.S. 52, was unavailable, because the only remedy on money claims against the United States was by petition to Congress, in 1803. Gouverneur Morris suggested in the Senate that the case could be gotten into court by one of the judges assuming to do some judicial act, the validity of which could then be questioned in court. Annals, XII, 76. But it was not questioned that all the judges' duties had been taken from them with complete constitutionality. *Cf.*, Warren, I, 224 note, and Annals, XII, 432. If what Morris suggested was really possible, it was apparently decided by the Federalists that to attempt it would put the Justices of the Supreme Court into too perilous a position.
66. Annals, XII, 31, 33, 51–78, and 427–41.
67. *Dred Scott* v. *Sanford*, 19 How. 393 (1857).
68. The two cases mentioned in the text are unreported; but were mentioned in both the argument and the opinion in *Marbury* v. *Madison*. *Cf.*, 1 Cranch 149 and 171–72.
69. 1 Cranch 174.
70. *Cf.*, pp. 486–87 *supra*.
71. *Loc. cit.* note 68 *supra*.
72. *The* [Philadelphia] *Aurora*, December 22, 1801.
73. *Ibid.*
74. Annals, XI, 595–96 and 662.
75. *Cf.*, Warren, I, 227 *et seq.*
76. *Ibid.*, 229–30.
77. Annals, XII, 438.
78. B. Ind. Chr., March 10, 1803. This was after the actual decision, refusing the mandamus; but the tenor of the item shows it was written from Washington before the decision.
79. These expectations were realized by the Jeffersonians in the 1804 election; and they immediately made their nearly successful attempt to remove Justice Chase by impeachment.
80. 1 Cranch 154.
81. *Cf.*, *Wilson* v. *Mason*, 1 Cranch 91–92 (1801); *Ex parte Crane*, 5 Pet. 190, 200 (1831).
82. *Cf.*, p. 802 *supra*.
83. *Cf.* note 67 *supra*.
84. Records, I, 124.

NOTES TO CHAPTER XXX

1. The beginning of "substantive due process," in the Supreme Court, is generally dated from *Chicago, M. & St. P. R. Co.* v. *Minnesota*, 134 U.S. 418 (1890). It was fully established by the date of *Lochner* v. *New York*, 198 U.S. 45 (1905).
2. *Slaughter-House Cases*, 16 Wall. (U.S.) 36, 80–81 (1872).
3. *Cf.*, the discussion herein at pp. 1096–1119 and 1146–58.
4. *Twining* v. *New Jersey*, 211 U.S. 78, 101 (1908); *Heiner* v. *Donnan*, 285 U.S. 312, 326 (1932); *cf.*, *Wight* v. *Davidson*, 181 U.S. 371, 384 (1901).

5. See, on the "equal-protection" point, the following cases, among others: *Detroit Bank* v. *United States*, 317 U.S. 329, 337–38 (1942); *Hirabayashi* v. *United States*, 320 U.S. 81, 100 (1943); *Korematsu* v. *United States*, 323 U.S. 214, 216 (1944). The Court customarily concedes that there is no "equal-protection" guaranty in the Fifth Amendment, and then observes that, therefore, that Amendment "restrains only *such* discriminatory legislation by Congress as amounts to a denial of due process." 320 U.S. 100. In state cases, whenever possible, inequalities are condemned both as "unequal protection" and "want of due process of law." It is safe to say it would be an impossible task to make clear any real distinction between "unequal protection of the laws" and "*such* discriminatory legislation as amounts to a denial of due process." The Supreme Court cases that define "due process of law" as involving equality before the law as an essential element are legion. See, for example: *Leeper* v. *Texas*, 139 U.S. 462, 468 (1891); *Giozza* v. *Tiernan*, 148 U.S. 657, 662 (1892). For an unilluminating judicial attempt to discriminate between the two, see: *Truax* v. *Corrigan*, 257 U.S. 312, 331 *et seq.* And *cf.*, discussion herein at p. 1116. On the "contracts-impairment" point, see *Lynch* v. *United States*, 292 U.S. 571, 579 (1934); *Louisville Joint Stock Lank Bank* v. *Radford*, 295 U.S. 555, 589 (1935); and *cf.*, *Home Building & Loan Assoc.* v. *Blaisdell*, 290 U.S. 398 (1934). It should be remembered, of course, that the Lynch and Radford cases involved "ex post facto Laws" which the Constitution forbids. *Cf.*, chapter xi hereof.

6. *Twining* v. *New Jersey*, 211 U.S. 78 (1908); *Adamson* v. *California*, 332 U.S. 46 (1947).

7. *Murray's Lessee* v. *Hoboken Land and Improvement Co.*, 18 How. (U.S.) 272 (1856).

8. Frankfurter, J., in *Adamson* v. *California*, 332 U.S. 46, 62 (1947). The learned Justice does not specify which of his predecessors he means; but as the late John Marshall Harlan stubbornly maintained, throughout his career, the position which Frankfurter, J., condemns, it seems certain that it was to Justice Harlan that the epithet quoted in the text was applied.

9. *Adamson* v. *California*, 332 U.S. 46, 68 *et seq.*; especially 90 (1947).

10. *Cf.*, cases cited in note 36 to chapter ii *supra*.

11. The cases are collected in Hale, *The Supreme Court and the Contracts Clause* (1944), 57 HLR 512, 514–16, where the development is discussed. It has to be remembered, of course, that the state Ex-post-facto Clause would have covered this kind of thing, had the Court not destroyed it. See chapter xi hereof.

12. See *Campbell* v. *Holt*, 115 U.S. 620, 623 (1885); *Stewart* v. *Keyes*, 295 U.S. 403, 417 (1935); *Lynch* v. *United States*, 292 U.S. 571, 579 (1934); *Louisville Joint Stock Land Bank* v. *Radford*, 295 U.S. 555, 589 (1935).

13. *Home Building & Loan Assoc.* v. *Blaisdell*, 290 U.S. 398 (1934), represents the peak in this respect.

14. *Cf.*, discussion herein at pp. 352–60 *supra*.

15. *Cf.*, discussion herein at pp. 541–57 *supra*.

16. 7 Pet. (U.S.) 243 (1833).

17. The doctrine of *Barron* v. *Baltimore* has been reaffirmed times without number. See, for example, the following: *Spies* v. *Illinois*, 123 U.S. 131, 166 (1887); *Brown* v. *New Jersey*, 175 U.S. 172, 174 (1899); *Adamson* v. *California*, 332 U.S. 46, 51 (1947).

18. See note 4 to chapter xxii *supra*.

19. DHC, II, 377 *et seq.*

20. Records, II, 318; Madison, V, 269, 272.

21. 4 Call (Va.) 135 (1788); and *cf.,* p. 957 *supra.*

22. 1 Stat. at L., 97; Gaz. U.S:, October 3, 1789.

23. Annals, I, 433, 436; Gaz. U.S., June 13, 1789.

24. *Ibid.*

25. The vote of the 8th of June was to refer to a committee of the whole House. The next known record is the report of the select committee, on July 28th. Annals, I, 450 and 672; Gaz. U.S. June 10, and August 1, 1789.

26. Gaz. U.S., August 1, 1789.

27. Annals, I, 707, 717; Gaz. U.S., August 15, 1789.

28. In Annals, I, 766, this is recorded as occurring on August 19th. In Gaz. U.S., August 22, 1789, it is recorded as occurring on August 20th. There appears to be no way of telling which date is correct.

29. Annals, I, 713.

30. *Loc. cit.* note 26 *supra.*

31. Annals, I, 729–31; Gaz. U.S., August 19, 1789.

32. Annals, I, 753; Gaz. U.S., August 22, 1789.

33. Article V.

34. Gaz. U.S., August 22, 1789.

35. *Journal of the First Session of the Senate of the United States* (New York, 1789), 103, 106; Gaz. U.S., August 29, 1789.

36. Senate Journal, *cit.* note 35 *supra,* 105, 121.

37. *Ibid.,* 104; Gaz. U.S., August 29, 1789.

38. The restriction that trials shall be held in the state where the offense is alleged to have been committed would of course be needless, except as to federal prosecutions. The particular provisions of the amendment were apparently intended to be taken *reddenda singula singulis. Cf.,* chapter xxiii *supra.*

39. *Loc. cit.* note 35 *supra.*

40. *Op. cit.* note 36 *supra.*

41. See note 38 *supra.*

42. *Loc. cit.* note 22 *supra.*

43. Senate Journal, *cit.* note 35 *supra,* 116, 117, and 129.

44. Annals, I, 433, 434; Gaz. U.S., June 13, 1789.

45. *Loc. cit.* note 26 *supra.*

46. *Loc. cit.* note 31 *supra.*

47. Annals, I, 766; Gaz. U.S., August 29, 1789; Senate Journal, *cit.* note 35 *supra,* 104.

48. *Cf.,* chapter xxii hereof.

49. *Bank of Columbia* v. *Okeley,* 4 Wheat. 235, 242, 244 (1819); and *Houston* v. *Moore,* 5 Wheat. 1, 32, 34 (1820).

50. *People* v. *Goodwin,* 18 Johns. (N.Y.) 187, 201 (1820).

51. See Rawle, chap. x, and Angell, *Restrictions upon State Power in Relation to Private Property,* 1 UNITED STATES LAW INTELLIGENCER AND REVIEW, 4, 64 (Providence, 1829).

52. See, especially, *Cohens* v. *Virginia,* 6 Wheat. (U.S.) 264, 413 *et seq.* (1821).

53. 7 Pet. (U.S.) 243 (1833).

54. Edmund Randolph, the first Attorney General of the United States, repeated these arguments in the report on the Judiciary Act of 1789, which he made to the House of Representatives, in December 1790. ASP, 23.

55. 1 Wheat. (U.S.) 304, 319, 323, 338 *et seq.* (1816).

56. 6 Wheat (U.S.) 264, 310, 315, 413, 416 (1821).

57. 3 How. (U.S.) 236, 252 (1845).

58. 12 Wheat. (U.S.) 64, 90 (1827).

59. The statement was made by Justice Johnson in a letter to Thomas Jefferson. An excerpt from the letter, containing the part quoted in the text may be found conveniently in 57 HLR 333.

60. *Cf.*, p. 372 *supra.*

61. *Cf.*, chapter x hereof.

62. *Adamson* v. *California*, 332 U.S. 46 (1947).

NOTES TO CHAPTER XXXI

1. 19 How. 393 (1857).

2. 16 Wall. 36 (1873).

3. *Ibid.*, 73.

4. 19 How. 403, 404.

5. *Ibid.*, 404, 406.

6. *Ibid.*, 403.

7. *Ibid.*, 405.

8. *Ibid.*, 405–7.

9. *Ibid.*, 406, 410–11.

10. *Ibid.*, 449, 450.

11. 7 Pet. 243 (1833).

12. See, for example, Grant, *Natural Law Background of Due Process* (1931) 31 COLUMBIA LAW REVIEW, 56, where it is said that the Fourteenth Amendment was "miserably drafted, as the wording of this clause is obviously incapable of the construction intended"; also, McGovney, *Privileges or Immunities Clause—Fourteenth Amendment* (1918), 4 IOWA LAW BULLETIN, 219.

13. McGovney, *op. cit.* note 12 *supra*, 225–26, 231–33.

14. *Selected Essays on Constitutional Law* (Chicago, 1938), I, v; II, 402.

15. McGovney, *op. cit.* note 12 *supra*, 225–26.

16. *Ibid.*, 231–33.

17. See the contemporary constitutions or bills of rights of New Hampshire, Massachusetts, Pennsylvania, Delaware, Maryland, Virginia, and North Carolina.

18. 19 How. 407.

19. *Ibid.*, 584.

20. *Ibid.*, 422.

21. *Livingston* v. *Van Ingen*, 9 Johns. (N.Y.) 507 (1812).

22. See, for example, *Truax* v. *Corrigan*, 257 U.S. 312 (1921); *Stewart Dry Goods Co.* v. *Lewis*, 294 U.S. 550 (1935).

23. *Cf.*, *Blake* v. *McClung*, 172 U.S. 239, 260–61 (1898).

24. Hamilton, IV, 231–32.

25. See McKechnie, *Magna Carta* (2d ed.; Glasgow, 1914), 379–81; cf., *Davidson* v. *New Orleans*, 96 U.S. 97, 102 (1878).

26. 2 Co. Inst. 50–51; Blackstone, I, 127–40.

27. See pp. 500–501 and 541–57 *supra.*

28. See Story, III, 655–66.

29. 18 How. 272 (1855).

30. *Ibid.*, 276–77.

31. *Ibid.*, 277.

32. *Reiche* v. *Smythe*, 13 Wall. 162, 164 (1871); *Case of the Sewing Machine Companies*, 18 Wall. 553, 584 (1873).

33. *Adamson* v. *California,* 332 U.S. 46 (1947).

34. Rawle, 128–33.

35. Kent, II, 9–10.

36. Story, III, 652–61; *cf.,* McKechnie, *op. cit.* note 25 *supra,* 385.

37. *Wynehamer* v. *The People,* 13 N.Y. 378 (1856).

38. 19 How. 450, 452.

39. *Loc. cit.* note 37 *supra.*

40. See Corwin, *The Doctrine of Due Process of Law before the Civil War* (1911), 24 HLR, 366, 460, 471 *et seq.*

41. *Ibid.,* 474; and see, especially, *State* v. *Keeran,* 5 R.I. 497 (1858).

42. *Cf.,* cases cited note 5 to chapter xxx *supra.*

43. See Flack, *op. cit.* note 45 to chapter xvii *supra,* chap. 5.

44. These are conveniently collected in an appendix to the opinion of Black, J., in *Adamson* v. *California,* 332 U.S. 46, 92 (1947).

45. *Slaughter-House Cases,* 16 Wall. 36, 73 (1873); *United States* v. *Wong Kim Ark,* 169 U.S. 649, 682 (1898); *Elk* v. *Wilkins,* 112 U.S. 94, 102 (1884).

NOTES TO CHAPTER XXXII

1. *Colgate* v. *Harvey,* 296 U.S. 404 (1935).

2. *Madden* v. *Kentucky,* 309 U.S. 83 (1940).

3. See Stone, J., in 296 U.S. 404, 443 *et seq.,* and 307 U.S. 496, 520 note, cited with approval by the Court in 309 U.S. 83, 90 (1940); also Jackson, J., in 314 U.S. 160, 182–83.

4. 16 Wall. 36 (1873).

5. *Ibid.,* 80.

6. *Ibid.,* 96, 129–30.

7. *Ibid.,* 118–19.

8. *Ibid.,* 97 and 116–18.

9. *Ibid.,* 117–18.

10. *Ibid.,* 97, 98, 100, 101.

11. *Ibid.,* 101.

12. 144 U.S. 323 (1892).

13. 123 U.S. 131, 151–52 (1887).

14. 144 U.S. 323, 337, 361–63.

15. *Ibid.,* 370.

16. *Lemmon* v. *The People,* 20 N.Y. 562, 580–81 (1860).

17. Speech of John A. Bingham, of Ohio, on a bill for the admission of Oregon as a state, February 11, 1859. THE CONGRESSIONAL GLOBE, 35th C., 2d S., pt. 1, pp. 981–85, especially 984.

18. 4 Wash. C.C. 371 (1823).

19. 18 How. 591 (1855).

20. 19 How. 405–7, 422–23, 580–84.

21. It is, apparently, a fear that this is the only and true alternative which produces the emotion on this subject displayed by certain modern Supreme Court Justices. *Cf.,* 296 U.S. 445; 307 U.S. 496, 520 note; and 332 U.S. 61–62.

22. 16 Wall. 74–76.

23. *Ibid.,* 117.

24. 8 Wall. 123 (1869).

25. 16 Wall. 79–80.

26. 6 Wall. 35 (1868).

27. *United States* v. *Cruikshank,* 92 U.S. 542 (1876).

28. *Gasquet* v. *Lapeyre*, 242 U.S. 367 (1917); *cf.*, *Barron* v. *Baltimore*, 7 Pet. 243 (1833), and discussion herein at pp. 1056–82 *supra*.

29. *Ex parte Royall*, 117 U.S. 241 (1886).

30. 92 U.S. 90 (1876).

31. *Cf.*, 332 U.S. 78.

32. 116 U.S. 252 (1886).

33. 176 U.S. 581 (1900).

34. 176 U.S. 594–96.

35. 176 U.S. 597–98; *cf.*, 211 U.S. 99.

36. 176 U.S. 601–2.

37. The three new Justices were William R. Day, of Ohio; and Oliver Wendell Holmes and William Henry Moody, of Massachusetts.

38. 211 U.S. 78 (1908).

39. Frankfurter, J., in *Adamson* v. *California*, 332 U.S. 46, 59 (1947).

40. Holmes, J., in *Baldwin* v. *Missouri*, 281 U.S. 586, 595 (1929).

41. 211 U.S. 98–99.

42. 16 Wall. 122 and 128.

43. 16 Wall. 80–81.

44. 92 U.S. 90 (1876).

45. *Cf.*, 332 U.S. 78–79.

46. 110 U.S. 516 (1884).

47. 18 How. 272 (1855).

48. See cases cited in note 32 to chapter xxxi hereof.

49. 18 How. 276–77.

50. *Cf.*, p. 1113 *supra*.

51. 18 How. 277–80.

52. See cases cited in note 32 to chapter xxxi hereof.

53. 110 U.S. 528–29.

54. *Cf.*, Frankfurter, J., in *Adamson* v. *California*, 332 U.S. 46, 59, 61, 62, 65 (1947).

55. 110 U.S. 534–35.

56. 110 U.S. 547–50.

57. *Twining* v. *New Jersey*, 211 U.S. 78 (1908); *Maxwell* v. *Dow*, 176 U.S. 581 (1900); *West* v. *Louisiana*, 194 U.S. 258 (1903); and other cases.

58. 211 U.S. 99–101.

59. *Ibid.*, 101.

60. 18 How. 277–80.

61. 211 U.S. 102–3.

62. *Ibid.*, 106–7.

63. *Ibid.*, 107–9.

64. *Ibid.*, 109–10.

65. Frankfurter, J., in *Adamson* v. *California*, 332 U.S. 46, 59 (1947).

66. 211 U.S. 114.

67. Frankfurter, J., in *Adamson* v. *California*, 332 U.S. 46, 62. Justice Harlan is not named; but the only other possible reference would seem to be Justice Bradley (*cf.*, 16 Wall. 118), who, since he is praised as a liberal by Justice Frankfurter (332 U.S. 62), was apparently not meant.

68. *Palko* v. *Connecticut*, 302 U.S. 319 (1937); *Adamson* v. *California*, 332 U.S. 46 (1947).

69. The last case in point is *Adamson* v. *California*, 332 U.S. 46 (1947).

70. *Cf.*, *ibid.*, 84 *et seq*.

71. 211 U.S. 99.

72. 13 N.Y. 378 (1856).

73. *Bartemeyer* v. *Iowa*, 18 Wall. 129, 133 (1874).

74. Pound, *Liberty of Contract*, 18 YALE LAW JOURNAL, 454 (1909). See *Powell* v. *Pennsylvania*, 127 U.S. 678, 684 (1888); *Allgeyer* v. *Louisiana*, 165 U.S. 578, 589 (1897); *Lochner* v. *New York*, 198 U.S. 45, 53 (1905).

75. Shattuck, *The True Meaning of the Term "Liberty" in Those Clauses in the Federal and State Constitutions Which Protect "Life, Liberty, and Property,"* 4 HLR, 365 (1891).

76. For a clear statement to this effect, see *Gillespie* v. *People*, 188 Ill. 176, 182 (1900).

77. See Blackstone, Bk. I, chap. i.

78. 13 N.Y. 383.

79. *In the Matter of Jacobs*, 98 N.Y. 98, 103, 112–14 (1885); *Mugler* v. *Kansas*, 123 U.S. 623, 661 (1887); *Adair* v. *United States*, 208 U.S. 161, 172 (1908).

80. 211 U.S. 99–100.

81. *Cf.*, note 1 to chapter xxx hereof.

82. 110 U.S. 535.

83. 16 Wall. 97.

84. 211 U.S. 106.

85. Frankfurter, J., in *Adamson* v. *California*, 332 U.S. 46, 59, 61–62 (1947).

86. 332 U.S. 61 and 63.

87. Frankfurter, *Law and Politics: Occasional Papers, 1913–1938* (New York, 1939), 13. See, also, 36 HLR, 913–14, and 41 *ibid.*, 124–26.

88. See cases cited in note 32 to chapter xxxi hereof.

89. *Butcher's Union Slaughter-House and Live-Stock Landing Co.* v. *Crescent City Live-Stock Landing and Slaughter-House Co.*, 111 U.S. 746, 765–66 (1884).

90. 16 Wall. 81.

91. *Cf.*, chapter xxvii hereof.

92. 16 Wall. 81.

93. *Civil Rights Cases*, 109 U.S. 3 (1883).

94. *Yick Wo* v. *Hopkins*, 118 U.S. 356 (1886).

95. *Barbier* v. *Connolly*, 113 U.S. 27 (1885); *Soon Hing* v. *Crowley, ibid.*, 703 (1885).

96. *Santa Clara County* v. *Southern Pacific R. Co.*, 118 U.S. 394, 396 (1886).

97. *Pembina Consolidated Silver Mining & Milling Co.* v. *Pennsylvania*, 125 U.S. 181 (1888).

98. See, for example, *Truax* v. *Corrigan*, 257 U.S. 312 (1921); and *Colgate* v. *Harvey*, 296 U.S. 404 (1935).

NOTES TO CHAPTER XXXIII

1. *Calder* v. *Bull*, 3 Dall. 386 (1798). *Cf.*, chapter xi hereof.

2. 5 How. 504, 574, and 582 (1847).

3. See, for example, "The Letters of Brutus, No. XI," in N.Y. Jour., January 31, 1788.

4. Records, I, 124.

5. *Erie R.R. Co.* v. *Tompkins*, 304 U.S. 64, 78 (1938).

6. *Southern Pacific Co.* v. *Jensen*, 244 U.S. 205, 221–22 (1917).

7. *Swift & Co.* v. *United States*, 196 U.S. 375 (1905), certainly belongs in the same category. For the developed form of this "liberalizing" doctrine, see *Stafford* v. *Wallace*, 258 U.S. 495 (1922).

8. See W. G. Hammond's edition of Blackstone's *Commentaries* (1890), I, 132–33; and Field, *Ex Post Facto in the Constitution*, 20 MICHIGAN LAW REVIEW, 315 (1922).

9. The nearest to a real questioning will be found in the various items cited in note 4 to chapter iii hereof *supra*.

10. The only at all recent challenge to this dogma known to the writer is Lawson, *The General Welfare Clause* (Washington, 1934). It offered, however, no explanation of the Congressional enumeration.

11. Fairman, *Does the Fourteenth Amendment Incorporate the Bill of Rights? The Original Understanding*, 2 STANFORD LAW REVIEW, 5 (1949); see, also, Morrison, *The Judicial Interpretation, ibid.*, 140. Entirely apart from questions of the adequacy, and of the handling, of the evidence which Mr. Fairman presents, it is to be remembered that a recurrence to evidence of the sort he presents, is illegitimate in the case of a provision, like the first section of the Fourteenth Amendment, which is clear in itself, or clear when read in the light of the prior law. It is doubly illegitimate when it is remembered that most of what the first section of that amendment requires, was also required by Amendments II–VIII. *Cf.*, discussion herein in chapters xxx and xxxi. Mr. Fairman apparently forgets that the ultimate question is not what the legislatures meant, any more than it is what Congress or the more immediate framers of the amendment meant: it is what the amendment means. *Cf.*, Holmes, *The Theory of Legal Interpretation*, 12 HLR, 417 (1899).

Index

Index

Adams, John: failure of, to appoint any Jeffersonians to judgeships under Judiciary Act of 1801, 761; ground of violent Jeffersonian opposition to, as President, 10; judicial appointments of, under Judiciary Act of 1801, 760–61; "Novanglus" papers of, of 1774–75, 175–78, 289; part taken by, in drafting of resolution on trade, by First Continental Congress, 160–65, 1308–10; participation of, in piracy trials, during colonial period, 1330; recommends changes in Judiciary Act of 1789, 759

Adams, John Quincy, on war power of Congress, 512

Adams, Samuel, position of, on Constitution, 1300

Adams v. *Storey*, 693

Adamson v. *California*, 1083 note

Addison, Alexander: impeachment and removal of, from office, 740; on meaning of Pennsylvania act relating to West Allegheny lands, 728 note

Administration of justice; *see* Law administration

Administration of Justice Act of 1774, 142

Admiralty, rules of decision in, 870–77

Agriculture: as "commerce" in eighteenth century, 85, 87, 90, 92, 94, 95, 98, 99, 100, 109; as "manufacture" in eighteenth century, 95, 1281; meaning of term, in eighteenth century, 109–12; as "trade" in eighteenth century, 87, 90, 92, 94, 96, 98, 99, 100; as "traffic" in eighteenth century, 1288

Alden, Roger, on effects of Supreme Court's decision in *Huidekoper's Lessee* v. *Douglass*, 733–34

Almy v. *California*, 314

Ambassadors, etc., powers with respect to, under Constitution, 417–18

Amendments to Constitution: certain of initial, in relation to Supreme Court's limited right of review, 1004; division of opinion on necessity of, in First Congress, 685–90; drafting of initial, 1066–76; power of Congress to propose, 497; purpose of initial, 675–79; to create states' rights urged by Virginia, 1350; unadopted preamble to initial, 1065–66

Amendments II–VIII: intended general application of, to the states, 1057–76; Supreme Court's destruction of, as limitations on the states, 1056–82

American Law Institute, 32

Ames, Fisher: on applicability of eighteenth-century rules of interpretation to Constitution, 370; in the Bank debates, in Congress, in 1791, 198, 200, 201–2; on general national legislative authority of Congress, 1313; on reasons for Southern opposition, in Congress, to Bank of the United States, 194, 195

"Among," more frequent use of, in eighteenth century, 76, 1275–79

Anderson v. *Jackson* ex dem. *Eden*, 839

Angel v. *Bullington*, 932

Angell, Joseph K., on general application of initial amendments to the states, 1076

Annals of Congress, as taken from Thomas Lloyd's *Congressional Register*, during initial period they cover, 702 note

Anti-picketing laws as infringements of free speech, 31, 1258

Archer, William S., on scope of national commerce power, 243

Armstrong v. *Carson's Executors*, 548

Army power, Congressional, reasons for enumerating, 413, 425

"Article of Commerce," meaning of, in eighteenth-century America, 92–93, 99, 101

Articles of Confederation, practical construction of election provision in fifth article of, 525

Attorney General v. *The Grantees*, 730, 731

Baldwin, Abraham, on addition of Congressional defining power with respect to offenses against law of nations, 458

Baldwin, Henry: dissents in *Green* v. *Neal's Lessee*, 750, 850; on *Sims' Lessee* v. *Irvine*, 828

Bank of North America, Continental Congress' power to incorporate, 42

Bank of the United States: act to organize, as regulation of commerce, 201, 204–5; debates on constitutionality of, in Congress, in 1791, 193–203; debates on constitutionality of, in Philadelphia newspaper press, 203–5; Alexander Hamilton's opinion upon constitutionality of, 217–27; Thomas Jefferson's opinion upon constitutionality of, 211–16; Edmund Ran-

nental Congress, bearing on scope of commercial regulation, 136–72, 1210–17; queries Lord Mansfield as to his opinion on correctness of *Rutgers* v. *Waddington*, 463 note; views of, in *Rutgers* v. *Waddington*, 963–64; writes Samuel Chase, on First Continental Congress, 166

Due Process Clause of Fifth Amendment, meaning of, 1103–15

Due Process Clause of Fourteenth Amendment: meaning of, 1102–16; Supreme Court's transformation of, 1135–55

Due process of law: general remarks on, 1051–53; as inclusive of equal protection of laws, 1375

Duer, William A., on scope of national commerce power, 287

Dulany, Daniel, on regulation of trade, 128

Du Ponceau, Peter S., on Common Law as law of United States, 1345–46

Durfee, Thomas: on equity in Rhode Island, 888; on practice of changing state of residence to get into national equity court, 896

"Duties," meaning of, in late-eighteenth-century America, 296, 309–10, 1317–18

Duval, Gabriel, appointed Justice of Supreme Court, 766

East India Co. v. *Sandys*, 414

"Economy," meaning of, in eighteenth century, 107, 1286

Edwards, Pierpont: appointed United States judge in Connecticut, 771; as Jefferson's agent in Connecticut, 770; as judge in Connecticut libel prosecutions by Jeffersonians at Common Law, 771–84

Ejectment, use of action of, to settle land-title controversies turning on disputed points of law, 786, 799

Election-of-Electors Clause: early practical construction of, 526; meaning of, 67–68; in ratification campaign, 537–39

Election provisions of Constitution, views on, in Federal Convention, 529–30, 534–36

Elections, powers of Congress over, 522–41; reasons for enumerating, 499, 505

Eleventh Amendment, in relation to Supreme Court's limited right of review, 1004

Elliot's Executor v. *Lyell*, 340, 1322

Ellsworth, Oliver: on *ex-post-facto* laws before Federal Convention, 325; interpretation of Contracts Clause by, in ratification campaign, 329–30; views on election provisions of Constitution, in Federal Convention, 535

Elmendorf v. *Taylor*, 843–45, 848, 849

Embargo acts as legislative precedents on scope of national commerce power, 230, 242–44

Employers' Liability Acts, national and state, jurisdictional litigation under, 22–31, 1257

Employers' Liability Cases, 23

Equal Protection Clause of Fourteenth Amendment: general remarks on, 1049, 1051, 1052; meaning of, 1096–1102; merger of, in "substantive due process of law," 1155–58, 1375

"Equalizing Court," proposal of, prior to Federal Convention, 976–78

Equity: lack of, in New England states when Government was formed, 887; lack of, in Pennsylvania when Government was formed, 897; in national courts, intentions of First Congress in respect to, 899; practice of changing state of residence to get into national court of, 896–97; rules of decision in, 870–74, 877–902; sense in which state laws were followed in national courts, in equity, 879–80

Erie R. Co. v. *Tompkins*, 627 note, 865–66, 912–37, 1365

"Exceptions," nature of, 1352

"Excises," meaning of, in late-eighteenth-century America, 296, 306–7, 309, 1317–18

Executive Article: applicability to, of eighteenth-century rules of documentary interpretation, 379; Supreme Court's application of eighteenth-century mode of interpretation to, in 1926, 385–86

Executive power, limitations upon: in Constitution, 408–67; in early state constitutions, 415

Executive removal power controversy in First Congress, constitutional significance of, 369, 370

"Exports"; *see* "Imports"

"Ex post facto," legal usage of, prior to Federal Convention, 330–32

Ex-post-facto Clause (state) as interpreted by New Jersey Supreme Court, in 1795, 340

Ex-post-facto Clauses: Hugh Henry Brackenridge on, in 1812, 349; Daniel Carroll on, before Federal Convention, 325; Congressional views of, even after *Calder* v. *Bull*, 349; Oliver Ellsworth on, before Federal Convention, 325; interpretation of, in Congress, in middle 1790's, 347; interpretation of, in Congress, in 1790, 338–39; interpretation of, in North Carolina convention, of 1788, 336–38; interpretation of, in ratification campaign,

tion, 1013–14, 1016–17; proposes change in amendment now the Tenth, 703

Gibbons v. Ogden, 52, 154, 240, 250–68, 270–80, 287, 288, 694, 695

Gibson, John Bannister, on correctness of United States Supreme Court's decision in *Huidekoper's Lessee v. Douglass,* 740, 752

Giles, William Branch, on *Marbury v. Madison,* 1043

Gilman v. Brown, 891–93

Gilman, Nicholas, as aware of New Hampshire state precedents for judicial review, in 1787, 971

Godden v. Hales, 941

Gold, Thomas R., on scope of national commerce power, 236

Golden v. Prince, 1361

Gordon v. United States, 696

Gorham, Nathaniel: on judicial dominance in council of legislative revision proposed in Federal Convention, 1371; on judicial review in Federal Convention, 1016

Government, main heads of, in eighteenth century, 1181–85

Granger, Gideon, as Jefferson's agent in Connecticut, 770

Graves v. Boston Marine Insurance Co., 889–90

Gray, John Chipman: on meaning of section 34 of Judiciary Act of 1789, 904; on Joseph Story and *Swift v. Tyson,* 904

Grayson, William: on initial amendments to Constitution, 686–87; on Tenth Amendment, 687

Green v. Neal's Lessee, 749, 750, 752, 753, 816, 817 note, 843, 849, 850, 851, 852, 853, 860, 862, 863

Griffin v. McCoach, 928, 930–31

Griffith, William: appointed circuit judge under Judiciary Act of 1801, 761; on effect of Supreme Court's decision in *Huidekoper v. Douglass,* 745–46; on practice of changing state of residence to get into national equity court, 896–97; with John B. Wallace, buys West Allegheny lands of Holland Land Company, 745

Grotius: on documentary interpretation, 364; on reprisals as sanction under law of nations, 1347

Groves v. Slaughter, 862

Guaranty Trust Co. v. York, 877–902, 931, 932, 933

Habeas corpus, provision on, in Constitution as indicative of an existing national law of the subject, 625

Hamilton, Alexander: on appellate jurisdiction of Supreme Court over courts of the states, 654; attempt of, to confuse objects

and powers of Government in *The Federalist,* 509 note; as counsel for defendant in *Rutgers v. Waddington,* 963, 964, 965; declines retainer in national-court litigation over Fairfax estate, 792; on due process of law, 1103; on Election-of-Electors Clause, 67–68, 526, 537–38; on executive power under Constitution, 418 note; *The Farmer Refuted* of, of 1775, 173–75, 289; on general character of government under Constitution, 66–67; ground of violent Jeffersonian opposition to, 10; inconsistency of, on judicial review, in *The Federalist,* 1026–28; on judicial review, 1010; on judicial tenure and salaries, in state governments, in 1787, 1343; on law-of-nations questions in cases within "party" categories of Judiciary Article, 650; on national commerce power in *The Federalist,* 220; on national commerce power in his Bank opinion, 217–27; on nature of judiciary power, 619; opinion on constitutionality of Bank of the United States, 217–27; on "party" categories of judiciary enumeration, 642; report to Congress recommending national bank, 193; on Supreme Court's general paramountcy to all other courts, both state and national, 711–12; theory of Common Defence and General Welfare Clause, 401–5, 408; on transfer of executive powers to Congress, in Constitution, 415

Hancock, John, on domestic tranquillity, 69

Harlan, John Marshall: delivers majority opinion in *Kuhn v. Fairmount Coal Co.,* 906; dissents in *Civil Rights Cases,* 1156; dissents in *Hurtado v. California,* 1139, 1140; dissents in *Maxwell v. Dow,* 1132; dissents in *O'Neil v. Vermont,* 1124; dissents in *Twining v. New Jersey,* 1145; as one of leaders in developing "substantive due process of law," 1146–47, 1151, 1154

Harrison, Benjamin, as participant in, and commentator upon, case of Josiah Philips, 946–47

Hazard's Lessee v. Lowry, 739

Heathfield v. Chilton, 463

Henfield, Gideon, case of, 629

Henry, Jabez, on law merchant, 1340

Henry, Patrick: on constitutional conditions in Virginia, in 1787, 1369; on Ex-post-facto Clauses before Virginia ratifying convention, 332–36; as participant in, and commentator upon, case of Josiah Philips, 944, 946

Hickey v. Kahl, 925, 927

Hicks, William, on power of Parliament over the colonies, 1295–97